St. Petersburg

BIBLIOPOLIS

St. Petersburg

*Photographs by Vladimir Sobolev
and Kira Zharinova
Introduced by Dmitry Likhachev
and Natalya Lanceray*

Translated from the Russian by TATYANA TIKHONOVA
Designed by ILDUS FARRAKHOV and LEO YEPIFANOV

© Dmitry Likhachev, 1992: A Window to Europe – a Gateway to Russia
© Natalya Lanceray, 1993: Introduction, notice
© Vladimir Sobolev, Kira Zharinova, 1993: Photographs
© Tatyana Tikhonova, 1993: Translation from the Russian
© Ildus Farrakhov, Leo Yepifanov: Design

ISBN 5-87671-028-8

A WINDOW TO EUROPE — A GATEWAY TO RUSSIA

St. Petersburg is named after the apostle Peter. Peter, according to popular conception is the gatekeeper, the keeper of the keys.

St. Petersburg not only a «window» to look outof at Europe, it was also the gate to our country. St. Petersburg was founded not only at the eastern extremity of the Baltic, but also in the western part of Russia's network of navigable rivers. While facing Europe, St. Petersburg was backed the Ladoga Lake, Novgorod, the Onega Lake and the White Sea, the Volga...

The rivers and the sea used to be the main highways of that period. It was for that particular reason that water, ships, embankments and landings played such an important role in the country's life.

Look, how high stays the water between the granite embankments in St. Petersburg, as if in a goblet lifted to the lips for a draught. The broad water expanse offers itself to the city to drink and never is its level low, even in the driest of summers. The Neva is not a river. It does not change with the seasons as rivers do: it does not flood in spring, nor does its level drop in summer. It can overflow its banks quite unexpectedly and inundate the nearby part of the city, but withdraw from the city, leave it altogether — that it never can. Ever large and generous, the Neva flows imperiously and majestically from month to month, from year to year: a thousand years — since the time when the main trading route of Europe passed this way connecting the North of the continent with the South — the route «from the Varangians to the Greeks».

The water expanses meet the land along a vast length of banks in the gigantic mouth of the Neva: its distributary arms, the Great and Small Neva, Great and Small Nevka; the many rivers, canals and channels. This permits the city not to crowd at the water's edge but to spread freely along the low banks handy for loading and unloading. The city touches the water not only with its buildings but also with its squares and gardens. Whole islands are taken up by parks and gardens, while the squares in the city continue to astonish, as they always have, all those coming to St. Petersburg for the first time. The main palaces are not cramped up along the streets but look out onto open spaces of land and water. The institutions of government, and first and foremost the Senate and Synod, the Twelve Collegia, the Academy of Sciences, the fortress and the Admiralty face the Neva.

The city merges with the expanse of water not simply because the water stands at such a high level, but because the low level of the streets and squares is flat and even like the water surface. In damp weather when it rains, or under the snow and ice of winter, the rivers look like squares and the squares like rivers. The Great Neva in front of the old Exchange is a square. The Fontanka and the Moika are streets; streets with houses pressed close against one another forming, as it were, a second set of banks and looking like deep canals.

And one more thing: the city seems to have no soil. The even, ever flat ground is bricked up in pavements of cobble-stones and wooden blocks, sheets of limestone and granite. The soil lies beneath a sort of «floor» which in days gone by was kept clean and carefully tended. And the Slavophiles' reproaches that the city was «groundless» and its construction on a marsh artificial seem to be justified. After all, even the lime-trees were brought in on the orders of Tsar Peter, not from Russia but from the Baltic lands.

But that is not the whole truth! The water in the Neva flows from Russia. It enters the Ladoga Lake from the Volkhov and Svir Rivers, and in the early years of St. Petersburg every cart coming to «Peter» was to bring a certain amount of stones for the pavements. And Yaroslav the Wise in the eleventh century and Alexander Nevsky in the thirteenth had both seen the banks of the Neva.

St. Petersburg is no mirage in the marshes. It is established here for centuries and millenia to come. It is steadfast and unshakeable.

Together with the Russians, foreign architects erected St. Petersburg, mainly Italians: Rastrelli, Quarenghi, Rossi, Rinaldi, Luchini... Here, on the broad expanses, the architectural genius of the Italians broke free. In Italy the creative efforts of Italian builders were cramped in between the constructions of three millenia of traditions. There, in Italy, they had little space, uneven sites and no mighty rivers. In order to understand the Italian constructional genius one must first of all visit Rome, Florence, Verona, and then travel via Venice to St. Petersburg to see here the ensembles of Rastrelli and Rossi and the ensemble of ensembles that is St. Petersburg. But St. Petersburg's most striking feature is the monumentality with which it was built — for the centuries to come.

Edifices — the palaces, the fortress, the towers and the two spires — surround the open space of the Neva. The building of the Exchange looms majestically in the path of the Neva. The Rostral Columns stand like two gigantic candles in some temple: symbols of Russia's mastery of the seas and rivers. The palace and the fortress face each other accross the river. Further down, closer to the sea, are the Academy of Sciences, the University, the Kunstkammer and the cathedral of that little-known saint, Isaac of Dalmatia, who became a giant through the fact that Tsar Peter was born on his feast-day.

And as if to assert its stability St. Isaac is raised above the plain on hudreds of gigantic monolithic columns of red granite, while in front of the Winter Palace the largest monolithic granite column in the world was set up. Red granite predominates in the city and binds it, as it were, into a single whole: red embankments like necklaces embrace the land. To match the red granite the state buildings in St. Petersburg were painted a deep shade of red. The sinister colour adorned a city of tragic beauty...

St. Petersburg is abundant in skies. Not only the spaces of the squares and the broad Neva, but also the receding vistas along the straight streets are everywhere open to the sky.

The keeper of the heavenly keys, the apostle Peter, guards his city that is split in two. Perhaps it is precisely at this moment that Peter has stopped admitting people to paradise. Paradise is only a fancy in St. Petersburg: in this city of holy places, this garden-city. But St. Petersburg is a city of growing slums with the highest level of criminality and a sharp clash of beauty and ugliness. Straight streets and embankments, and the snake of the Yekaterininsky canal suddenly winding in amongst them — the ditch of Dostoyevsky's *Crime and Punishment*. Dostoyevsky's city. You can find a spot in old Kolomna where the Yekaterininsky Canal is visible at the end of the street and at its beginning. It is chaos that has penetrated the city. The snake of the Yekaterininsky Canal is the same one that is being trampled by Peter's horse on Senate Square. Trampled, but not perhaps killed?

Everything that is immortal about the city already belongs to the age bygone. Everything looks towards the precious past: including the palace that has ceased to be a palace, the Admiralty that has ceased to command the seas or build ships, the Peter and Paul Fortress that has ceased to be either fortress or prison. And in the central and oldest place in the city — the Peter and Paul Cathedral, beneath the spire which strains towards Heaven, the tombs of the emperors lie sleeping. There are just as many of them as the cathedral could hold.

Only the Neva continues its majestic motion from the past into the past, unfolding the tremendous panorama of Russian culture between the eighteenth and the early twentieth centuries.

Dmitry Likhachev

ST. PETERSBURG
A brief outline of architecture

The history of St. Petersburg which goes back only as far as three centenaries is a comparatively short period for a city of the world importance. Founded by Peter the Great to be the new capital of the Russian Empire, it was built in all the magnificence of the principal city of the country. And, although Petersburg remained capital a little over two hundred years, during this period it was the focus of all the most important aspects of Russian life — spiritual, political and economic; and all events of their development, however important they were — army and navy, war and commerce, science and religion, medicine and education, — became reflected in the structure of the city.

The role of Petersburg was dominant for the history of Russian culture. On the one hand, Petersburg was the centre of the official art, for the Academy of Fine Arts, the Conservatoire, Opera and Drama theatres, the Academy of Sciences were Imperial not only by name, but in spirit as well. On the other hand, it was the place where a lot of innovative trends appeared in art and literature.

Work of many great writers, artists, musicians, whose names became symbols of Russian culture and of its highest achievements, was connected with Petersburg. They are Pushkin and Gogol, Dostoyevsky and Tolstoy, Block and Akhmatova, Brullov and Repin, Roerich and Malevich, Tchaikovsky and Mussorgsky, Rakhmaninov and Shostakovich, Pavlova and Ulanova, and many others.

The history of constructing the city can be considered a most interesting page in the history of Russian and universal architecture. Here almost all the greatest Russian architects worked in the eighteenth, nineteenth and early twentieth century. It is to their creations that Petersburg owes its fame of one of the exceedingly beautiful cities of the world, owes its aspect of a city of an unsurpassed harmony, although in its construction layers of different epochs can be traced, beginning from the first years of its existence.

Towards the end of the seventeenth century solving the problem of searches for Russia a way out towards the Baltic sea became quite pressing. Peter the Great succeeded to win back the Baltic Sea coast, in a trying war with Sweden. This happened in May 1703 and the city of Saint Petersburg was laid immediatelly at the estuary of the Neva, which since 1712-1713 became the new capital of Russia.

The city began growing at several centres almost simultaneously, which later formed the nuclei of the consrtuction and ultimately defined the aspect of the city.

One of these centres was St. Peter and Paul Fortress which was built on the Zayachy Island. In 1706 the earthen fortifications were exchanged for the brick ones, the project of the fortress with six bastions and straight curtains between them being made by the Tsar Peter the Great. The construction was supervised by the architect Domenico Trezzini, in whose creations the epoch of Peter the Great in the history of Petersburg manifested itself in the most brilliant manner. The construction of brick fortifications was protracted for long decades. Among Trezzini's buildings in the fortress, only the main entrance remained realized in the form of a triumphal arch, and the cathedral to commemorate the Saint Apostles Peter and Paul, the construction of which started in 1712 around the initially built wooden church. This is a three-nave basilica, whose silhouette is dominated by the multitier campanile with a tall spire. To comply with Peter's desire, the campanile 106 metres tall was completed much earlier than the cathedral itself; and since then it has become a symbol of Petersburg and one of the vertical dominants in its architecture. After reconstruction of 1857-1858 the campanile is 122,5 metres tall.

To enhance the defensive power of the fortress from the side of the land, from the north, the massive building of the arsenal was erected in the form of a horse shoe. However, the fortress had no chance of displaying its military power in any real action. It turned to be the principal prison of the Empire, and the most dangerous opponents of the Empire, political prisoners, were kept there. These people used to have their only exit from this prison through the Neva entrance by the water, either to their execution place, or to be shut in the eternal captivity in Schlusselburg. And it was also Peter the Great to have initiated the use of the fortress for that purpose: there his son the Tsarevitch Alexey perished, who had stood against his father's policy.

Several architectural monuments of the early Petersburg period remain in the Vasilyevsky Island. One of them is the building of the Twelve Collegia, constructed after the design by Trezzini; its butt-end faces the Neva Embankment. The building housed the Senate and twelve Collegia — prototypes of ministries established by Peter the Great to administer the country. From the outside the building looks to be twelve separate constructions put in a row close to each other, but inside all the rooms are joined together with a common long corridor.

Not far from this building the palace of Prince Alexander Menshikov the Governor of Petersburg can be seen on the embankment; the contemporaries were staggered with its dimensions and splendour. Quite close to the Point is the Kunstkammer, the first scientific institution in Petersburg, whose scientific purpose is proved by the observatory tower, much alike to a church bell-tower. All these constructions have features common to the northern baroque style: flattish pilasters, shallow facade segmentation, fancy pediments, profiled window platbands with minute cross-sections.

For his summer residence with a «vegetable garden» Peter the Great chose the area on the left bank of the Neva between the Moika and the Fontanka Rivers. In 1711-1716 the area was turned into an island by digging the Lebyazhya canal. This is the first regular park of the city, the Summer Gardens. Its original planning remains to this day; and its alleys are decorated even now with the marble statues brought principally from Italy on Peter's order. In 1771-1784 the architect Yuri Veldten placed along the Neva Embankment the famous cast-iron fence, one of the masterpieces of Petersburg architecture. Among numerous eighteenth century buildings within the precincts of the garden only the Summer Palace of Peter the Great remains, a small two-storey building many of whose interiors preserve their original aspect.

By contrast, the ensemble of palace and parks constructed during the same years thirty kilometres from Petersburg, on the southern bank of the Gulf of Finland, was not inferior to similar European ensembles. Peterhof, sparkling with thousands of jets issued by its fountains, with the golden domes of the Grand Palace, with gilded statues of antique and biblical characters, with the windows of numerous park pavilions among shady alleys became the first gem in the wreath of palaces and parks in Tsarskoye Selo, Pavlovsk, Gatchina, which appeared step by step around Petersburg in the course of the eighteenth century.

During the reign of Anna Ioannovna almost all the Admiralty sloboda (settlement) was annihilated by fire. This event was the cause of organizing the Commission for Construction in St. Petersburg, which played a major part in the history of the city's growth. It was the merit of this commission, and particularly, of the great architect Pyotr Yeropkin, that the general plan of St. Petersburg was created, the plan that defined the city's structure with its broad avenues and streets, squares, gardens and parks, canals and numerous bridges for decades in advance. The city assumed unity of planning, each of its structural parts having an individual project of construction developed for it. Owing to efforts of many great architects, this plan was being realized in the course of the whole eighteenth and the first half of the nineteenth century.

The flourishing of the baroque architecture coincided with the reign of Elizaveta Petrovna and was represented by the work of the outstanding architects Francesco Bartolommeo Rastrelli and Savva Tchevakinsky.

In the course of his few years of active creative work Rastrelli managed to construct such a great number of buildings stupendous in their artistic quality that it is hard to believe in this possibility: the Smolny monastery ensemble, the palaces of Vorontsov and Stroganov, the Winter Palace in Petersburg and the Catherine Palace in Tsarskoye Selo.

The Smolny monastery was built beyond the city boundary, in the point where the Neva makes a loop which defines rather a large area. The cathedral's domes tower over the mass of trees, they are seen from afar if Petersburg is approached to from the Ladoga. Tall, elegant, directed heavenwards, they herald the approaching city. The monastery complex has a centric composition. The dominant of the complex is the five-domed cathedral having an almost square section.

Another beautiful building of the church architecture of that epoch is the St. Nicholas' Cathedral in St. Petersburg, an outstanding monument of Russian baroque style designed by Tchevakinsky. The five-domed cathedral combining in a single building a winter (lower) and a summer (upper) churches, is of a rare picturesque decor, elegance and harmony. The greatest architect's success is the multitier campanile placed on the bank of the Kryukov canal: it combines in a most harmonious manner the architectural traditions of the ancient Russia with some of the ways which characterize the baroque style.

However, the most famous building of the Russian baroque style in Petersburg should be considered the Winter Palace built by Rastrelli in 1754-1762. According to Elizaveta Petrovna's desire, it was erected at the place of a former palace which served as the official residence of the tsar and had been often rebuilt. However, she did not live several months up to its completion. The chatelaine of the new Winter Palace became Catherine the Great; but by the time the orientation of the society in art had changed, and the reign of Catherine the Great and her successors is characterized with the flowering of classicism.

Many interiors of the palace were decorated to comply with the new ideas. But of those interiors not a single one remains to our day, for in 1837 the Winter Palace burned out completely. It was restored by a large group of builders after the designs by the architects Vasily Stasov and Alexander Brullov, and with a few exceptions, the interiors of the Winter Palace preserve the aspect they assumed in the second half of the nineteenth century.

The period of classicism which began in the Petersburg architecture after Catherine the Great ascended the throne had to solve a great town-building task: to complete forming the city centre. Architects were expected not only to erect single buildings, more or less separate, but to design and build huge complexes, whole ensembles or even systems of such ensembles.

A particular attention was given to the Neva embankments and squares abutting them, — the Field of Mars, Palace and Senate Squares.

Near the Winter Palace on the Neva Embankment the ensemble of the Hermitage buildings appears. One after another residences of the nobility appear along the embankment, among which by a particular nobleness, beauty of decor and, so to say, by a spirituality of aspect the Marble Palace stands out created by Antonio Rinaldi. On the square below the Admiralty an equestrian statue of Peter the Great is placed, the *Bronze Horseman*, the celebrated creation of the French sculptor Etienne Maurice Falconet.

The building of the opposite bank continues, where, not far from the Menshikov Palace, the building of the Imperial Academy of Fine Arts is constructed, designet by Alexander Kokorinov and Jean Vallin de La Mothe (1784-1788). Large roost that covers the walls of the ground floor, which serves as base for the columns and pilasters connecting the two upper floors, gives monumentality to the aspect of the building.

The Point of the Vasilyevsky Island, one of the most spectacular and festive ensembles of Petersburg, assumes in these years its present aspect. The building of the Exchange, constructed after the design by Thomas de Tomon (1805-1810) has its prorotype in the antique temple, enclosed by columns on the circumference and decorated with statues above the portico. The tall basis of the building, with stairs of the same width as the facade, carries a powerful colonnade of the severe Doric order. The impression of a majestic solemnity is enhanced by the rostral columns placed at the slopes to the rounded promontory of the island which divides the Neva into two branches. From here an unforgettable vista opens of the wide river surface with the St. Peter and Paul Fortress on the left and the Winter Palace on the right.

In the early nineteenth century Adrian Zakharov rebuilt one of the first constructions of Petersburg, the Admiralty. The new Chief Admiralty preserved its former planning. The architect managed to create the building that became dominating in the city aspect and its symbol. Erected according to severe classic norm, simple and serene, it nonetheless brought a romantic note into the city construction.

A romantic atmosphere shrouds the Mikhailovsky Castle, the residence of the Emperor Paul I erected by Vincenzo Brenna near the Summer Gardens. The severe monolithic construction which reminded of impregnable medieval fortresses was separated from the city by canals and rivers with draubridges; but it failed to save its imperial master — death from the hands of the conspirators overtook Paul I here.

A year before the Napoleonic invasion into Russia and beginning of the 1812 Patriotic war Andrey Voronikhin finished construction of the Kazan Cathedral (Cathedral of Our Lady of Kazan), whose semi-circular colonnade, directed towards Nevsky Prospect with its giant arms, reminds of the St. Peter's Cathedral in Rome. After the victorious ending of the war, the cathedral became the Pantheon of Russian military glory. Here were preserved banners of the conquered Napoleonic armies, keys of the cities surrendered to the Russian armies, Kutuzov's remains were brought here.

After the war a new period begins in the history of construction of Petersburg — the period of a systematic reconstruction of the capital, of creating architectural complexes, which involved whole city districts, the period which is associated with the names of Vasily Stasov, Auguste Montferrand and Carlo Rossi.

The reconstruction of the central Petersburg squares — Palace, Mikhailovskaya, Theatre and Senate —

was performed by Rossi with a might and, at the same time, with a tactful regard for buildings constructed by his predecessors. One of his most famous creations is the Palace Square ensemble. Opposite the Rastrelli's baroque Winter Palace Rossi builds the classical construction of the Headquarters which embraces the space of the square in a semi-circle, and atteins a complete harmony in their contrast confrontation.

Senate Square also acquired wholeness and completion when, having erected the buildings of the Senate and Synod, connected with an arch thrown over Galernaya Street, Rossi put the last stroke, unifying in a harmonious composition a side Admiralty facade, the monument to Peter the Great created by Falconet, and the new St. Isaac's Cathedral, one of the greatest buildings in Petersburg, designed by Montferrand. This was one of the last constructions of classicism.

The next stage in the construction of the city is connected with its rapid growth. The city expanded including into its borders suburban villages and estates, and it also grew upwards increasing the number of storeys in hausing estates, and condensing the urban building. The leading role was played in that period by the architects of the eclectic trend: Andrey Stackenschneider, Alfred Parland, Nikolay Efimov, Nikolay Benois, Leo von Klenze, and others. They combined in their designs some elements of classicism, baroque, Gothic, Byzantine, and ancient Russian architectural styles.

Towards the end of the century, multy-storey rooming houses occupy a place of importance, and in the early twentieth century the predominant architectural style is modernist; banks, trading houses, hotels are created in this style. These buildings bring into the city atmosphere new feelings, joining old districts or forming whole new districts as for example Kamennoostrovsky Prospect or estate buildings on the Kamenny and Krestovsky islands.

Petersburg architects paid a tribute to constructionism after the 1917 revolution, and to neo-classicism, and to the ponderous pompous style which seemed in keeping with the «victorious march of socialism» (an example of this style can be seen in the buildings of Moskovsky Prospect).

In the course of its brief historical period of three hundred years the city lived throgh many dramatic events, becoming the arena of political actions and bloody battles. Here in the 1917 revolution began, which led to overthrowing of the Russian tsarism. During the World War II, the city lived through the tragedy of an unparalleled blockade, which took the lives of millions of people.

To satisfy ideological aims of different periods, St. Petersburg was renamed three times: at the beginning of the World War I, it was renamed Petrograd, and after Lenin's death in 1924, it was renamed Leningrad to commemorate the founder of the Soviet State. At present, the name given the city at its foundation is returned to it.

Today the city grows impetuously and without restraint. The suburbs of yesterday are converted into huge districts built with standard, absolutely identical dwelling houses, identical cinemas and supermarkets, identical schools and hospitals. Architects' fancy finds some use only on those seldom occasions when they are asked to build something unique — a Metro stations, for example, an airport building, or a sporting and concert complex.

However, in its heart, in its central districts, on the Moika, Fontanka or Yekaterininsky Canal embankments, in Liteiny or Zagorodny Prospects Petersburg remains its very self. It continues to live and to win with its harmony, beauty and majesty the hearts of every person who sees it.

Natalia Lanceray

1   *St. Peter and Paul Cathedral seen from the western gate of the Fortress.*
2   *Neva by night. Palace Bridge and St. Peter and Paul Fortress* →

3, 4   St. Peter and Paul Fortress.
       The Naryshkin Bastion

5   Palace Bridge. A white night

6 Palace Bridge seen from the Admiralteyskaya Embankment
7 St. Peter and Paul Fortress. The Nevsky Gate
8 St. Peter and Paul Fortress. St. Peter's Gate

9 St. Peter and Paul Fortress. The square in front of the Cathedral
10 St. Peter and Paul Fortress. The Boat house
11 Trinity Bridge →

12 Arsenal (The Artillery Museum)
13 St. Peter and Paul Fortress.
    St. John's Bridge

14 St. Peter and Paul Fortress.
    St. John's Ravelin

15 St. Peter and Paul Fortress and Trinity Square seen from the campanile of the Cathedral
16 St. Peter and Paul Cathedral. The interior
17 St. Peter and Paul Fortress. A winter evening
18 St. Peter and Paul Fortress seen from the Point of Vasilyevsky Island. *Sunrise*

19 Naryshkin Bastion of the St. Peter and Paul Fortress seen through the clock of the campanile of the Cathedral
20 St. Peter and Paul Fortress. Lamp post

21 St. Peter and Paul Fortress seen from the Point of Vasilyevsky Island. A misty morning →
22 St. Peter and Paul Fortress seen from the raised Palace Bridge. A white night →
23 Winter Palace →
24 Winter Palace. The Main Staircase →
25 Old Hermitage. The Nevsky enfilade →
26 New Hermitage. The Main Staircase →
27 Winter Palace. The White Hall →
28 Small Hermitage. The Pavilion Hall →
29 Winter Palace. Evening lights →

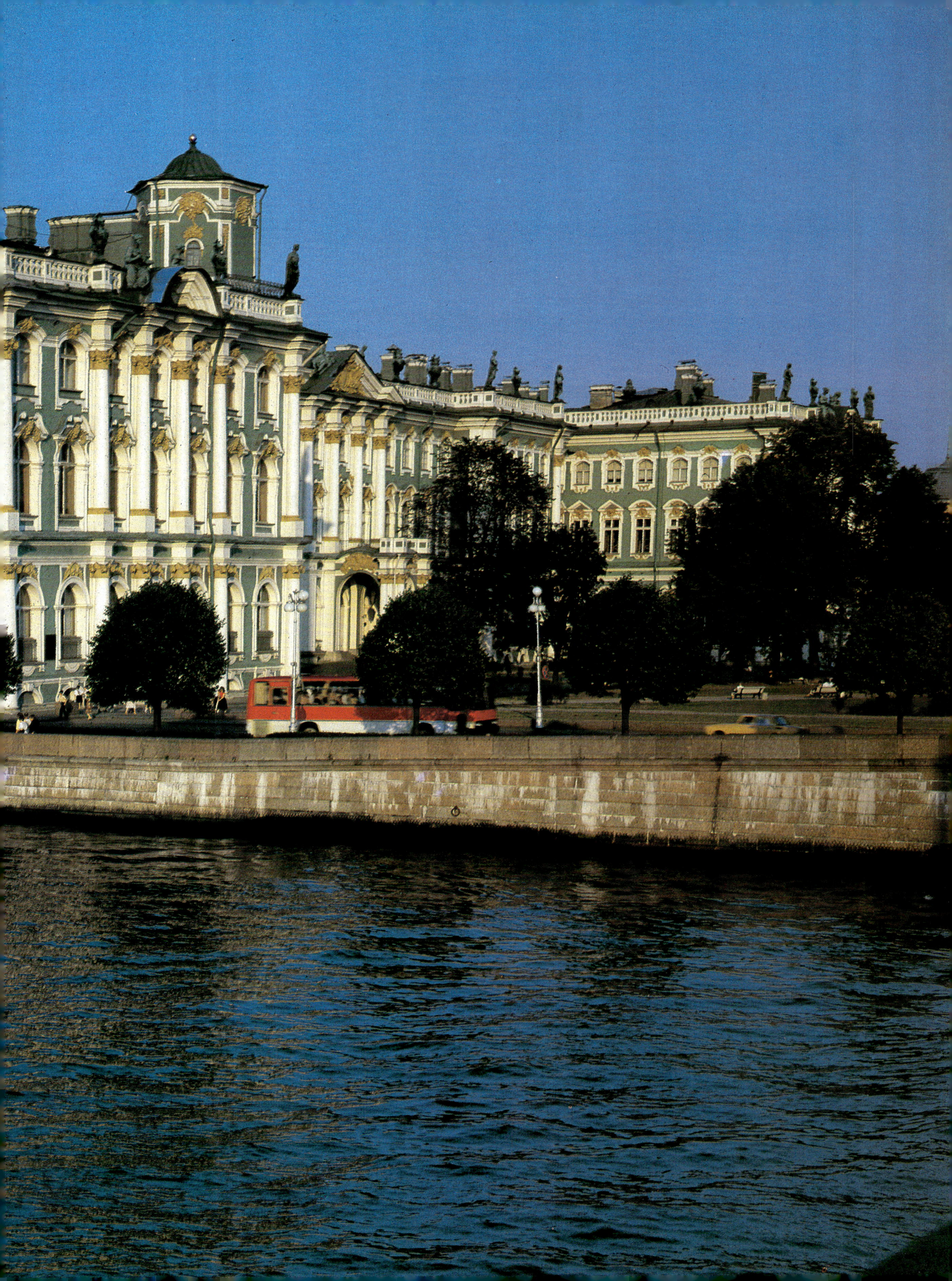

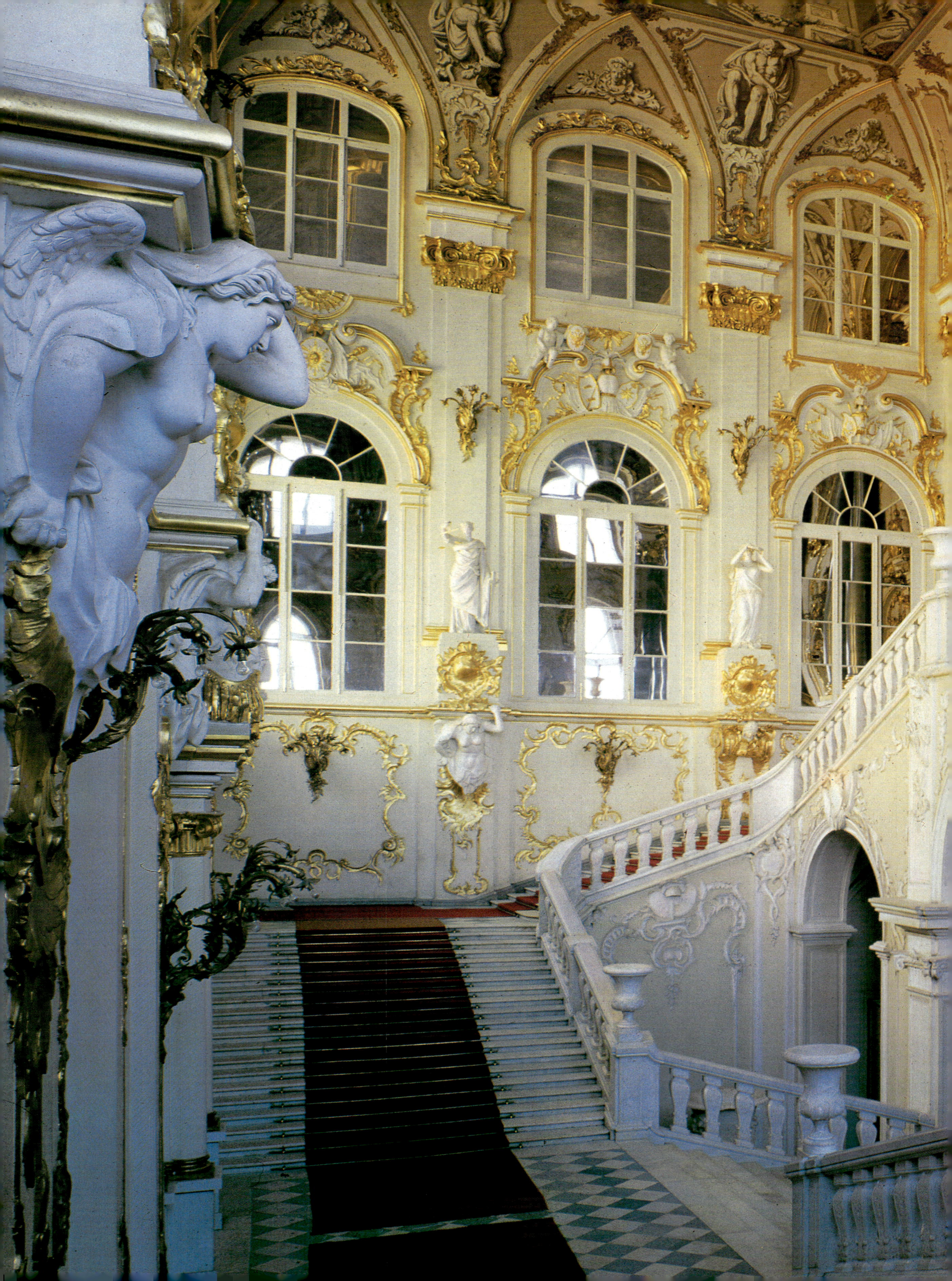

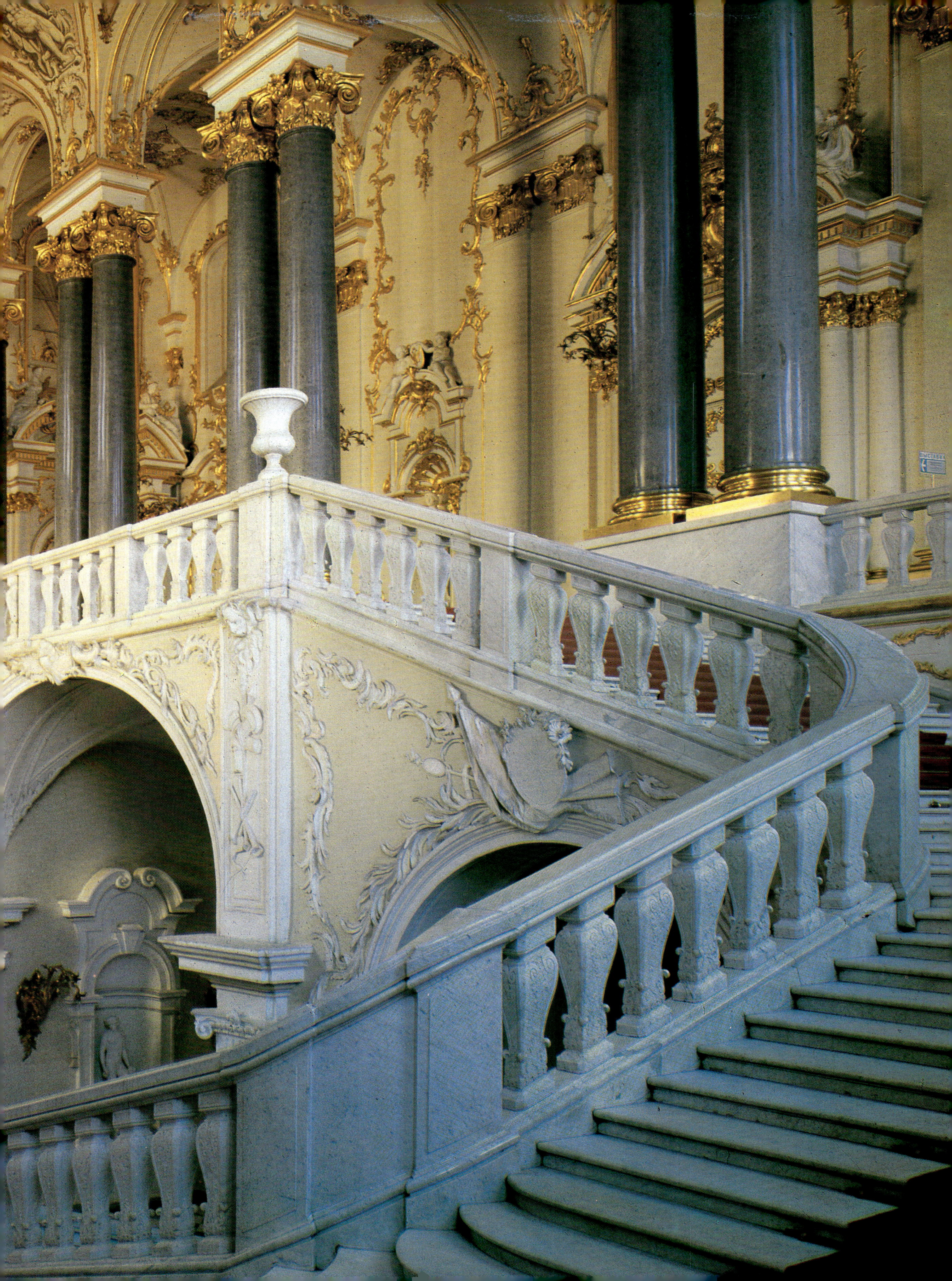

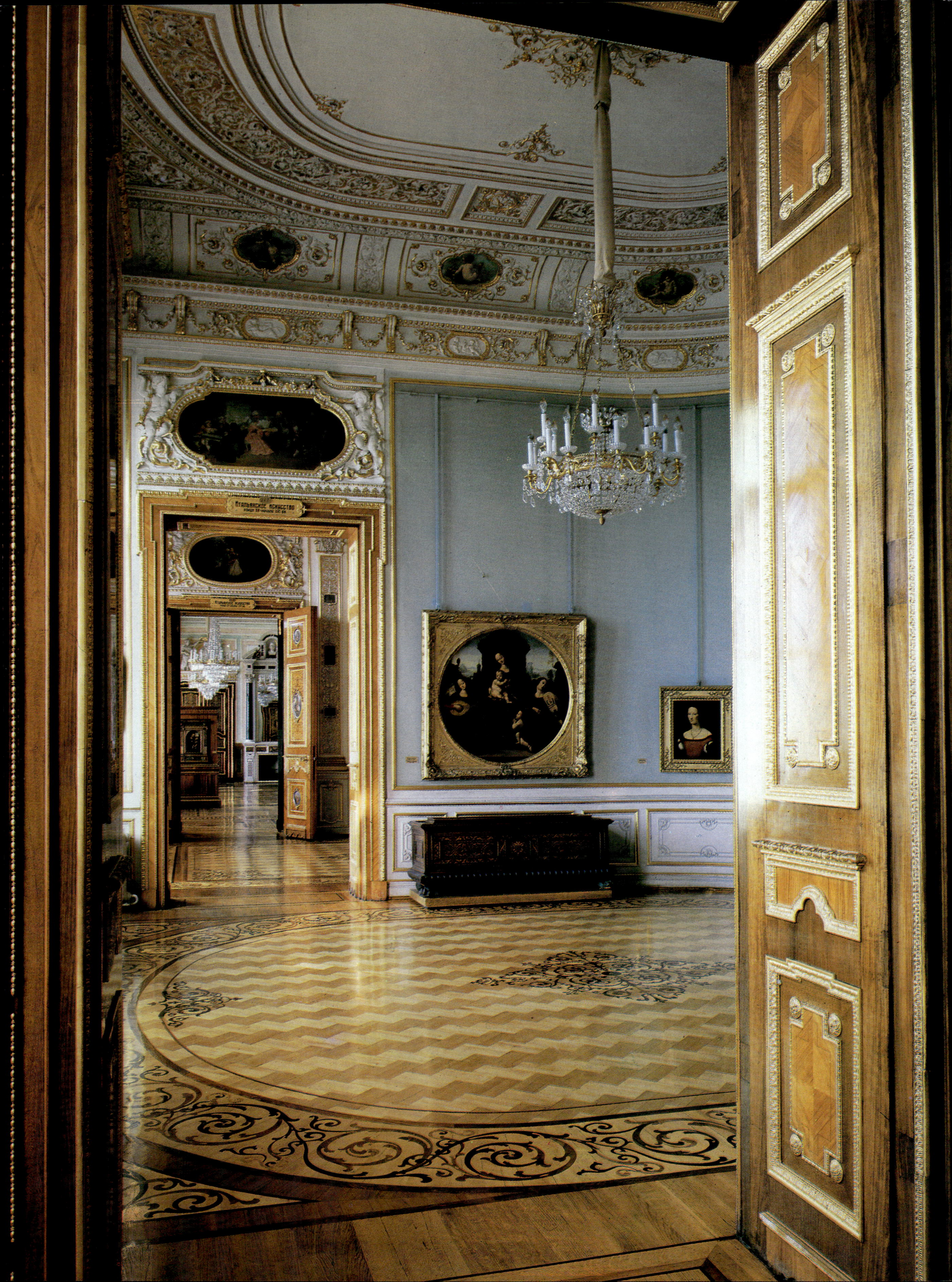
ИТАЛЬЯНСКОЕ ИСКУССТВО

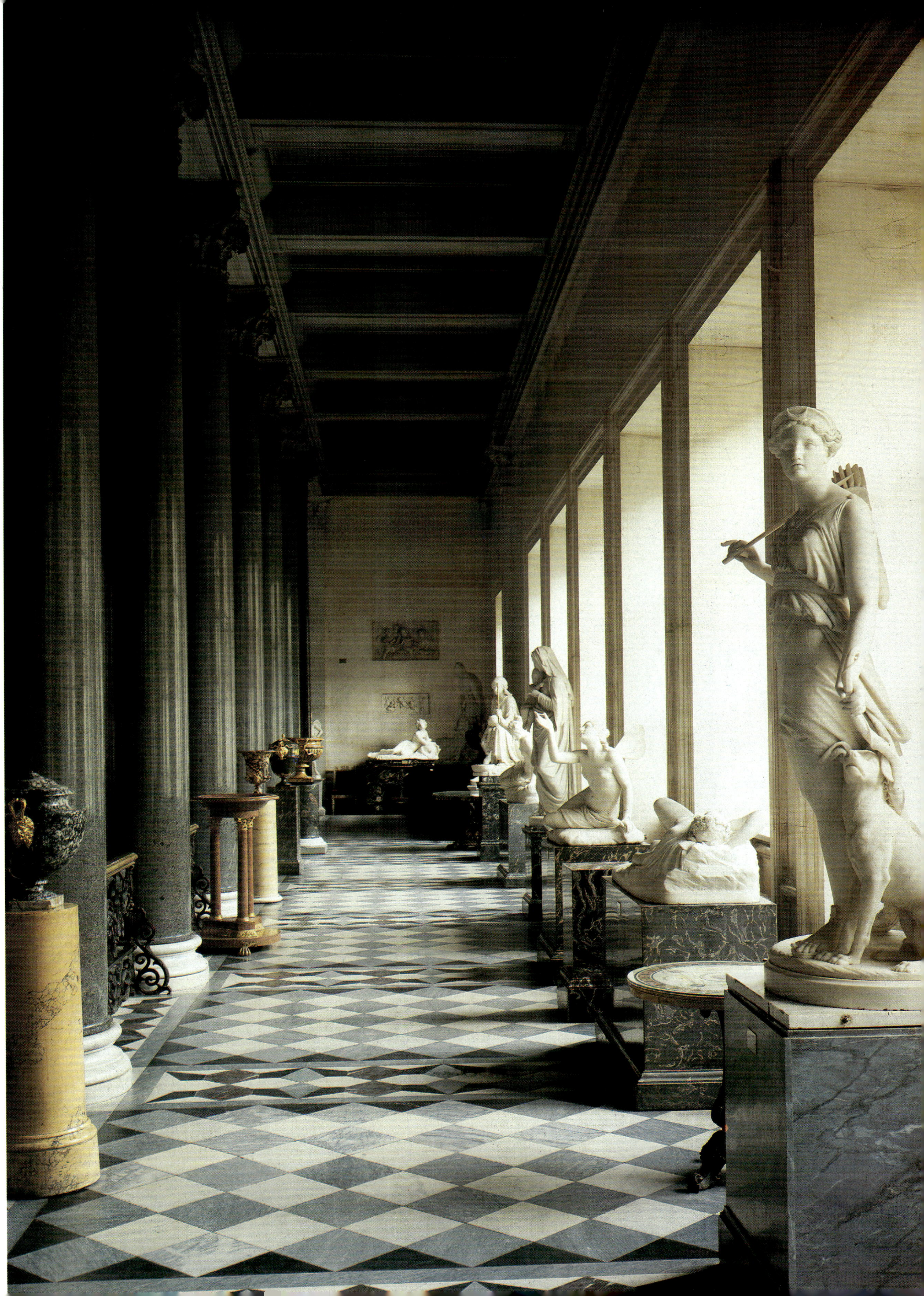

← 25

26

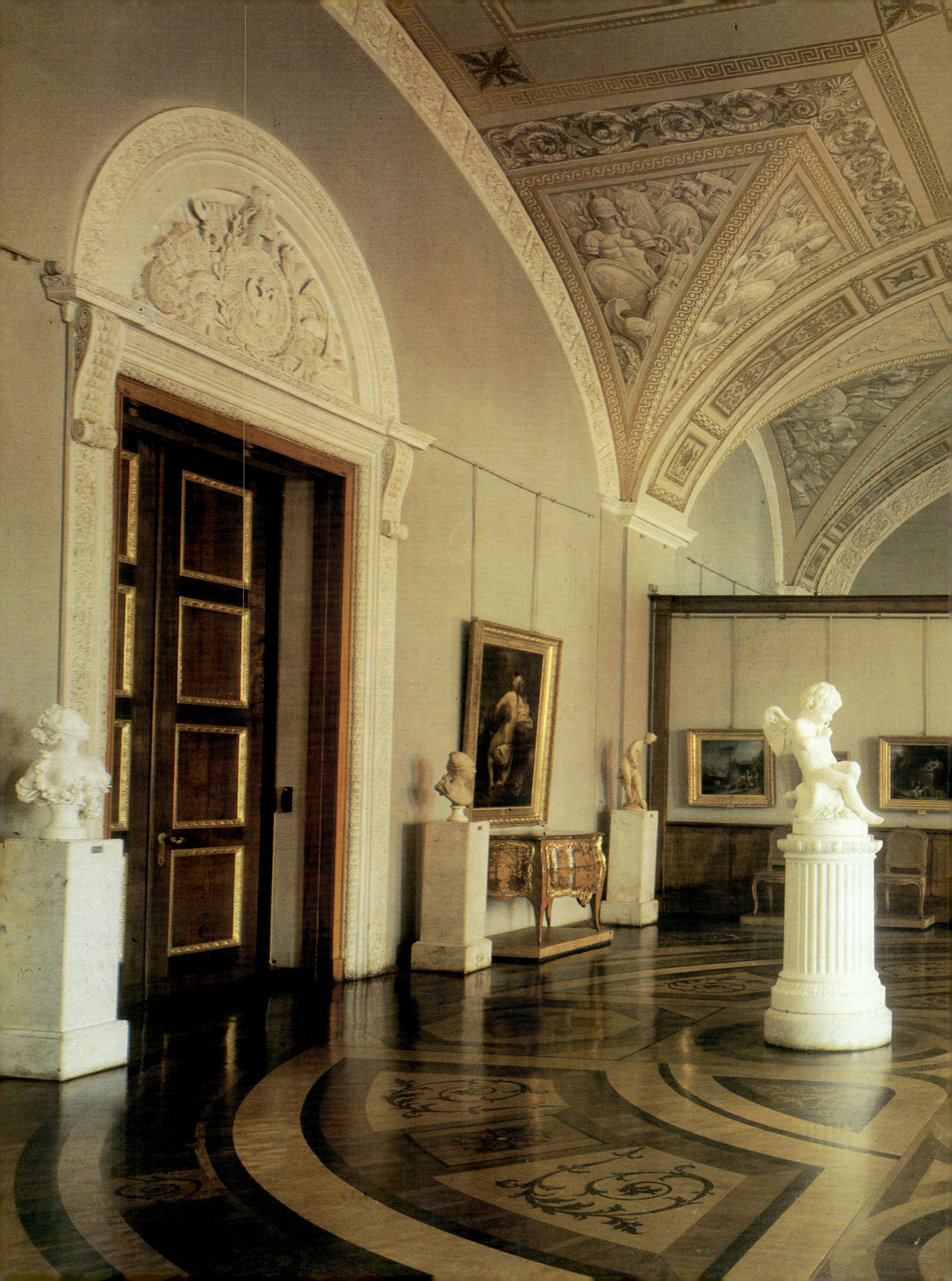

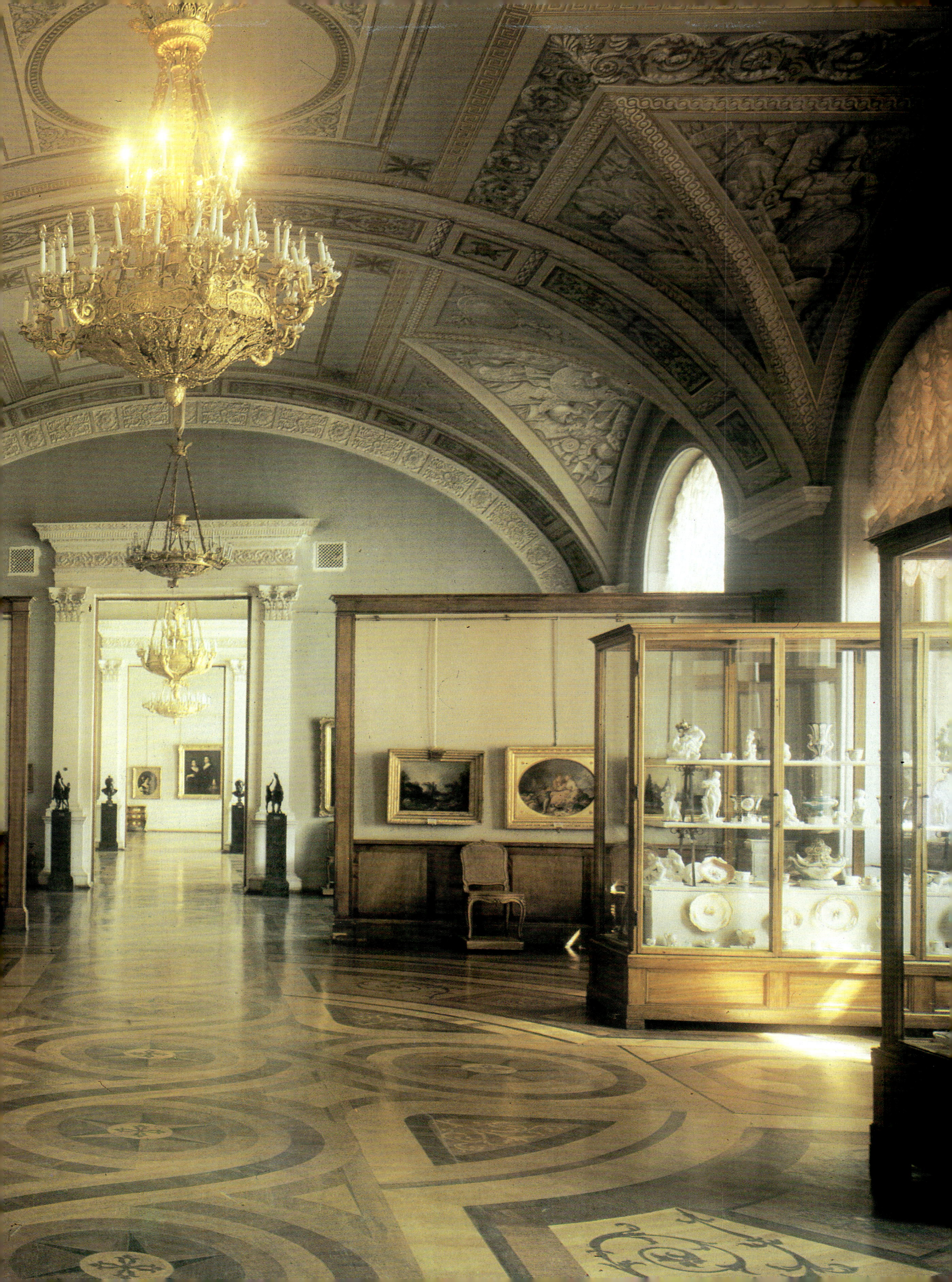

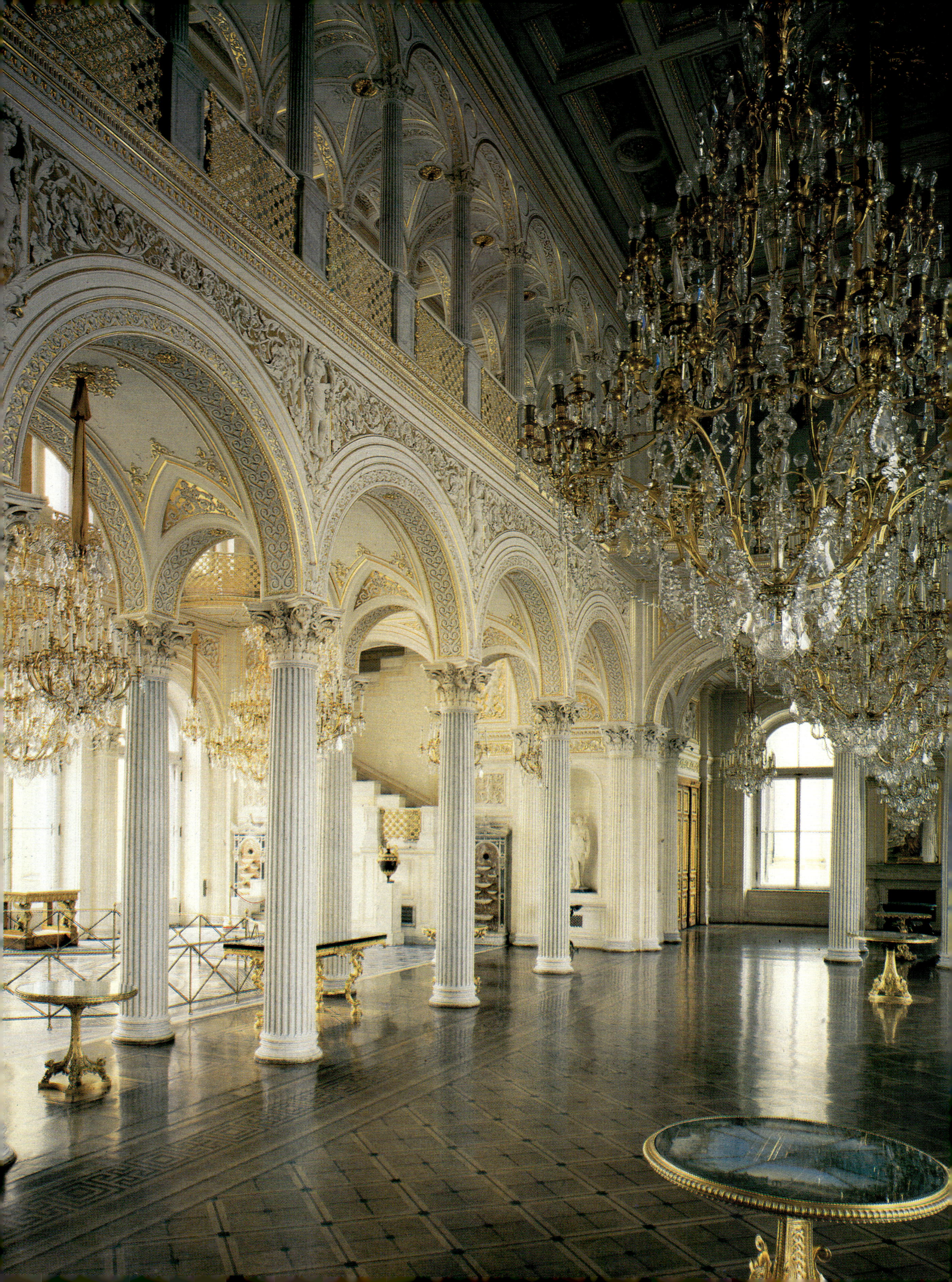

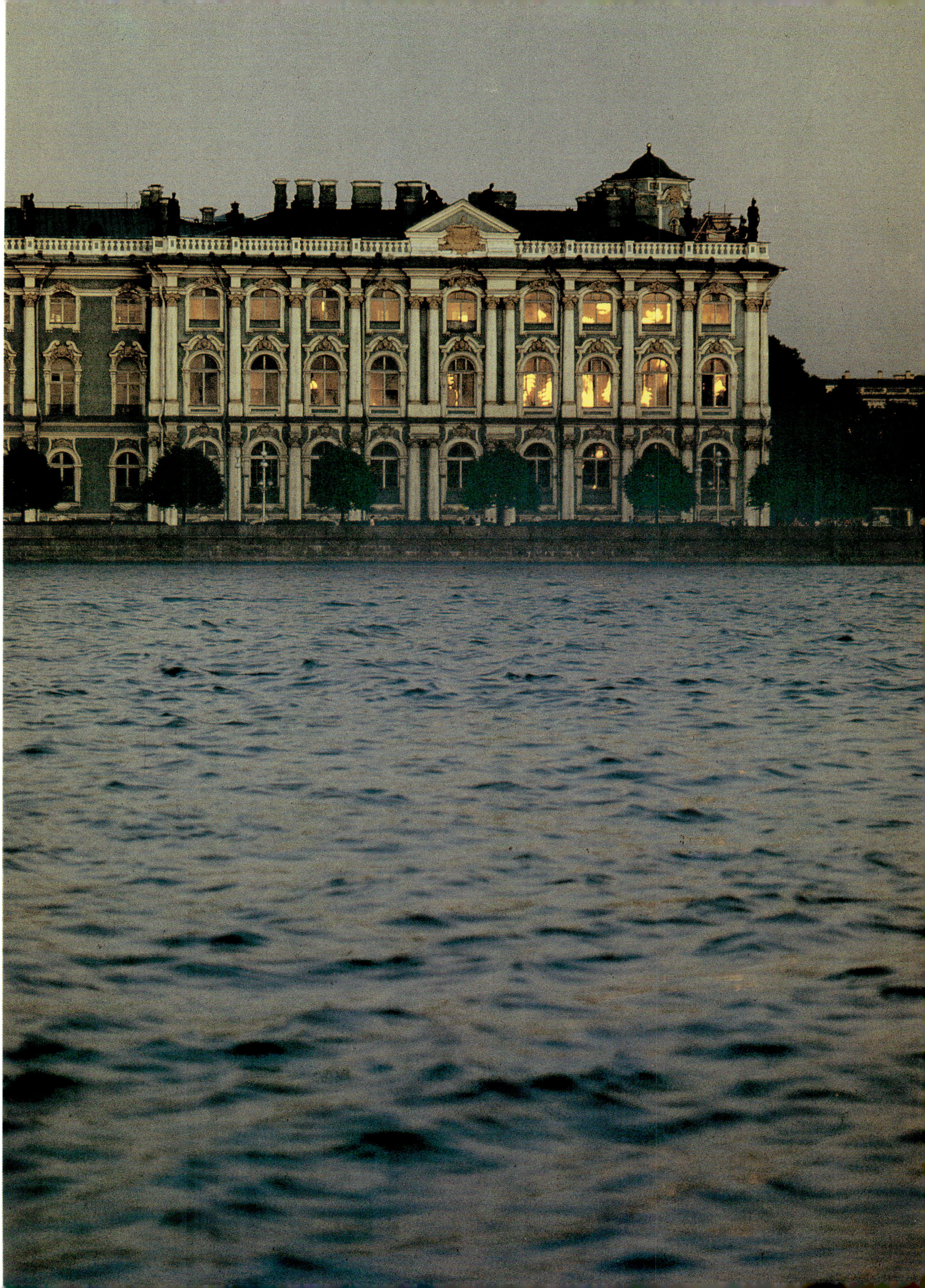

← 28

29

30, 32   New Hermitage. The portico with Atlantes
31   Winter Canal

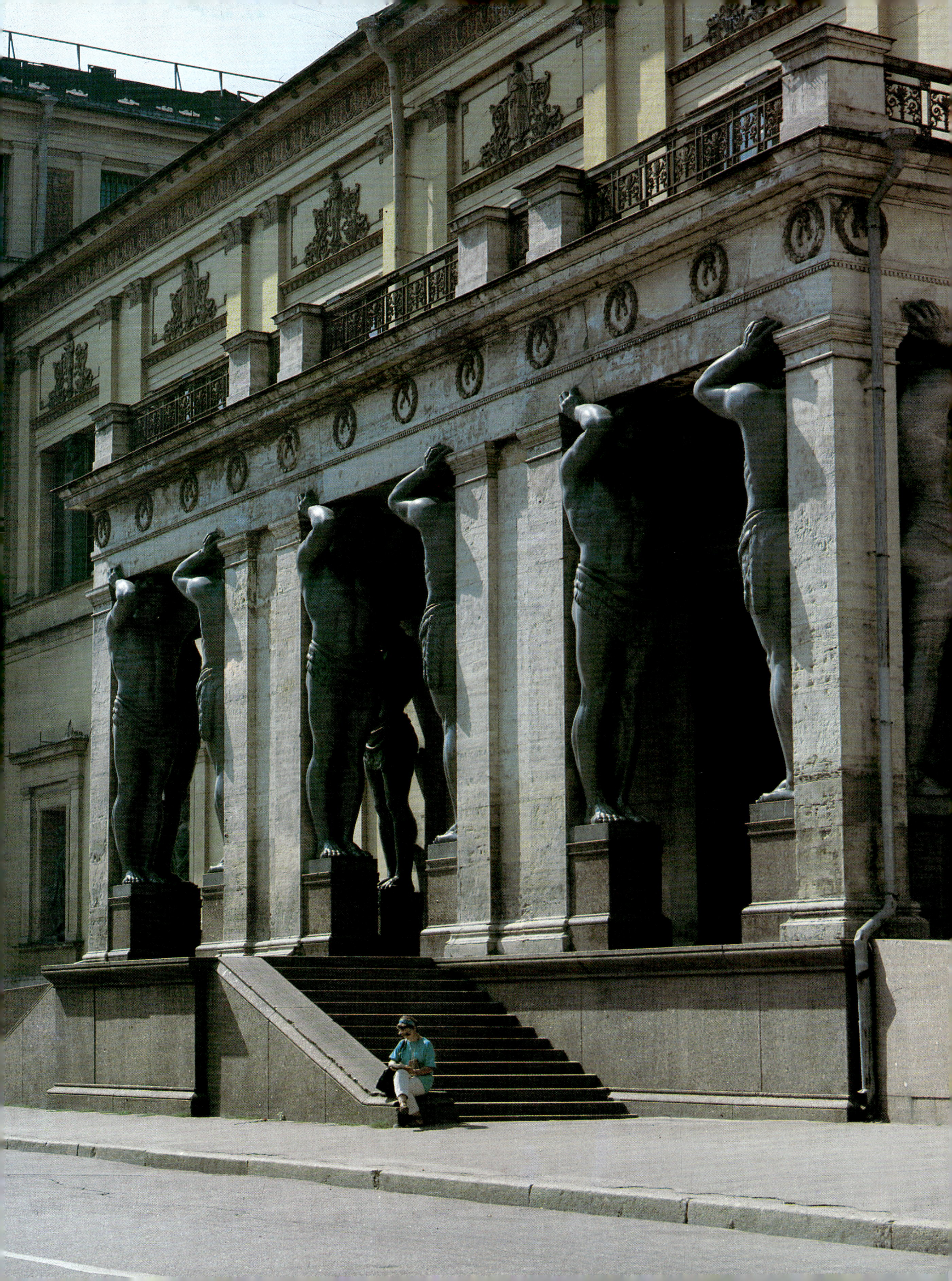

33 Hermitage Theatre
34 Winter Palace.
   The Saltykov Porch

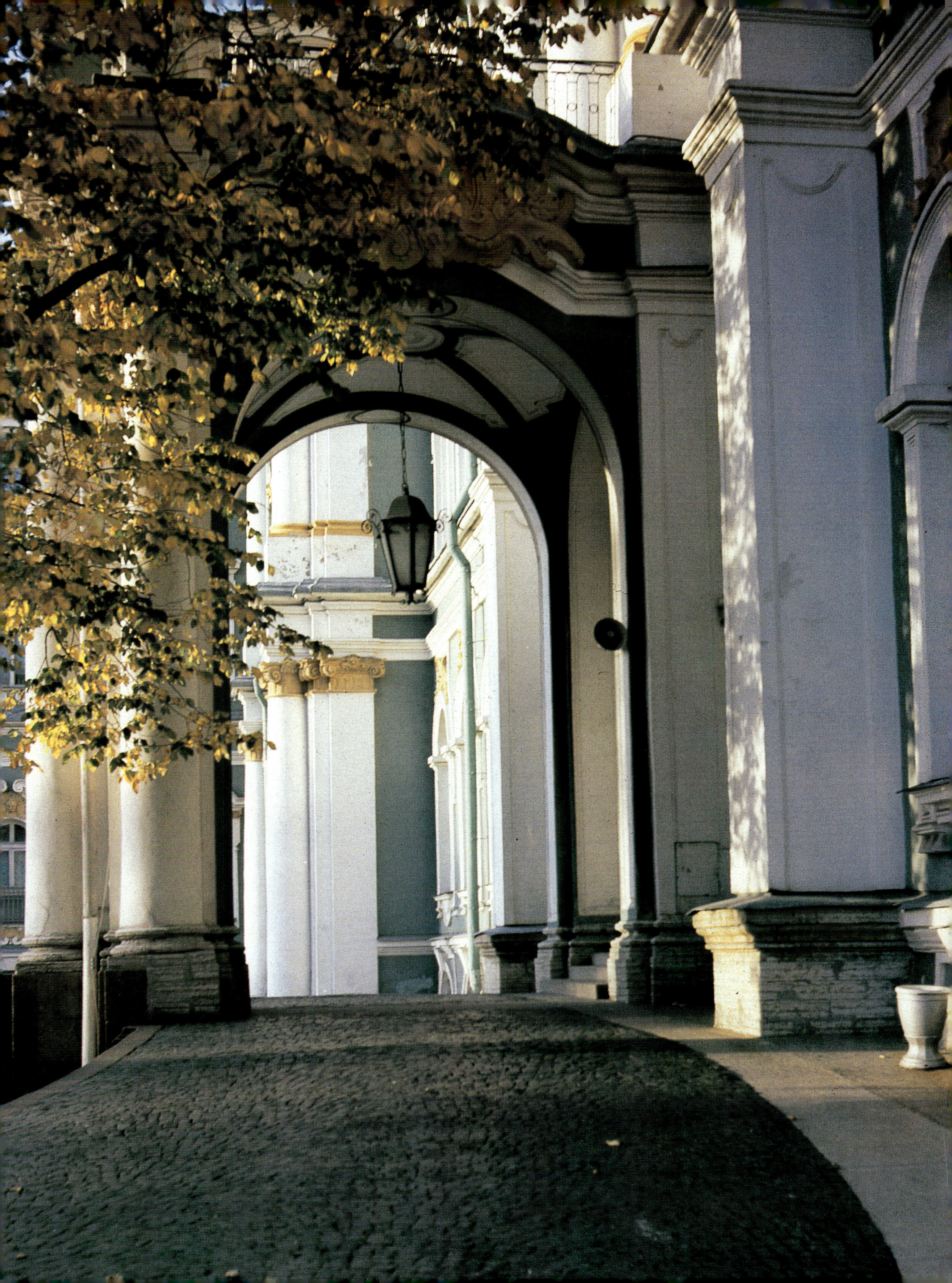

35

35 Palace Square and St. Isaac's Cathedral
    seen from the New Hermitage portico
36 Novomikhailovsky Palace

37 Winter Canal at night →
38 Palace Embankment.
    Lamp post →

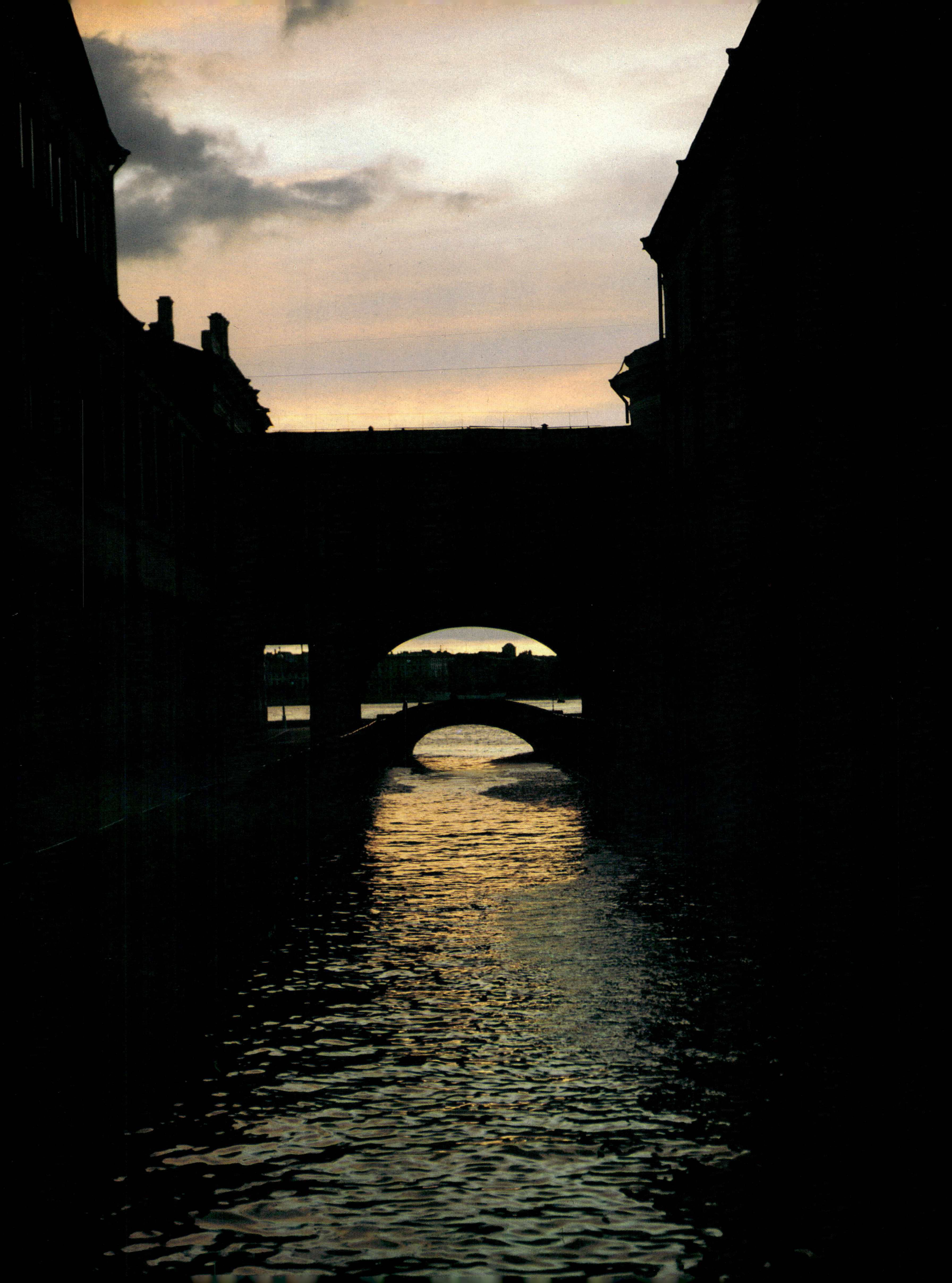

← 37

38

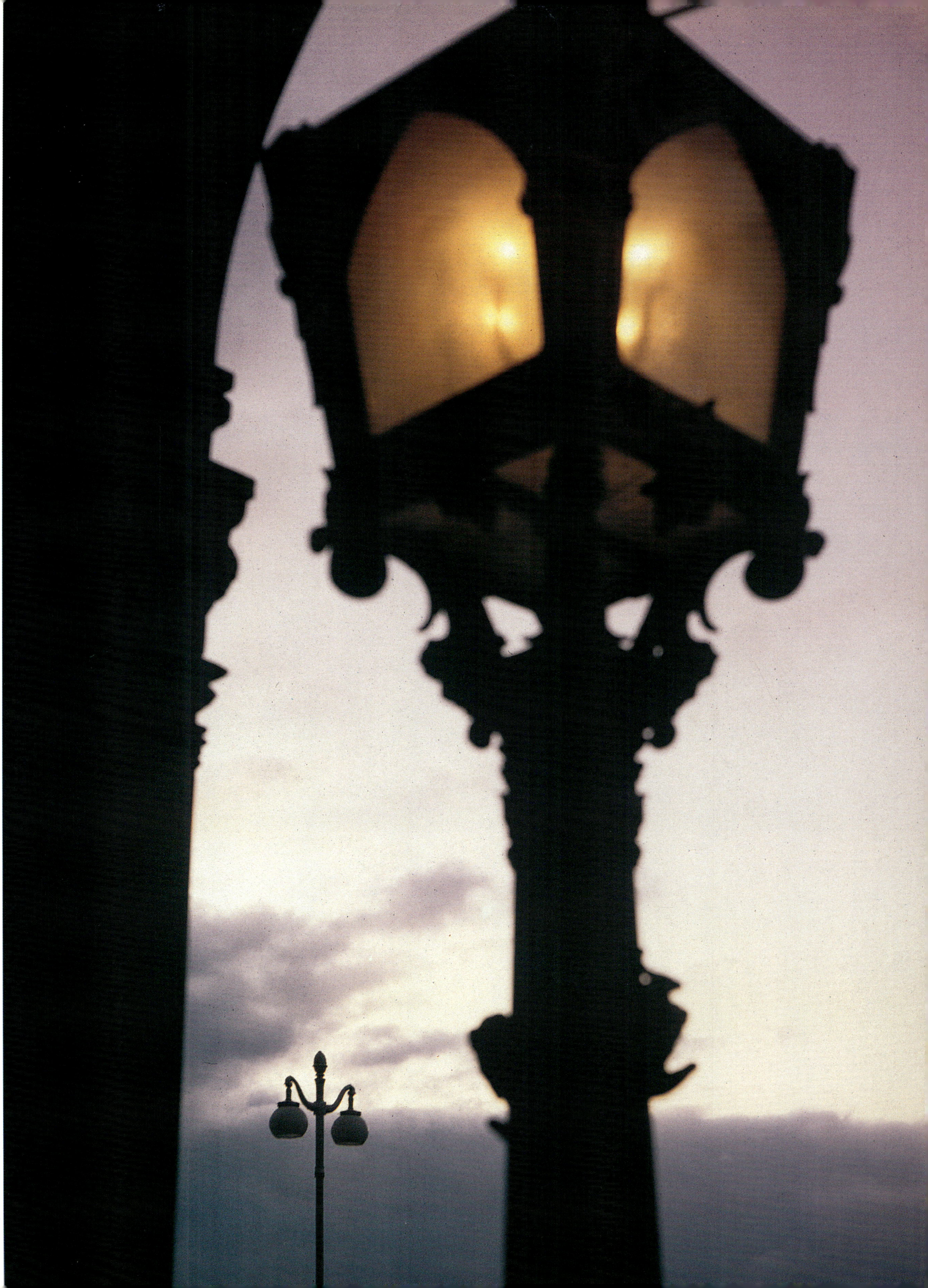

39 *Admiralty. The Eastern Pavilion*
40 *Admiralty. Tower and Steeple*

41 *Admiralteysky Prospect* →
42 *Admiralty* →
43 *Admiralty Tower. White frost* →
44 *Arch of the Headquarters. Detail* →
45 *Palace Square seen through the Arch of the Headquarters* →
46 *Palace Square* →

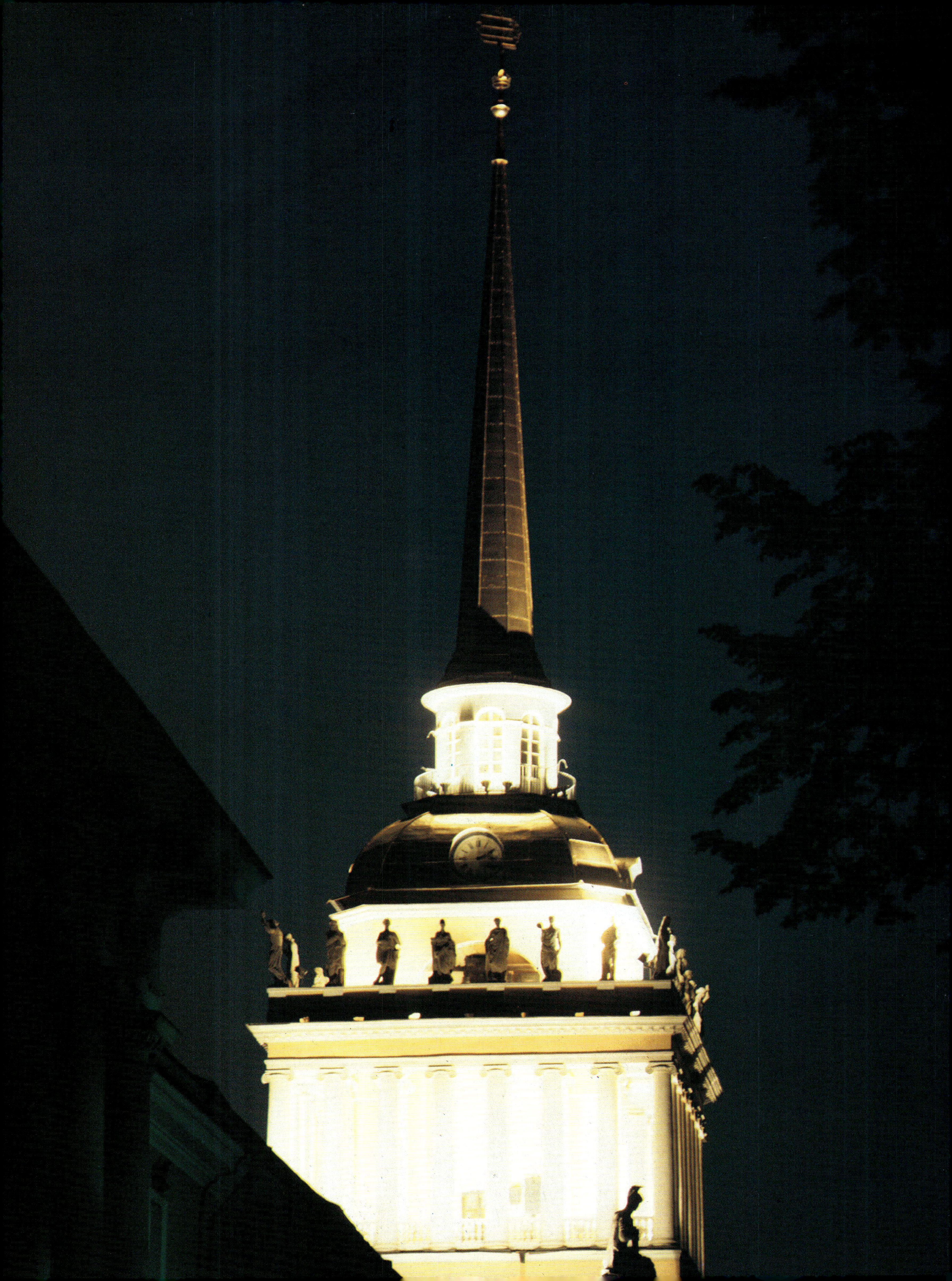

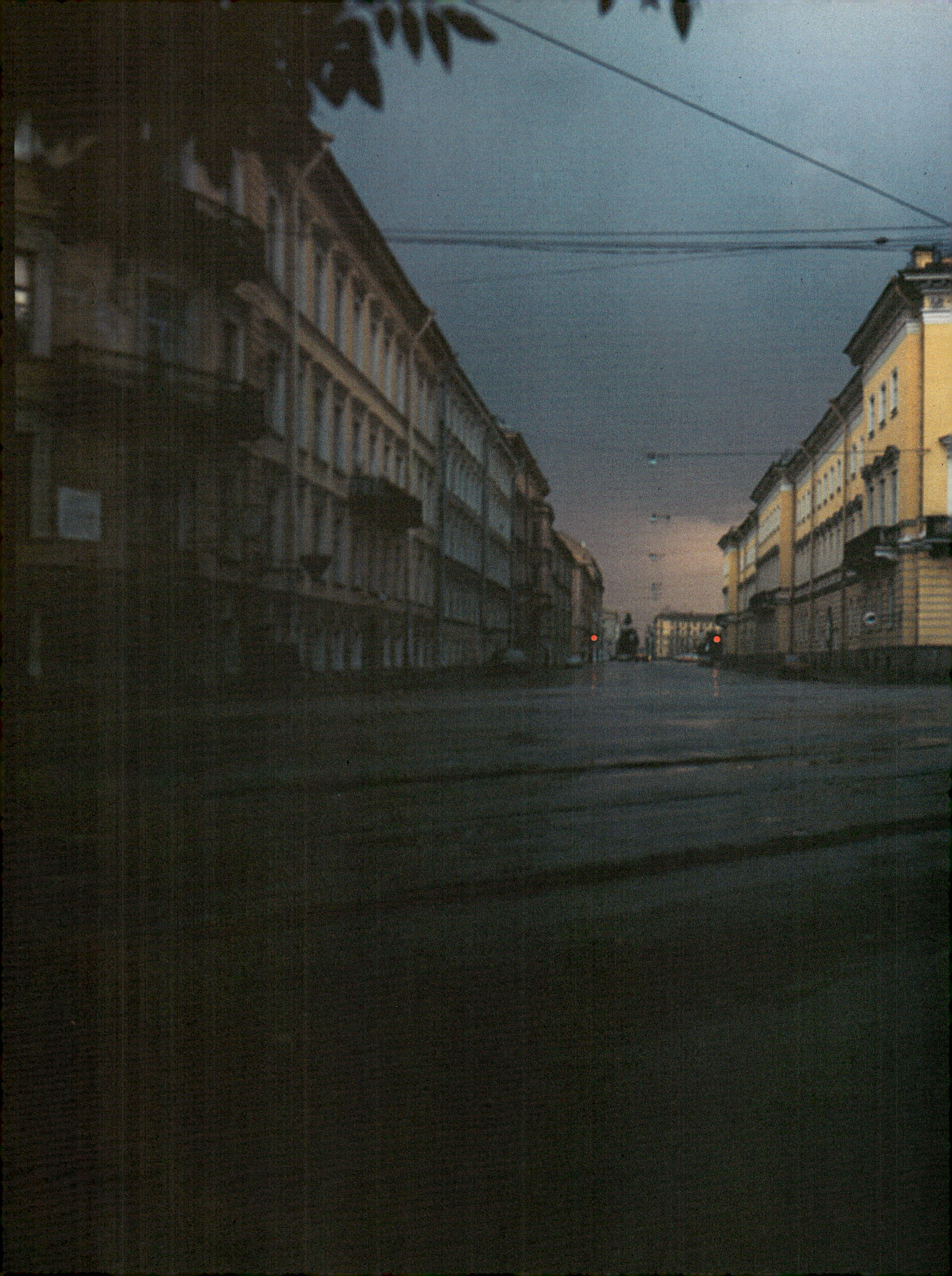

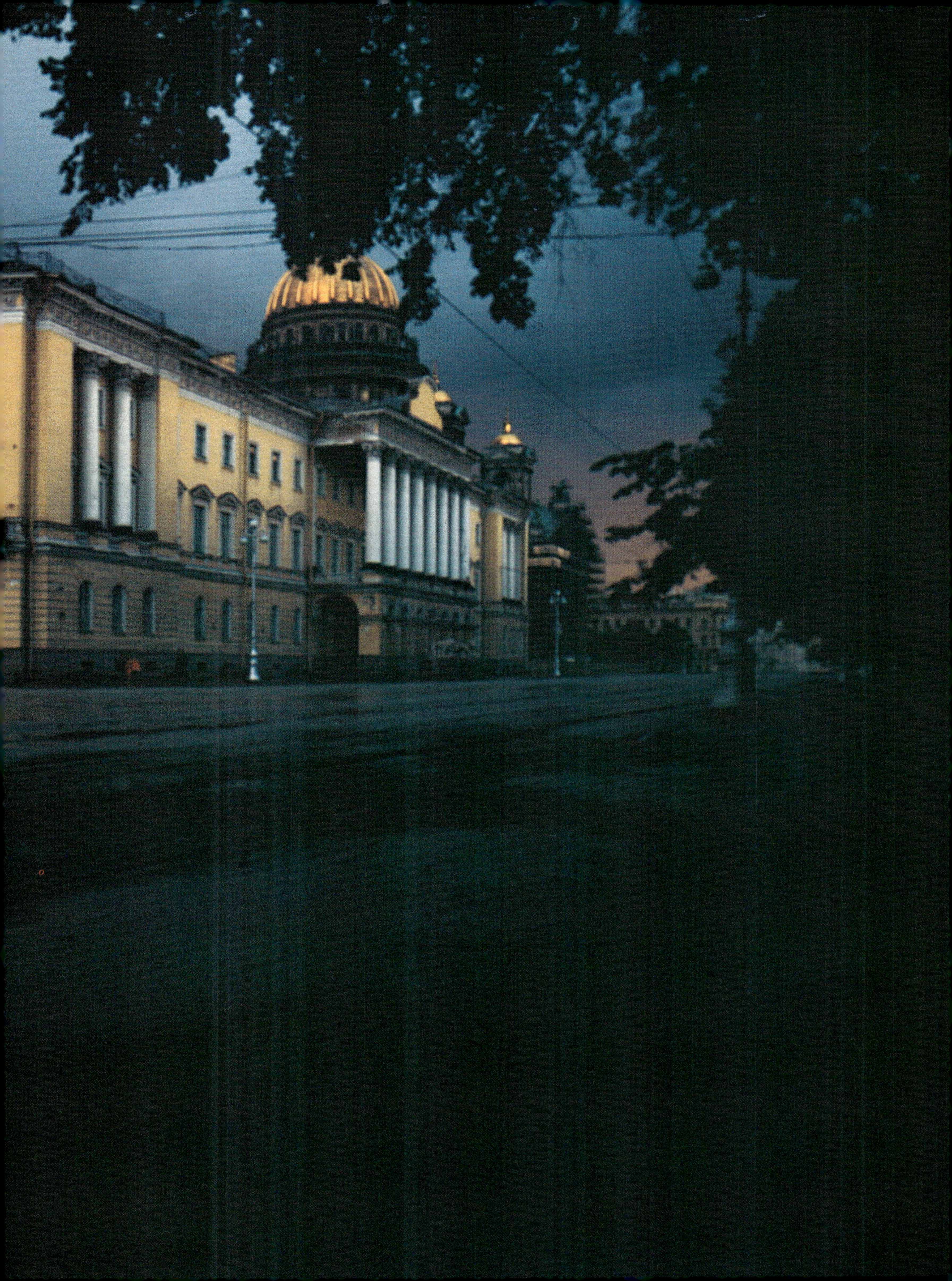

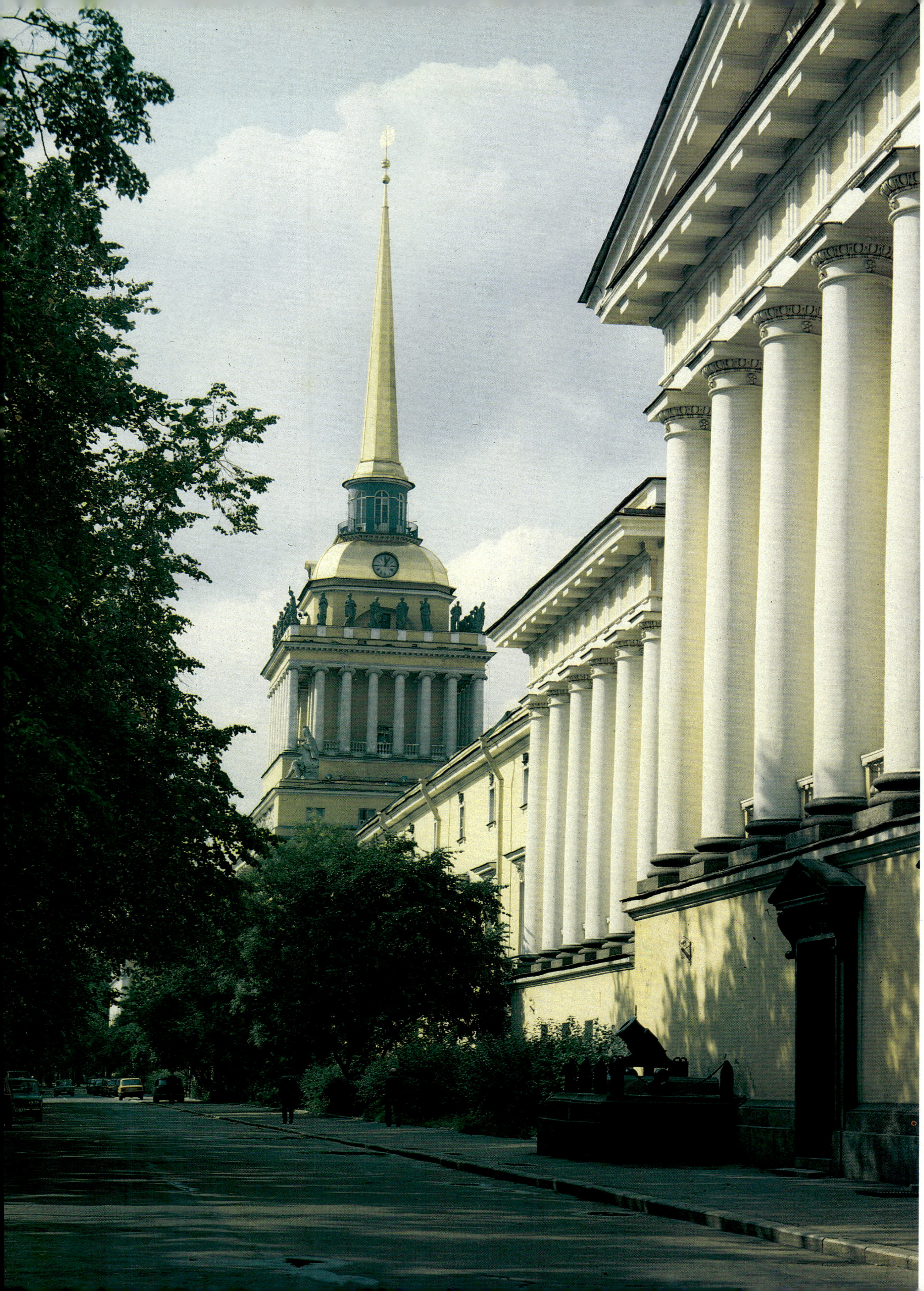

42
→
43

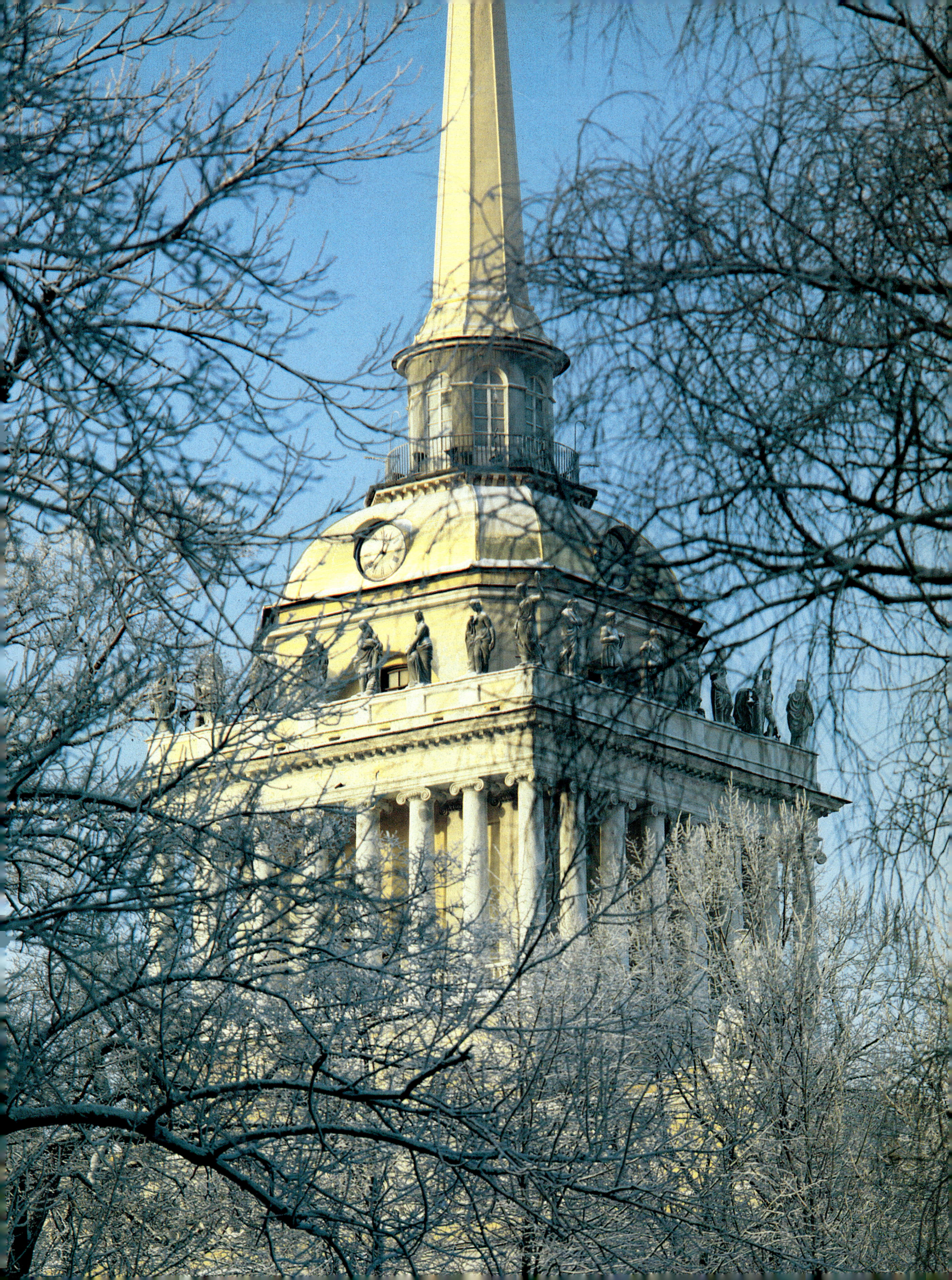

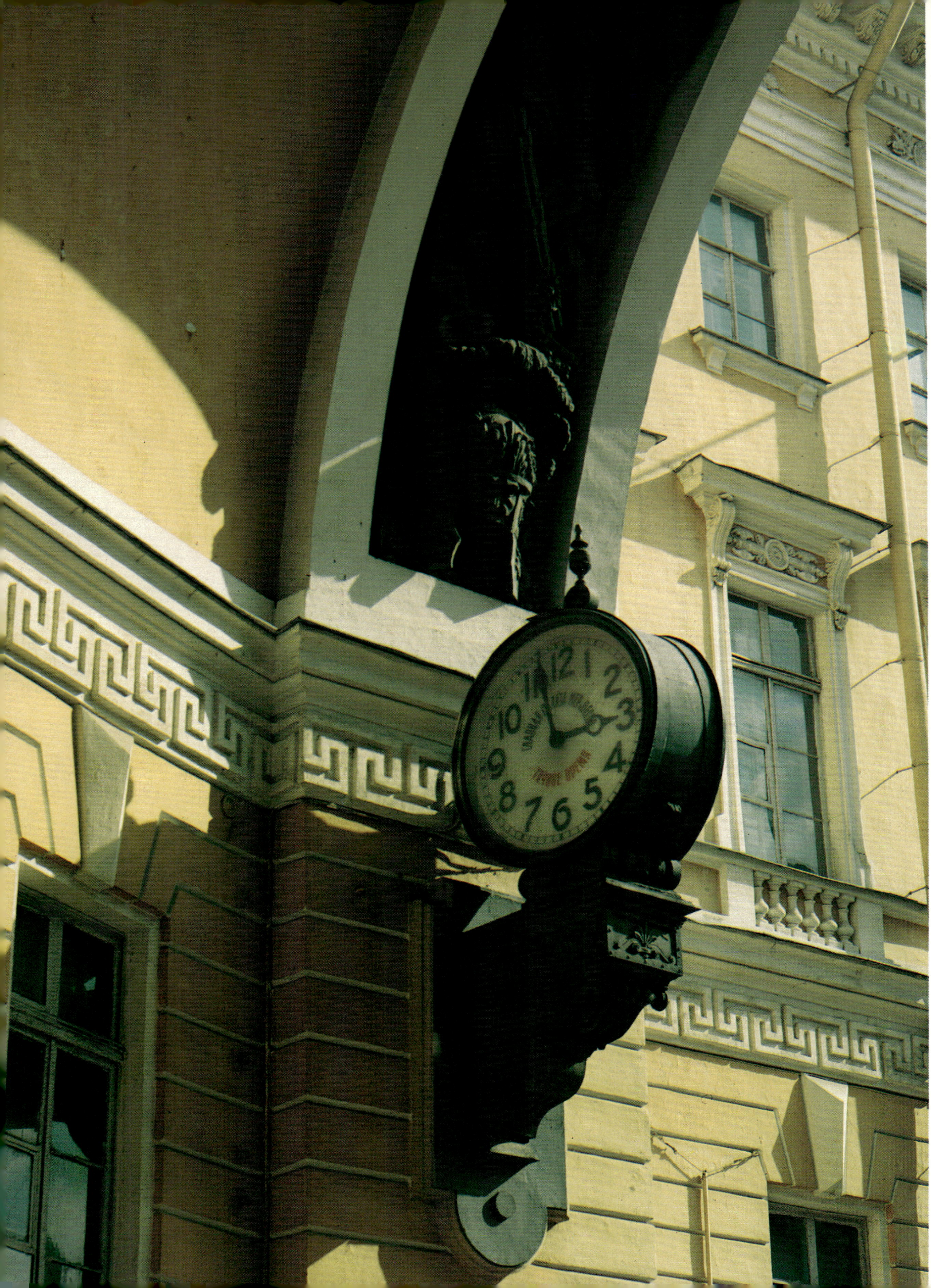

44
→
45

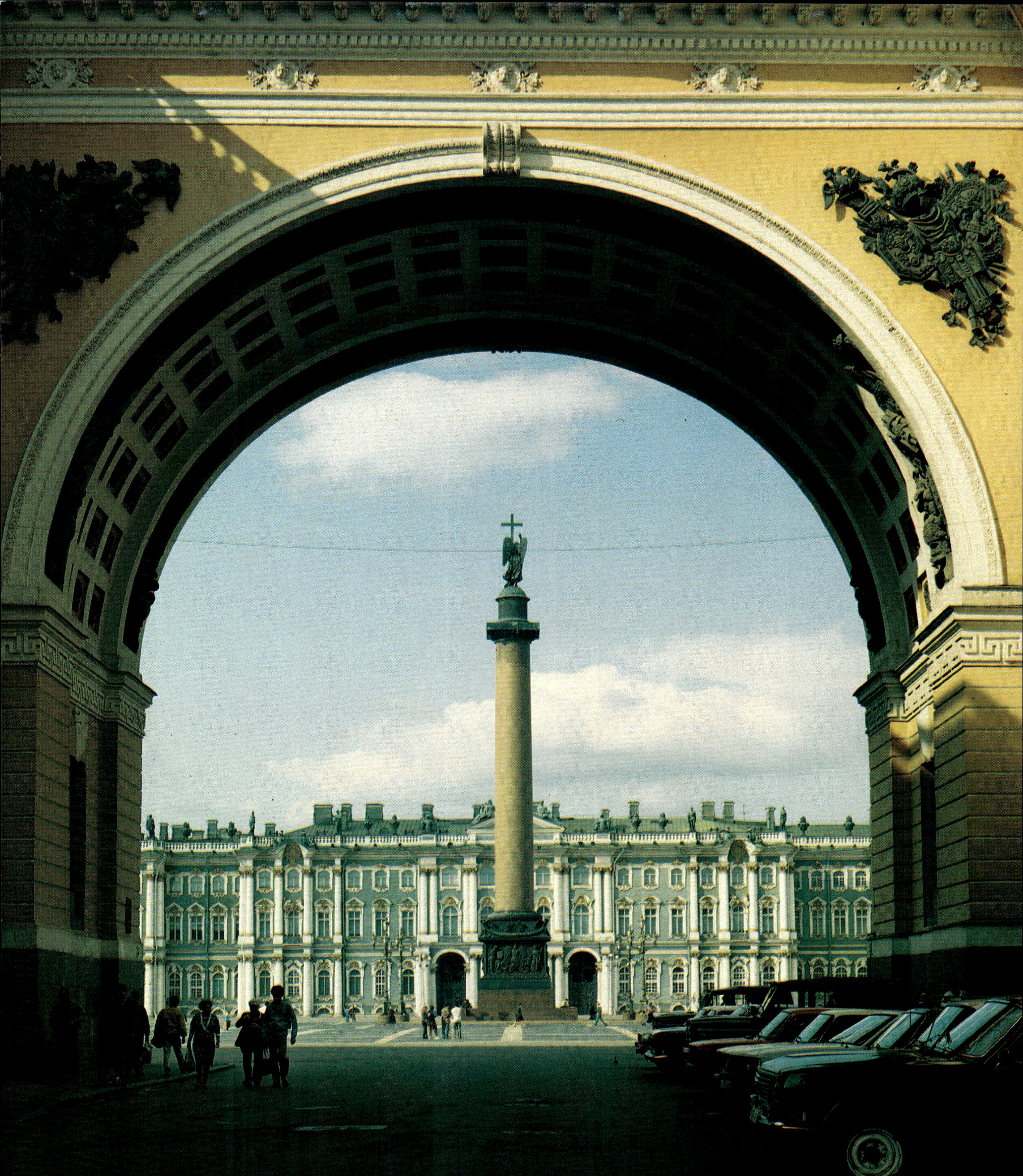

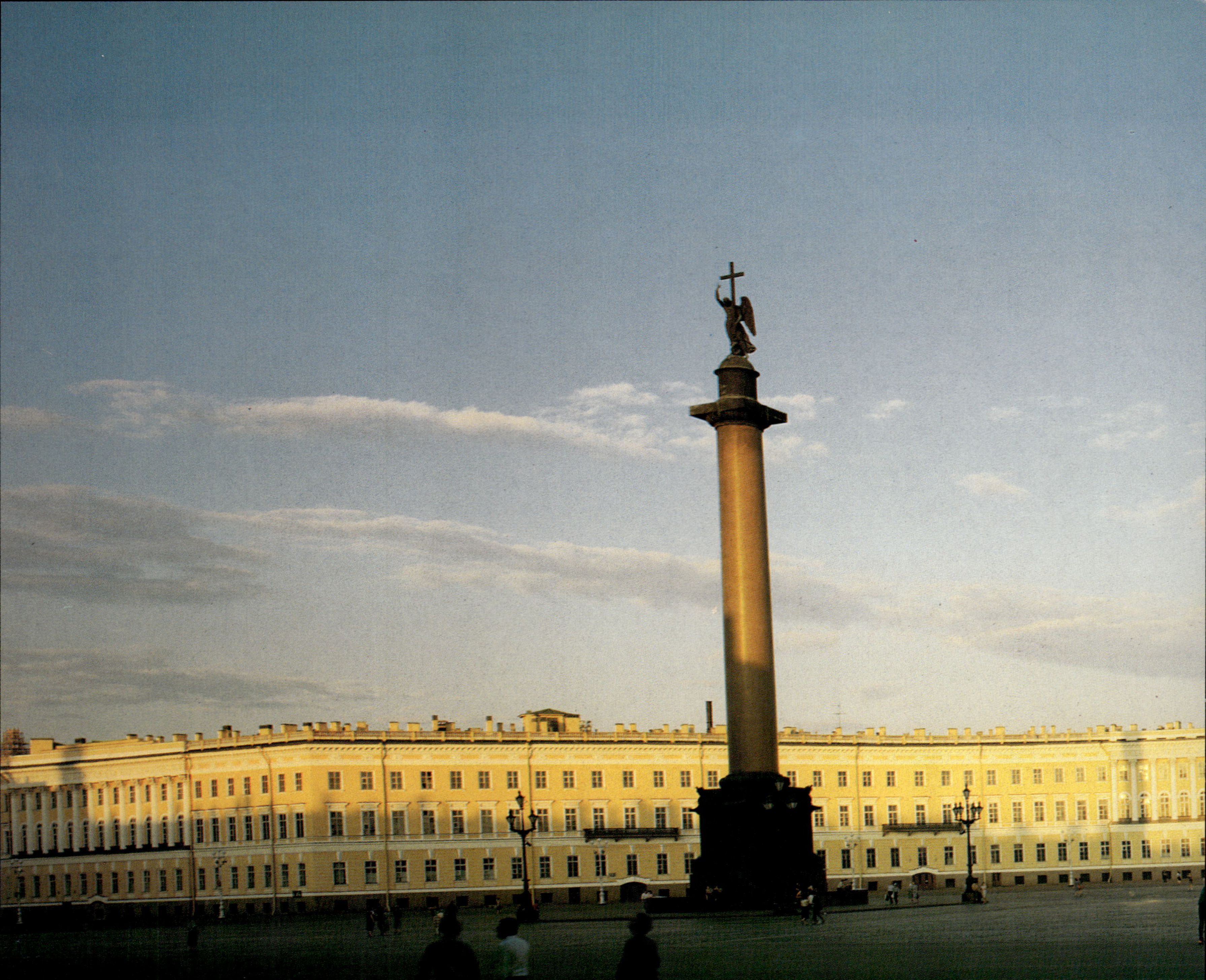

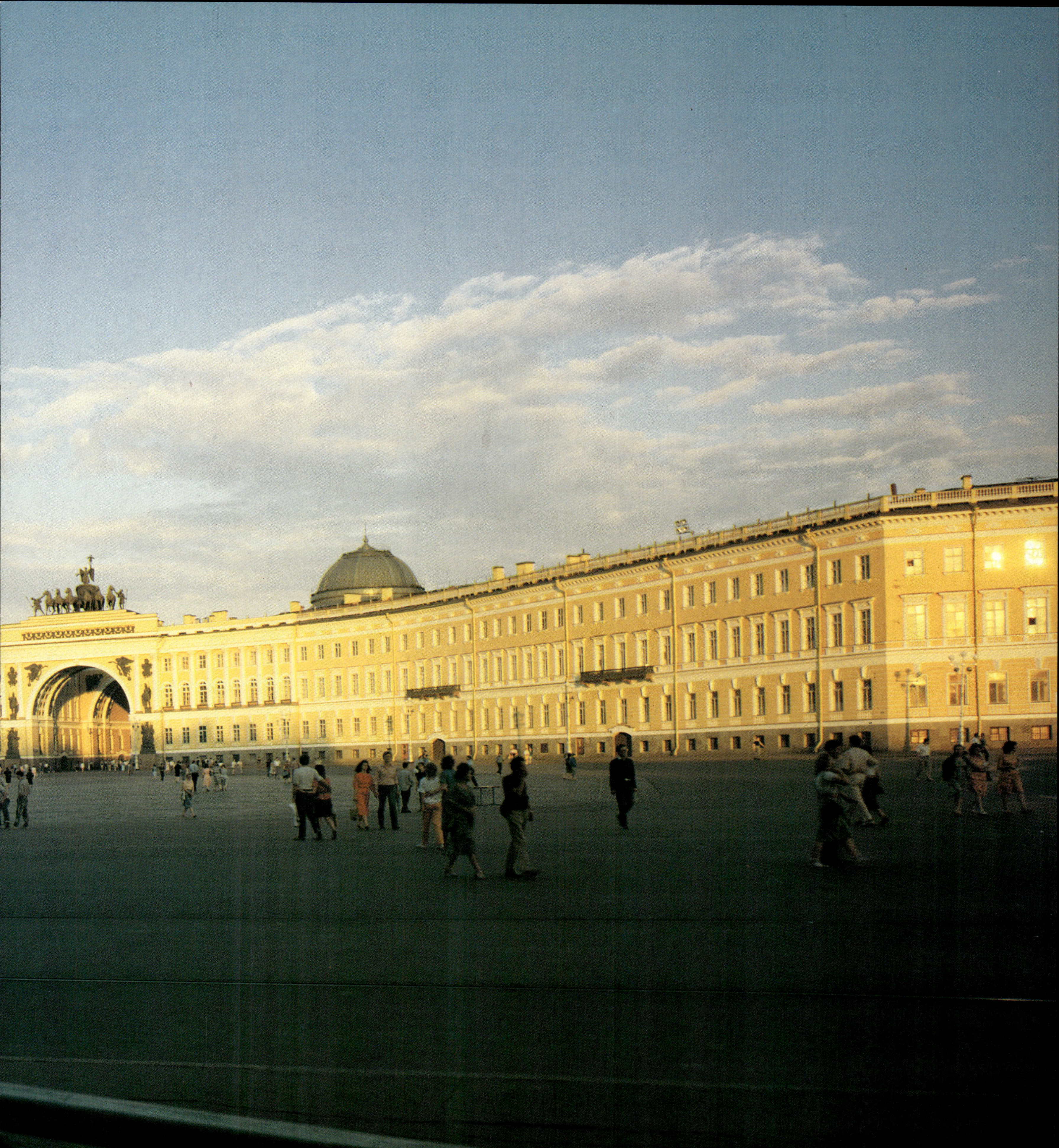

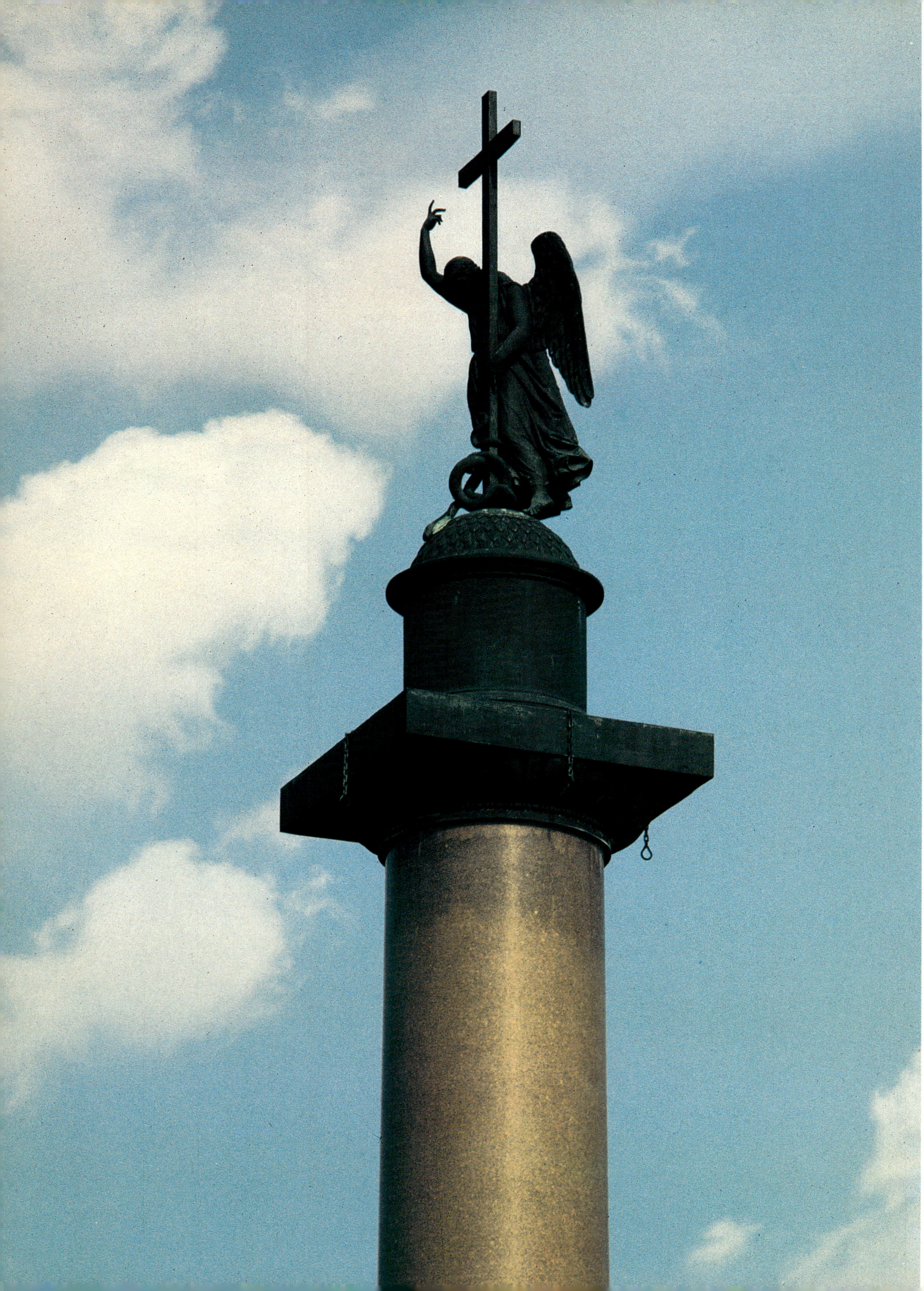

47
→
48

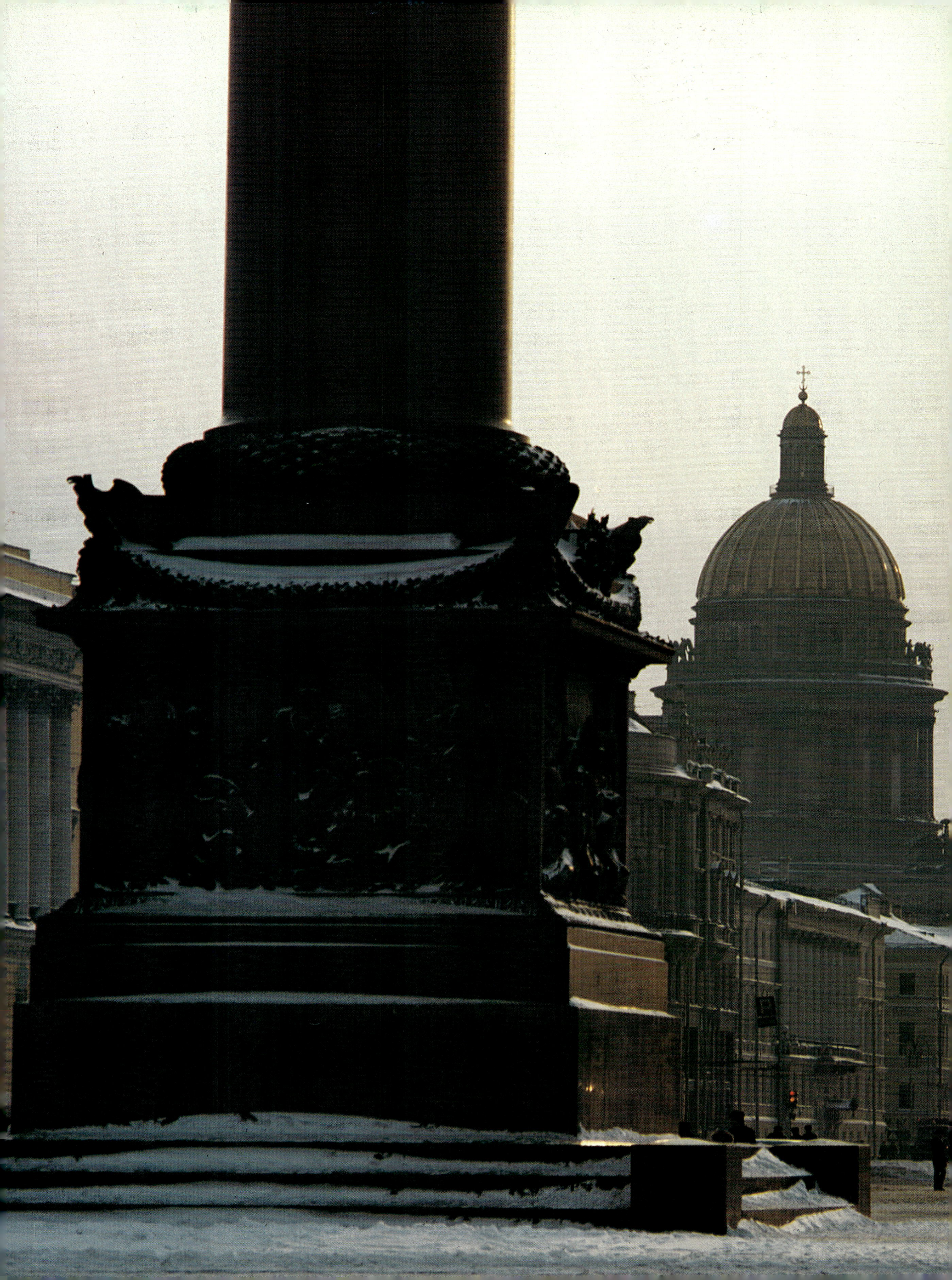

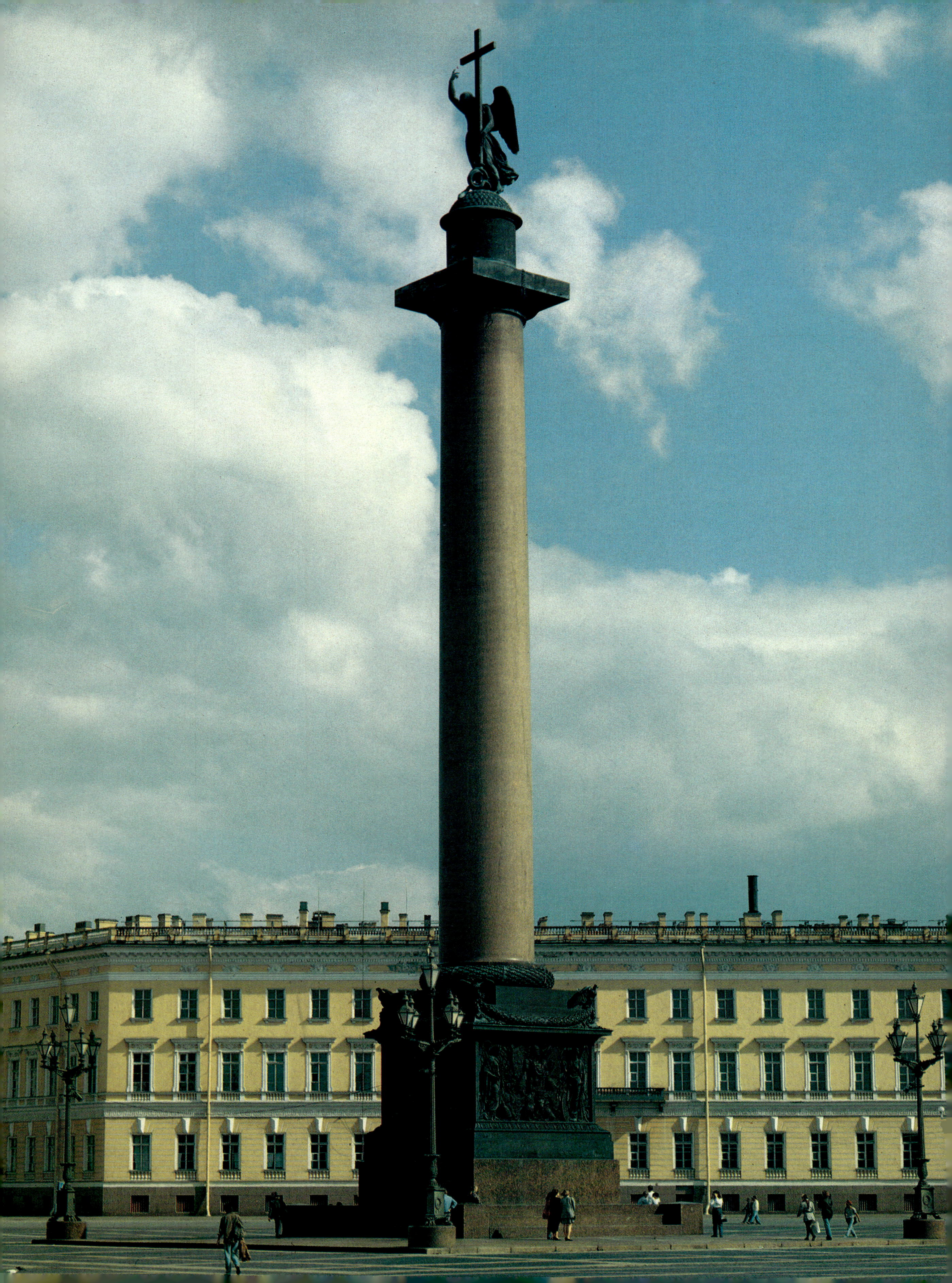

47—49 *Alexander Column*
50, 51 *Arch of the Headquarters*

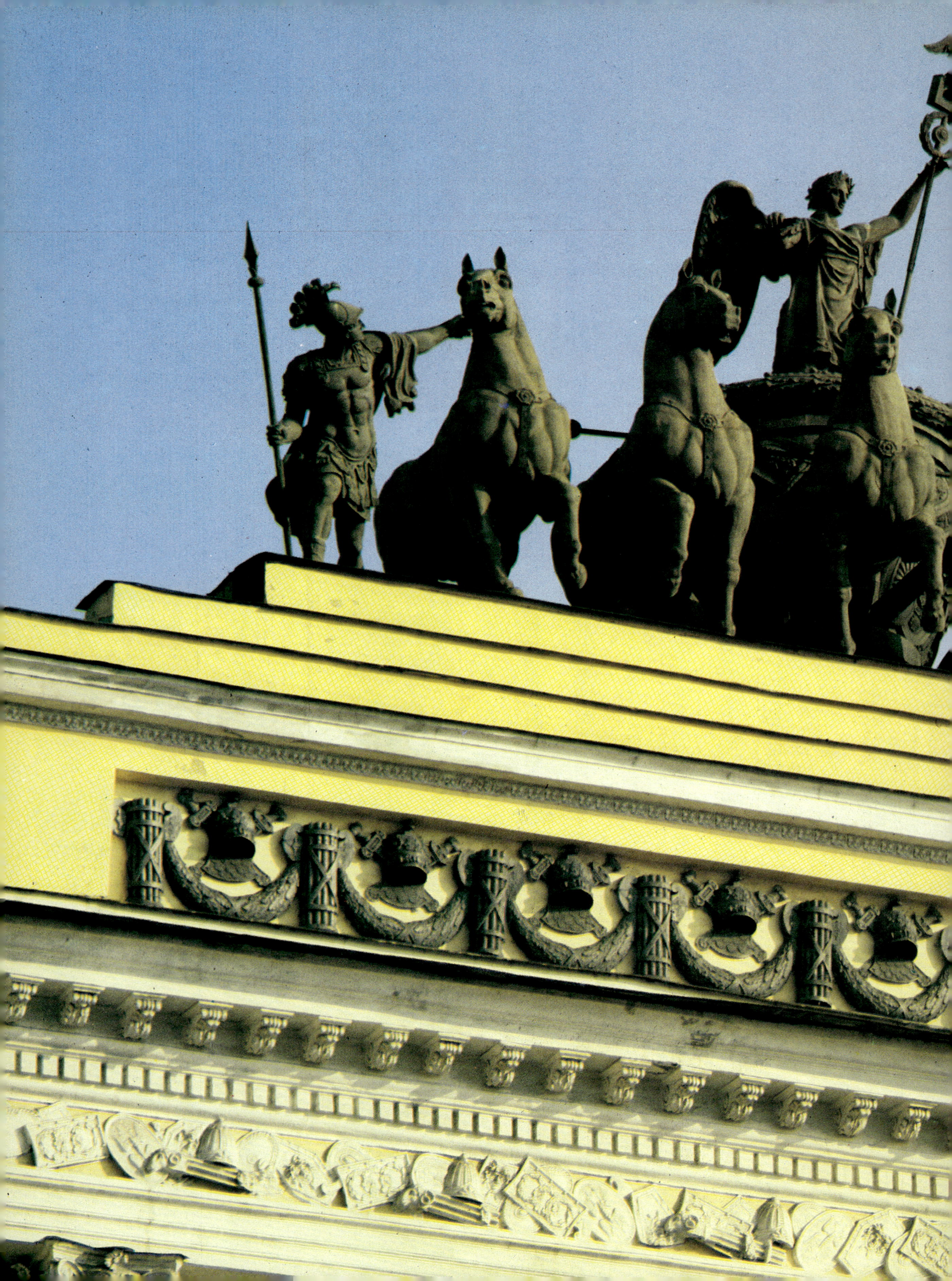

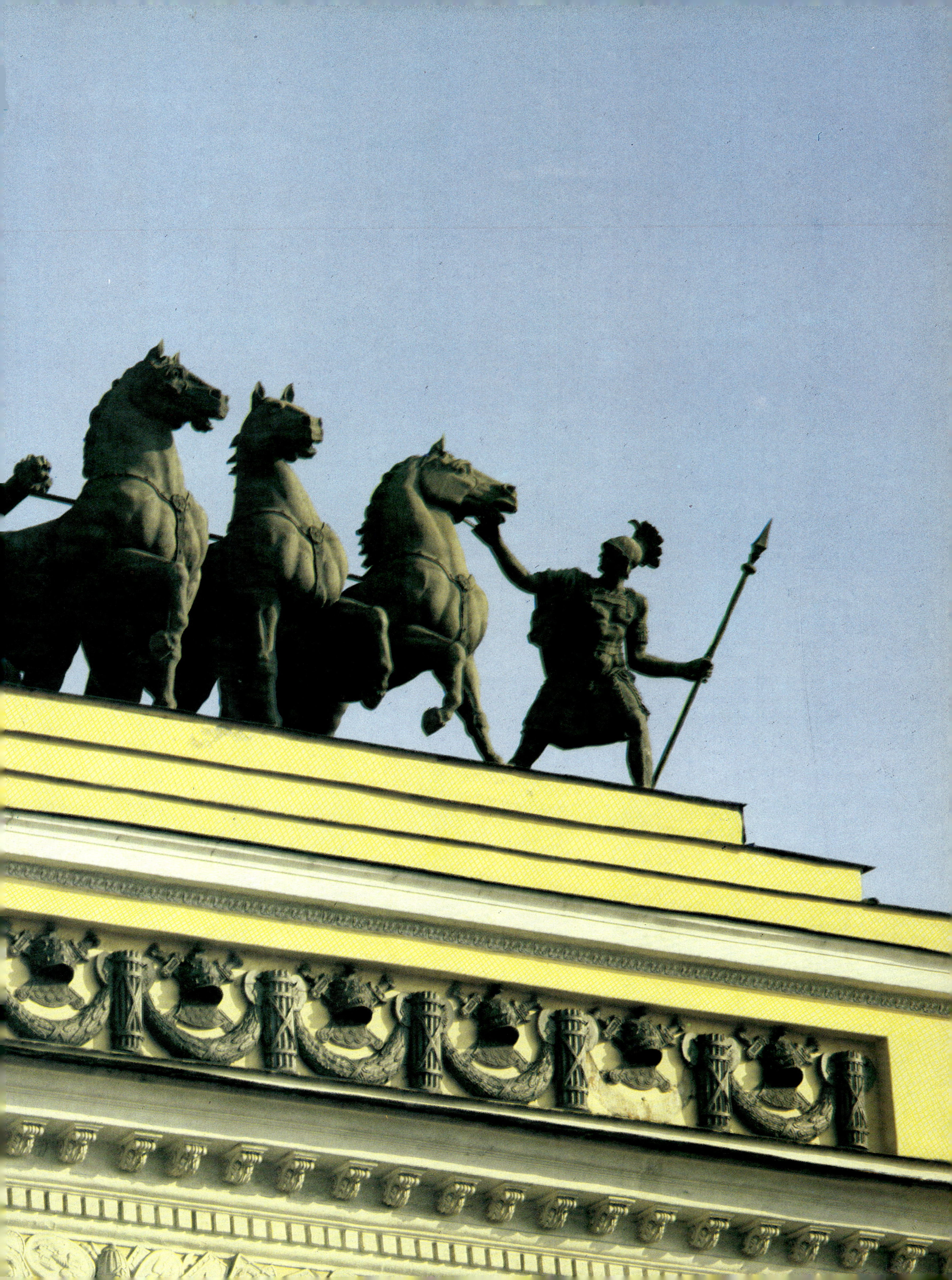

52 St. Isaac Square
53 St. Isaac's Cathedral seen from the Manege

54 St. Isaac's Cathedral.
    Cupola drum: a detail →
55 Monument to Nicholas I →
56 St. Isaac's Cathedral seen from the Neva →

57 St. Isaac's Cathedral. The Iconostasis →
58 St. Isaac's Cathedral. Apostle John →
59 Vasilyevsky Island seen from St. Isaac's
    Cathedral →
60 St. Isaac's Cathedral.
    Angels holding a lamp →
61 St. Isaac's Cathedral
    seen from St. Isaac Square →

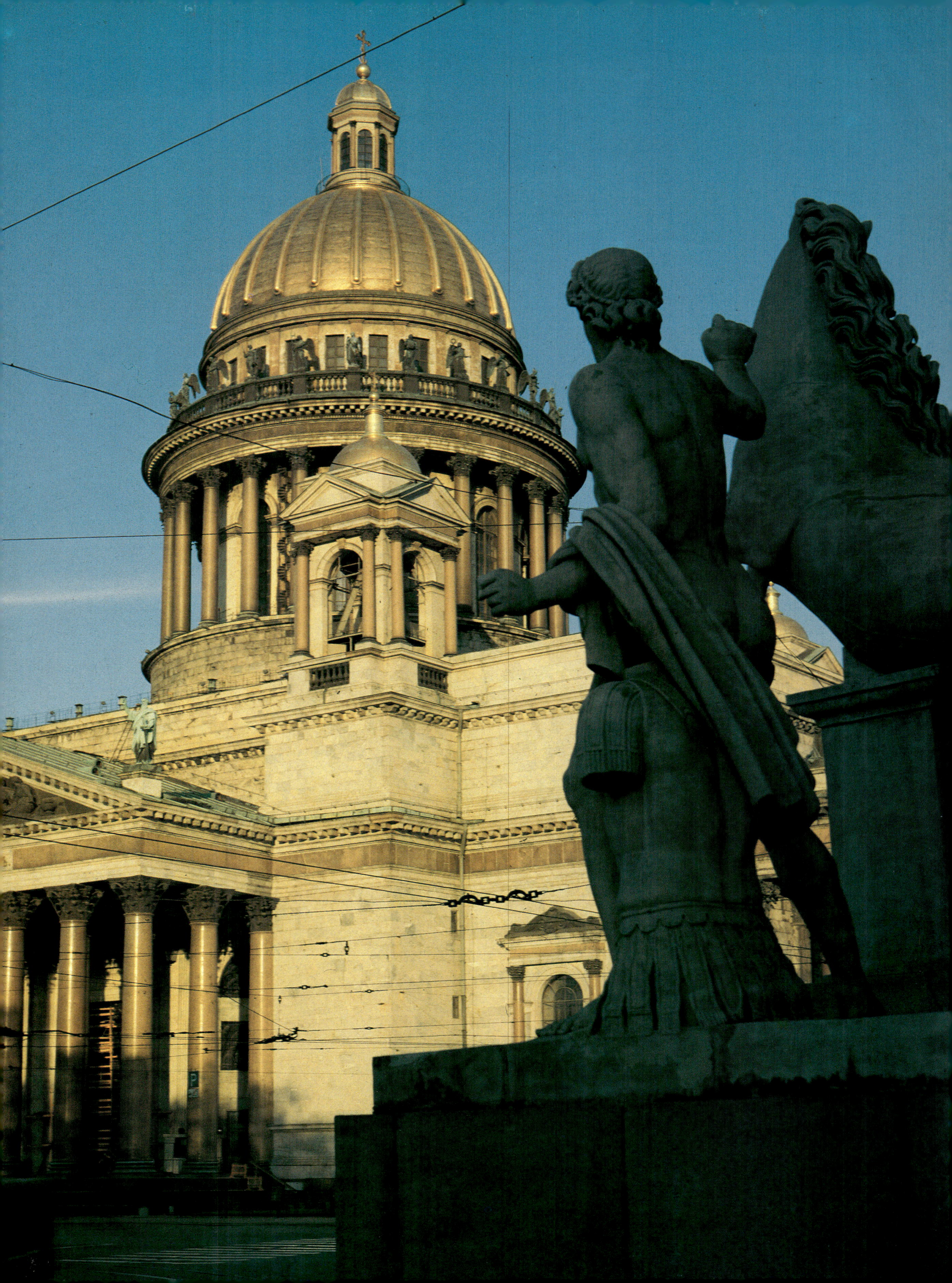

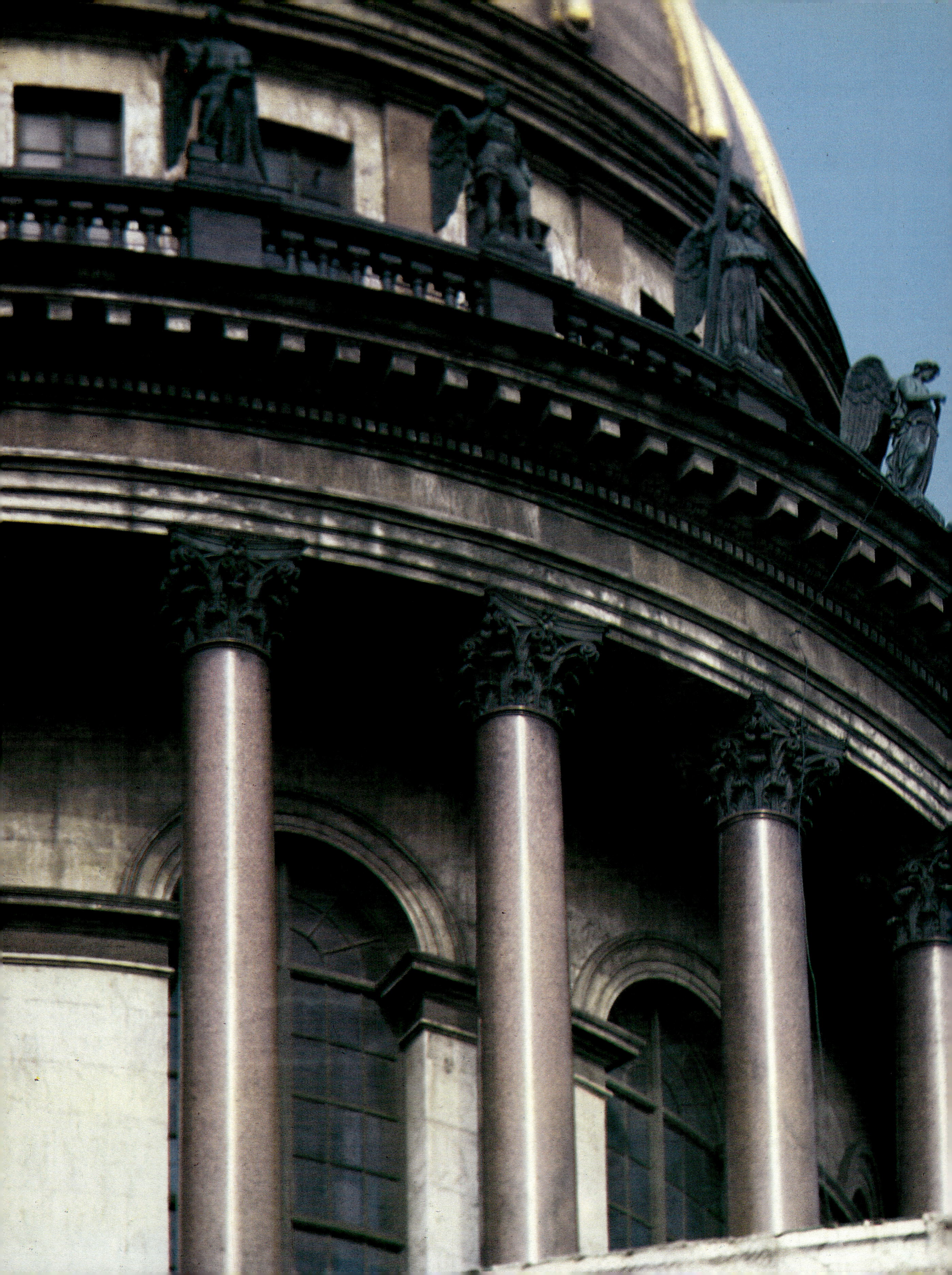

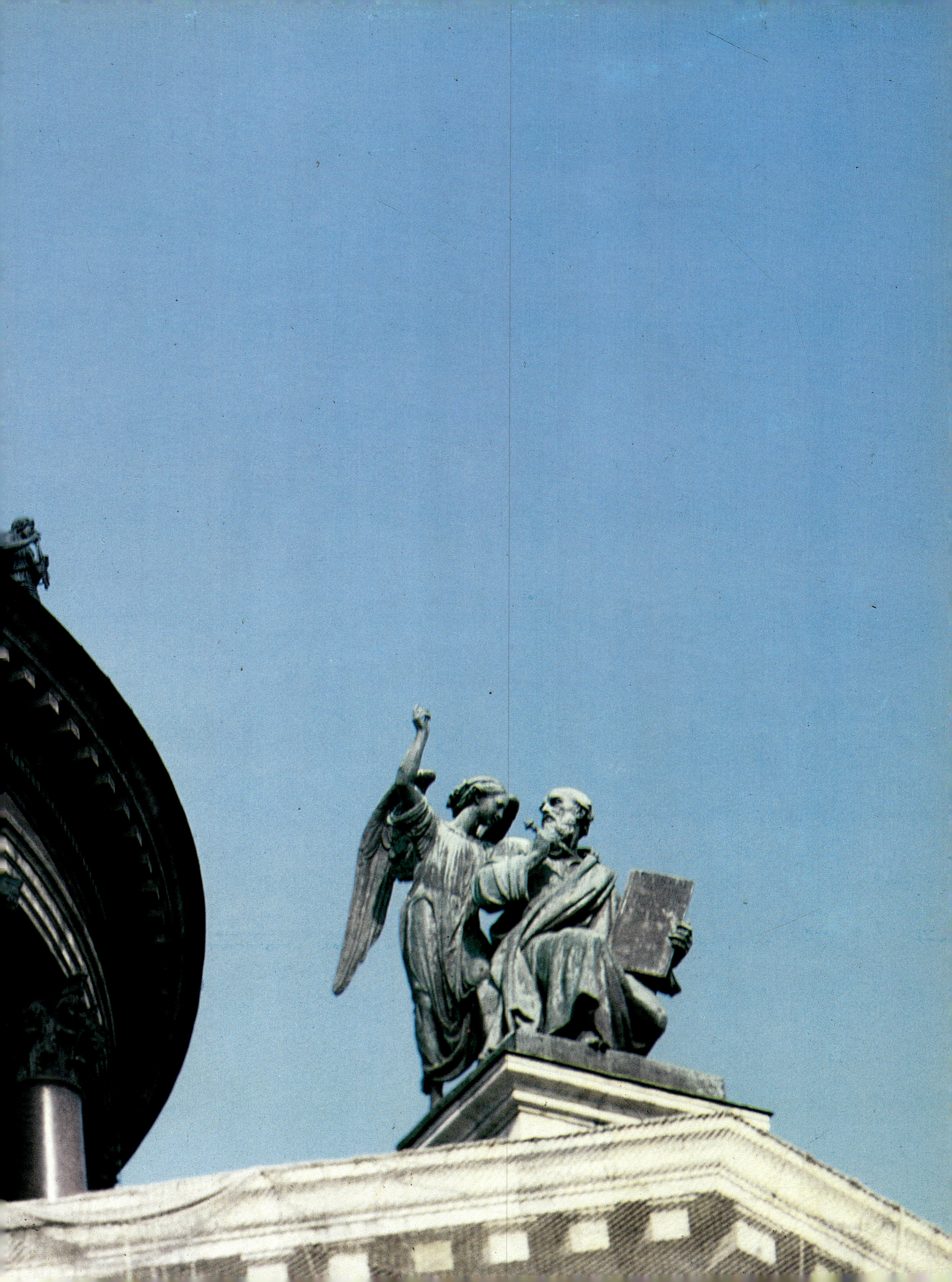

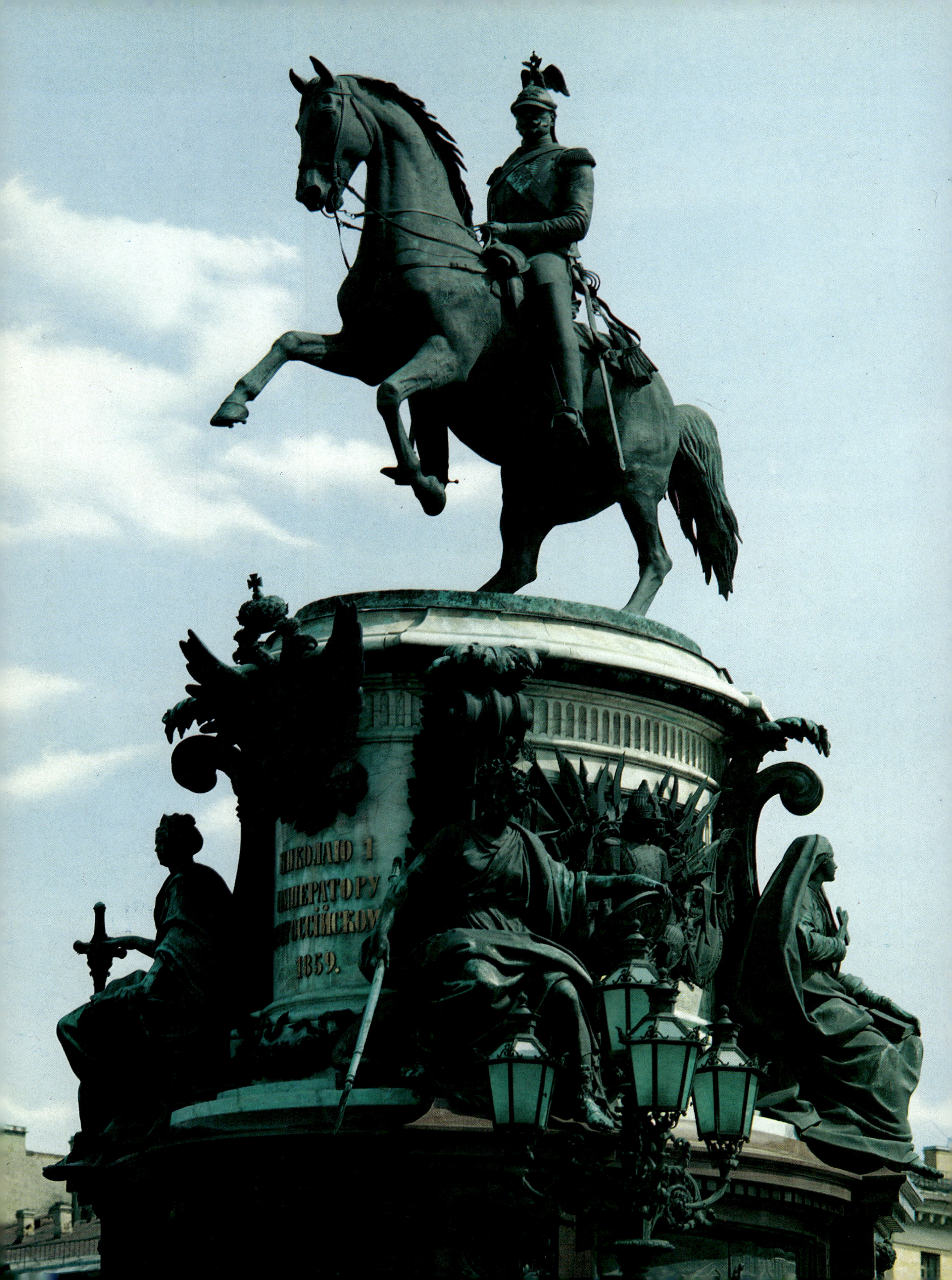
ИКОЛАЮ 1
ПЕРАТОРУ
ОССІЙСКОМ
1859.

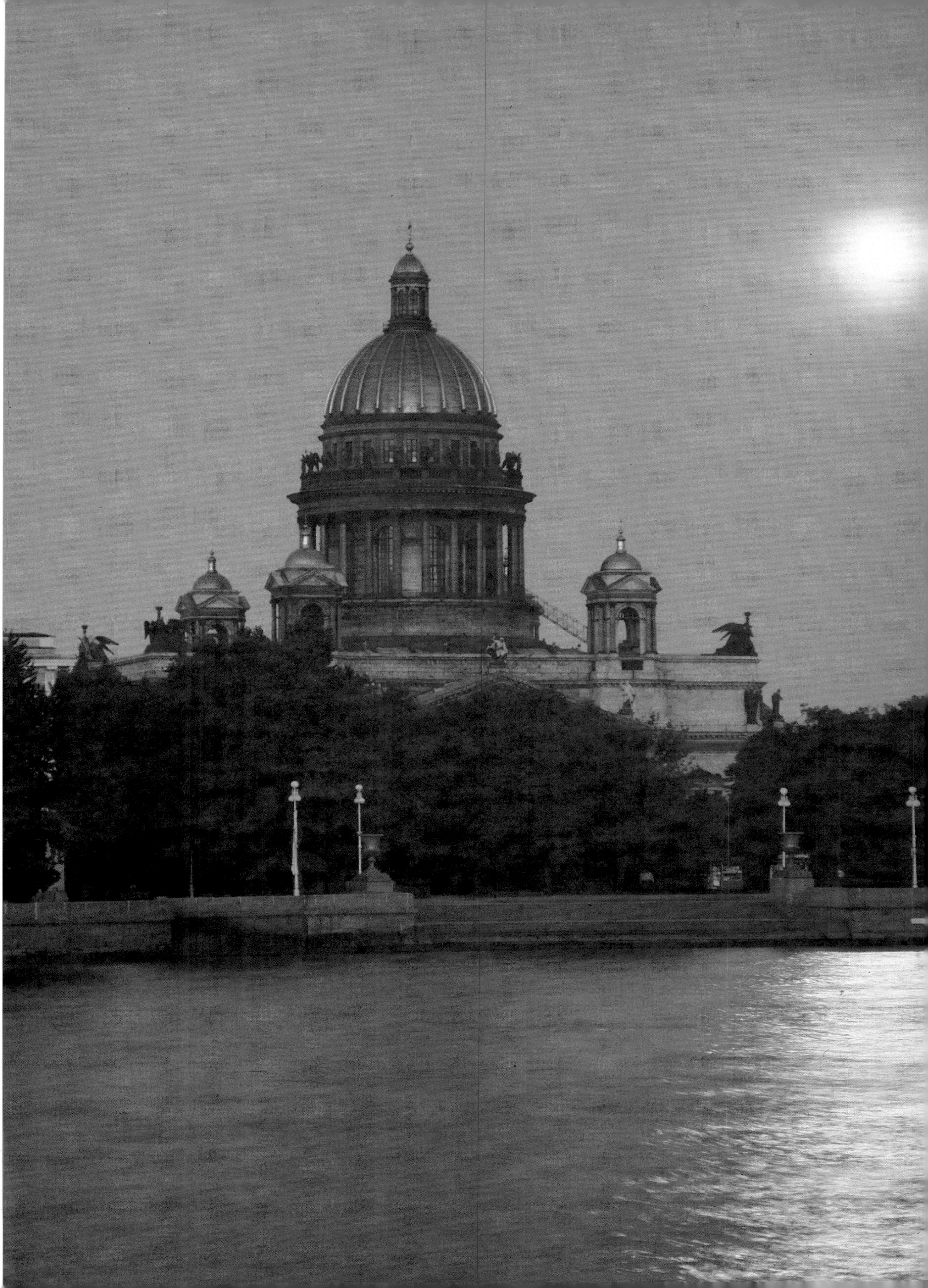

← 55

56

57
→
58

ЧУДЕСА ... БУДИ ГСПОДН

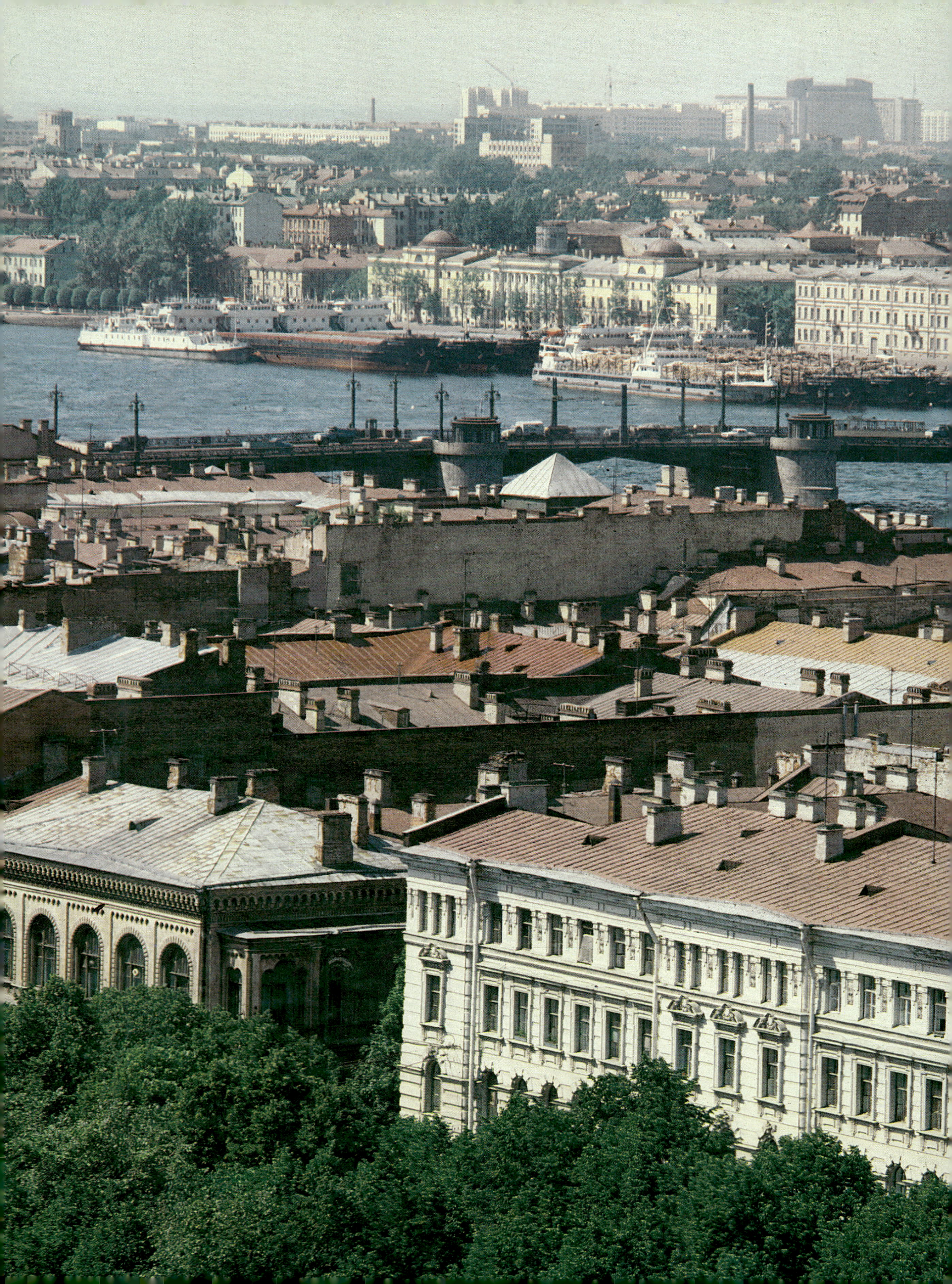

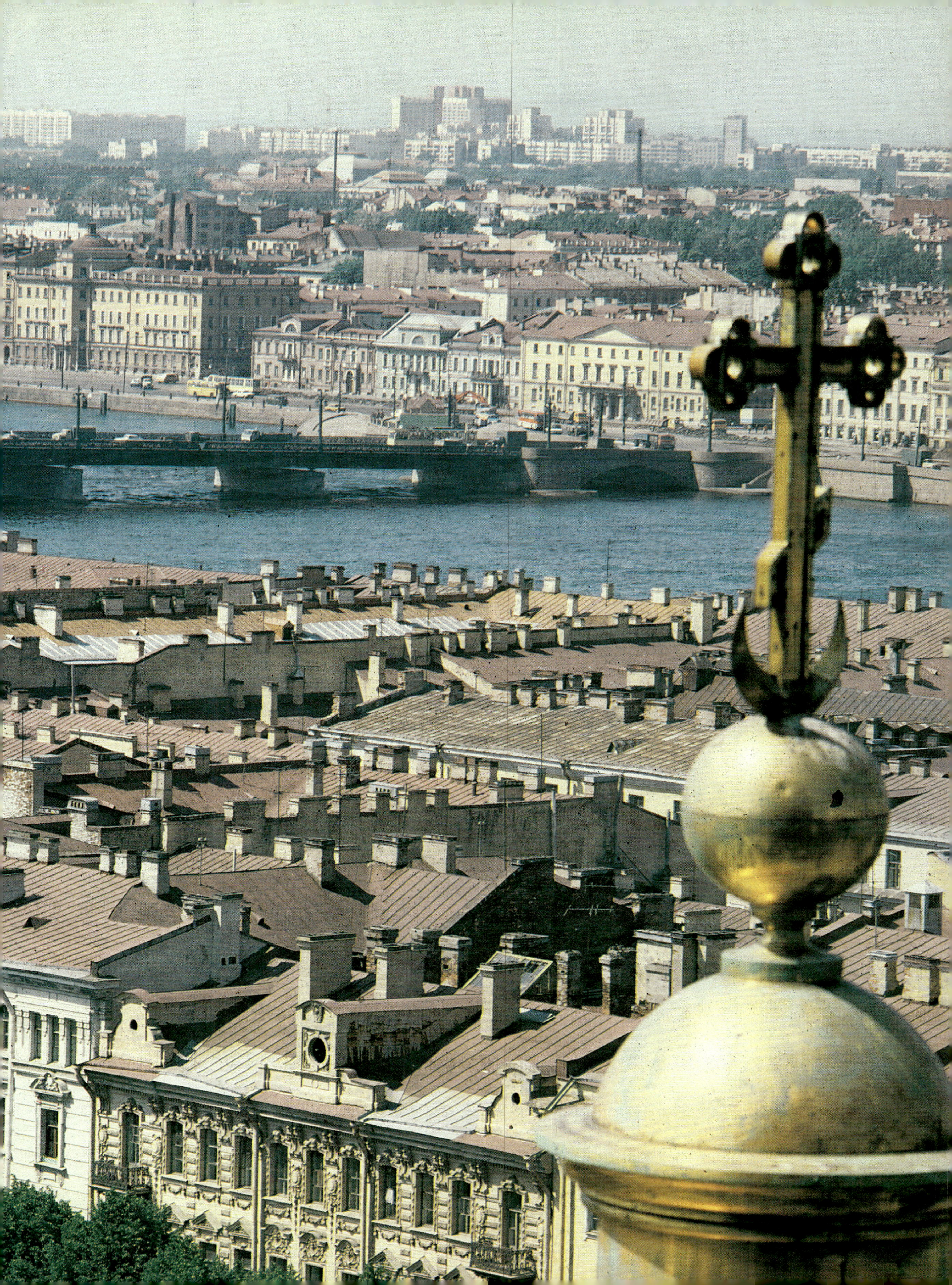

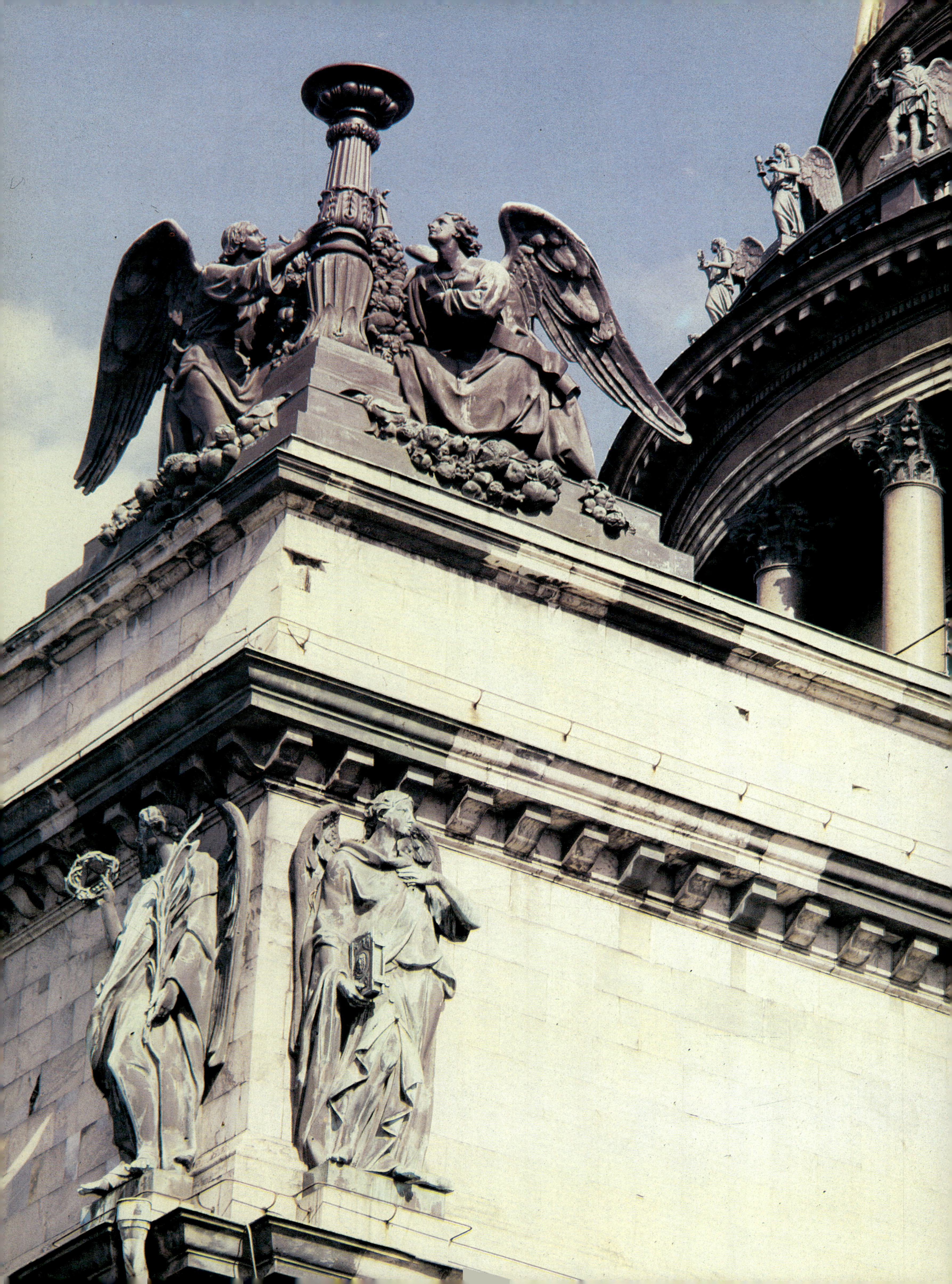

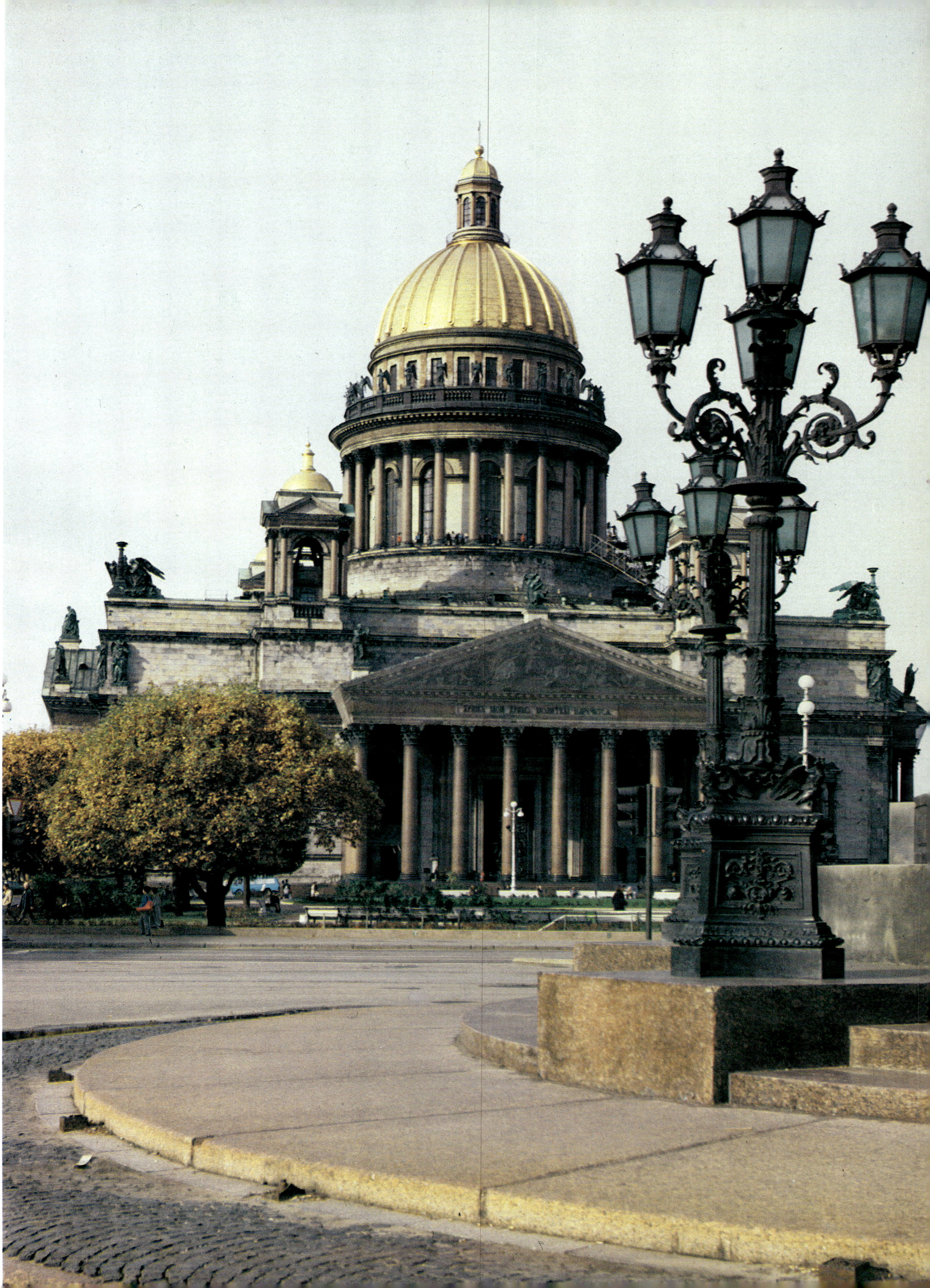

← 60

61

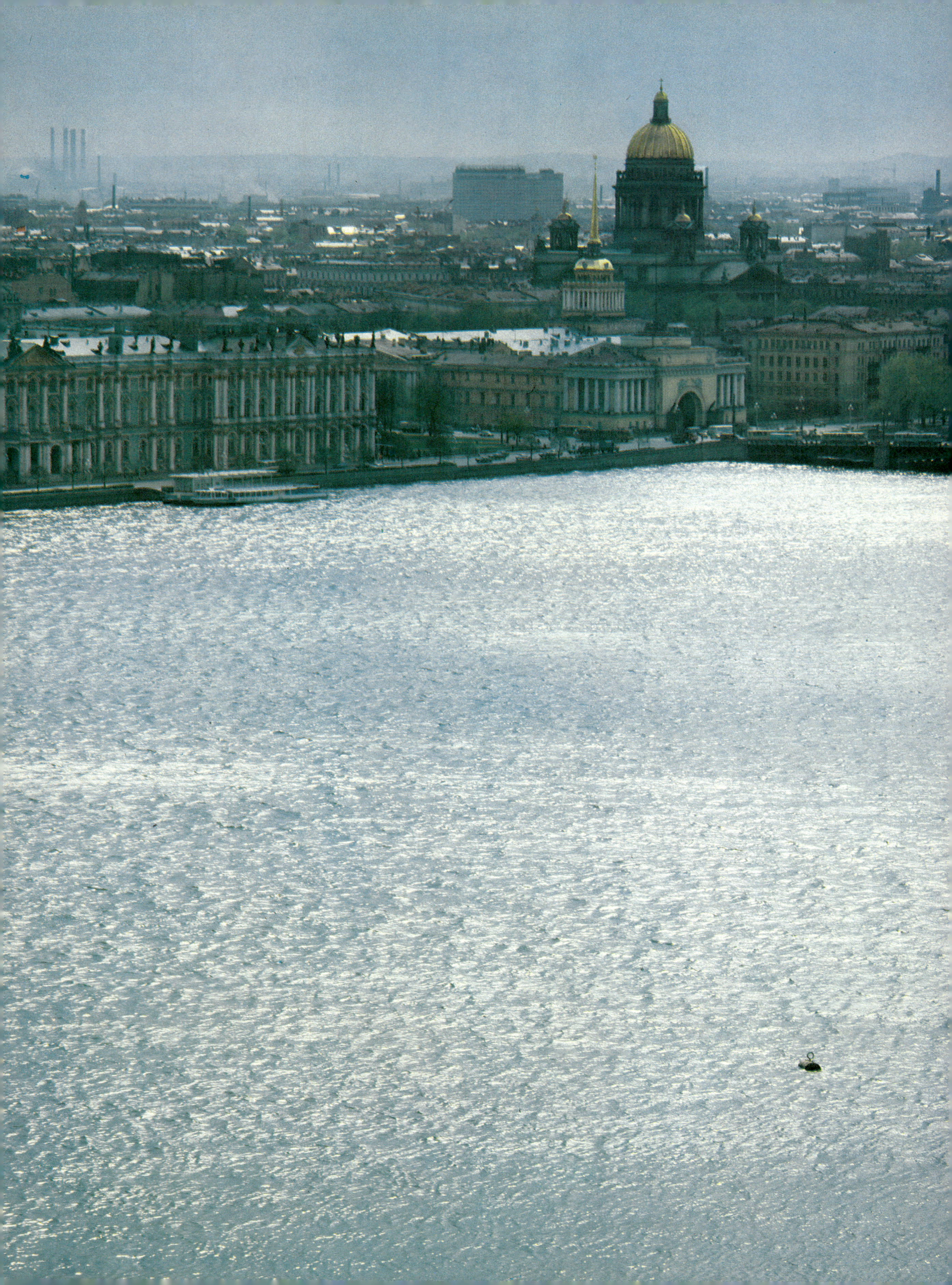

62
63

64

62 *Panorama of Petersburg seen from the campanile of St. Peter and Paul Cathedral*

63 *Ice-drift on the Neva*
64 *English Embankment seen from the St. Nicholas' Bridge*

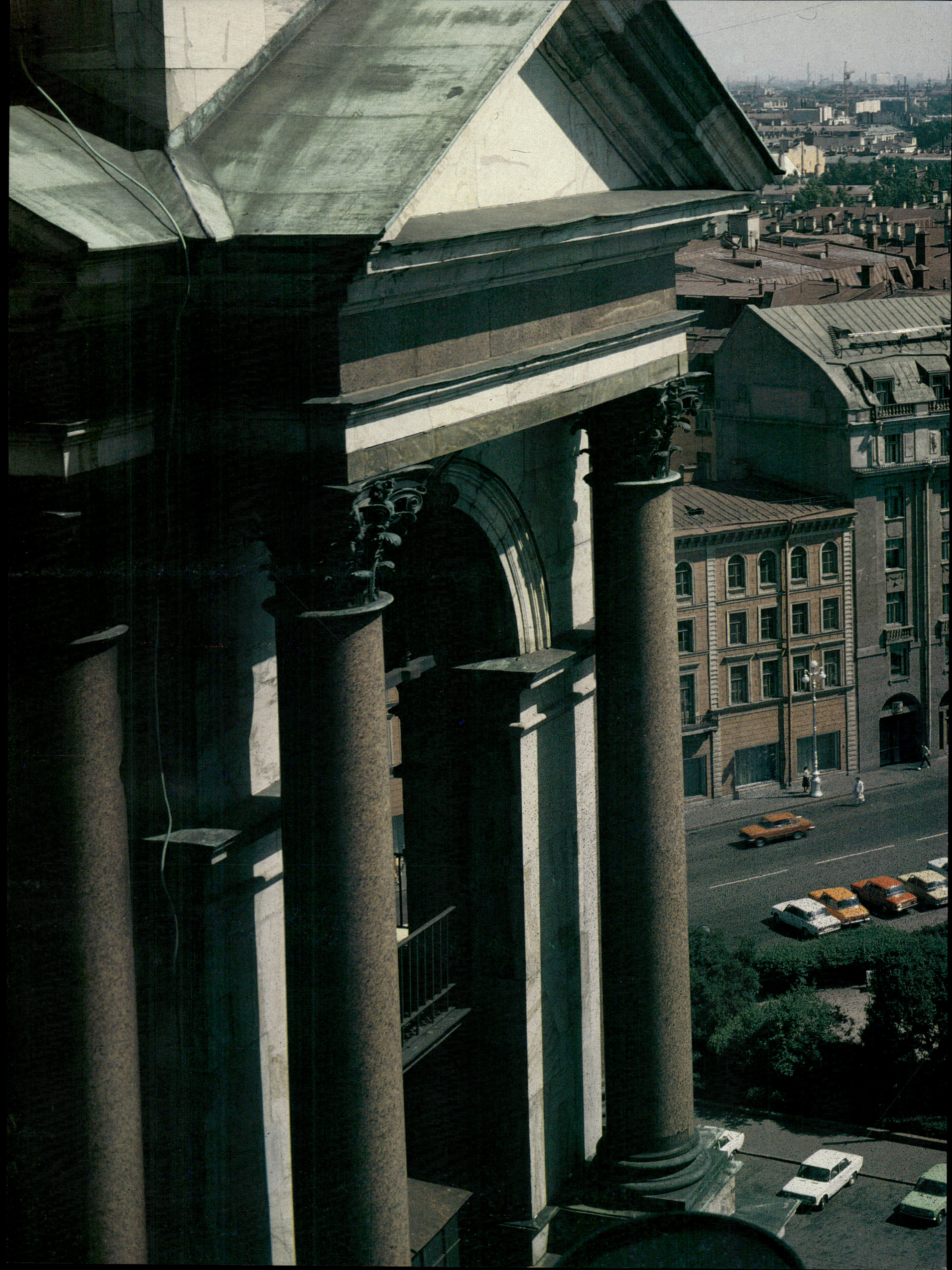

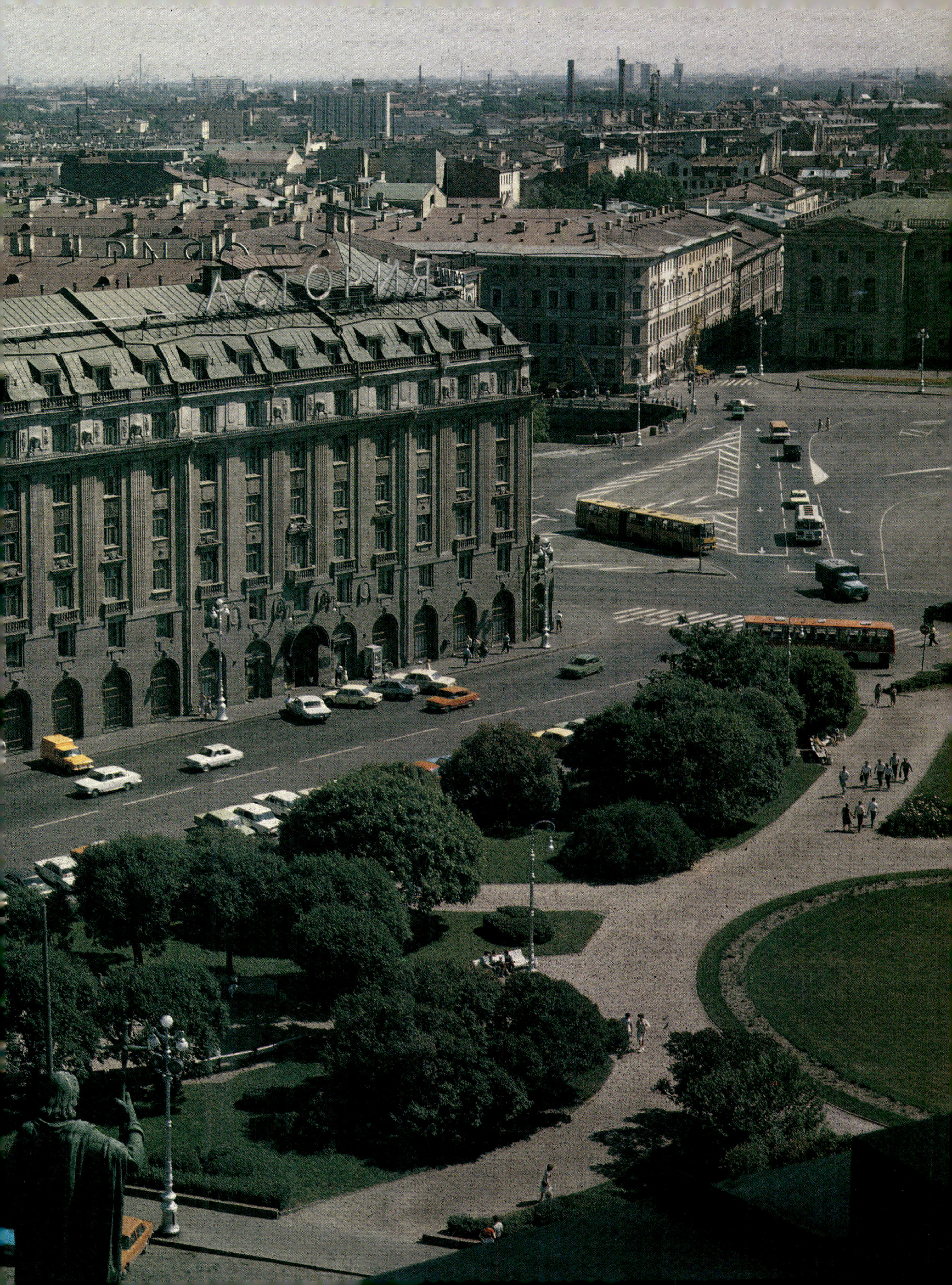
АСТОРИЯ

*65   St. Isaac Square seen from St. Isaac's
       Cathedral*
66, 69   Pier on the Neva near Senate Square *67, 68   Senate and Synode*

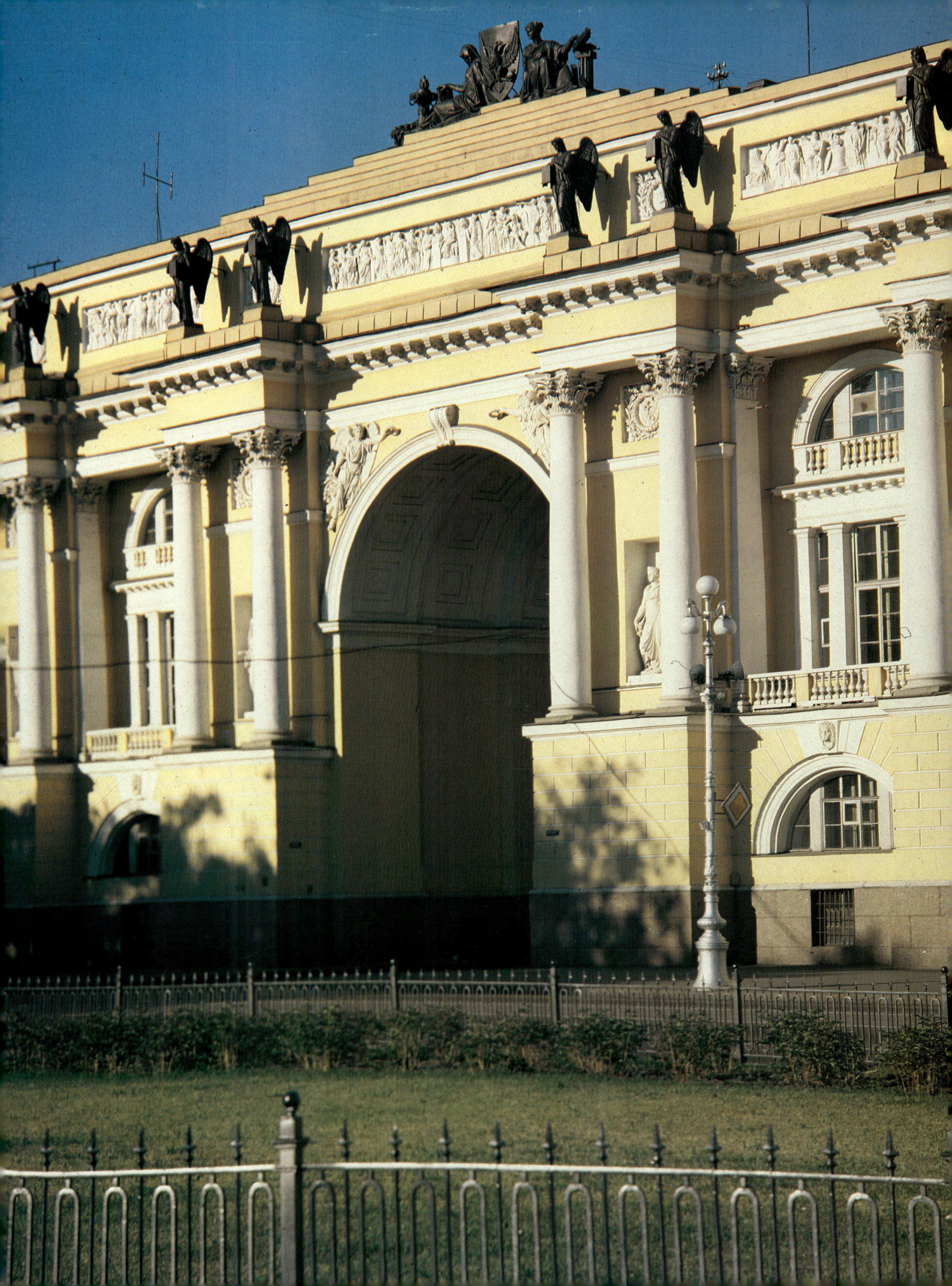

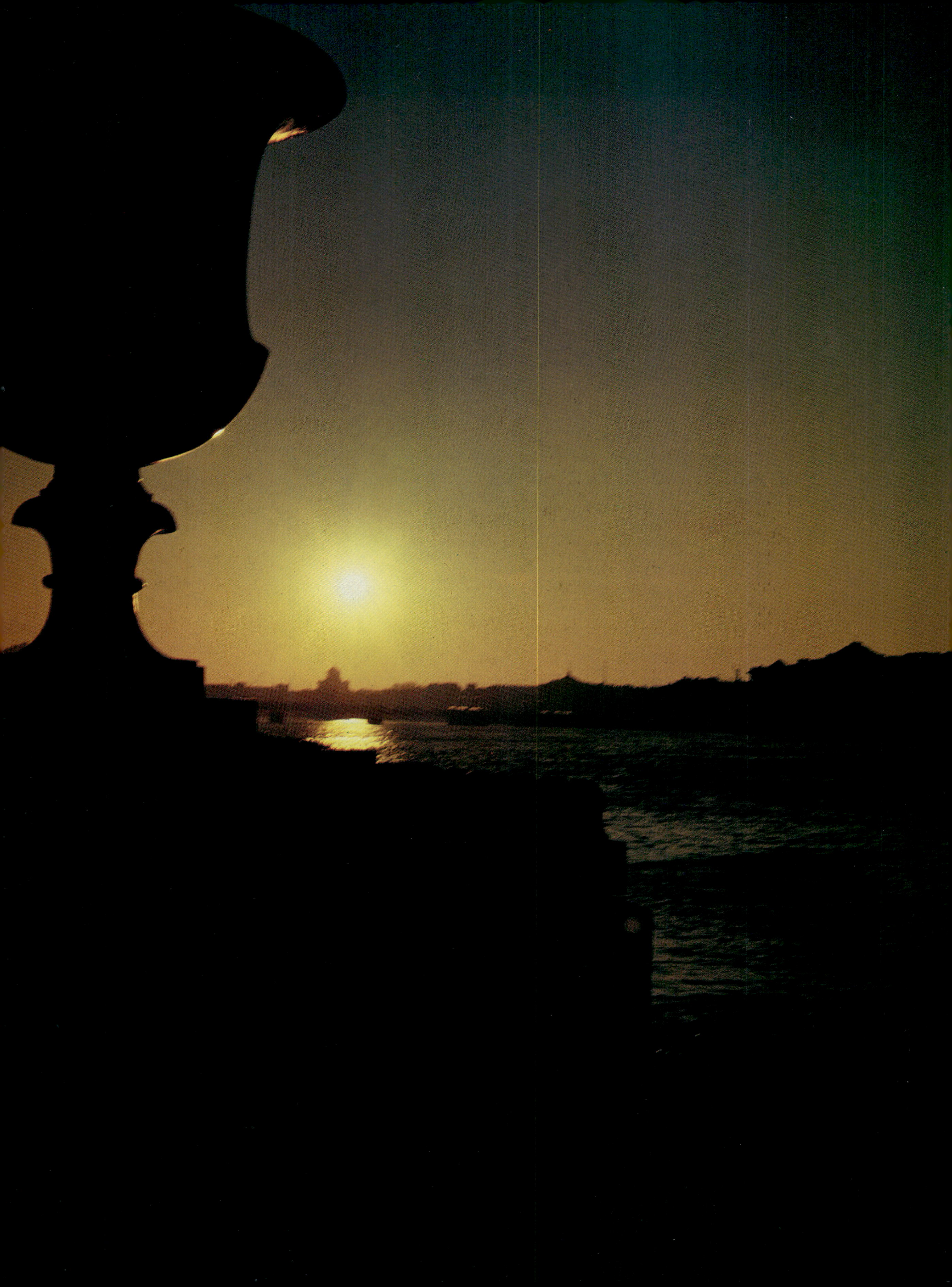

70 *Lion at the Admiralteyskaya Embankment*

71—73 Statue of Peter the Great
(The «Bronze Horseman»)

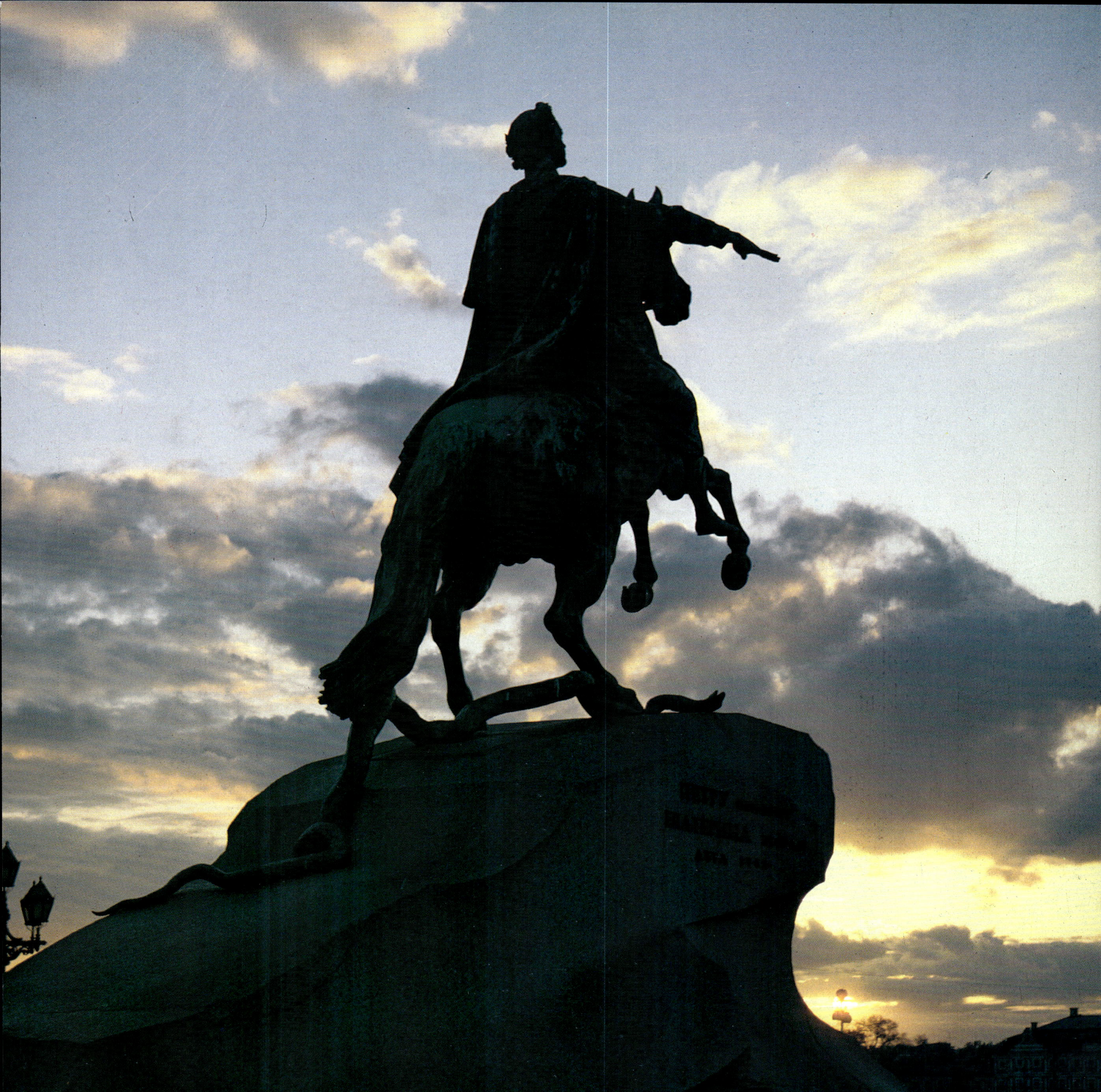

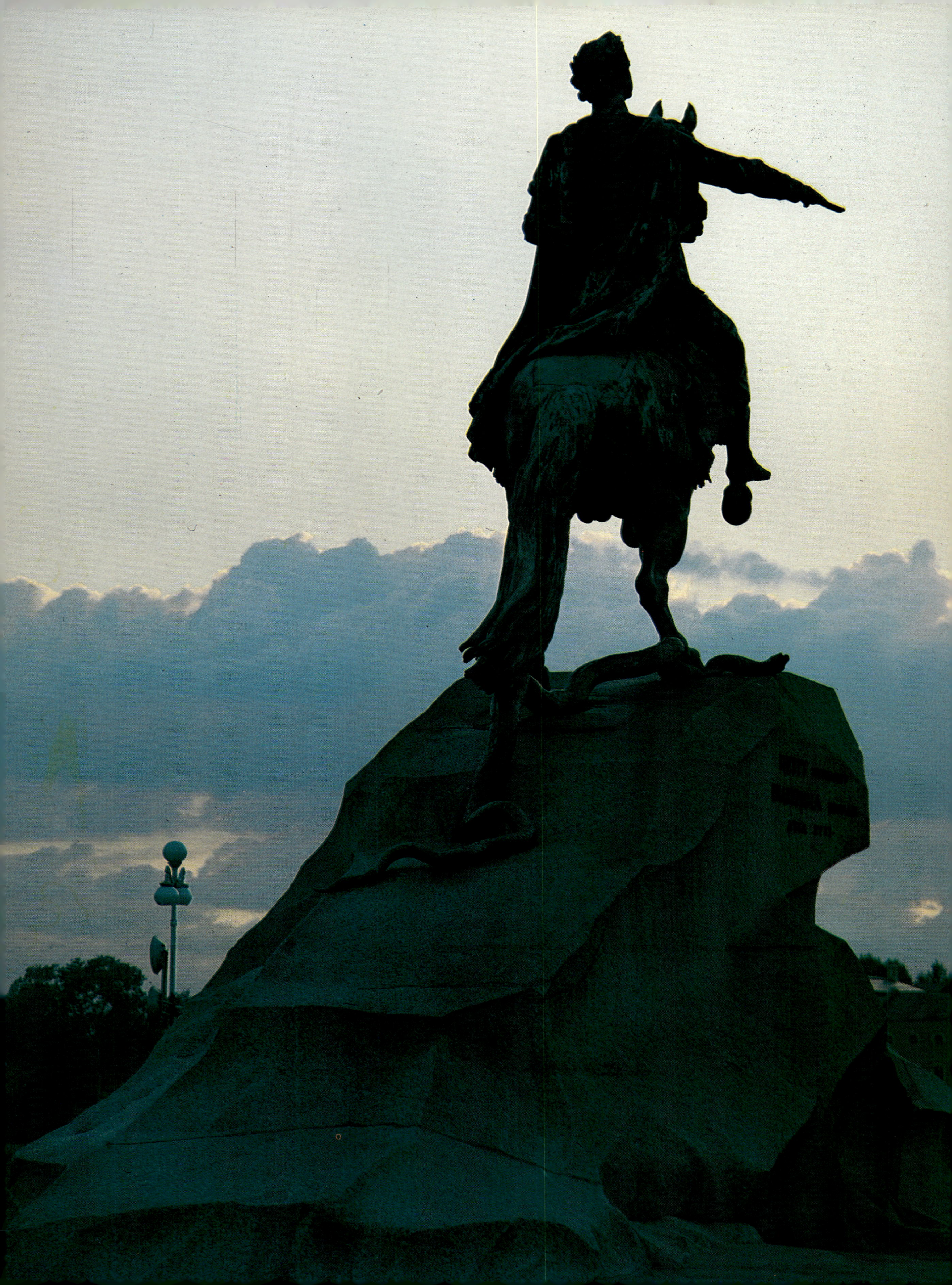

74 Naval Parade on the Neva

75 *Academy of Fine Arts*
76 *Winter Palace*

77 Pier near the Academy of Fine Arts.
   The Griffin
78 St. Nicholas' Bridge.
   A detail of the railing
79 Lieutenant Schmidt Embankment
   seen from the St. Nicholas' Bridge

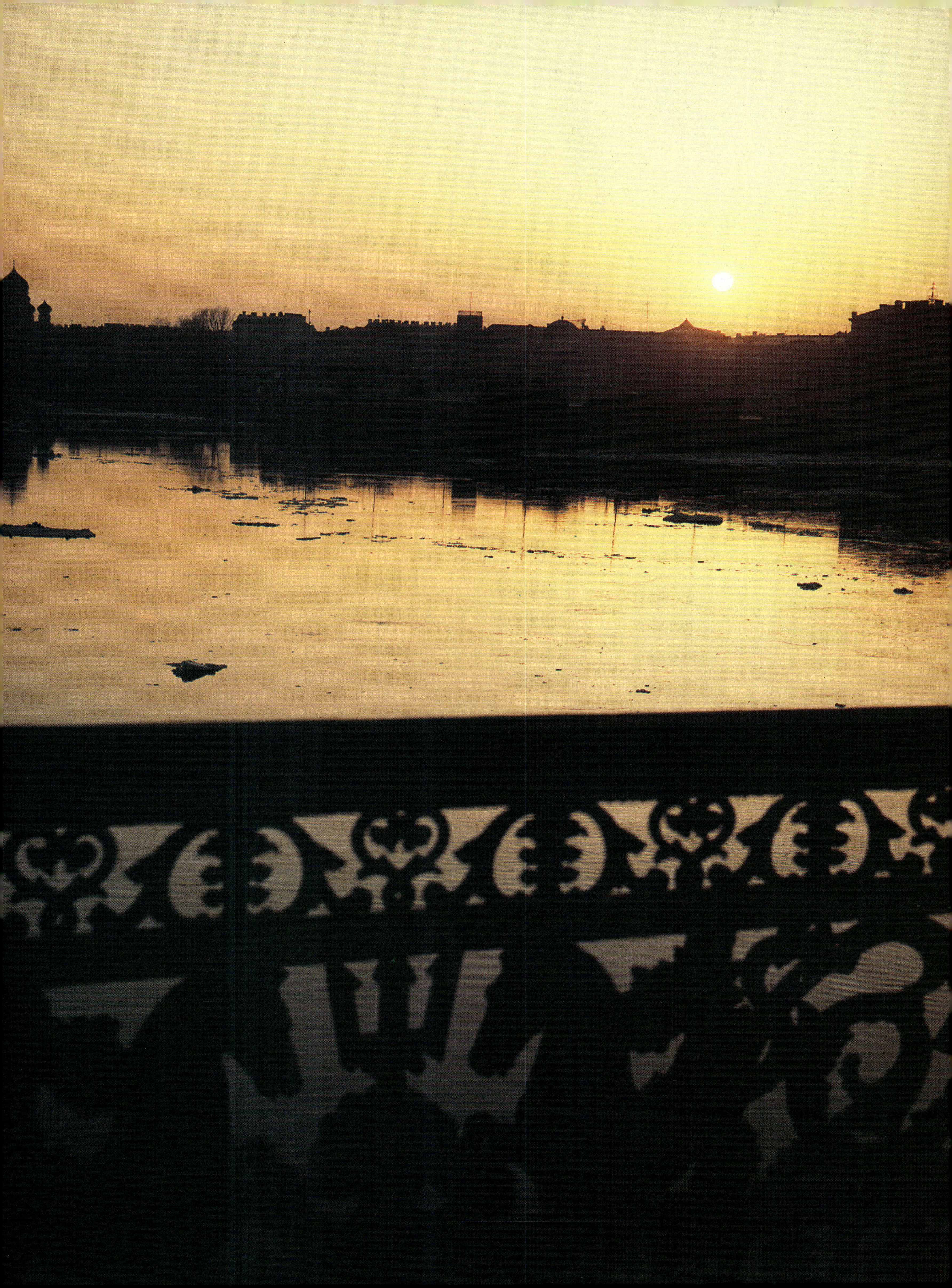

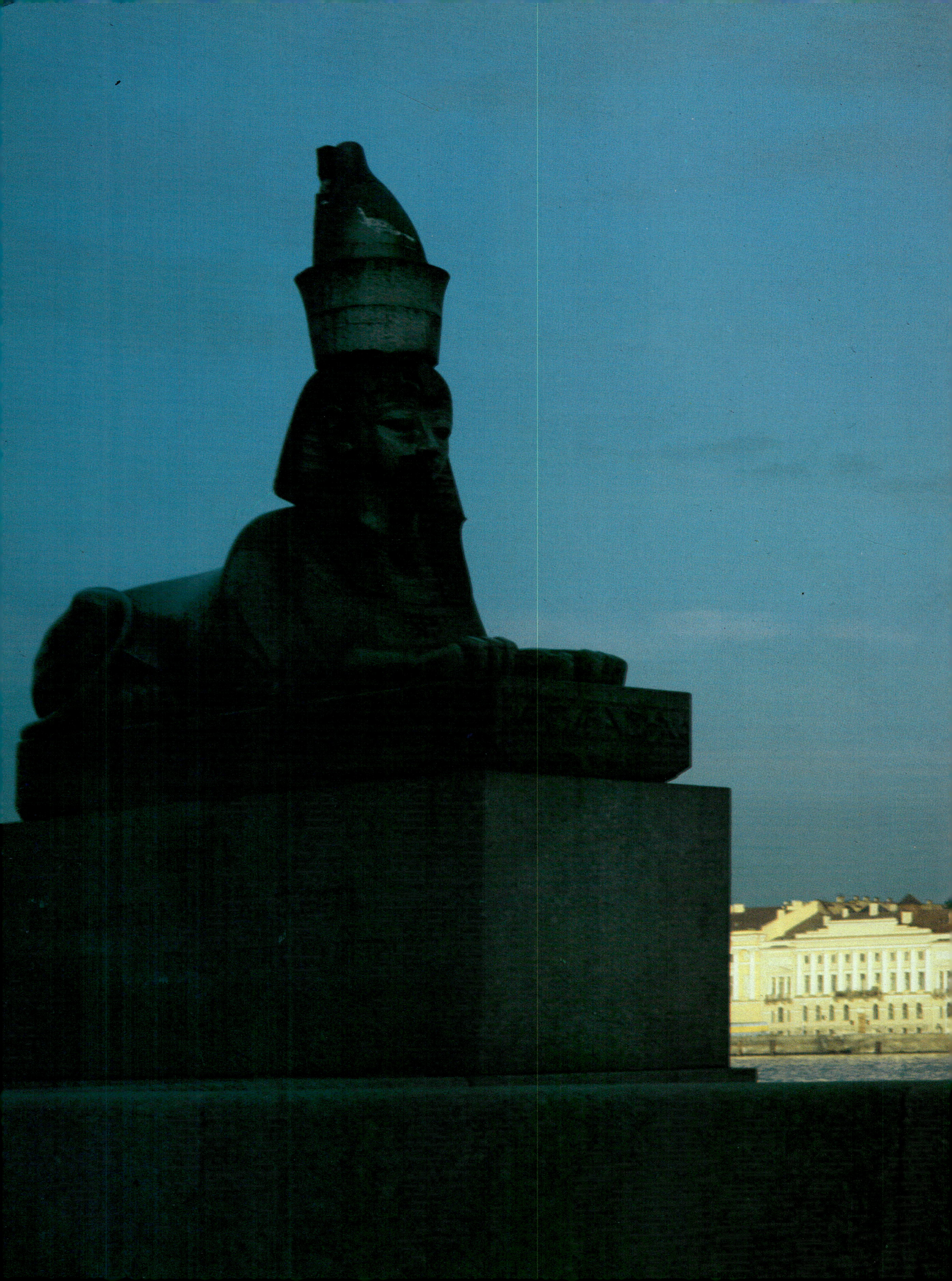

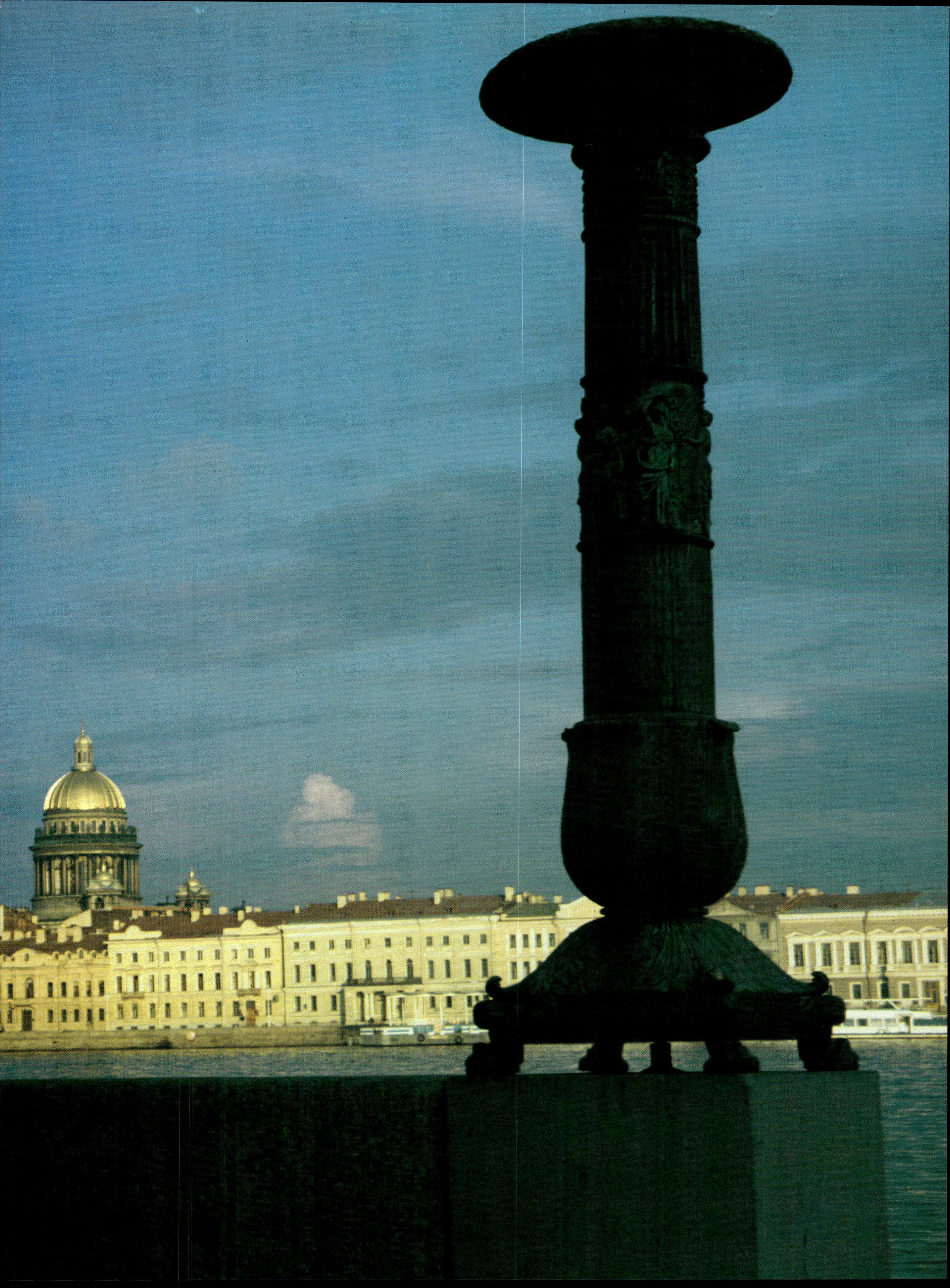

80—82   *Pier near the Academy of Fine Arts*

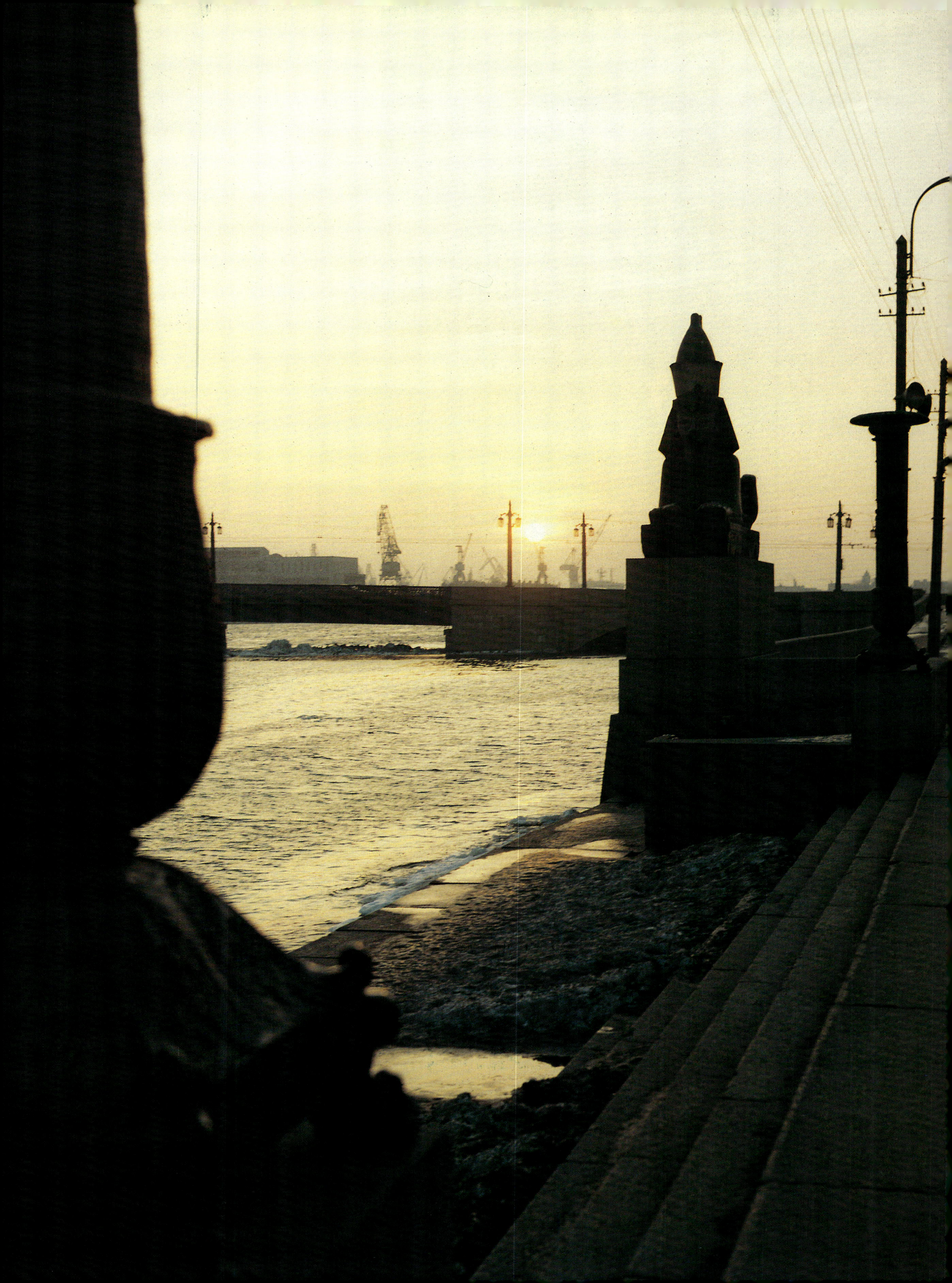

83 Academy of Fine Arts seen from the pier
   near Senate Square

84—87 St. Peter's Embankment. Shi-tsu on the
      embankment near the Hut
      of Peter the Great
88 Point of Vasilyevsky Island seen from the
   Palace Embankment →

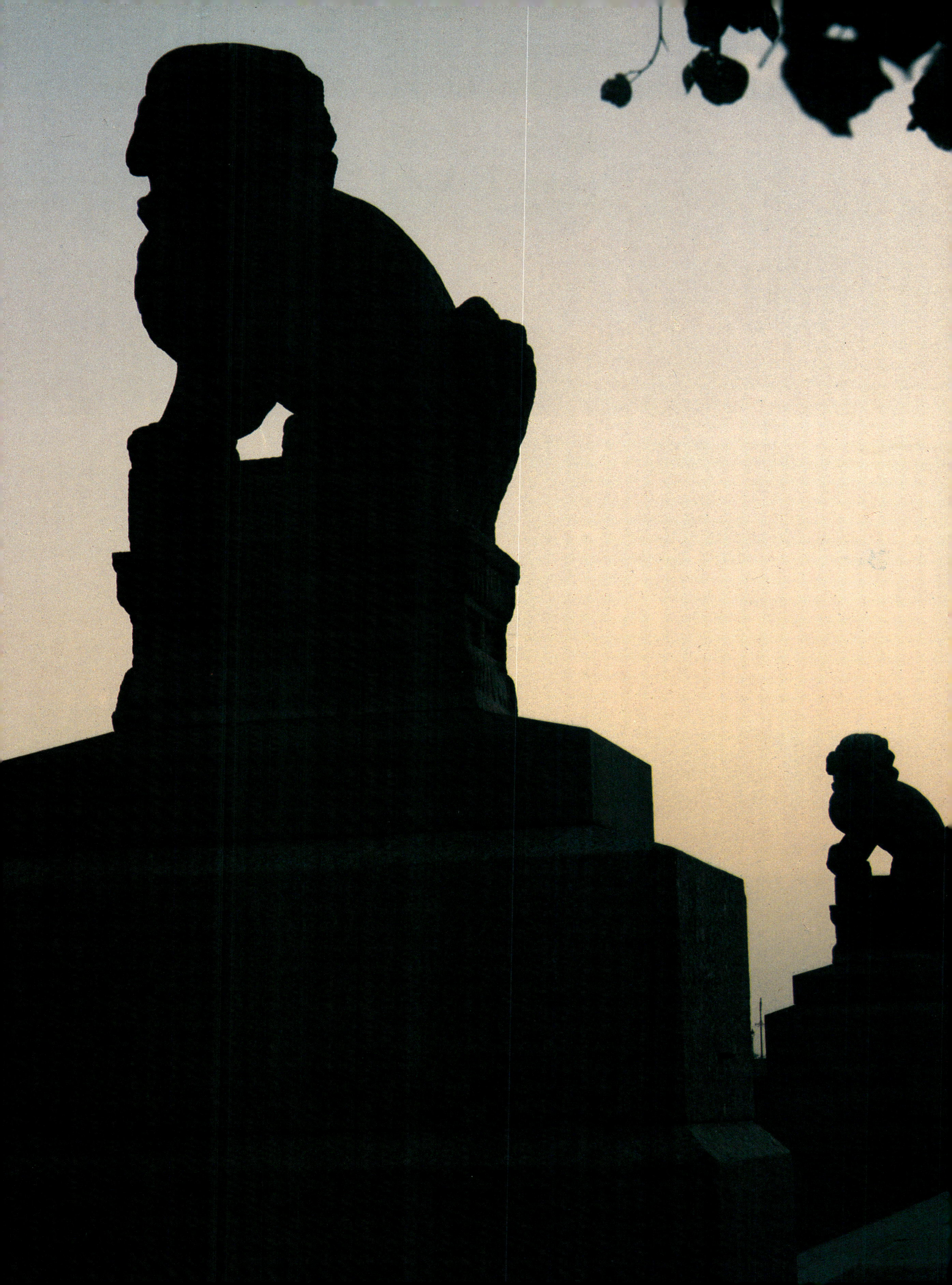

85

86

87
88

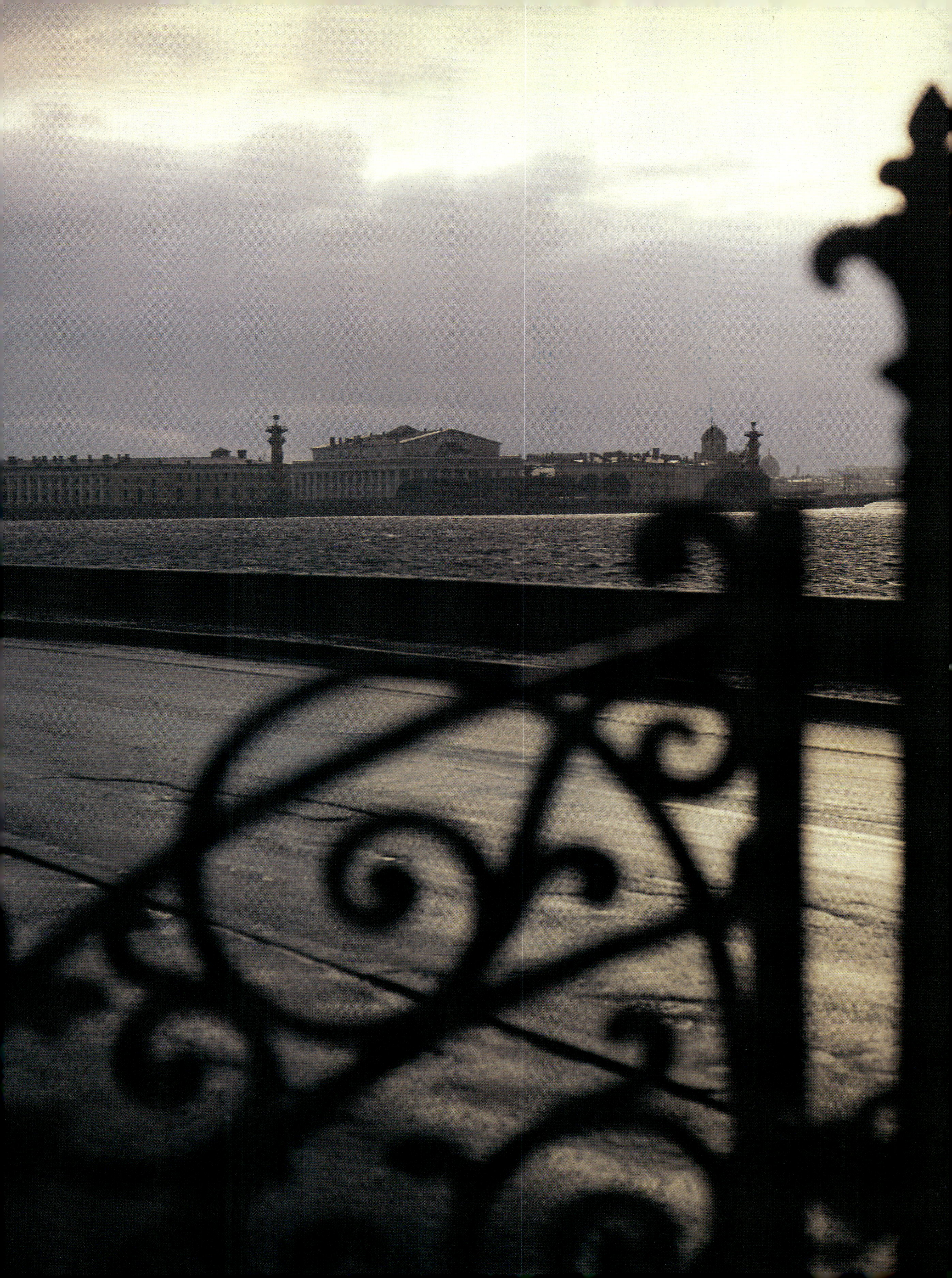

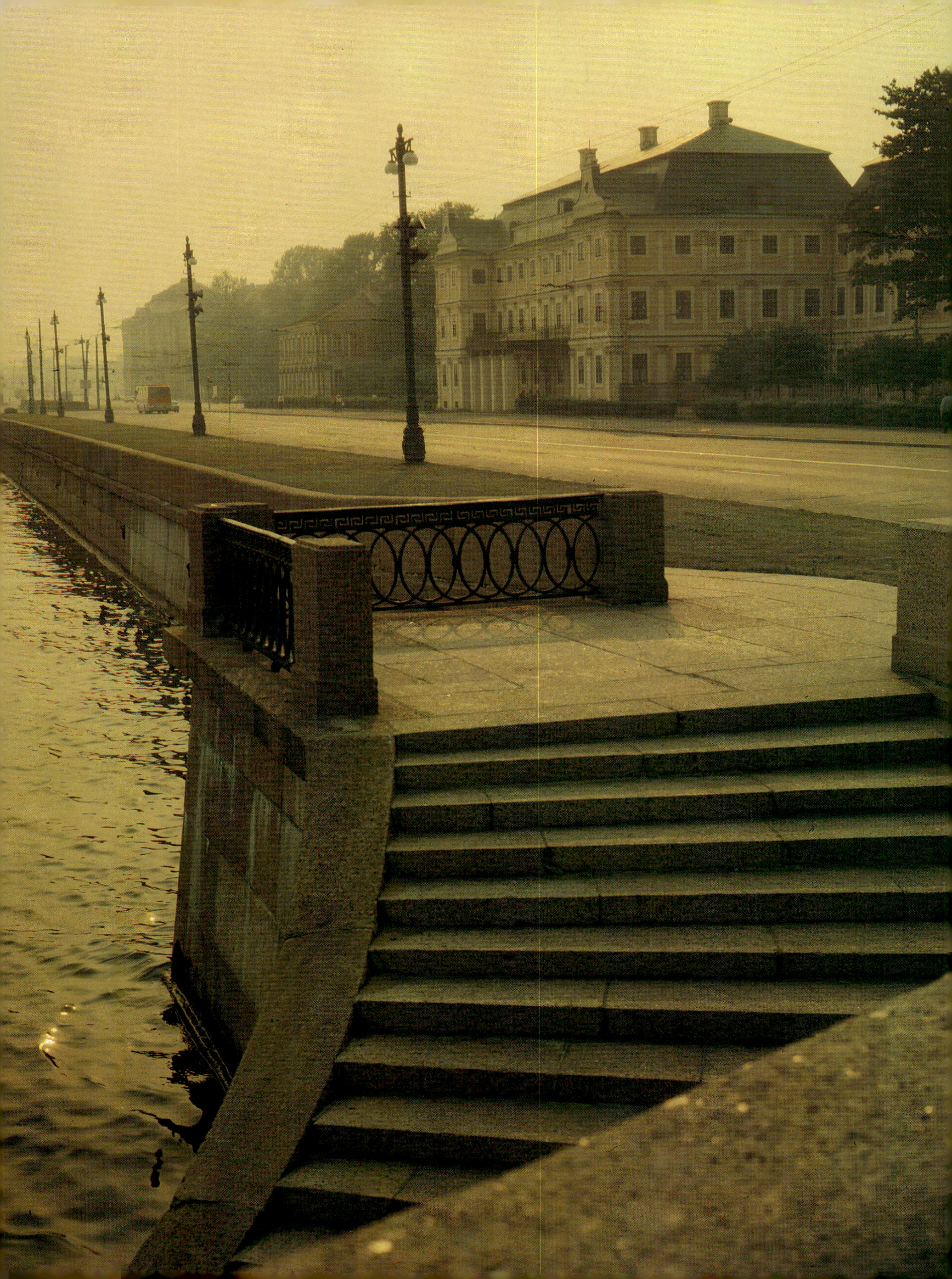

89 Universitetskaya Embankment
90 Menshikov Palace

91 Kunstkammer seen from the
 Admiralteyskaya Embankment →

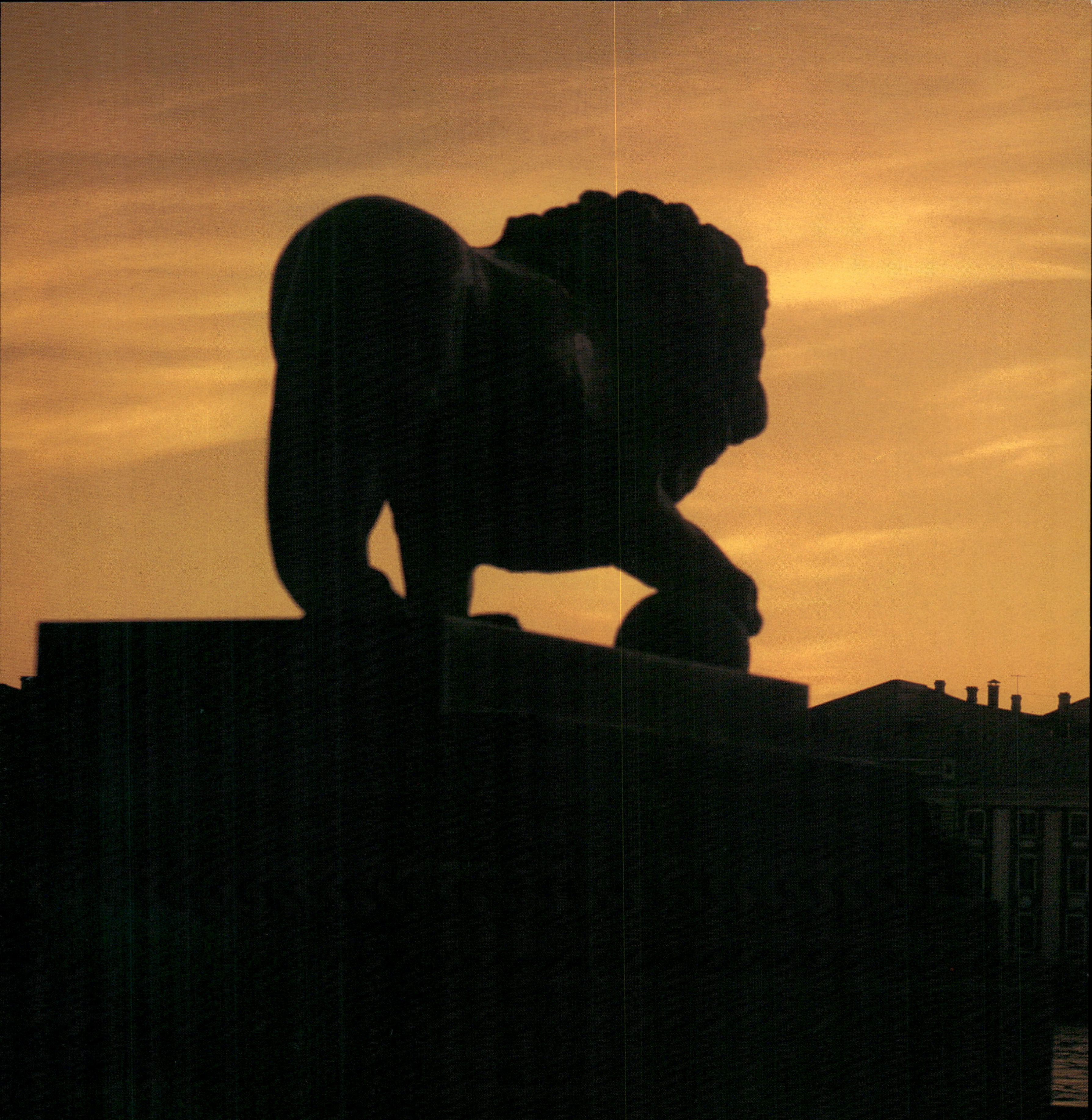

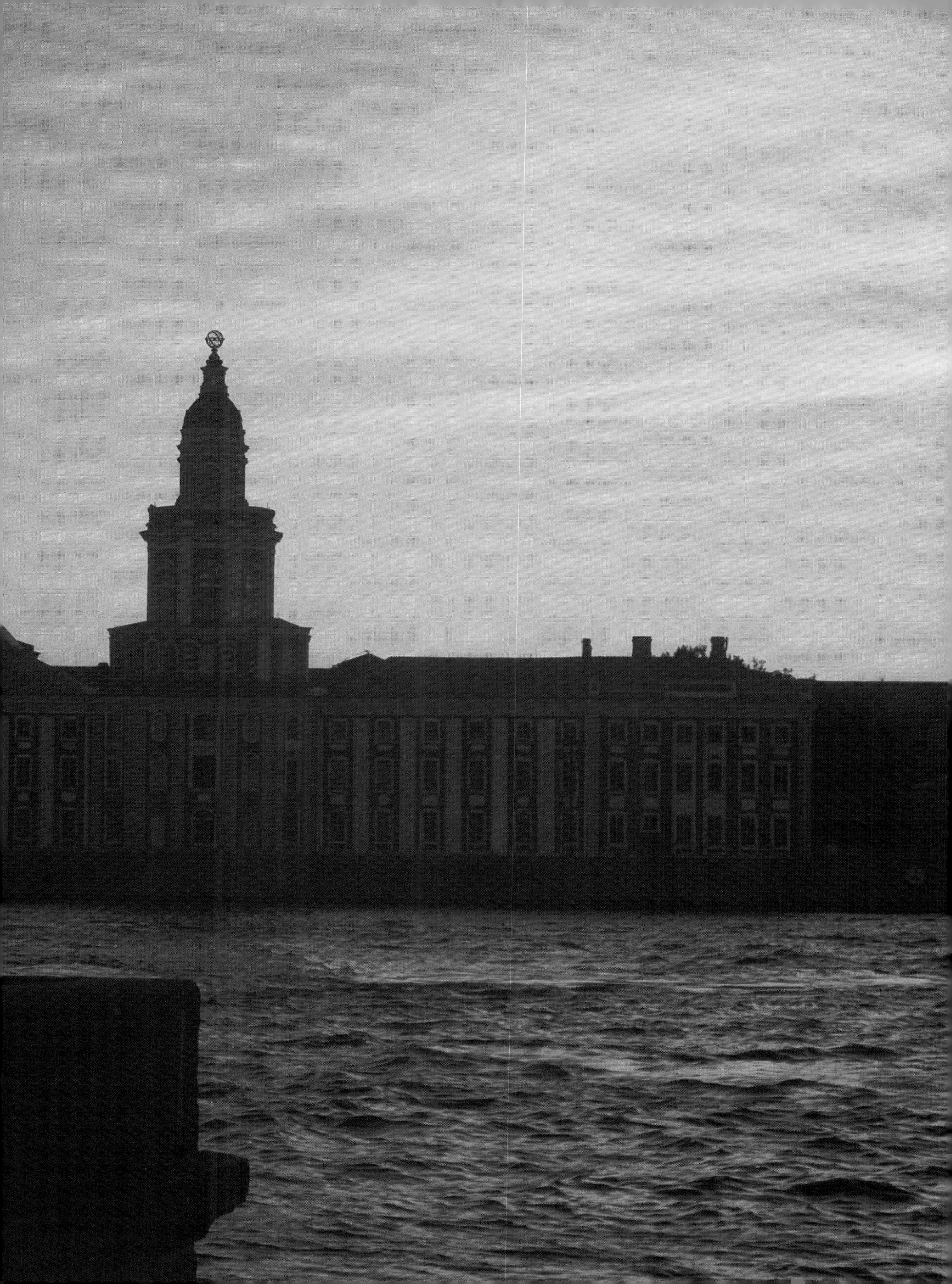

92 *University (The Twelve Collegia)*
93 *View of the Universitetskaya Embankment, Point of Vasilyevsky Island and St. Peter and Paul Fortress*
94 *Point of Vasilyevsky Island seen from the Palace Embankment* →
95 *Vasilyevsky Island. The Lieutenant Schmidt Embankment* →
96 *Panorama of Point of Vasilyevsky Island* →
97, 98 *Rostral Columns* →

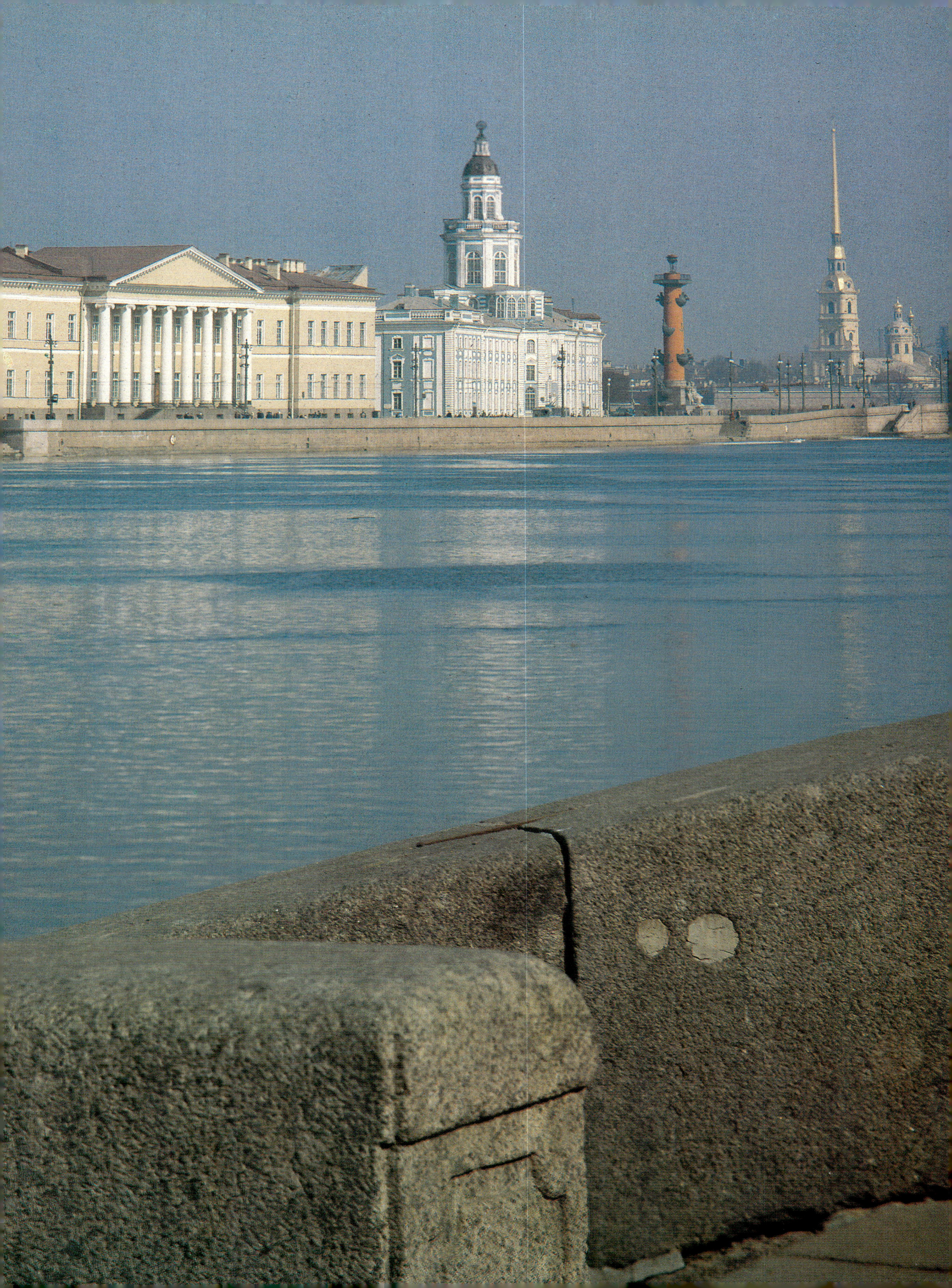

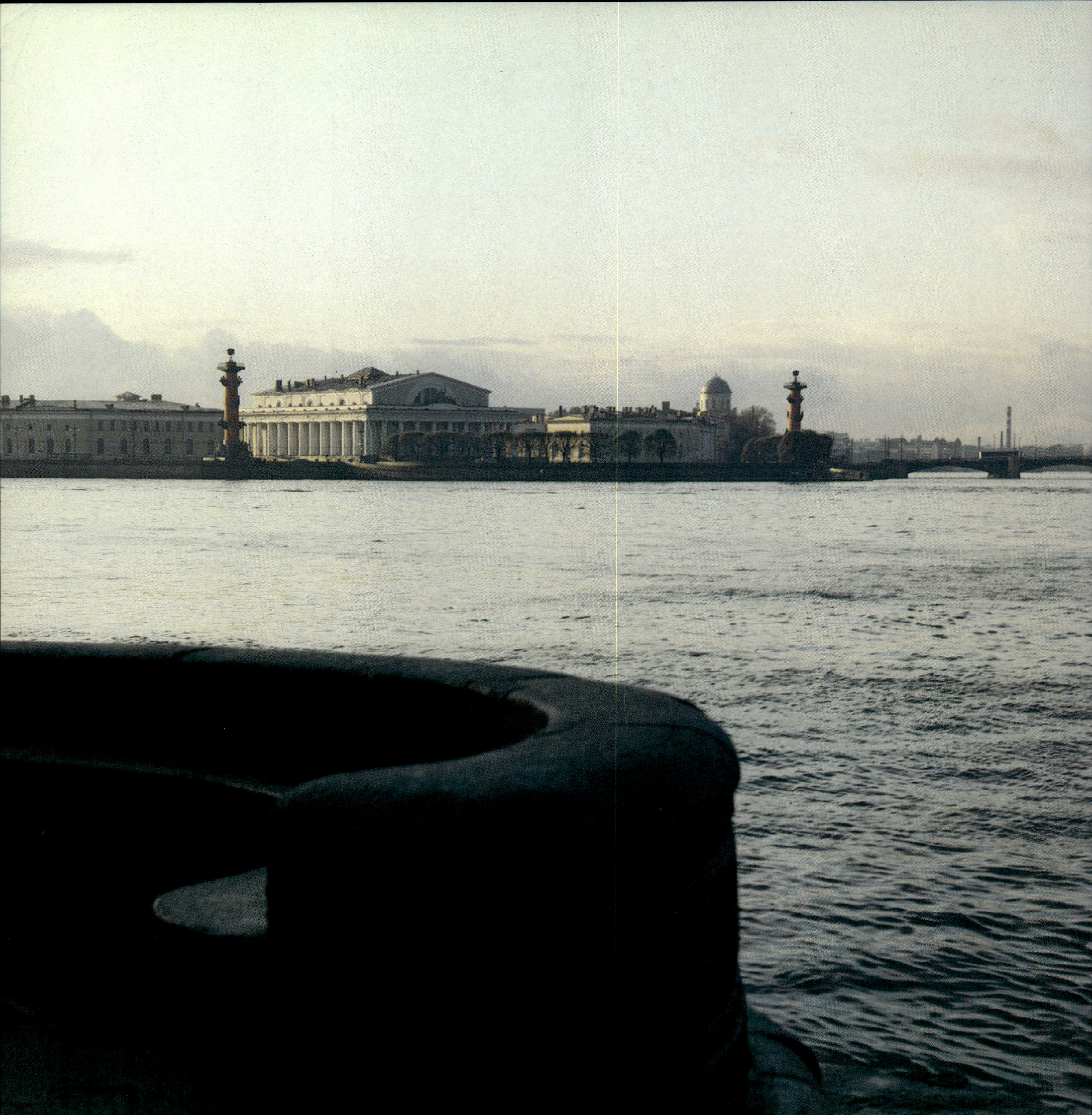

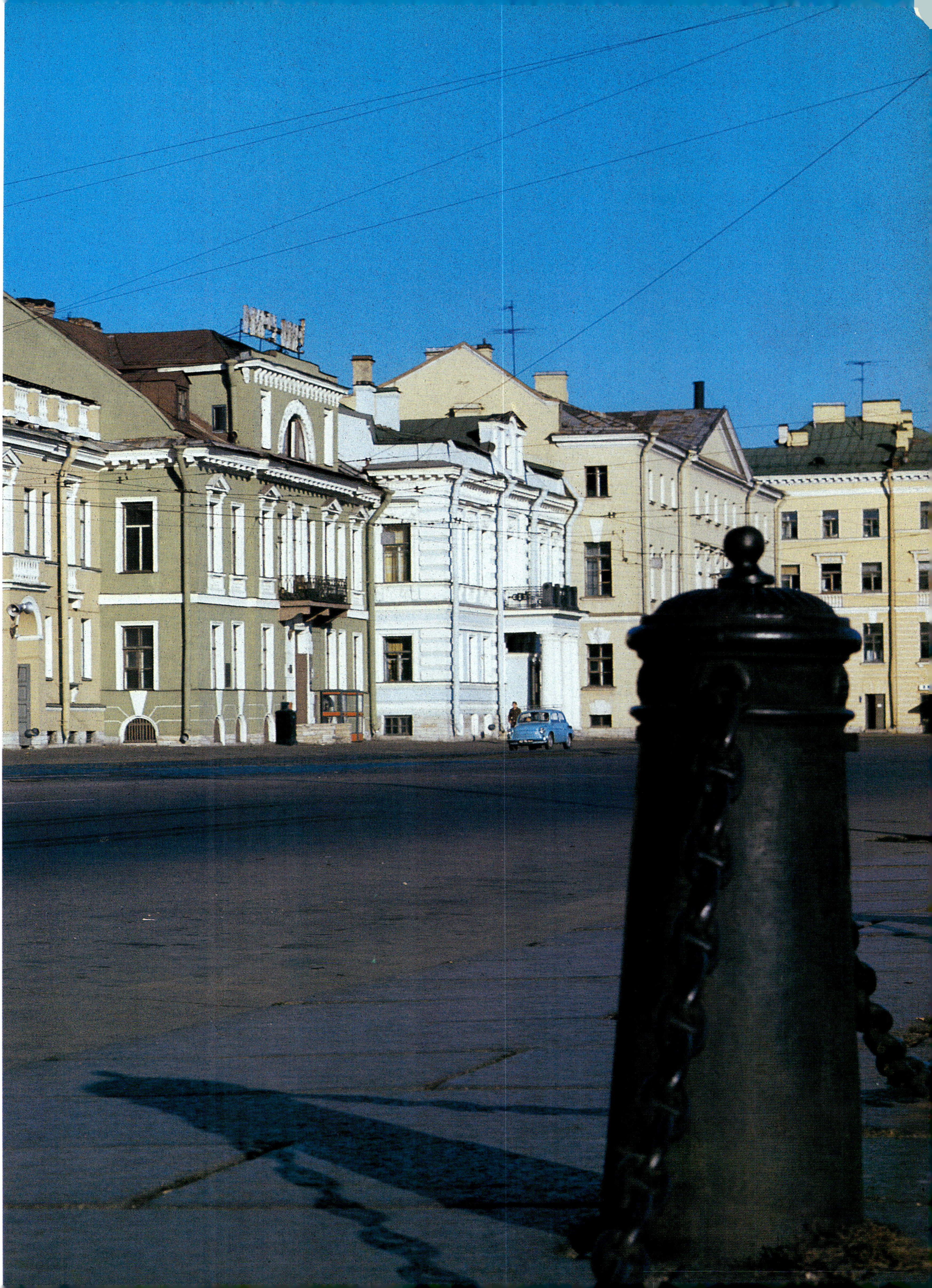

←
94

95

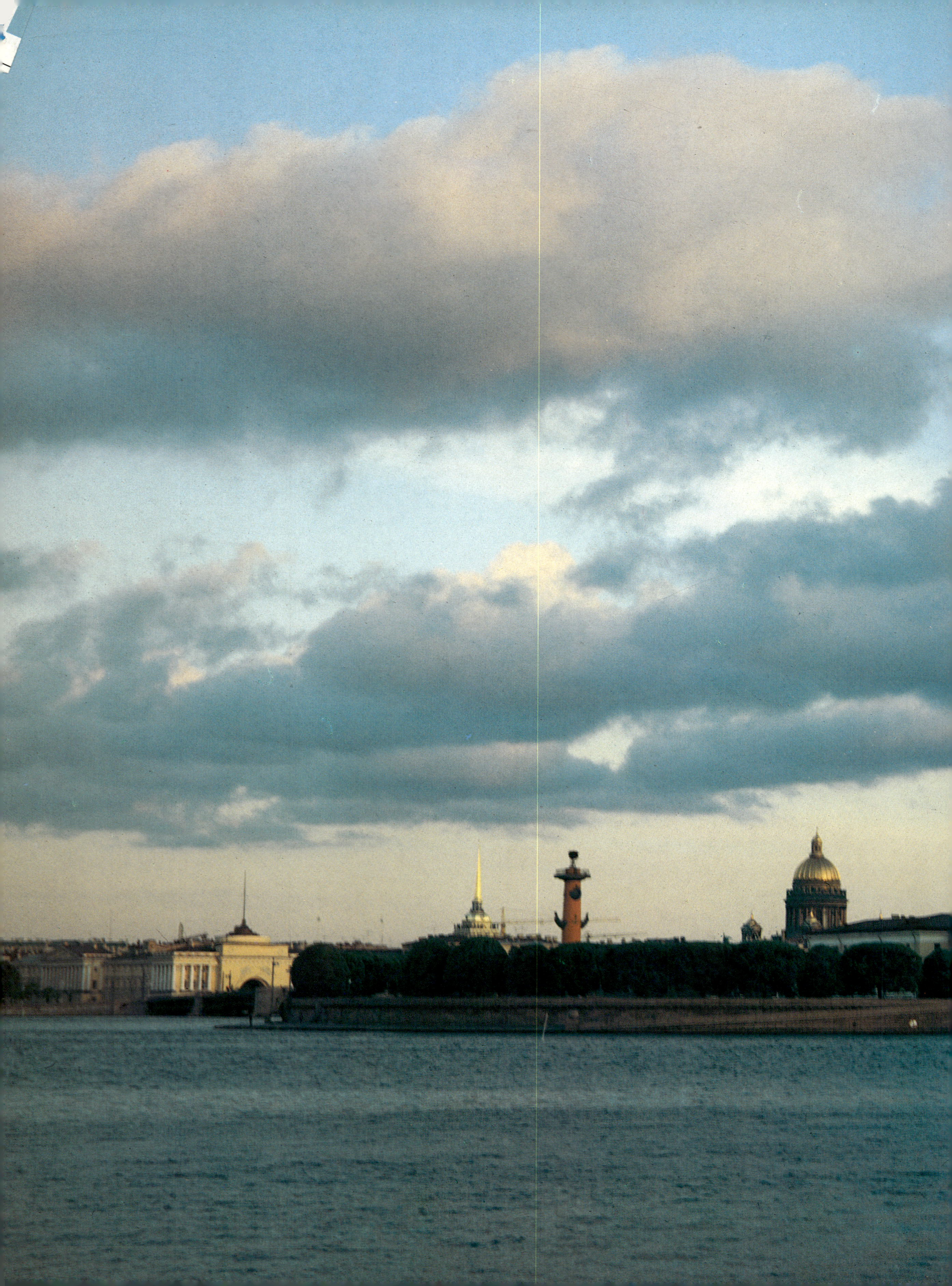

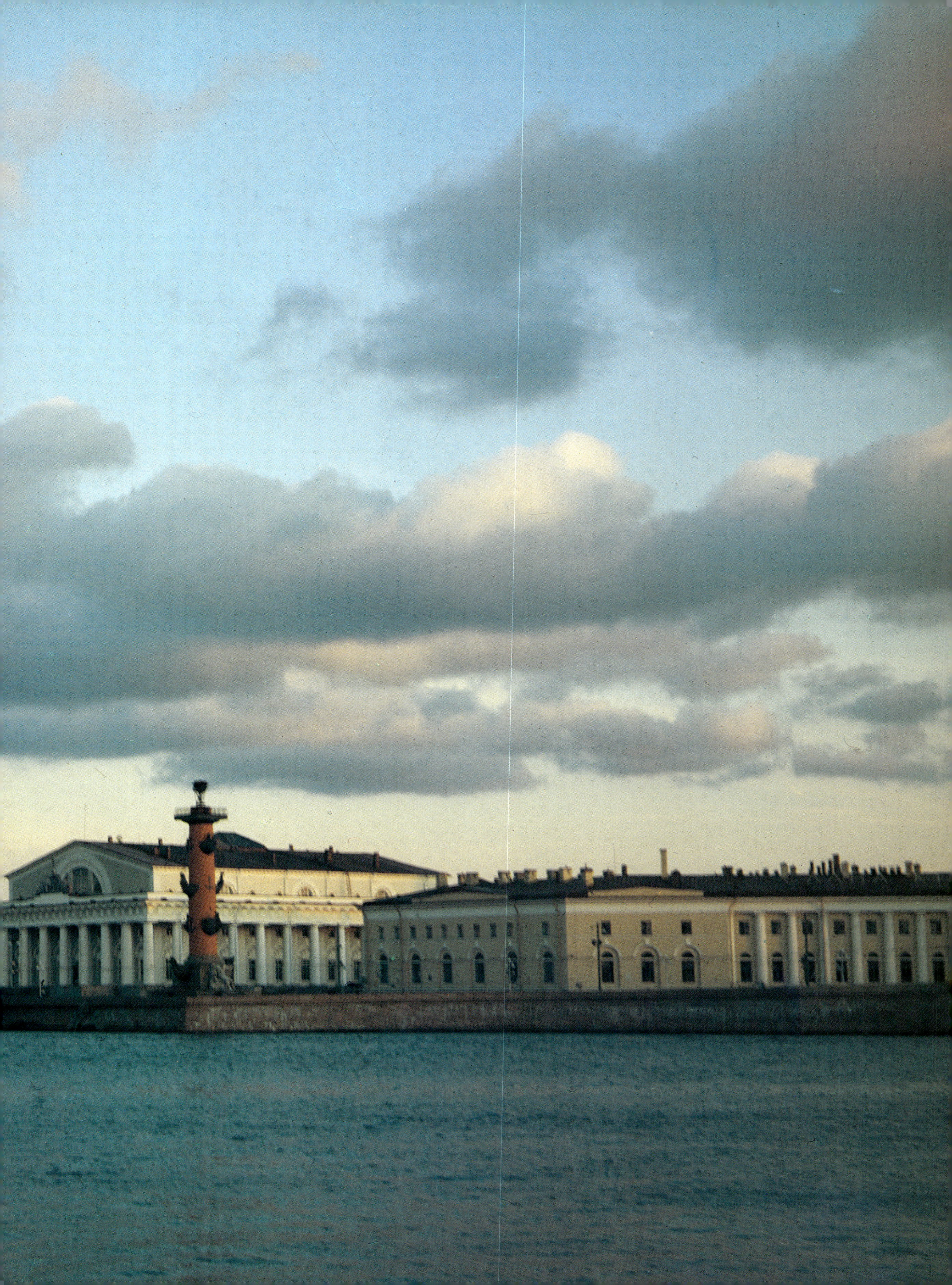

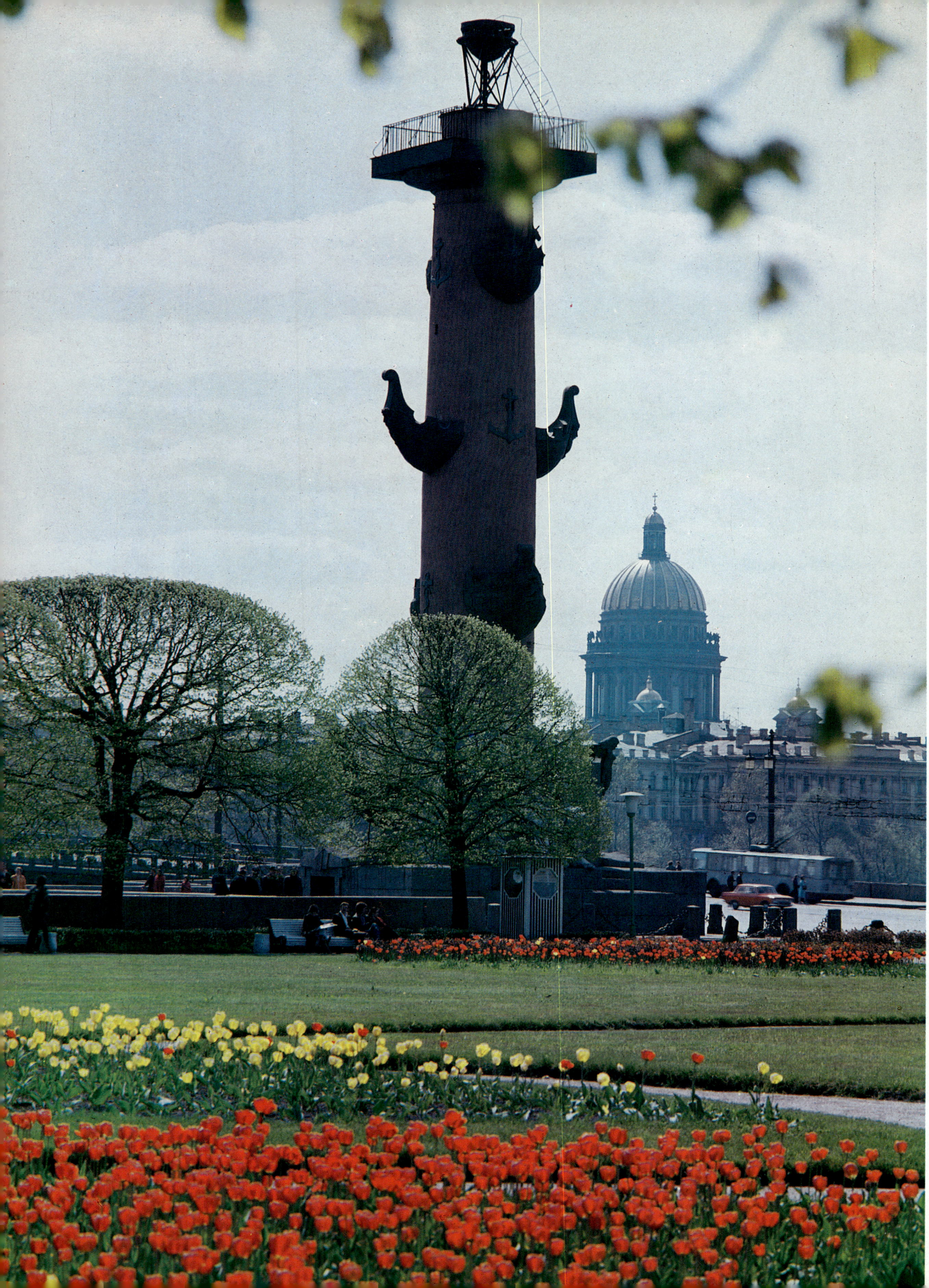

97
→
98

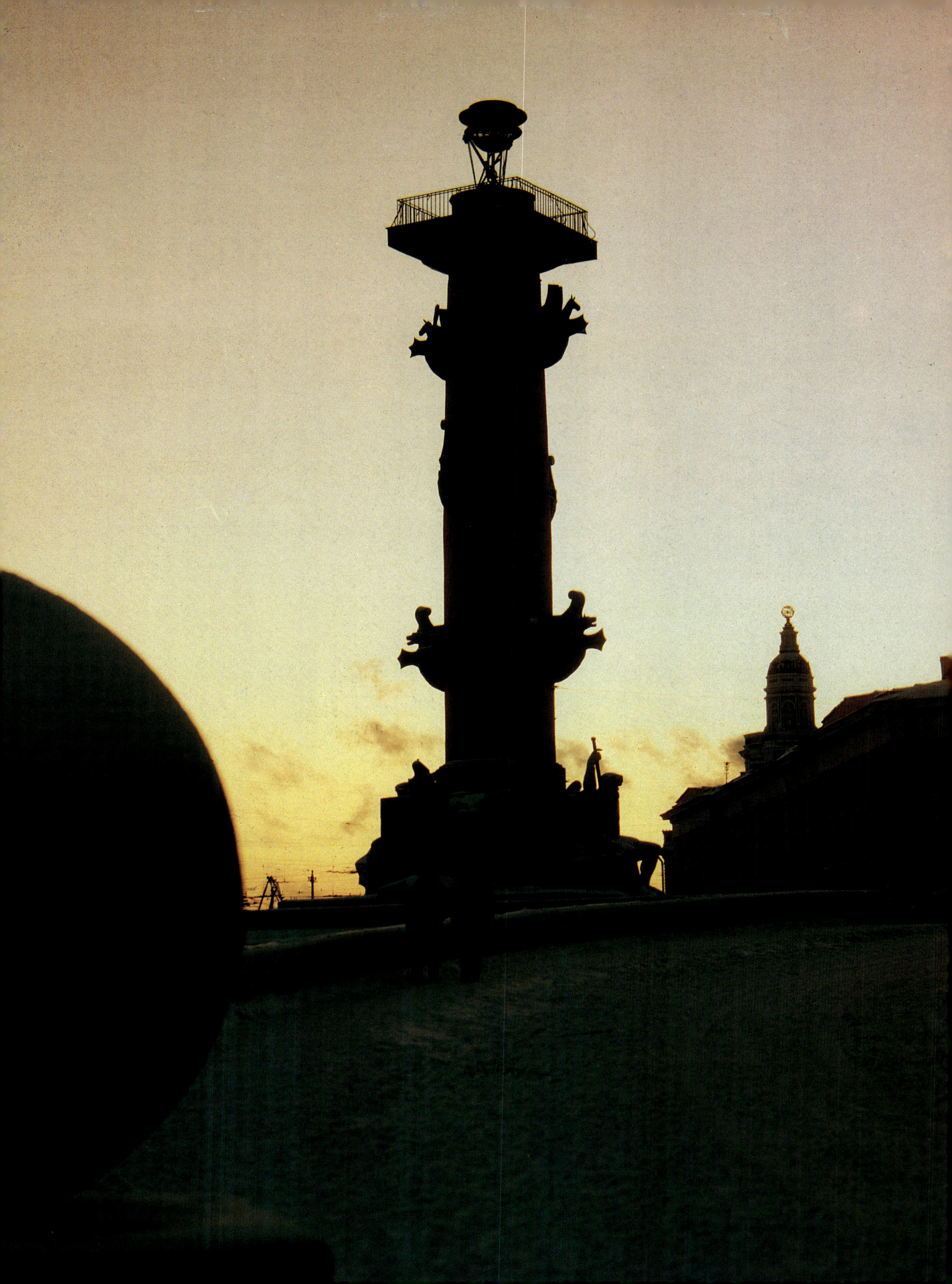

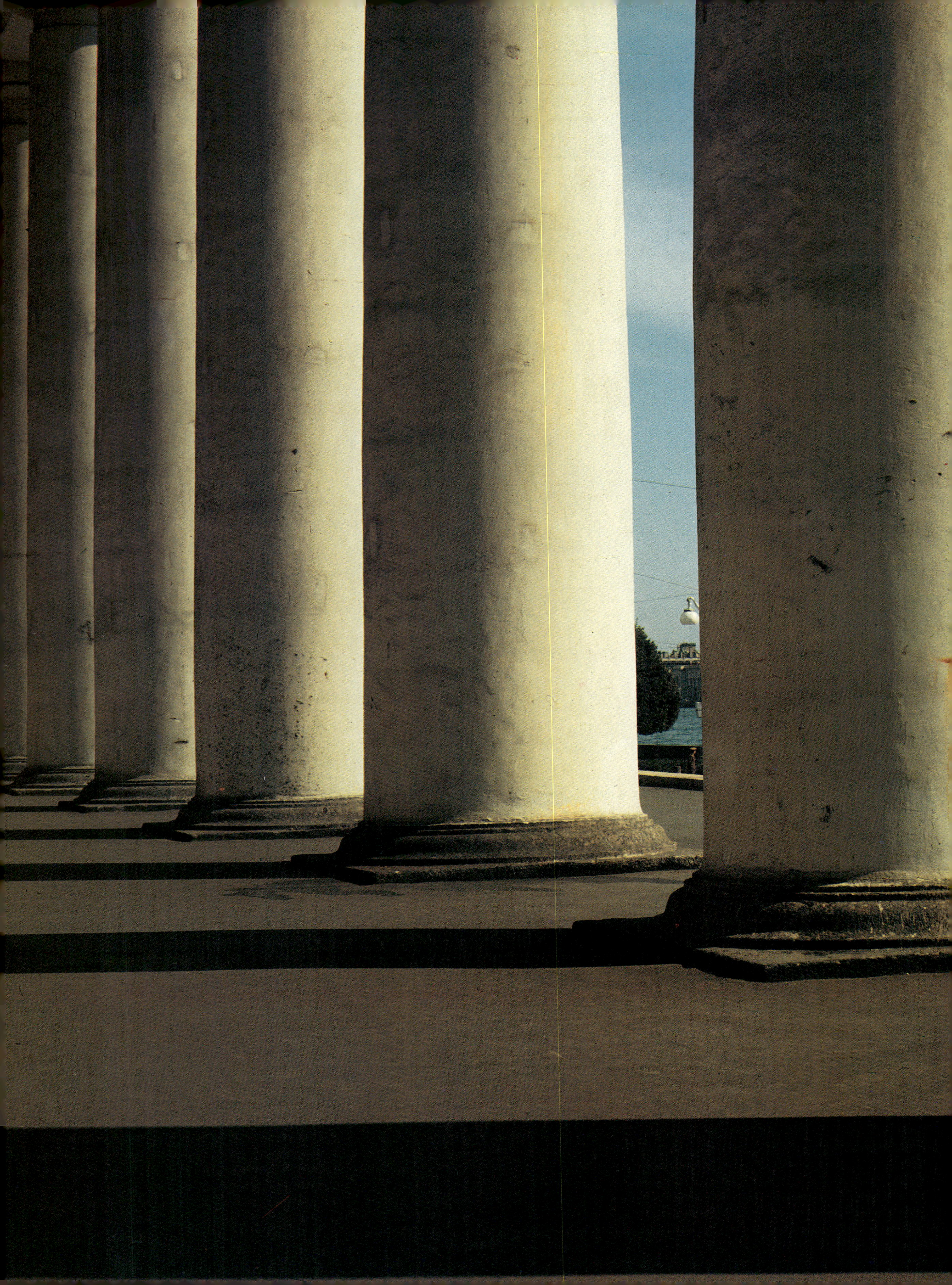

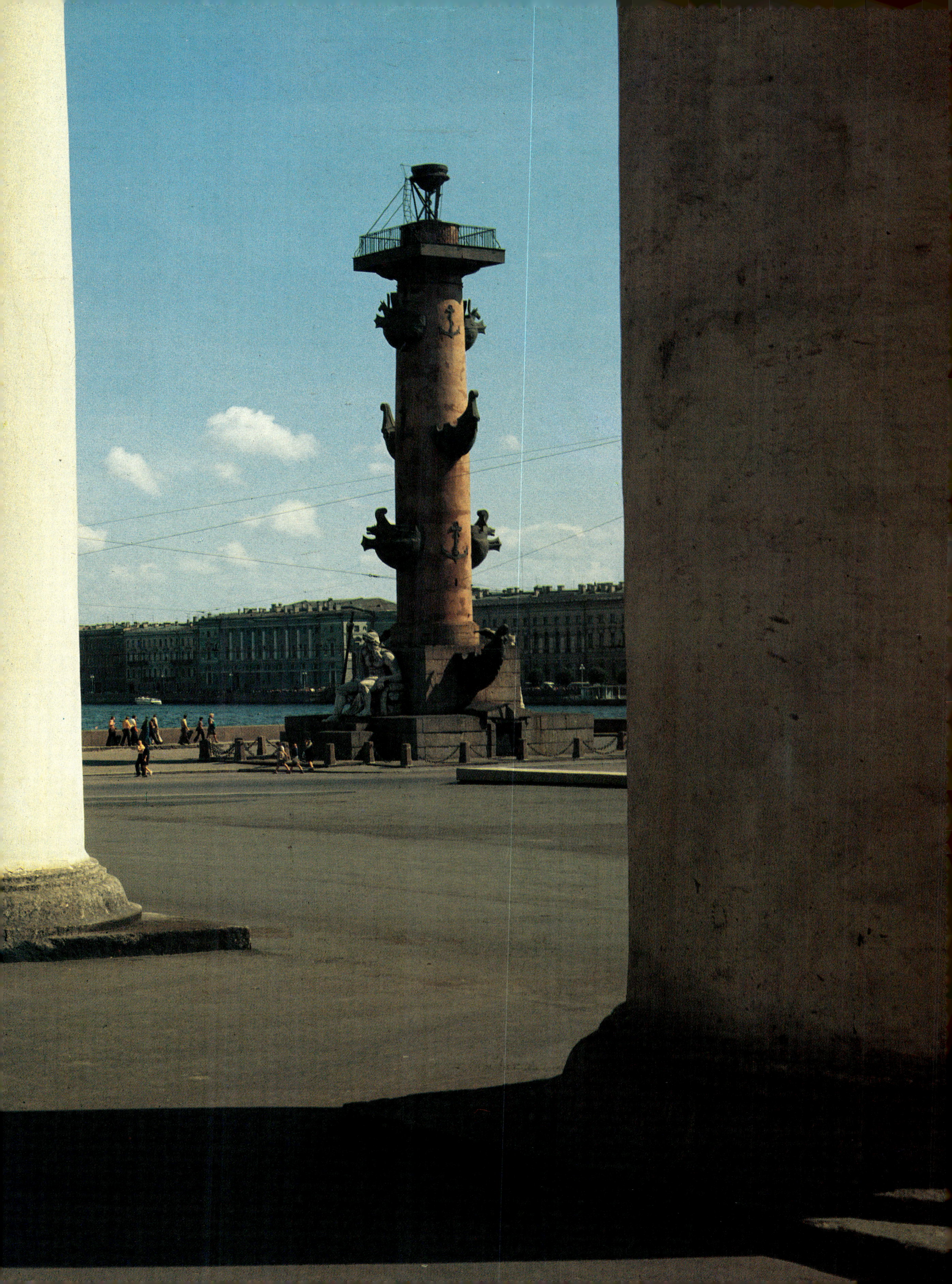

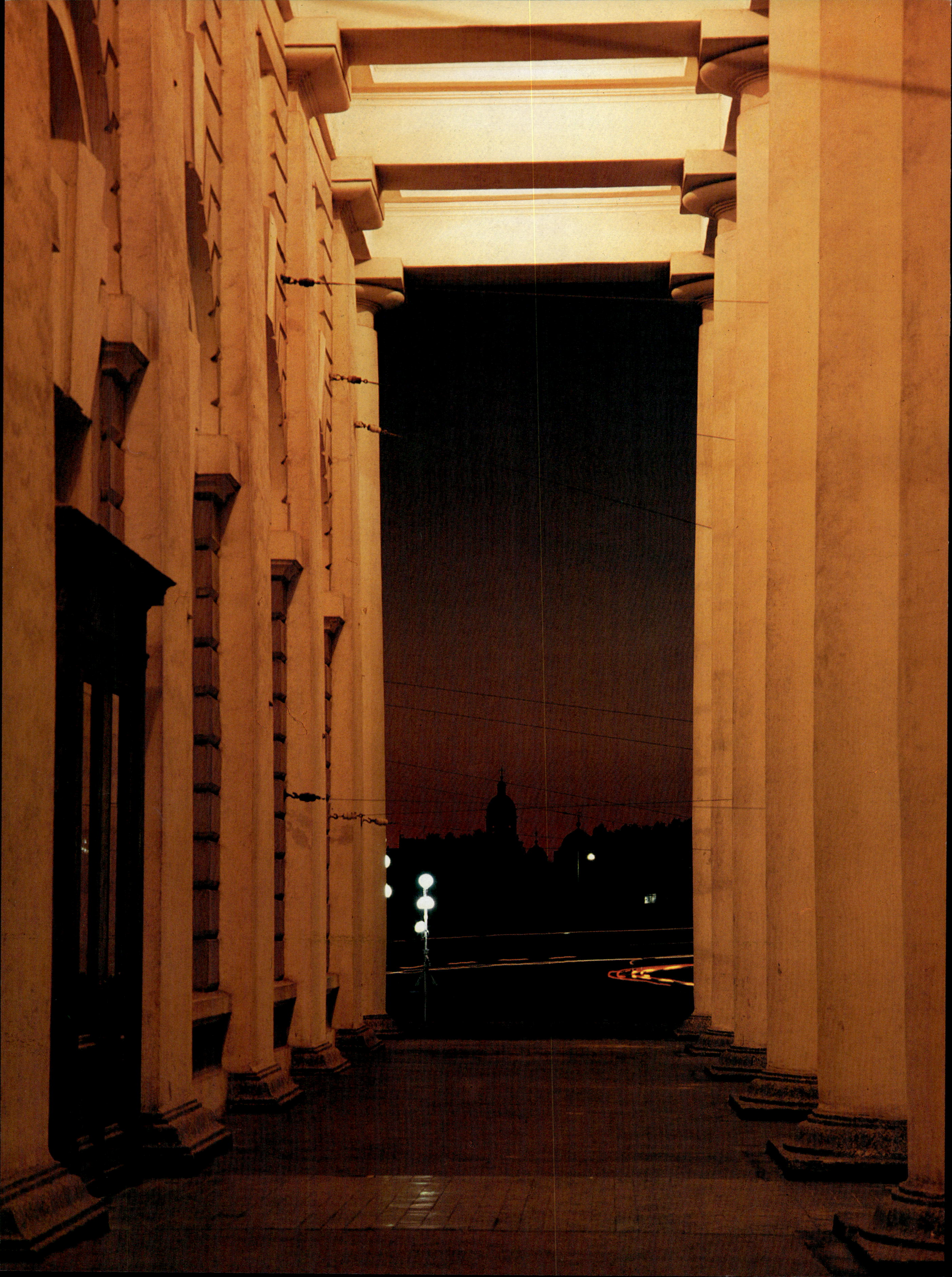

99, 100   *Colonnade of Stock Exchange*
101   *Stock Exchange*

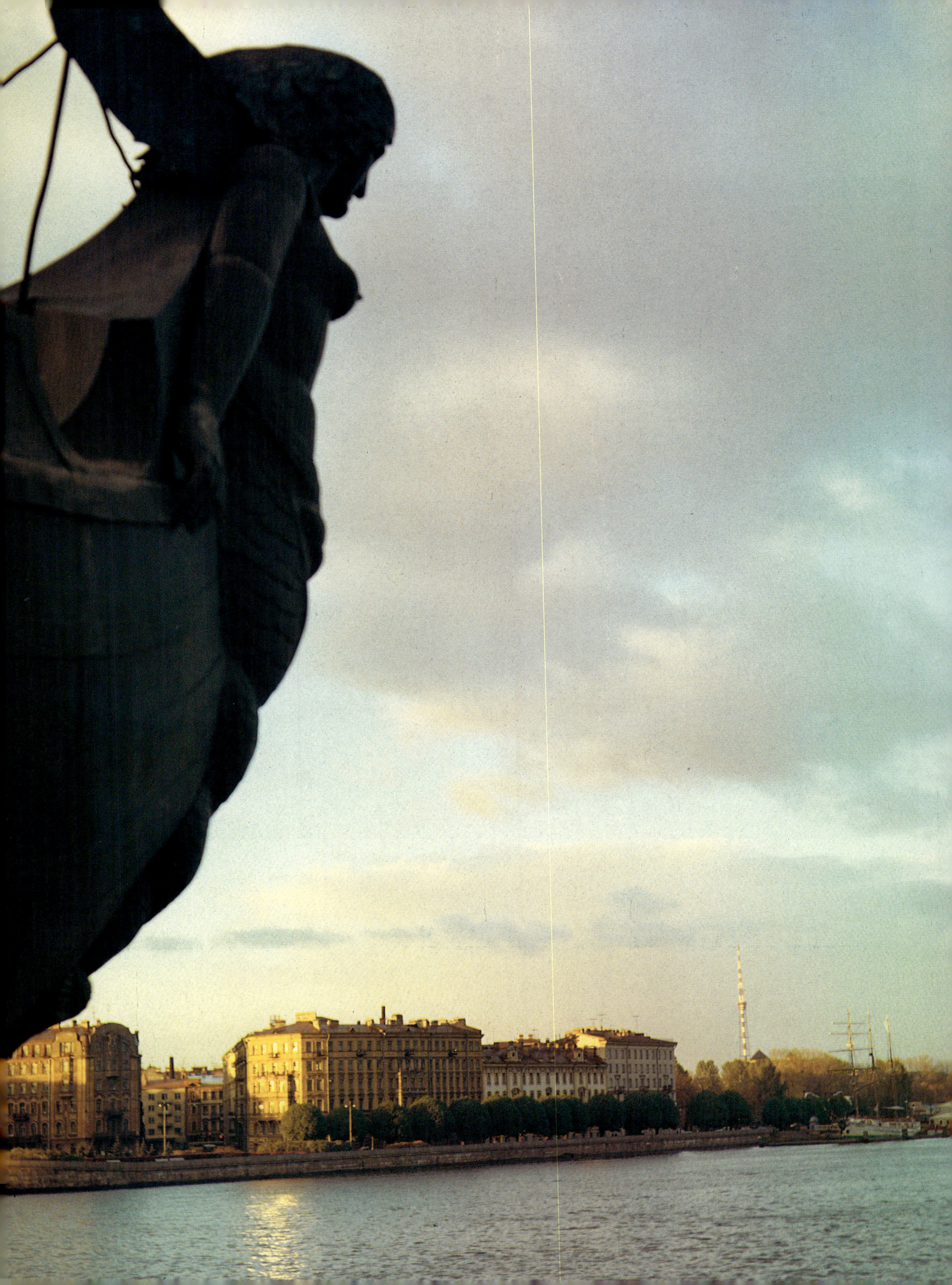

102　*Mytninskaya Embankment*

103, 104　*Point of Vasilyevsky Island seen from the park near St. Peter and Paul Fortress*

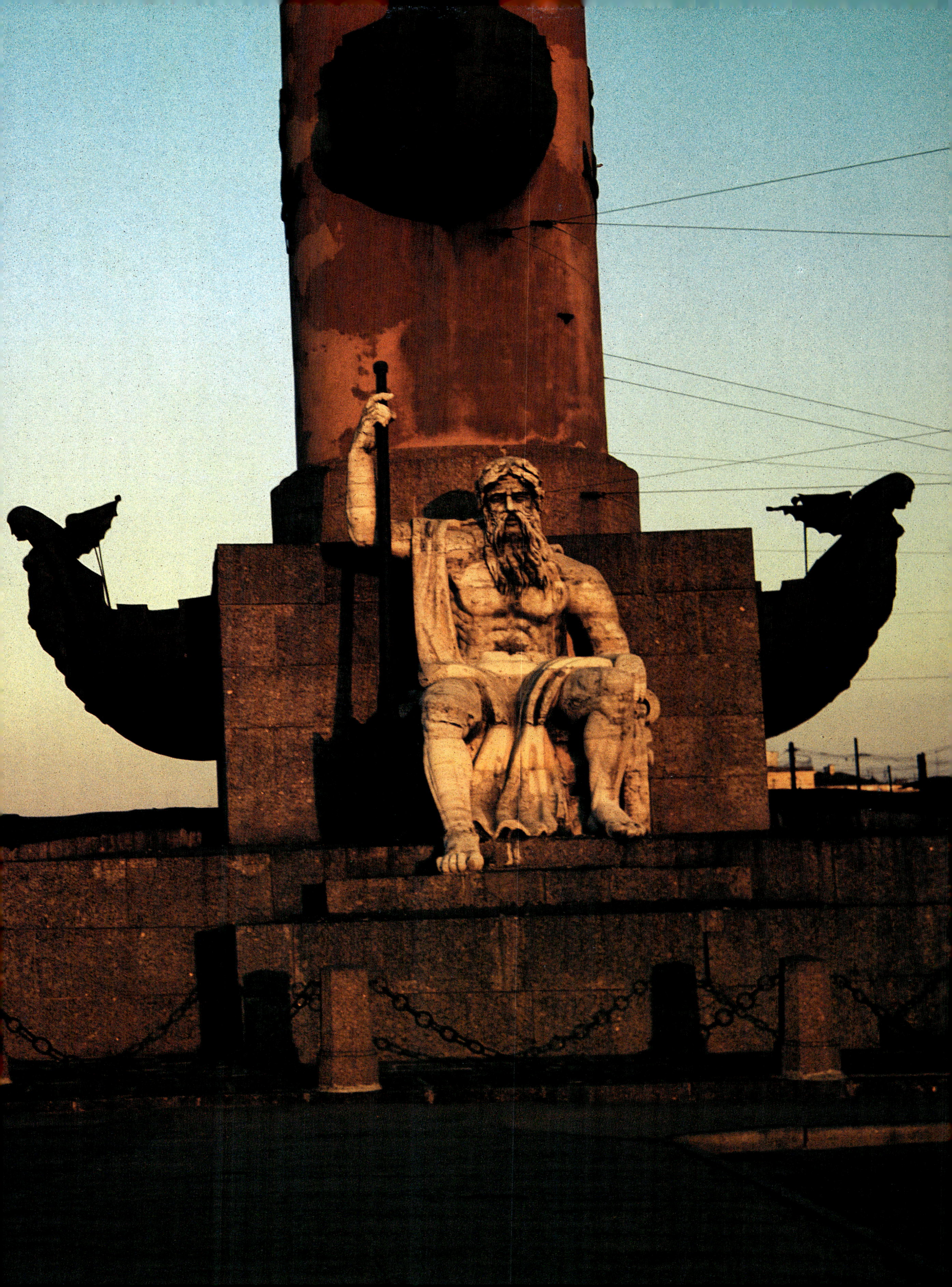

105 Rostral Column

106 Vasilyevsky Island. Makarov's Embankment
107 Winter tracery. A detail of the Summer Gardens' railing

108 — 110   Park near St. Peter and Paul Fortress

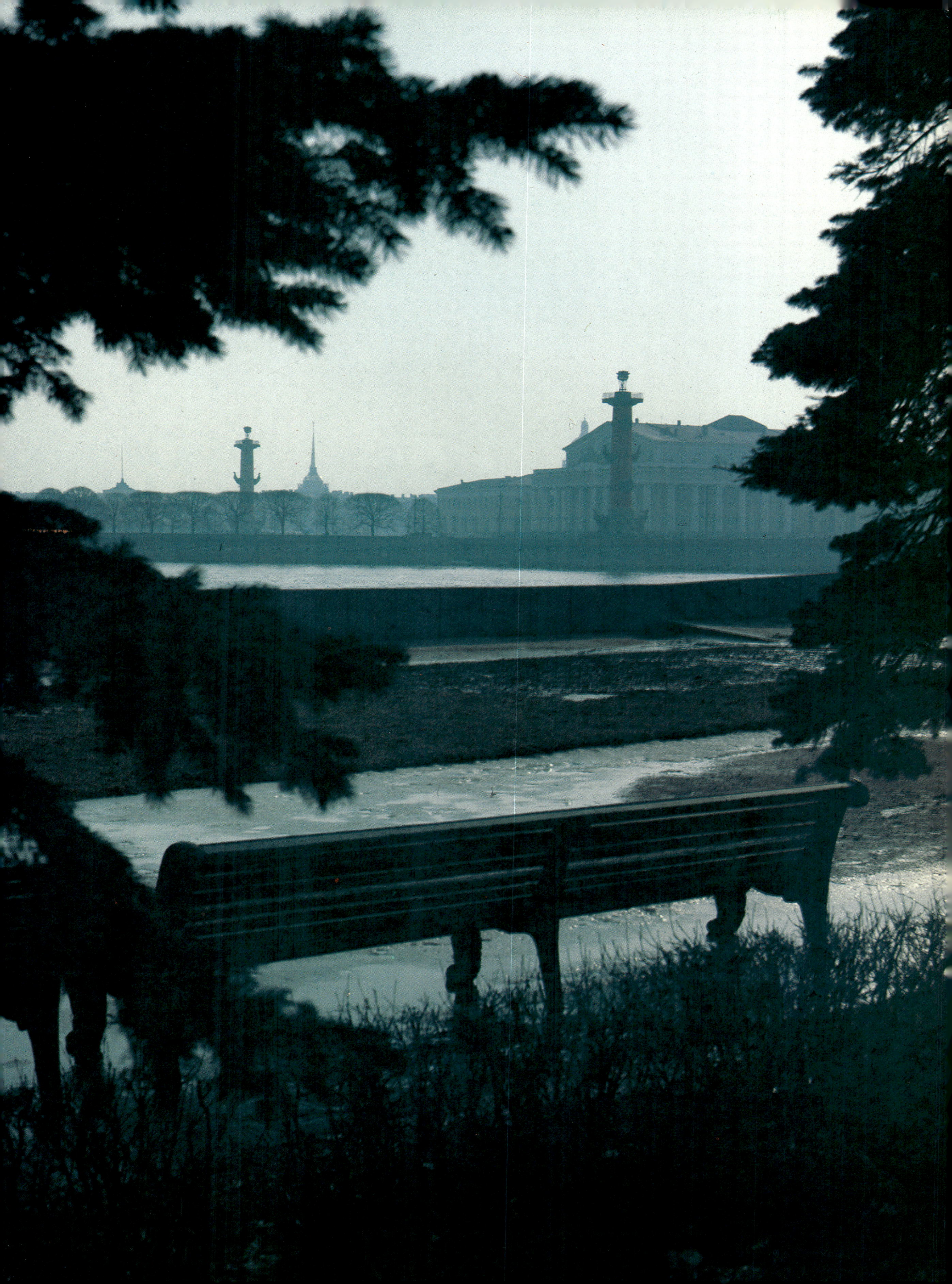

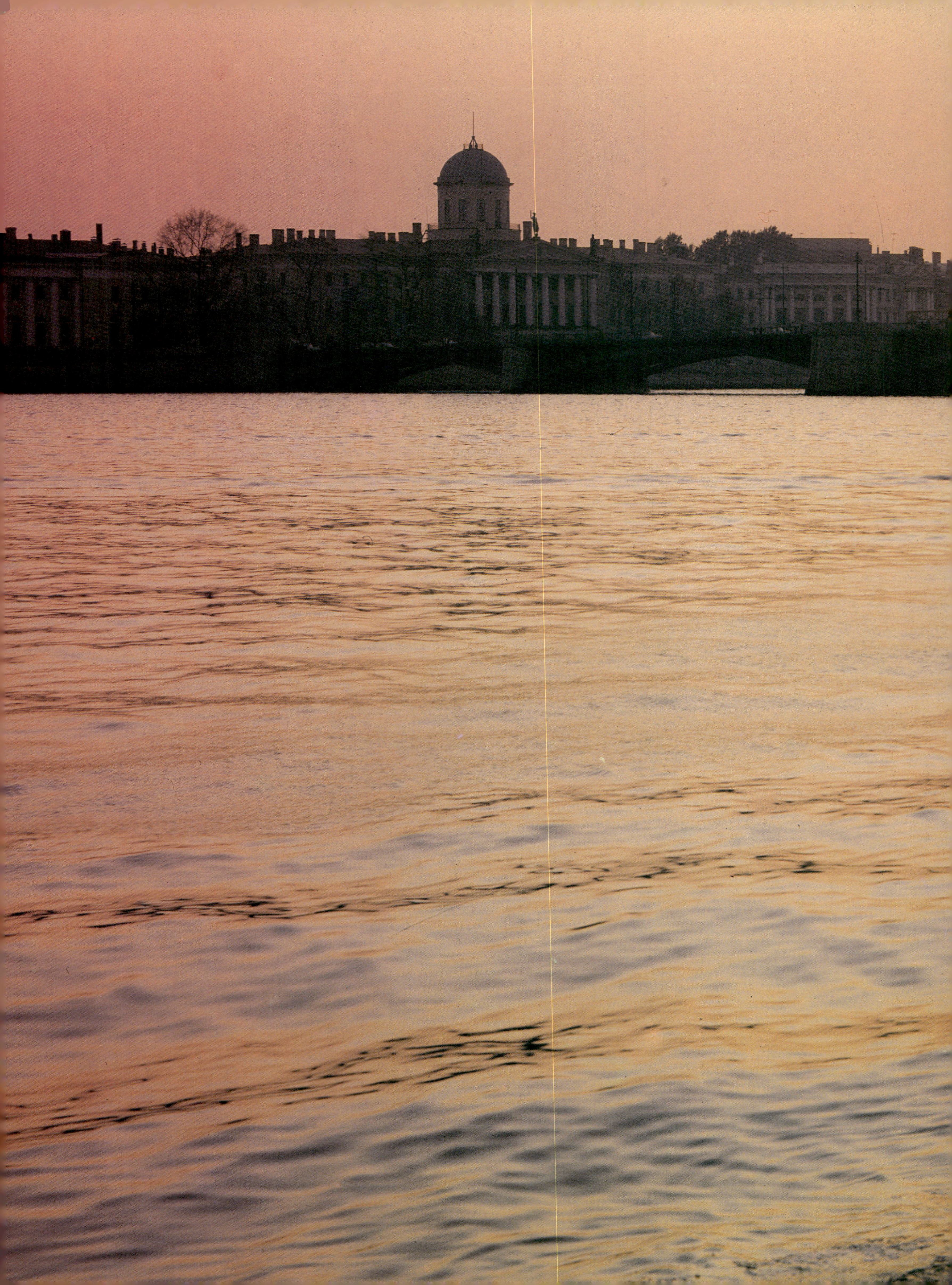

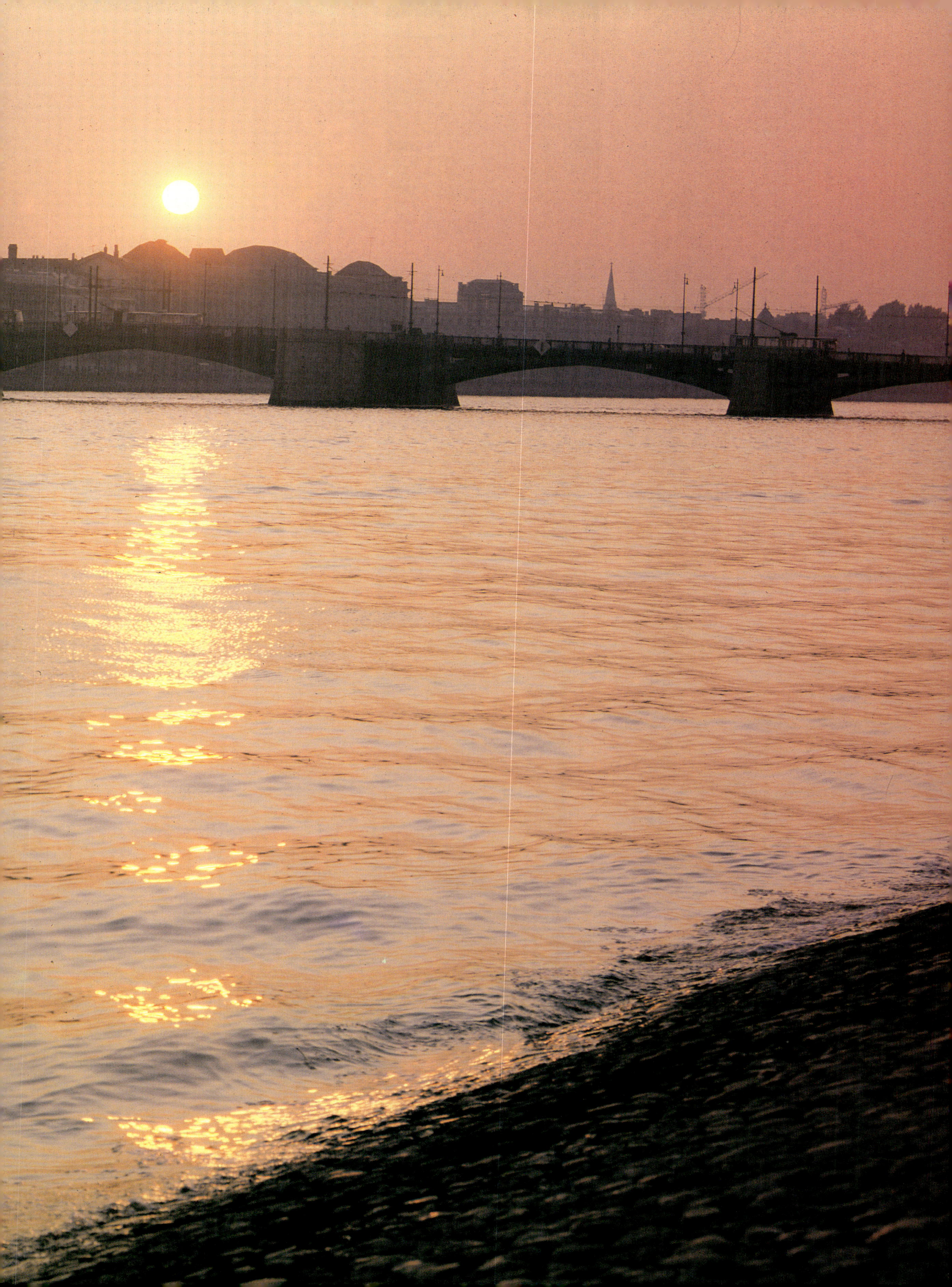

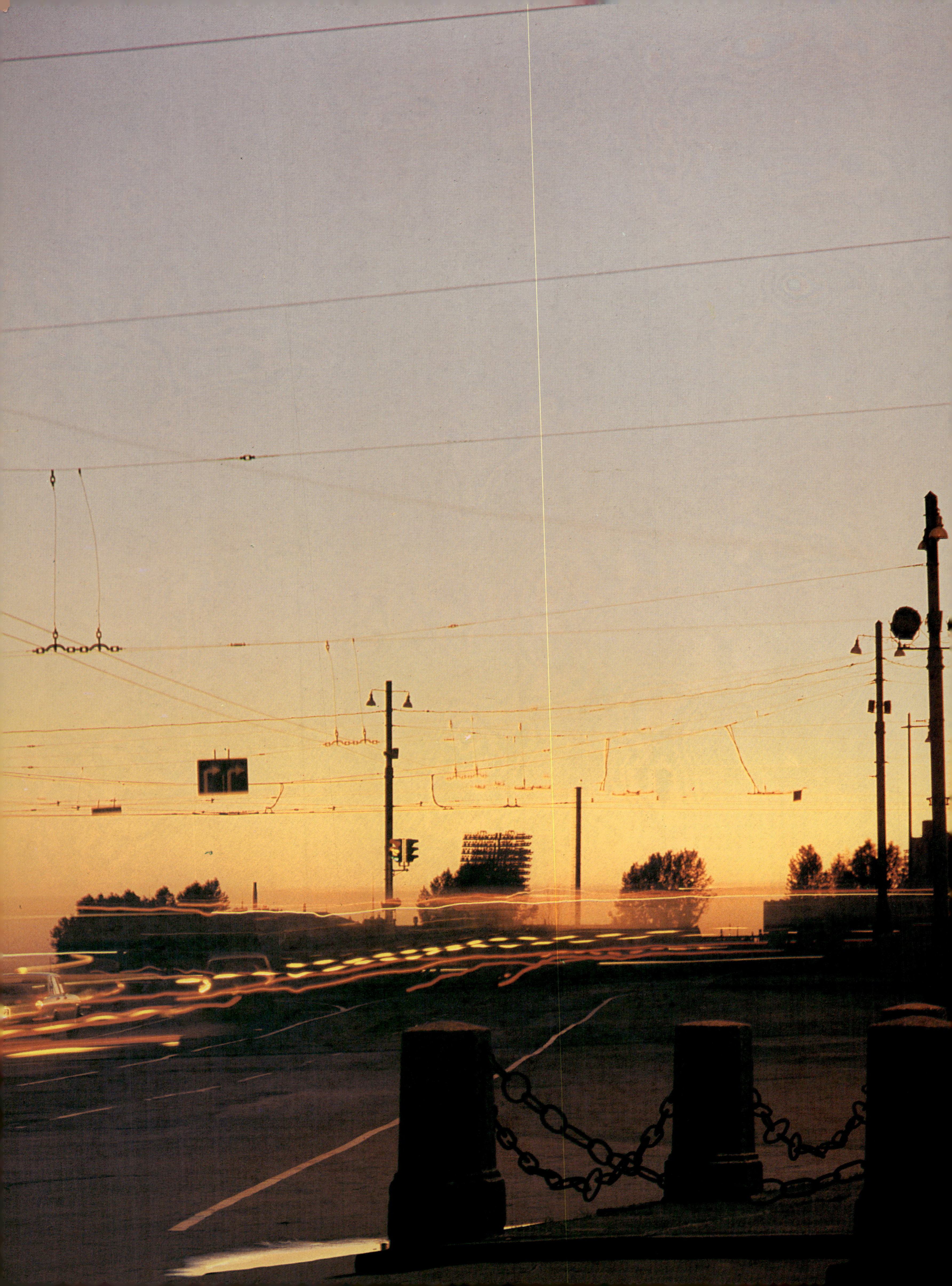

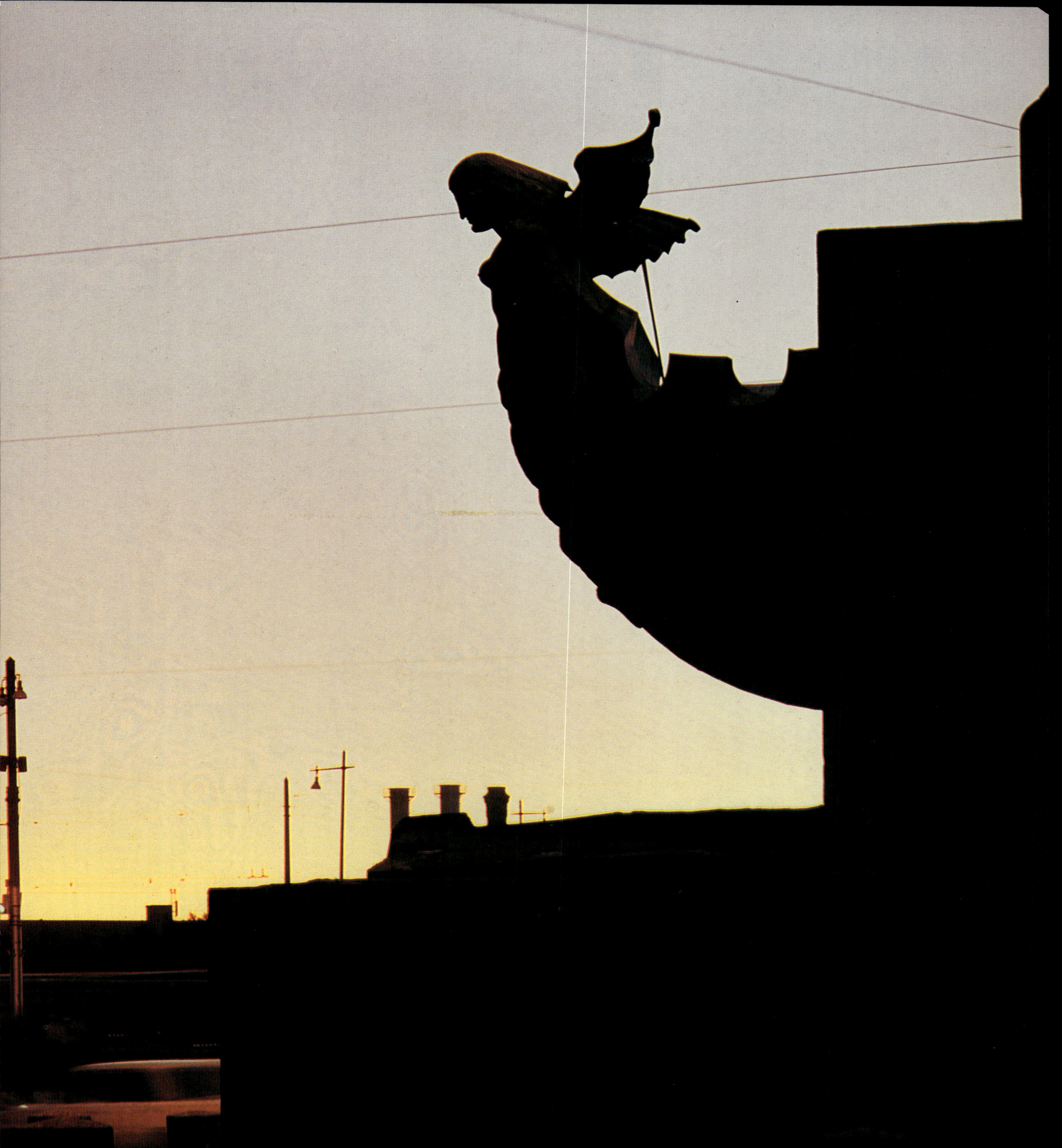

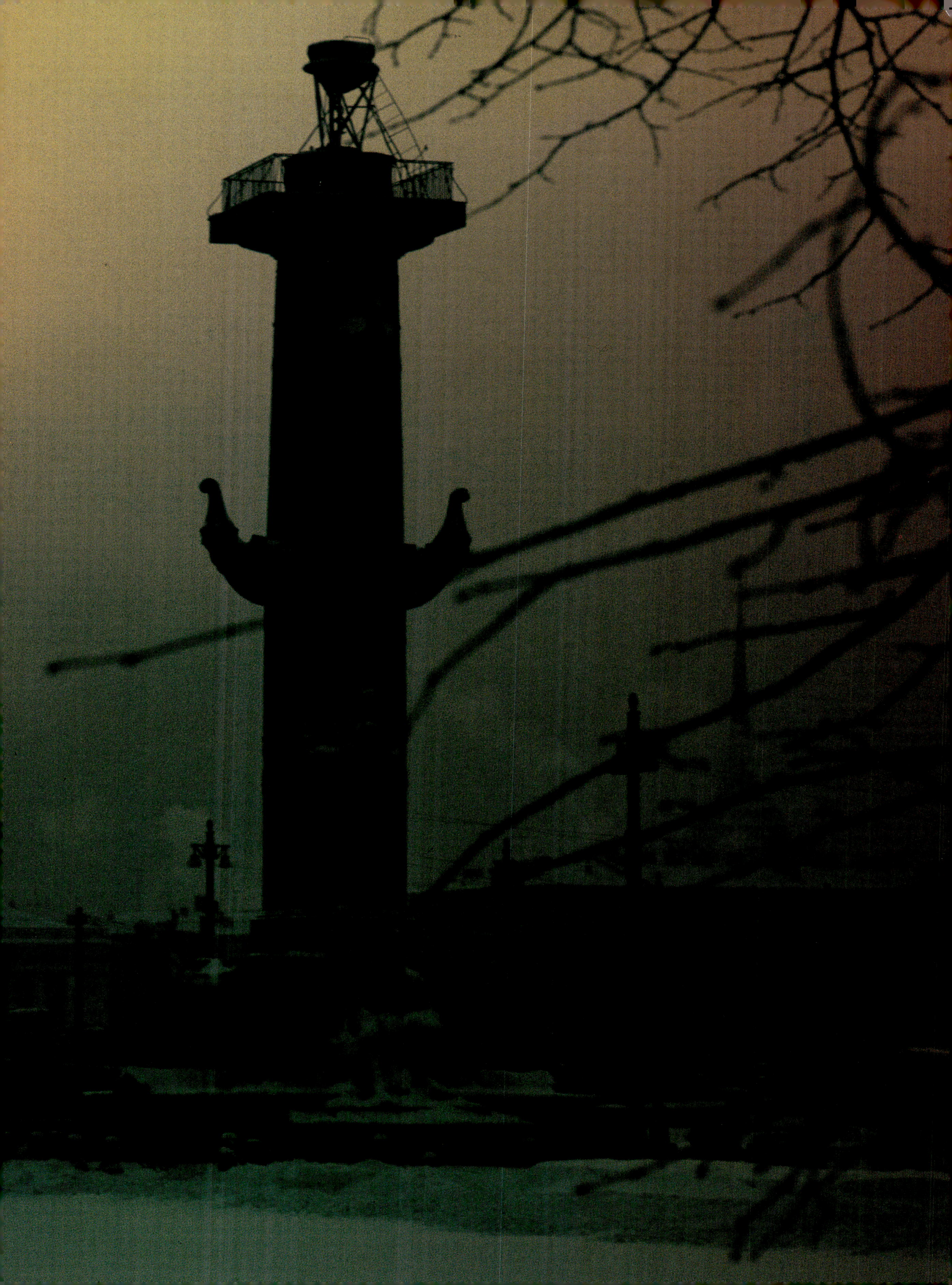

114
→
115

111, 112, 115   Builders' Bridge

113   Rostral Column by night
114   St. John's Bridge

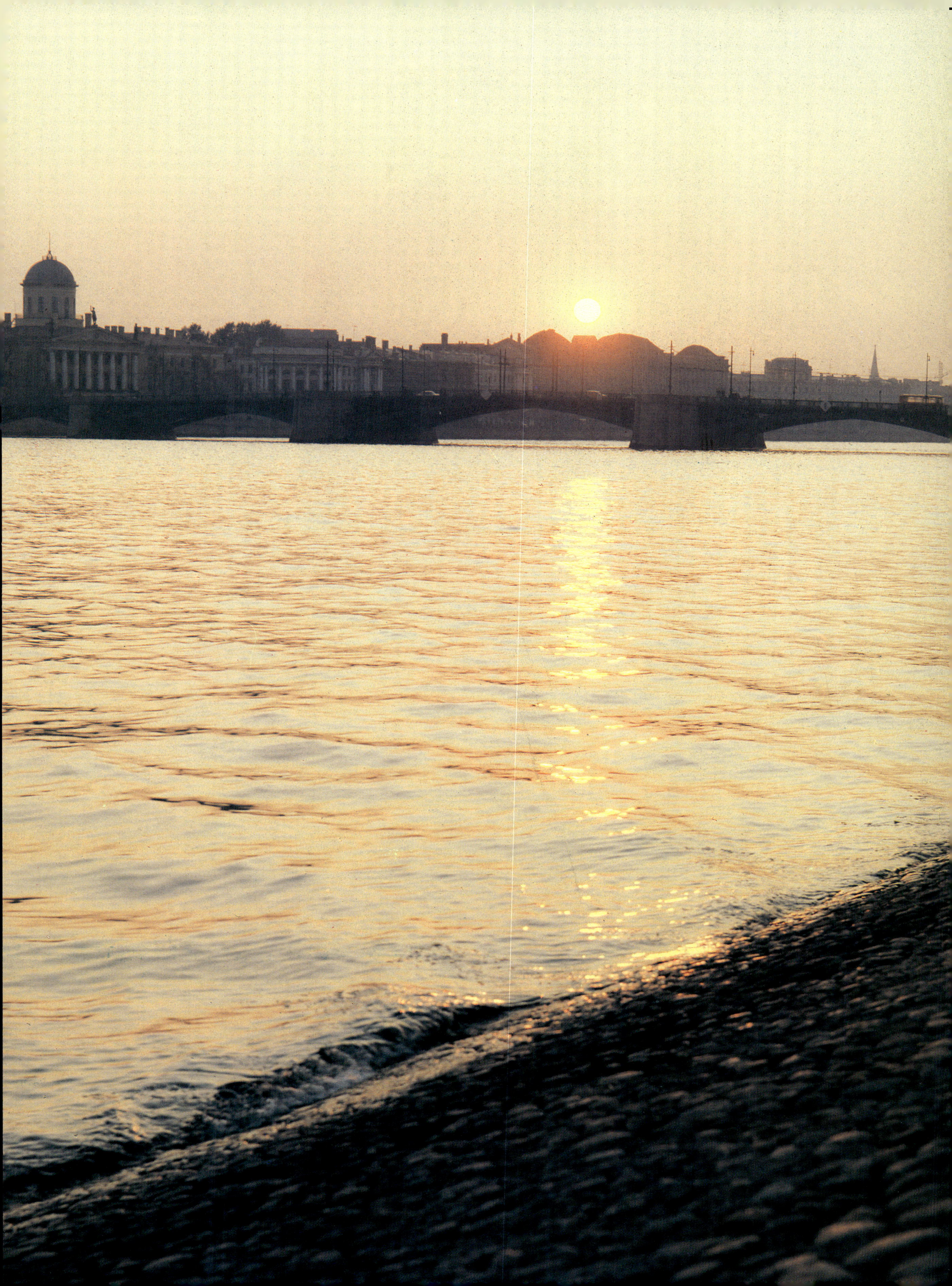

118	Summer Gardens. Railing →
119	Statue of Peter the Great (The «Bronze Horseman») →
120	Summer Palace of Peter the Great in the Summer Gardens →
121	Castle of Engineers. Southern entrance →
122	Swans' Canal near the Castle of Engineers →
123	Summer Gardens. Railing at a Swans' Canal →
124	Moika by the Field of Mars →
125	Castle of Engineers. Northern entrance →
126	Castle of Engineers. Detail of the decor →
127	Summer Gardens. Autumn →

116, 117 Allegorical statue of Suvorov near the Field of Mars

КНЯЗЬ
ИТАЛІЙСКОЙ
ГРАФЪ
СУВОРОВЪ
РЫМНИКСКОЙ.
1801 г.

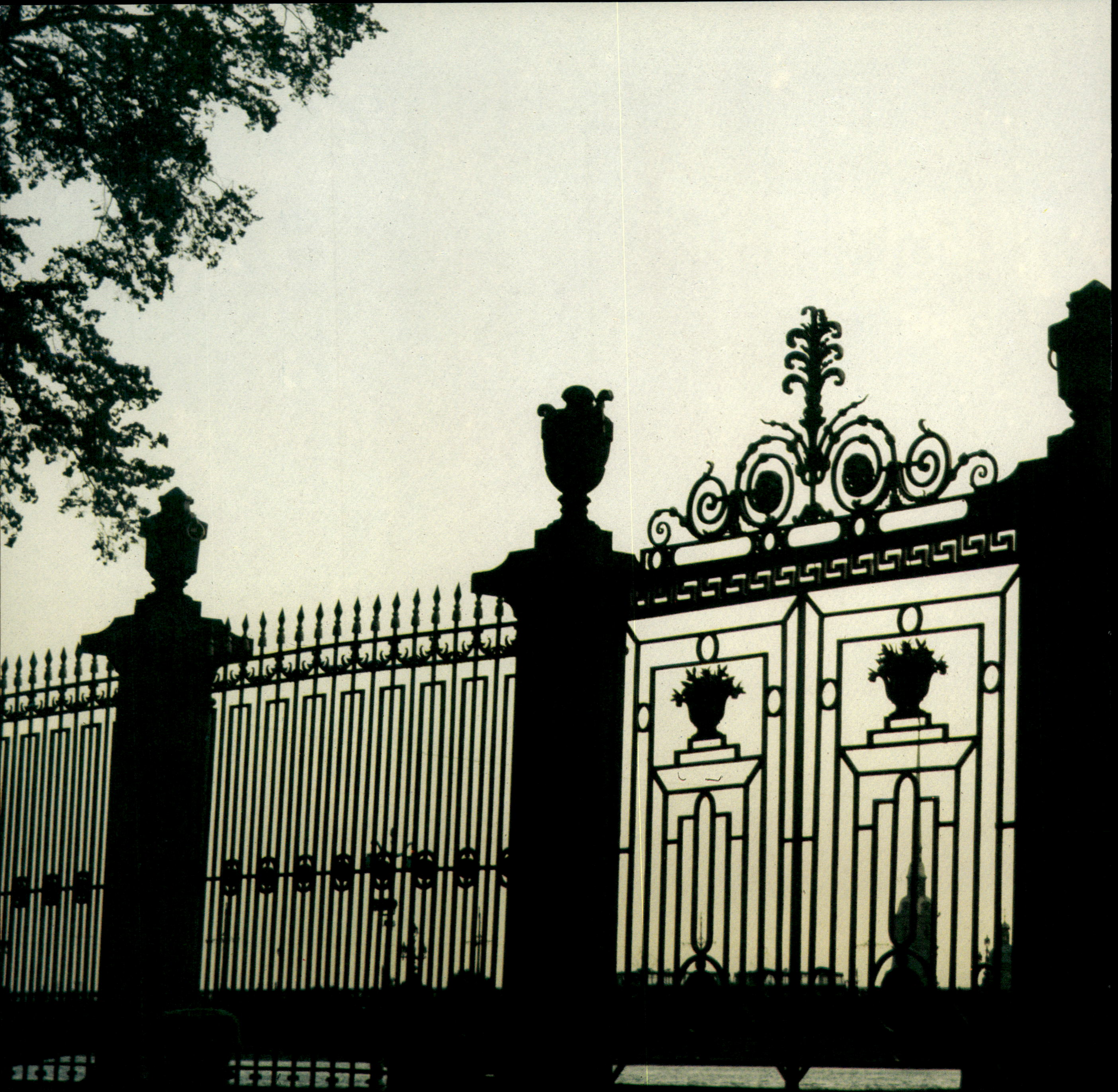

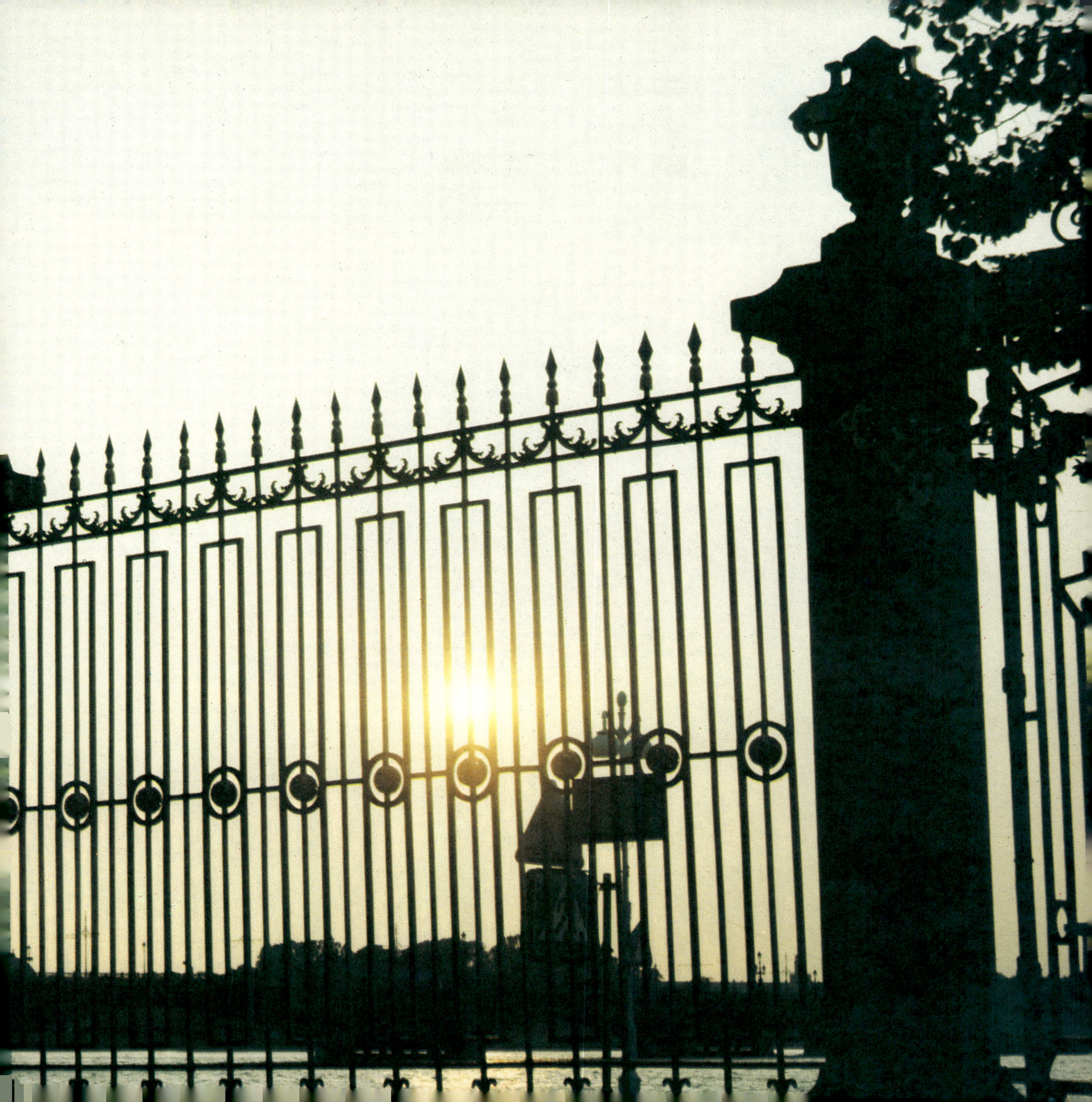

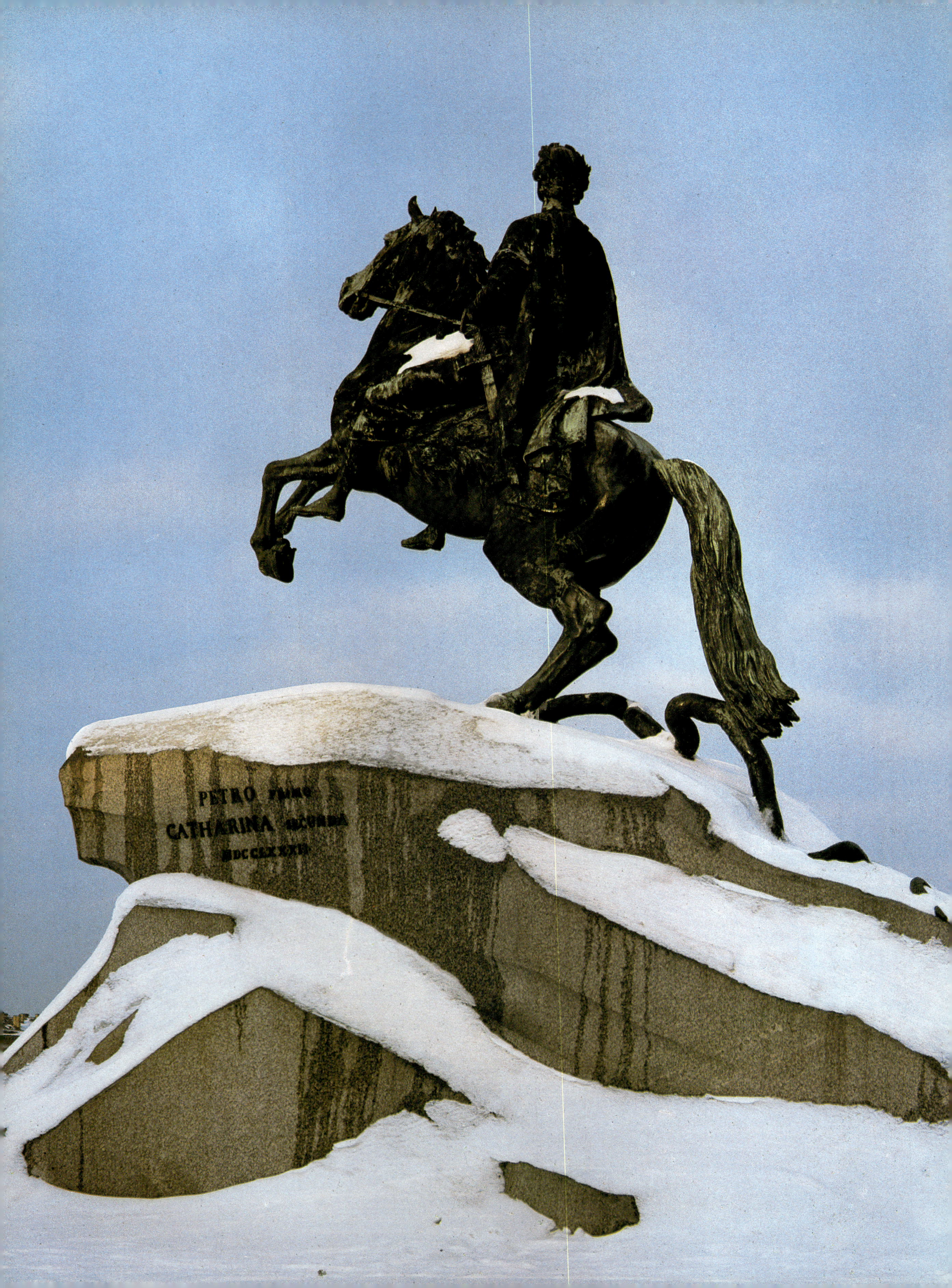
PETRO
CATHARINA

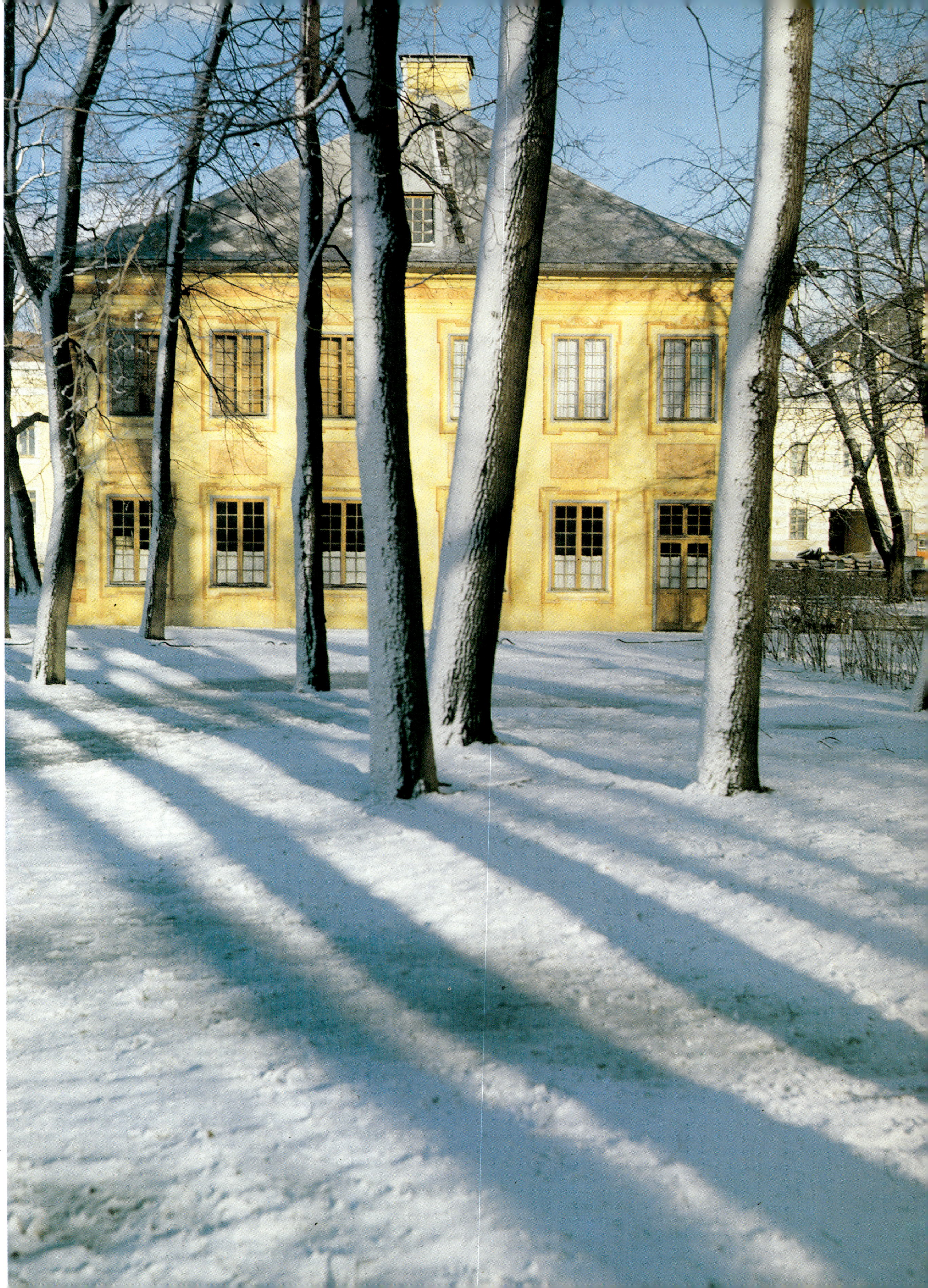

← 119

120

121 →
122

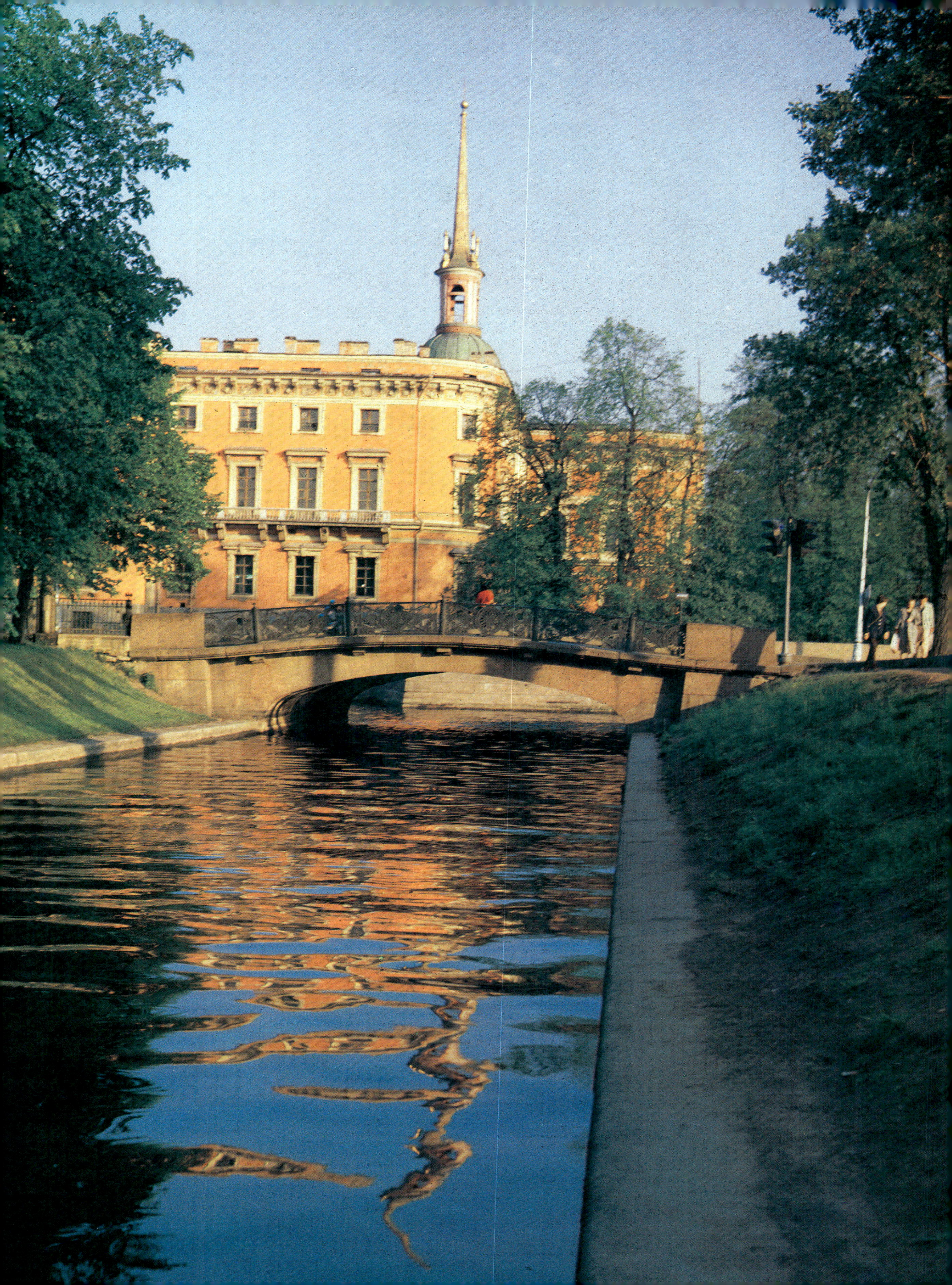

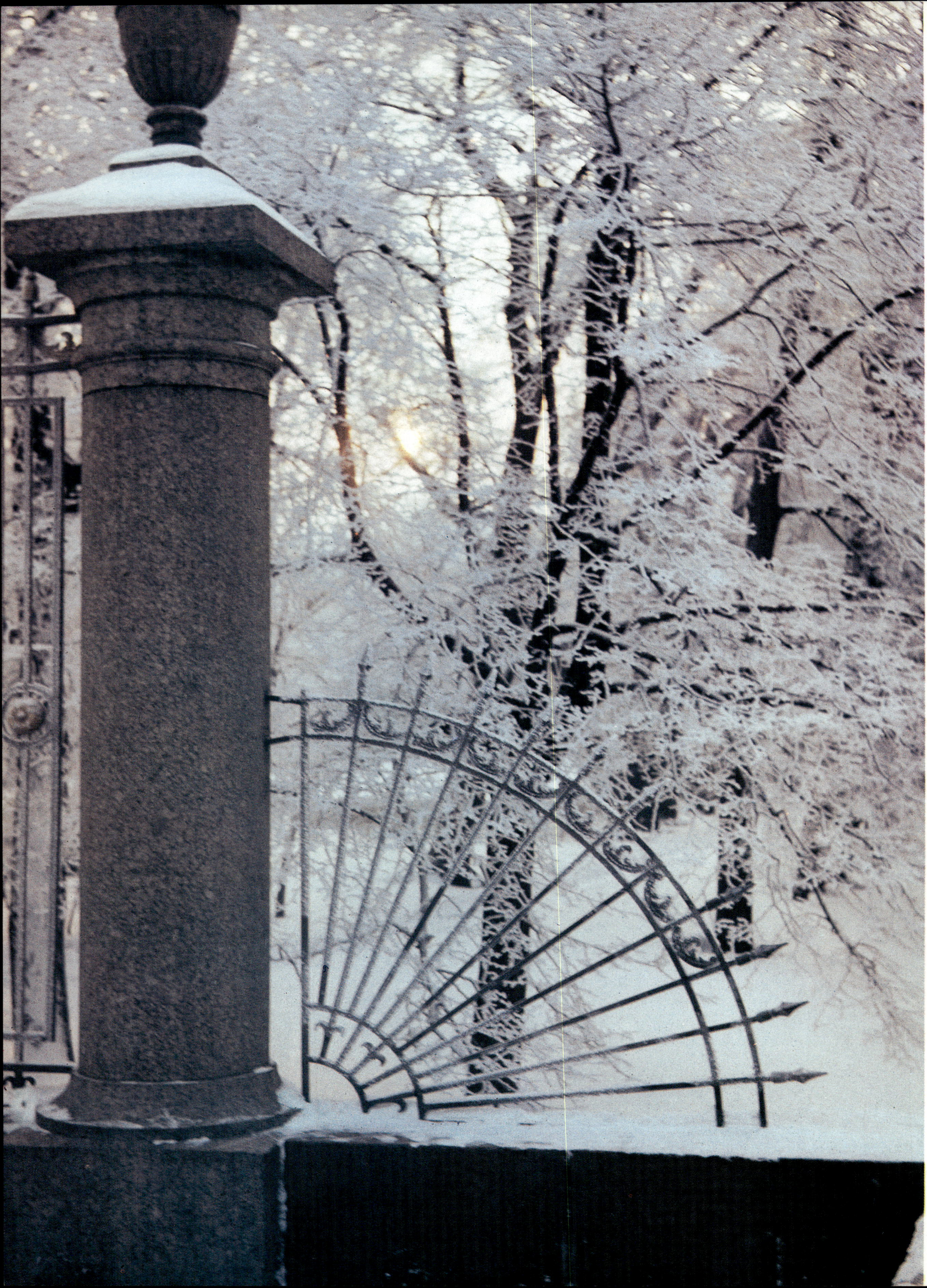

123

→
124

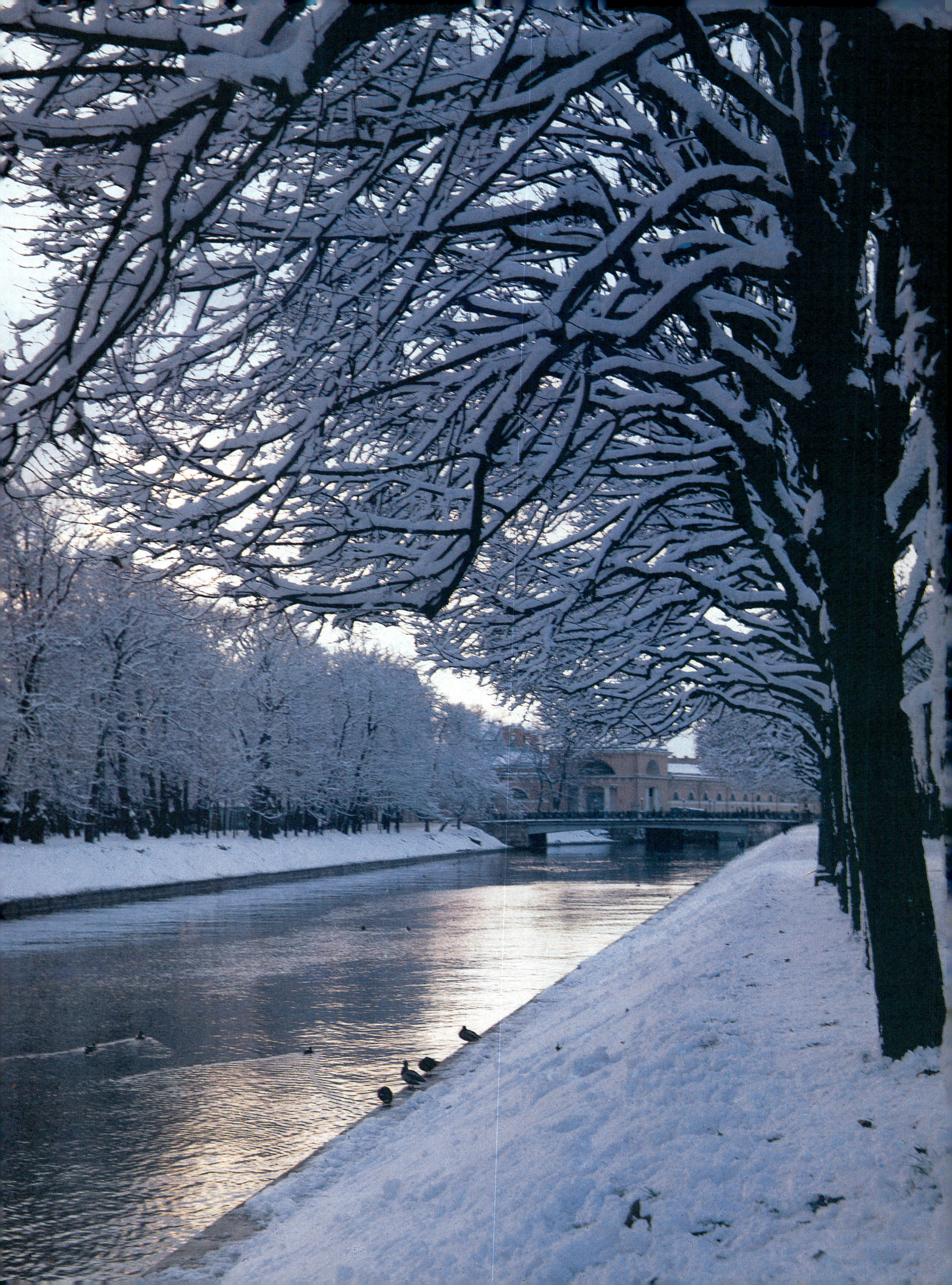

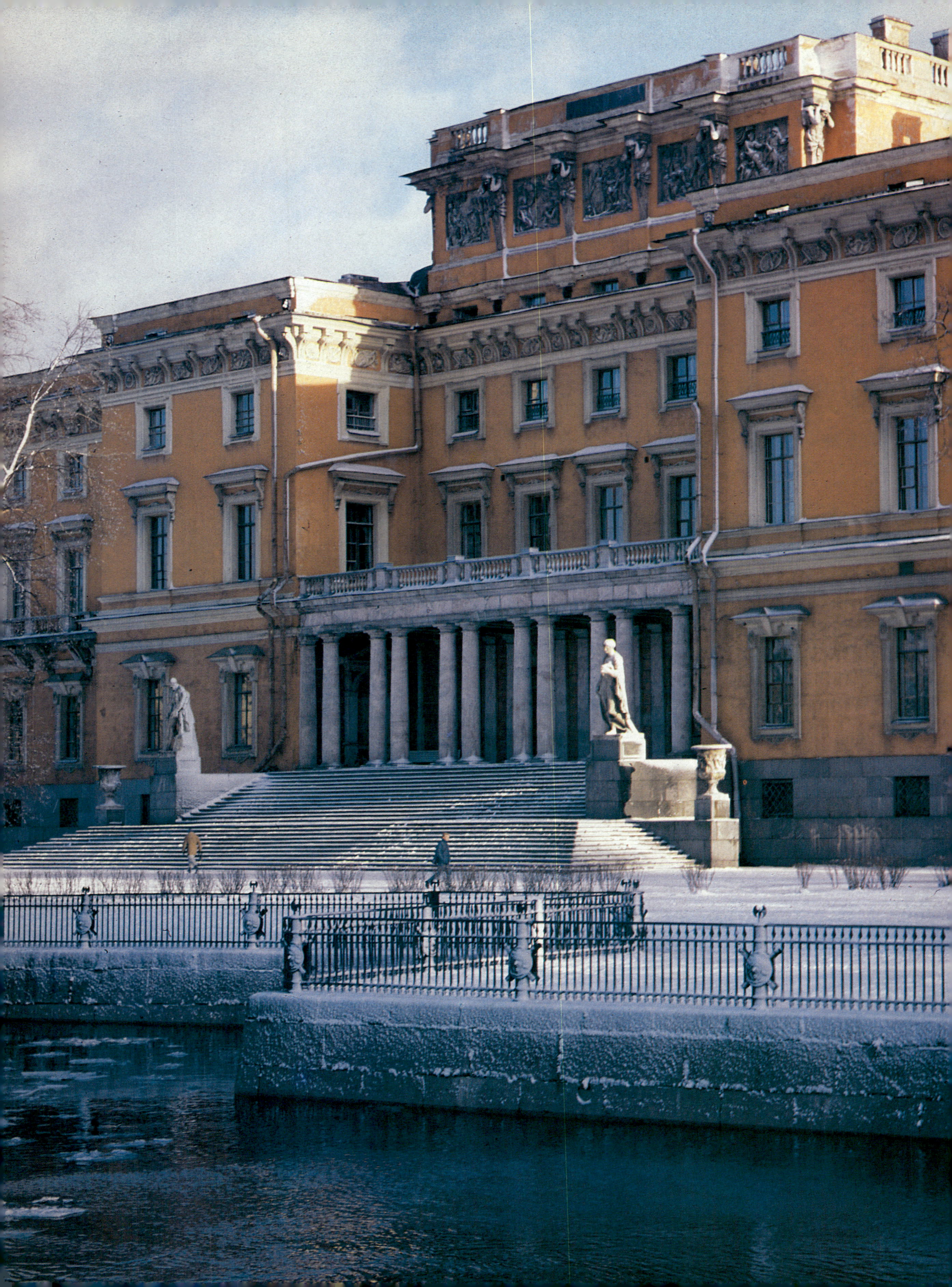

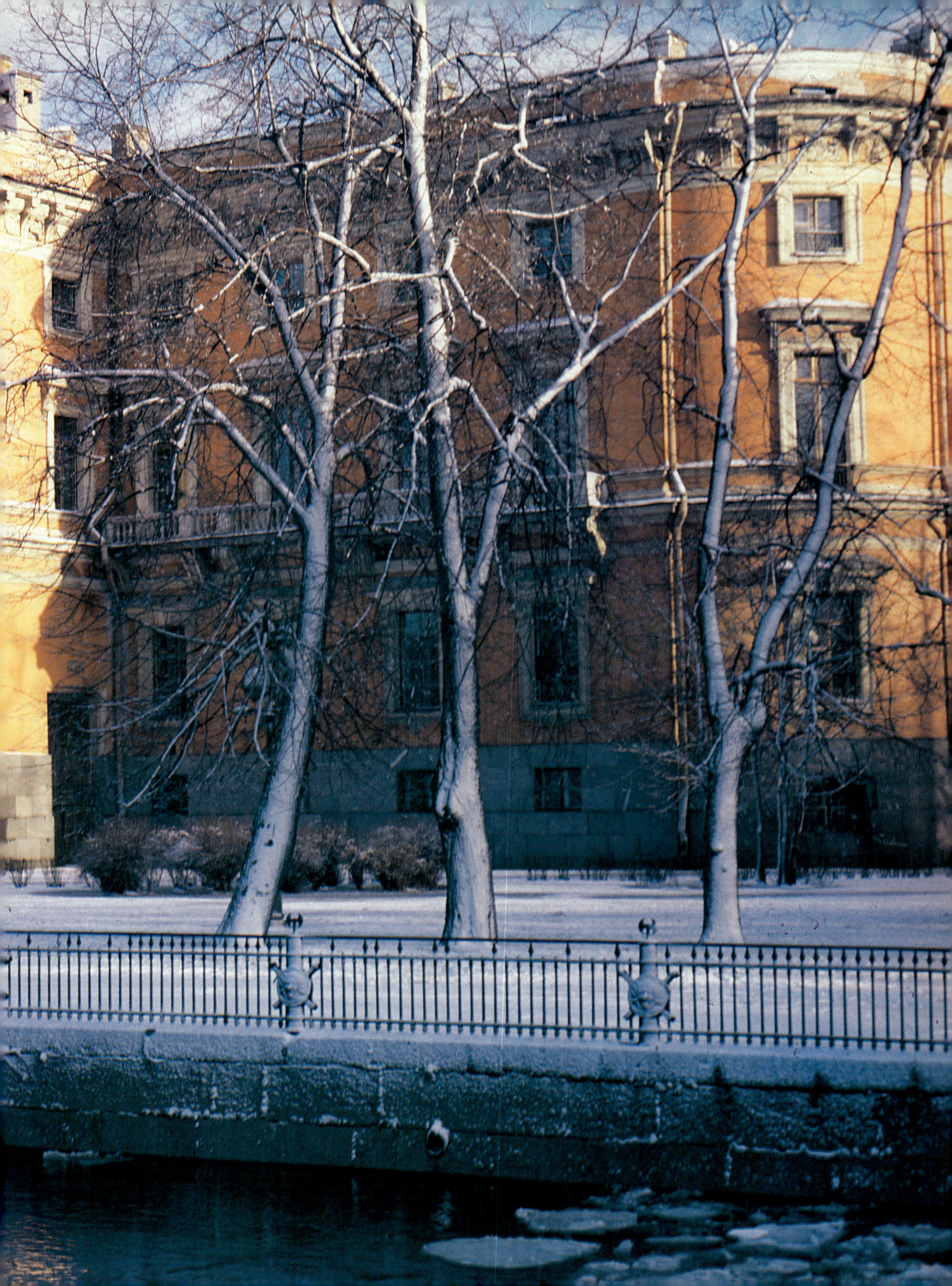

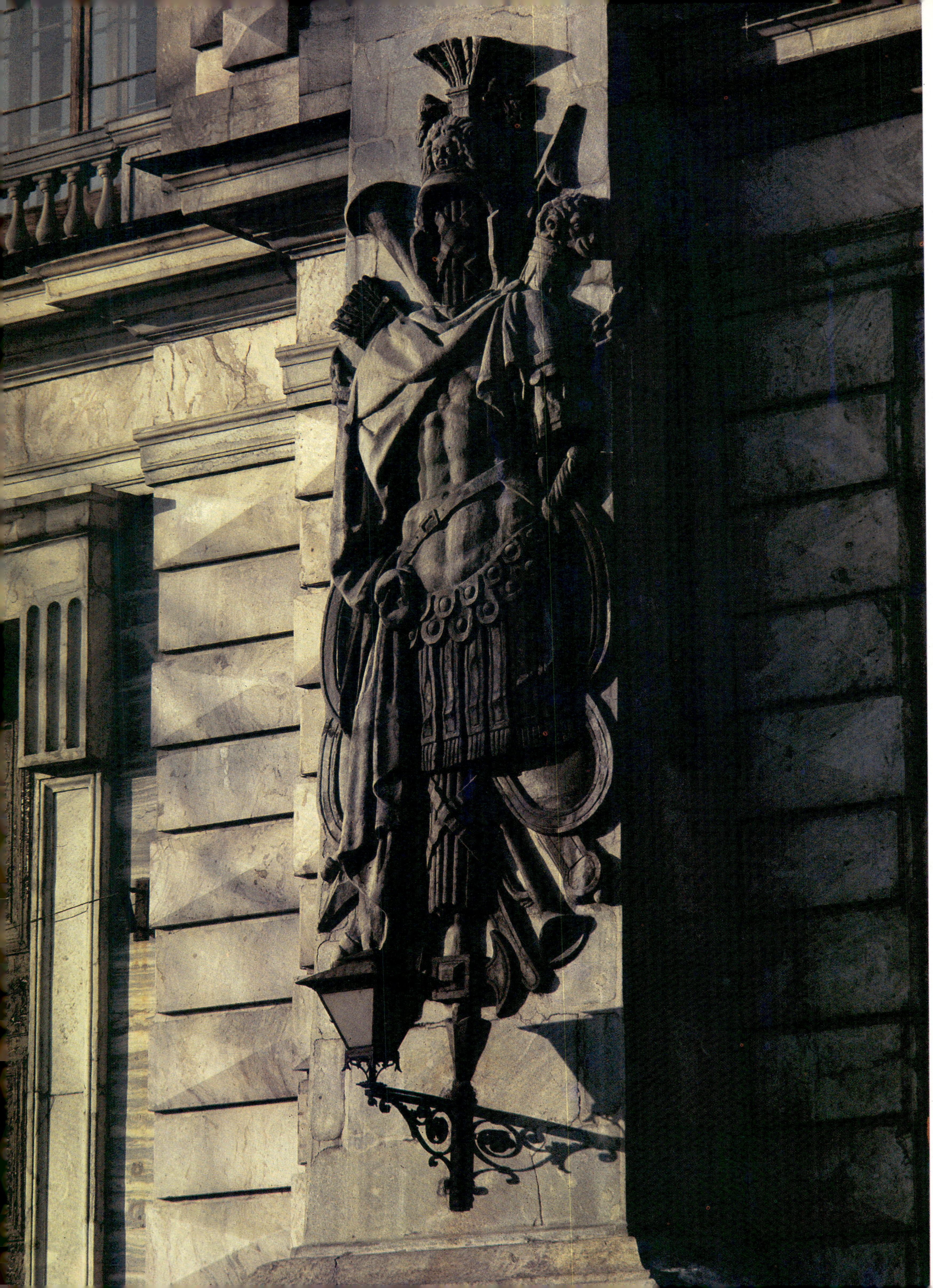

12

→
12

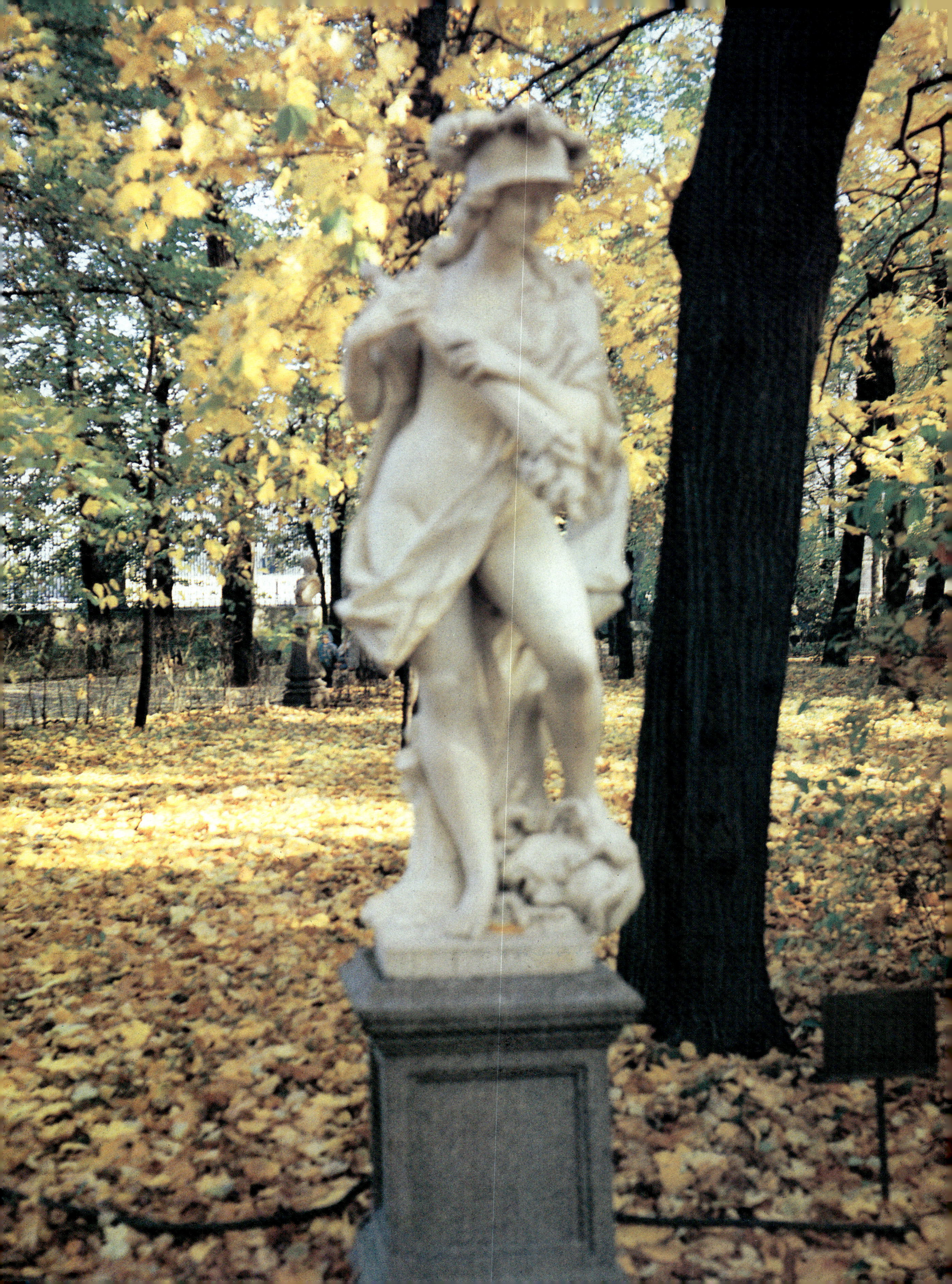

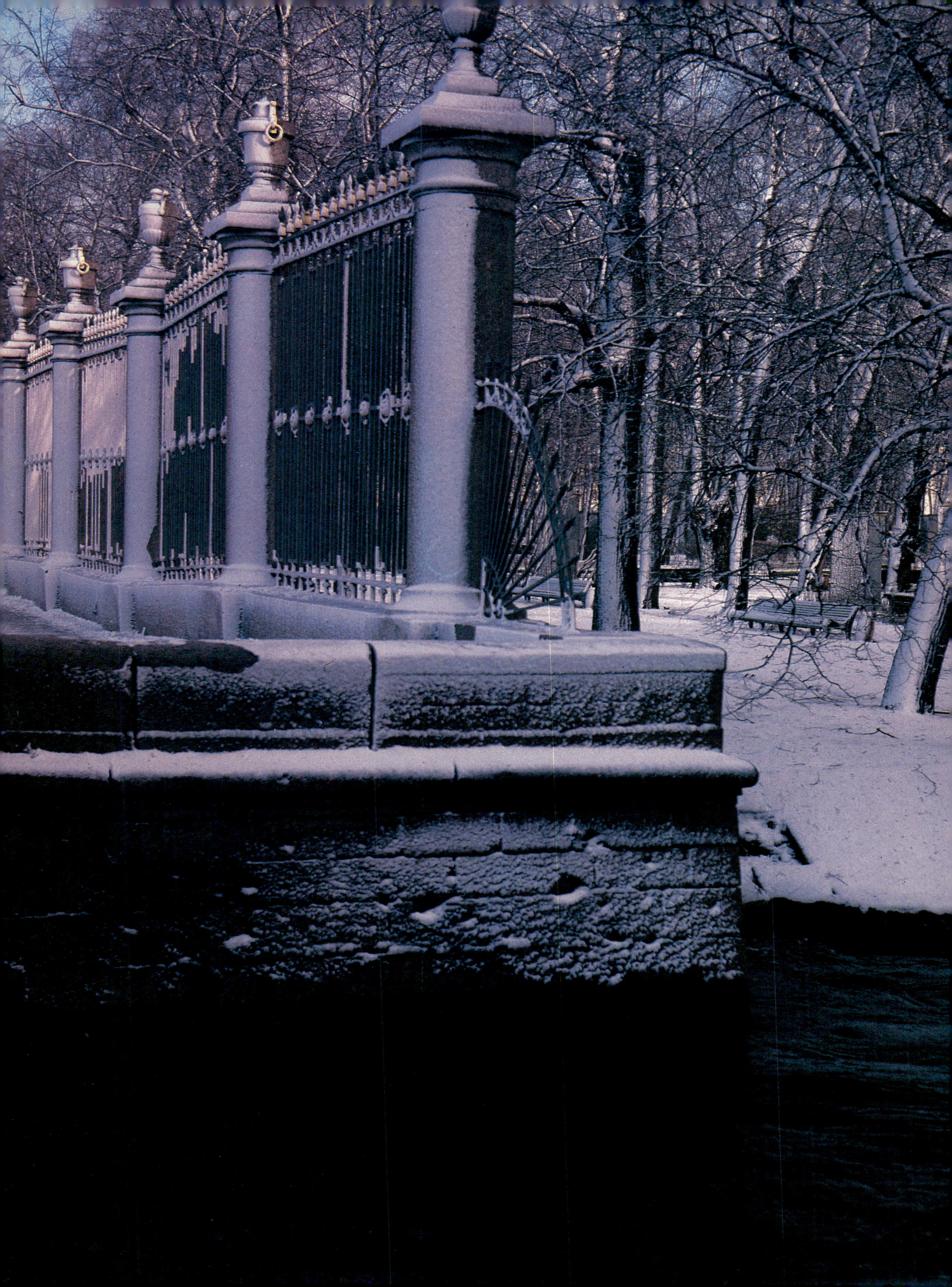

128 *Summer Gardens. Early snow*
129 *Castle of Engineers. Early snow*

130 Castle of Engineers seen from the Summer Gardens

131, 132 Statue of Peter the Great near the Castle of Engineers

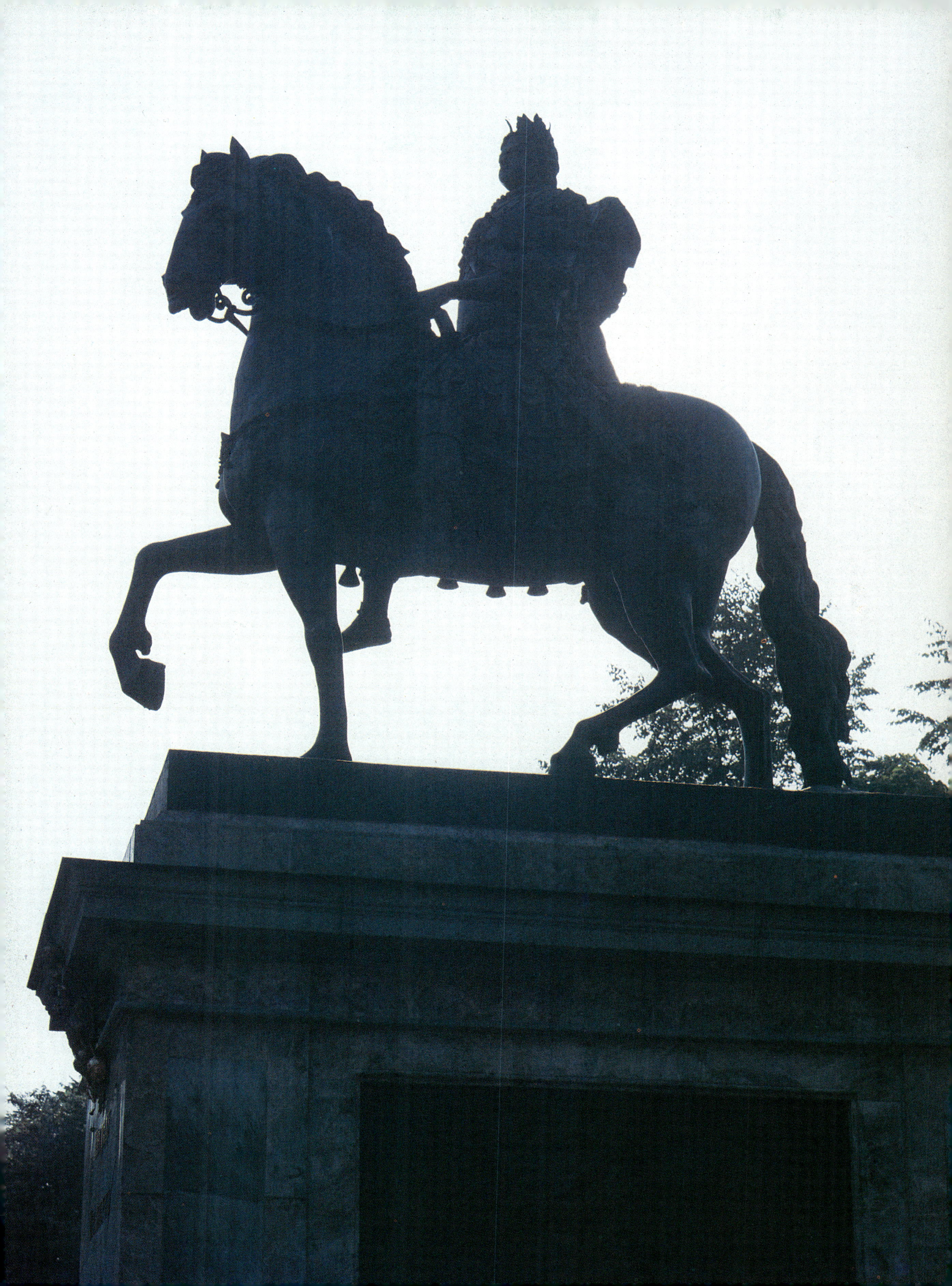

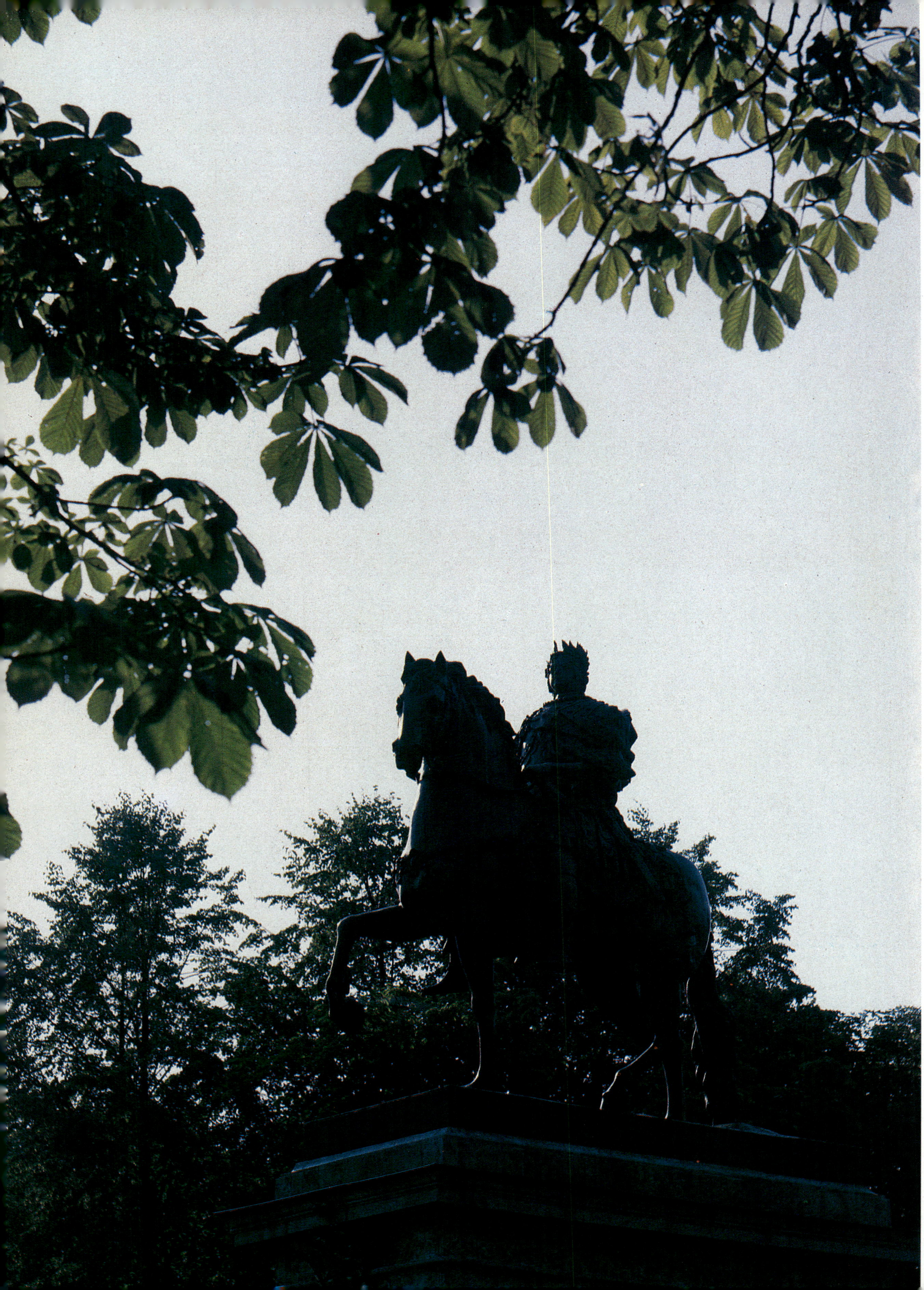

133   Summer rain

134   Mikhailovsky Gardens →
135   Castle of Engineers →
136   Field of Mars →
137   Castle of Engineers seen from
      the Mikhailovsky Gardens →
138   Smaller Opera Theatre (Mikhailovsky
      Theatre) →
139   Cathedral of the Resurrection
      (The «Savior on the Blood») →

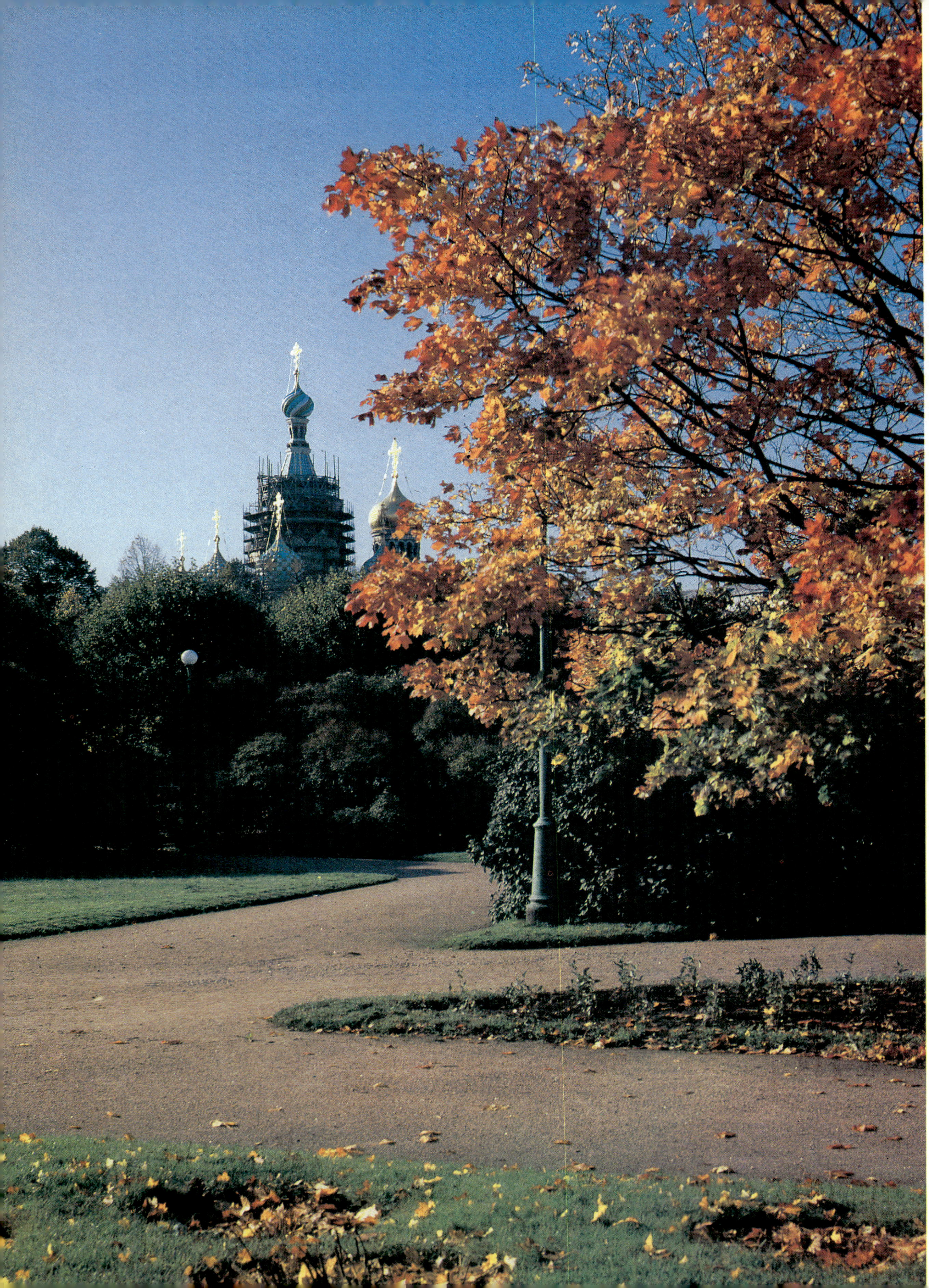

134
→
135

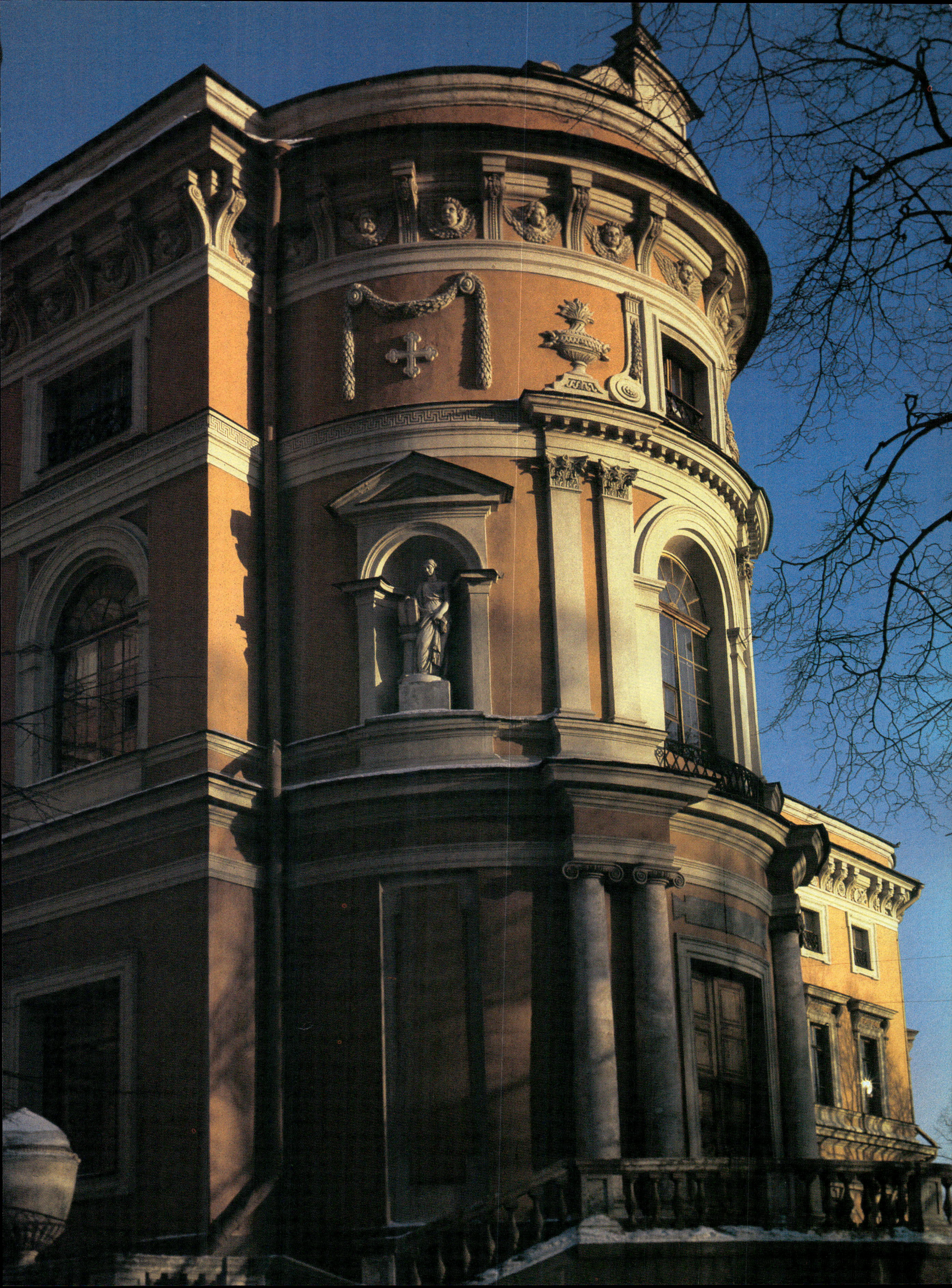

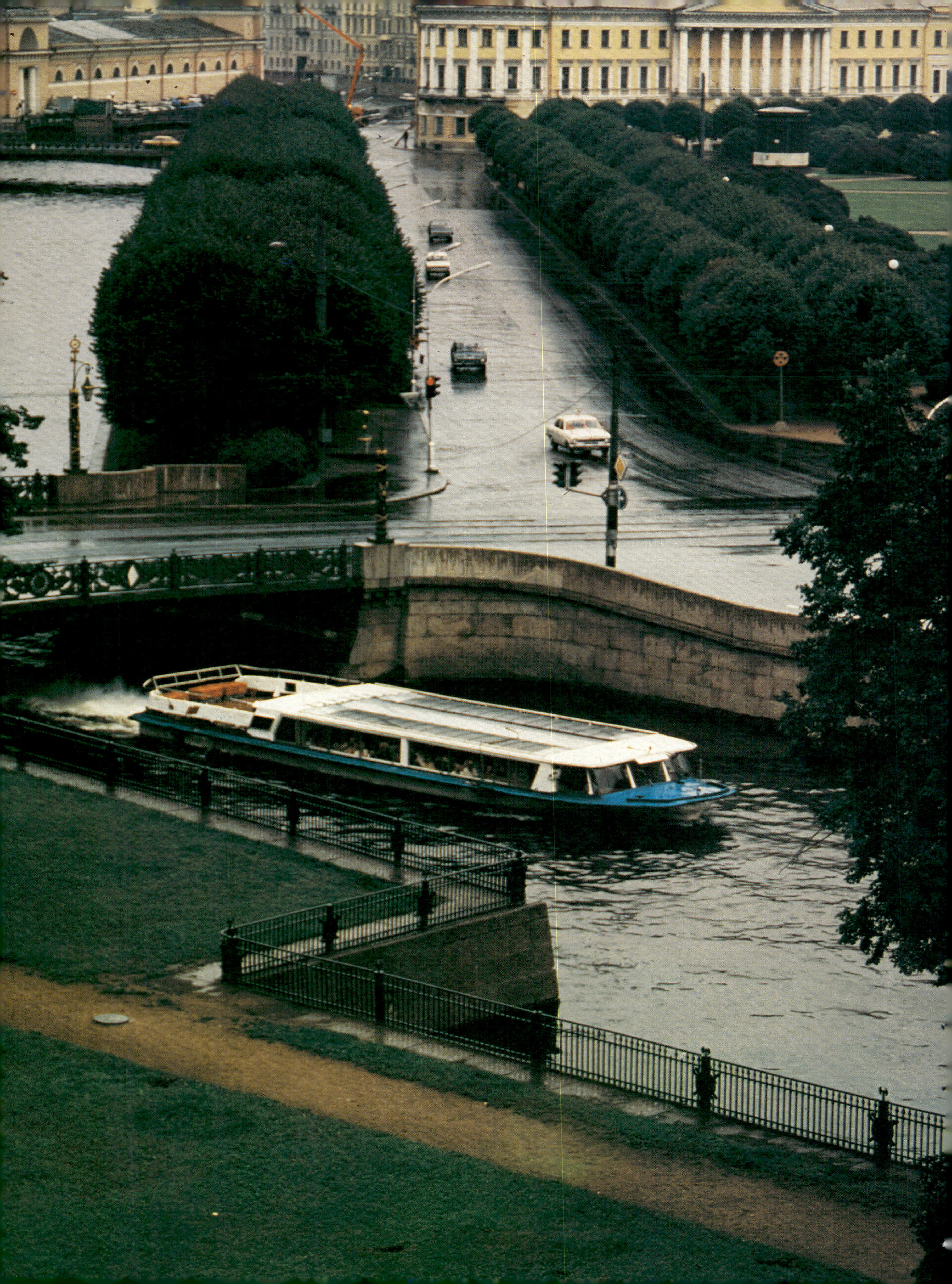

36
37

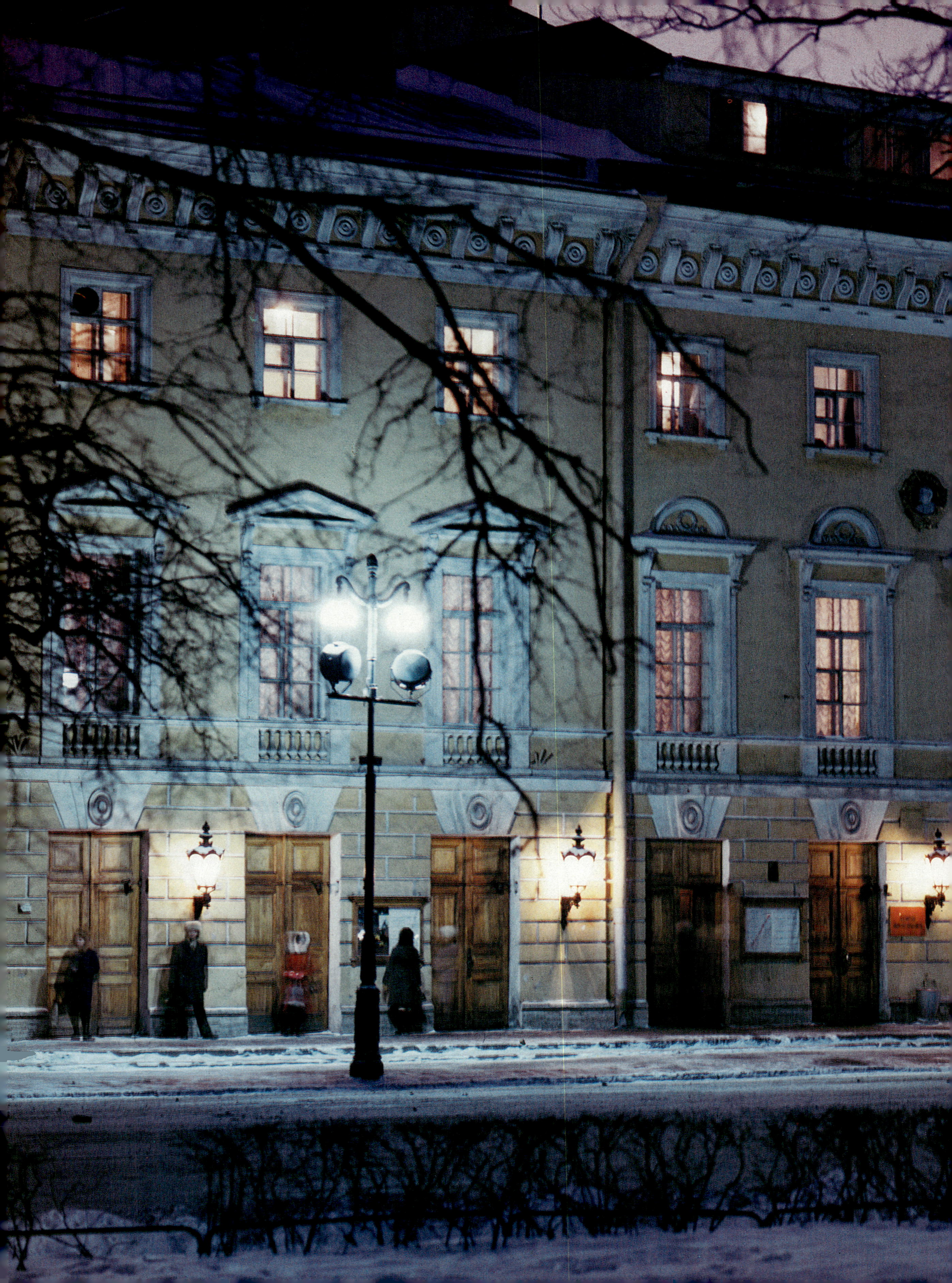

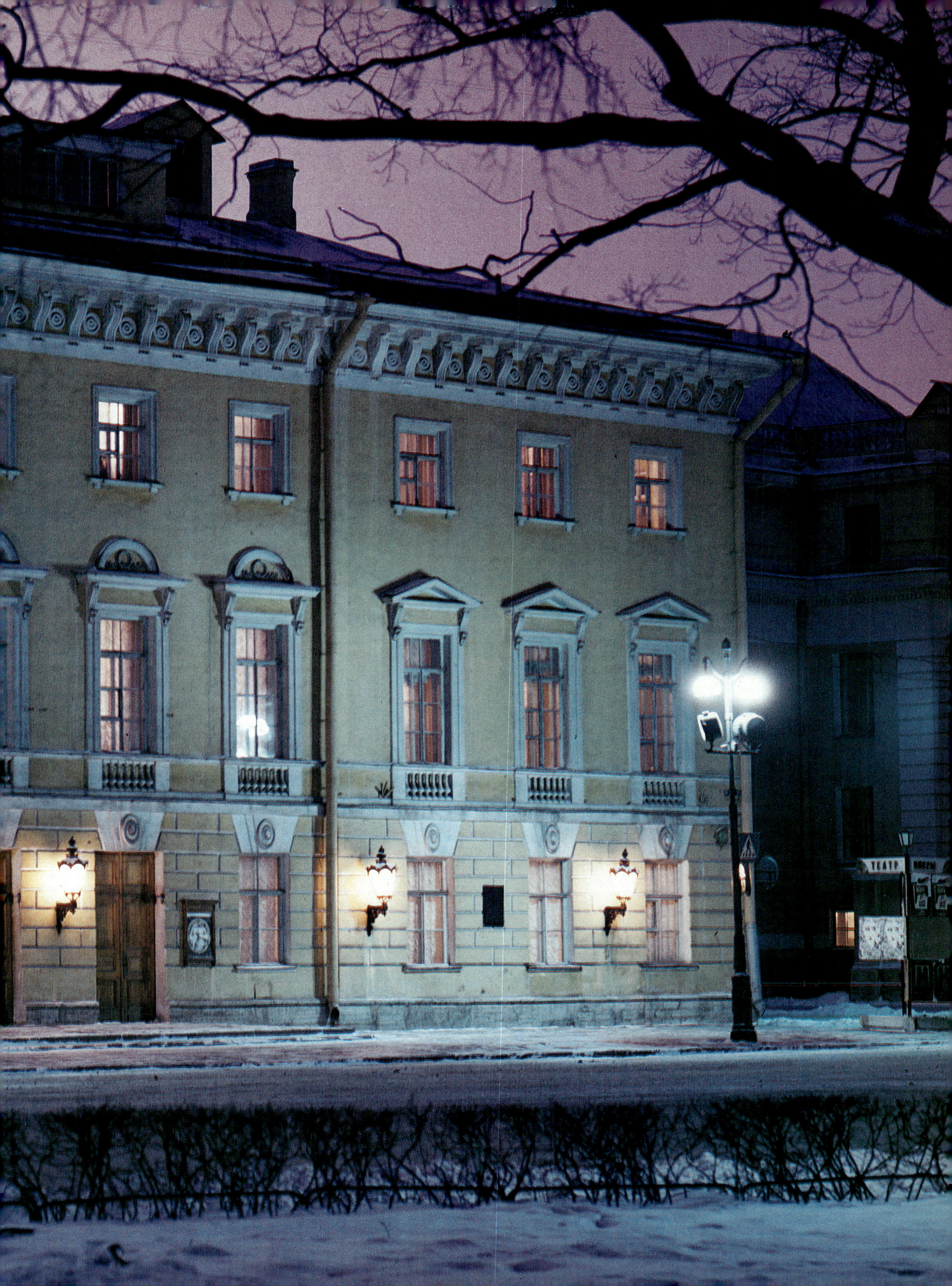
ТЕАТР

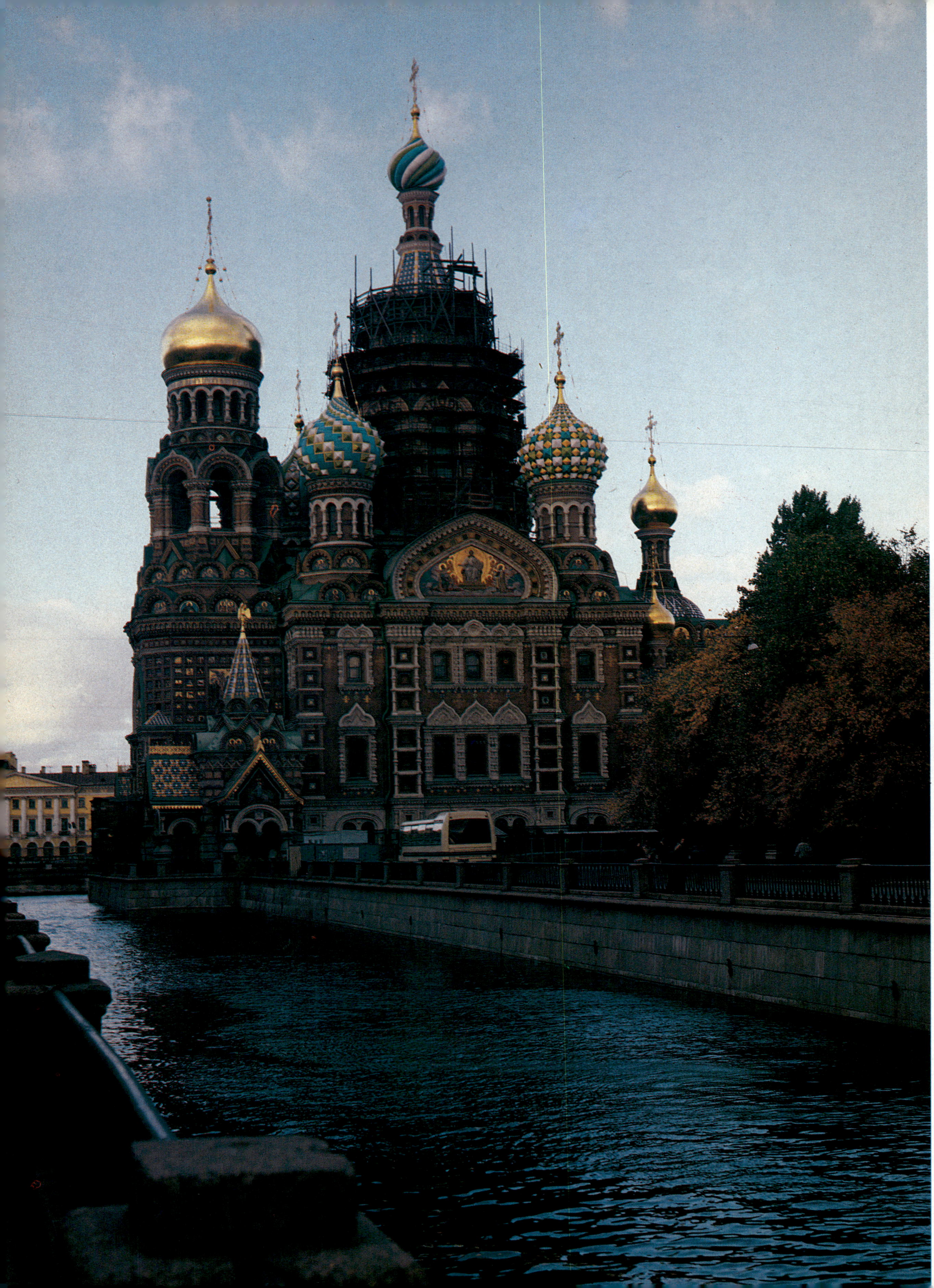

13

→

14

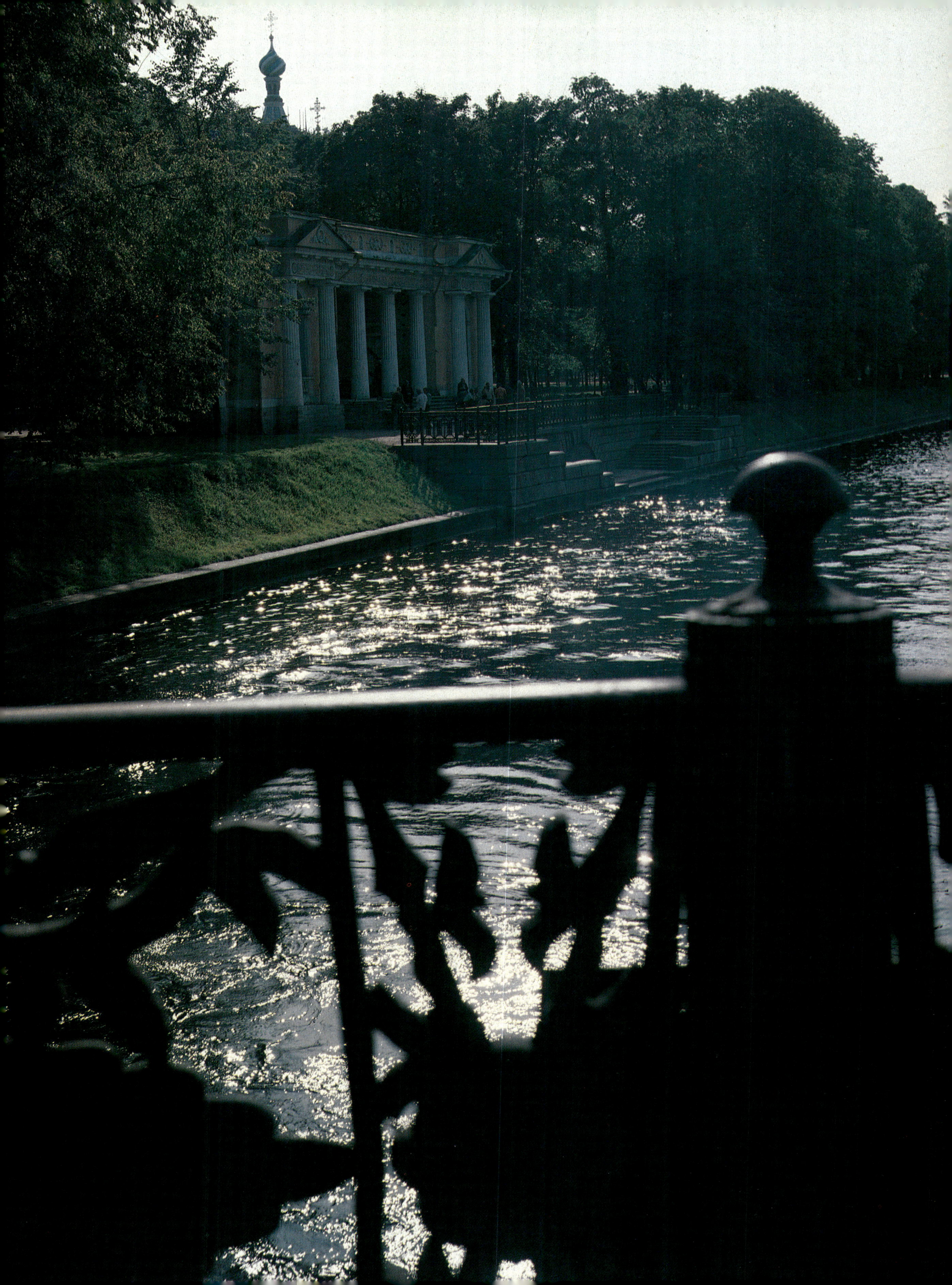

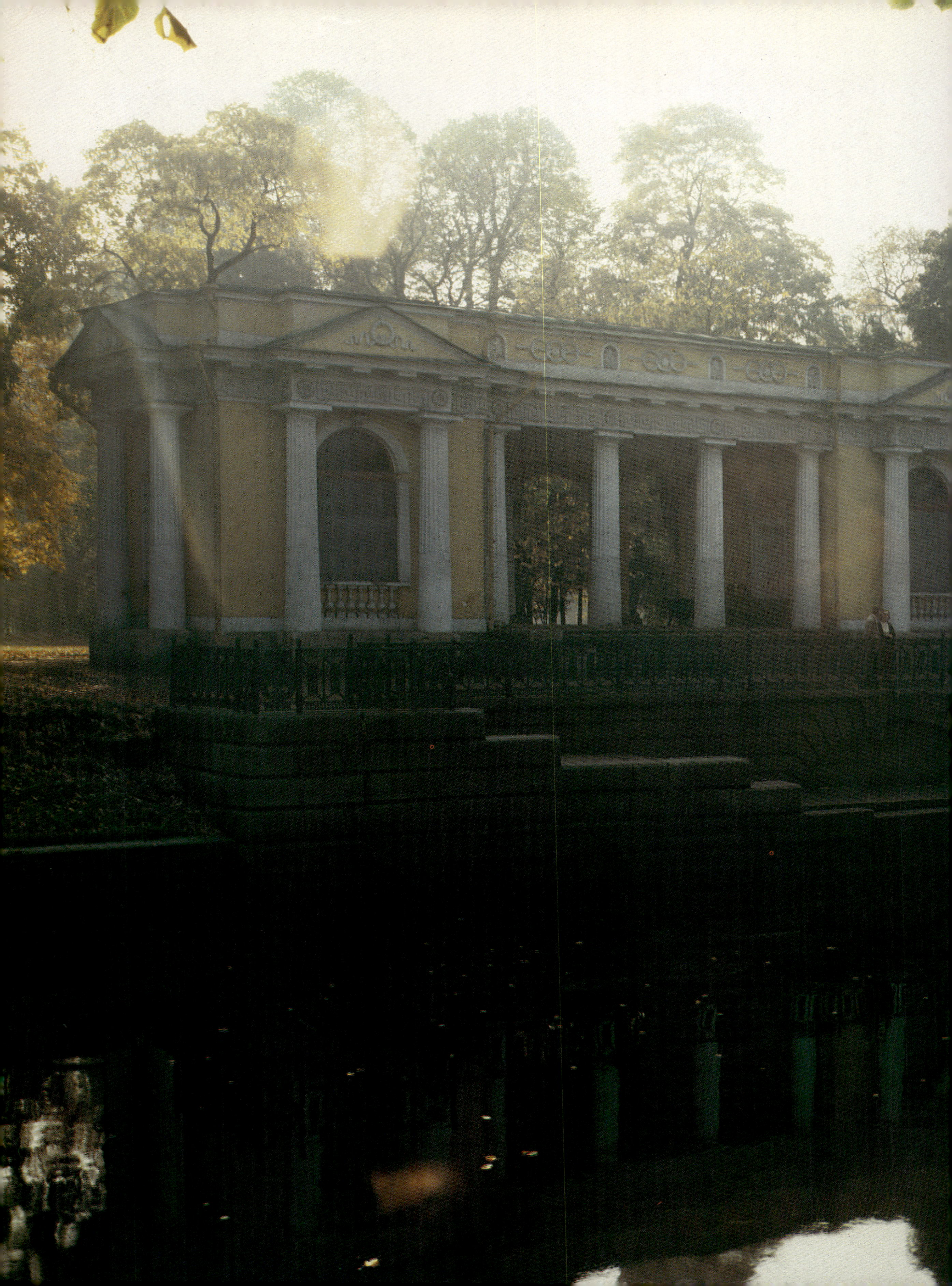

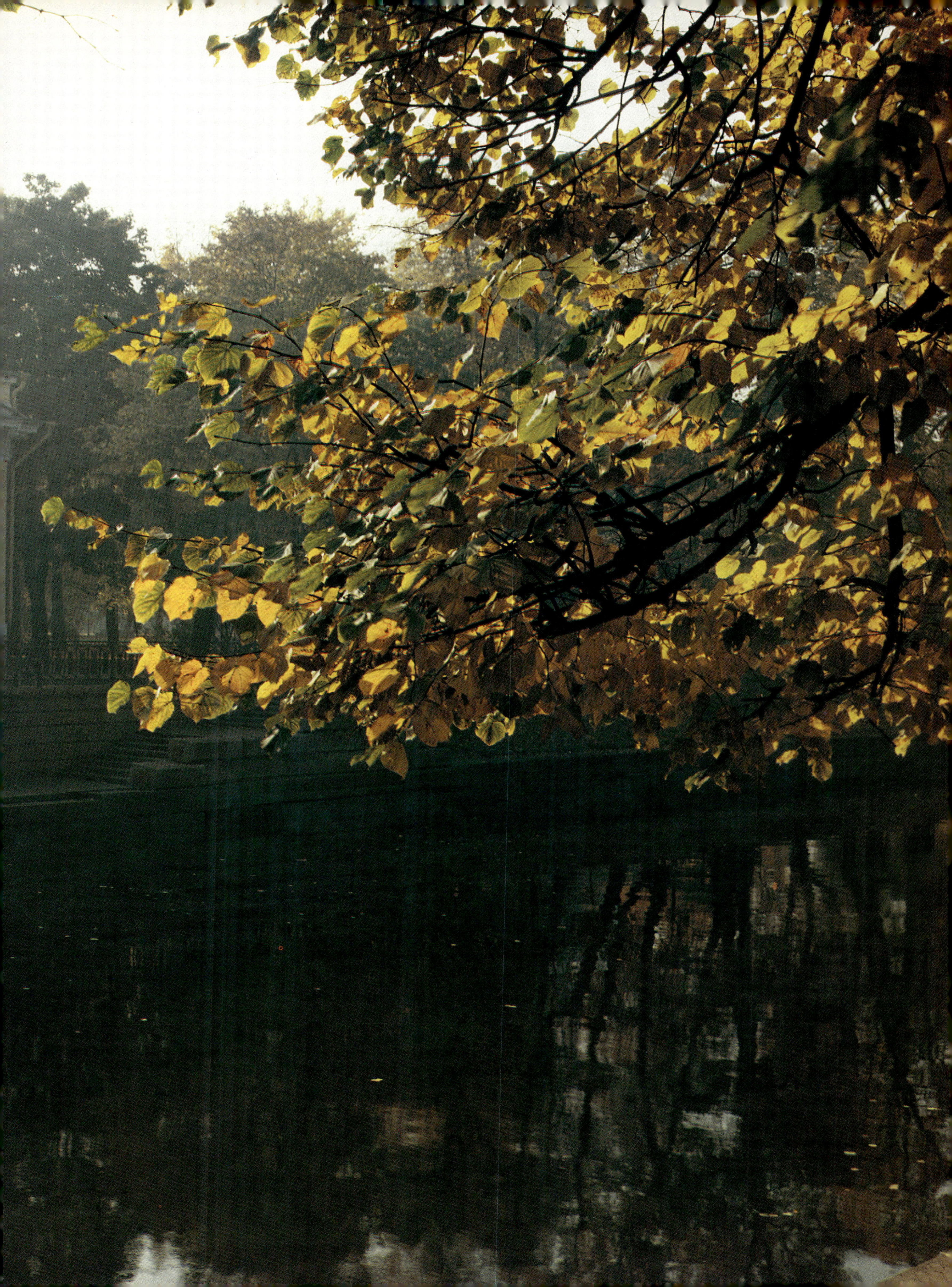

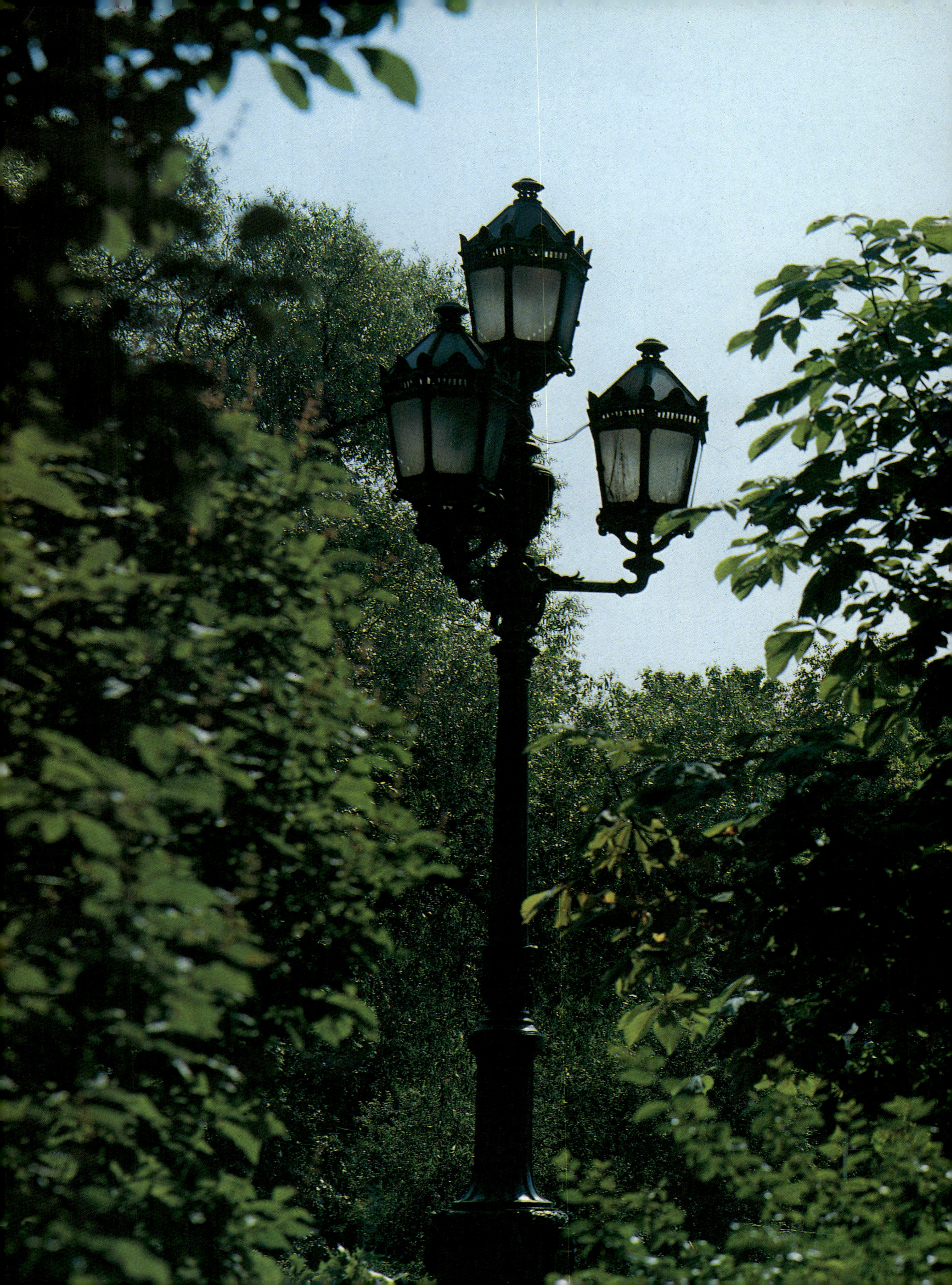

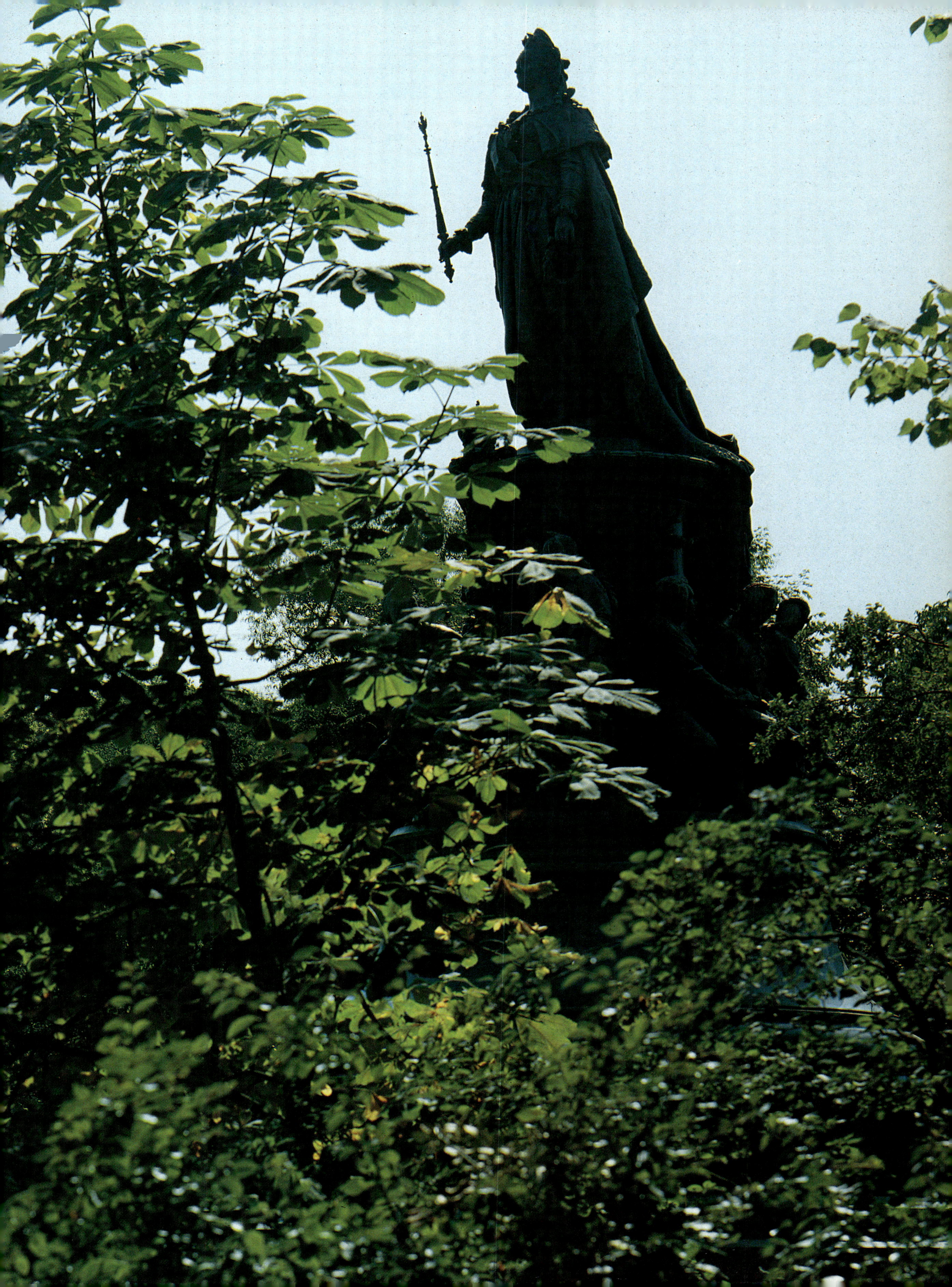

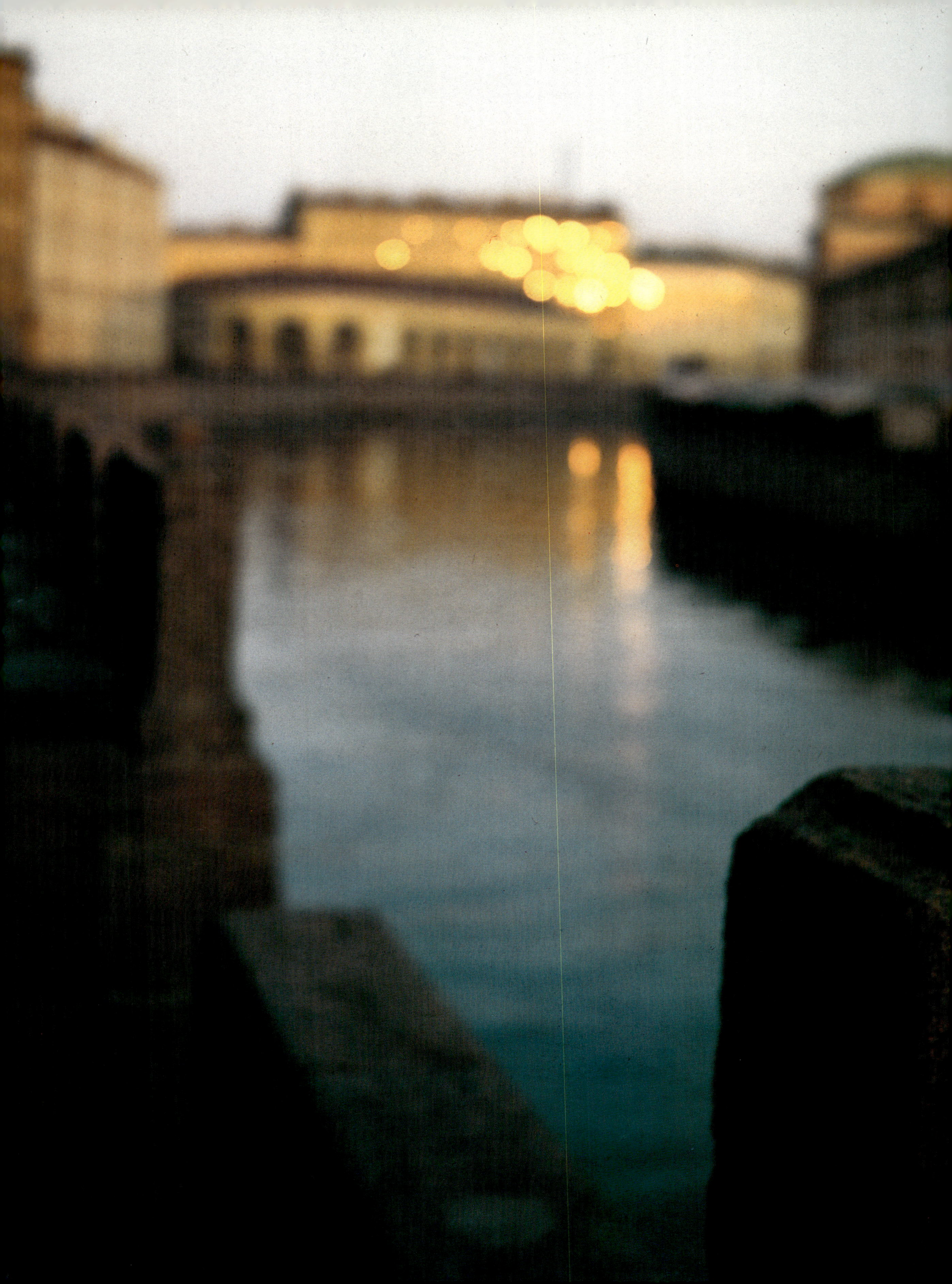

←
143

144

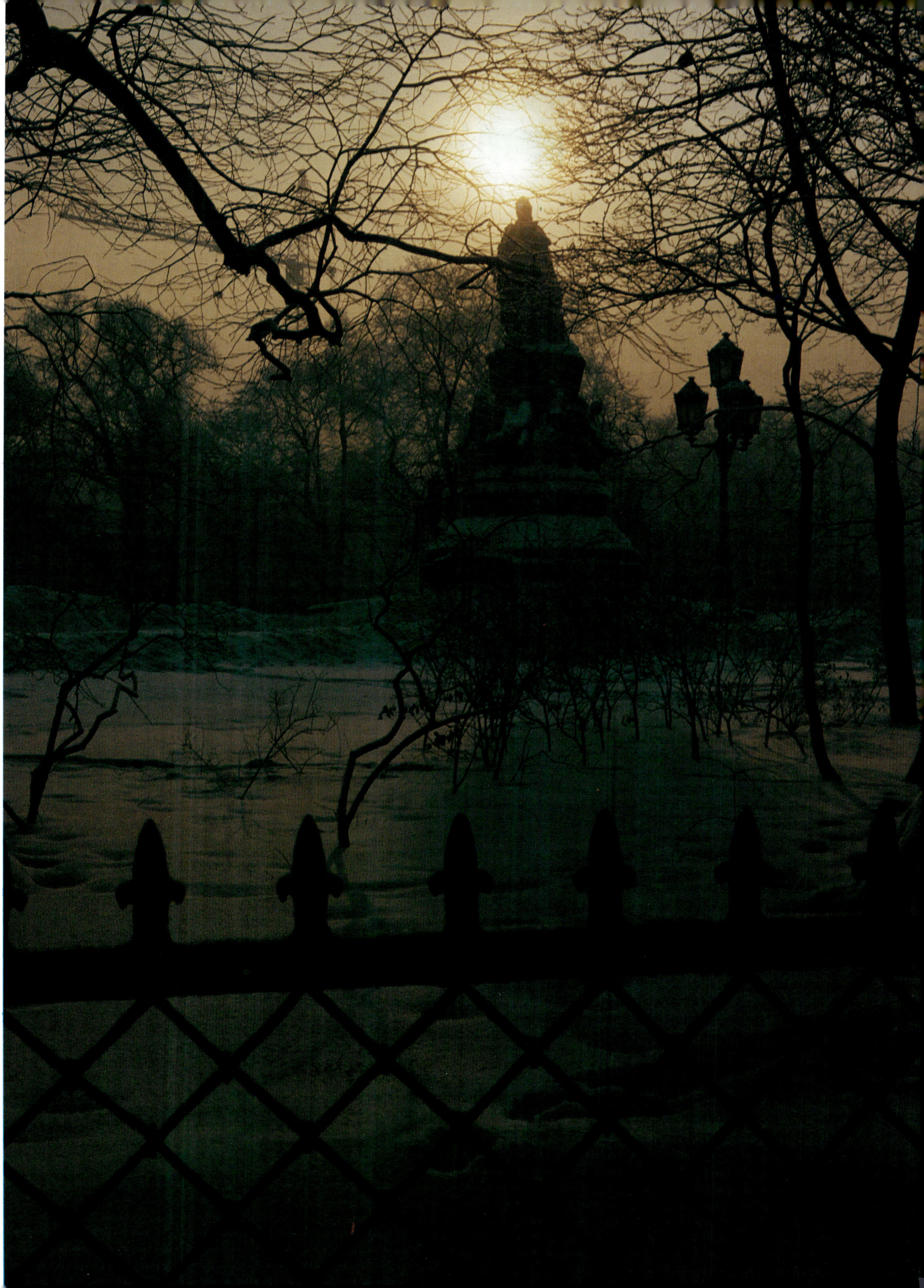

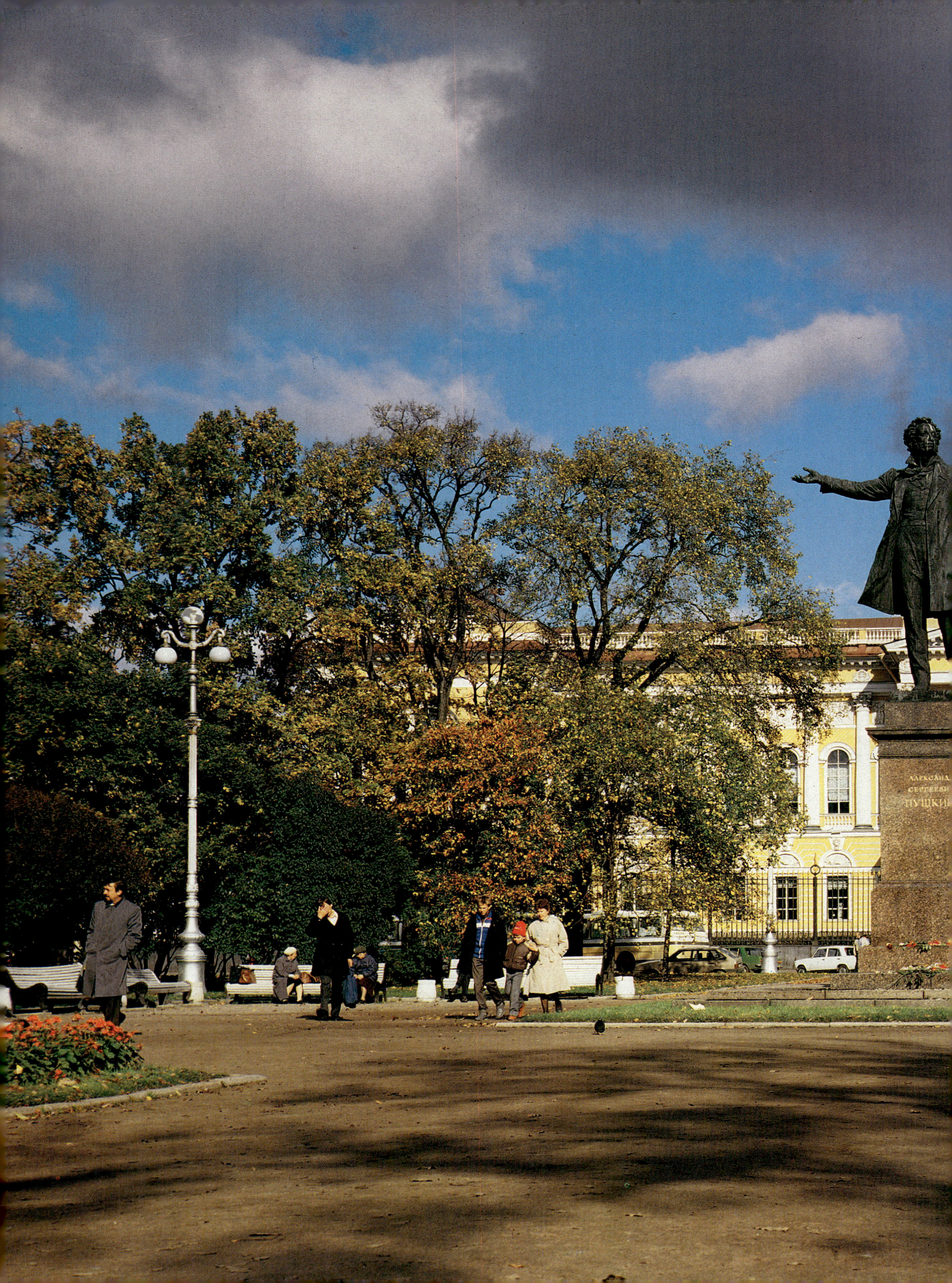

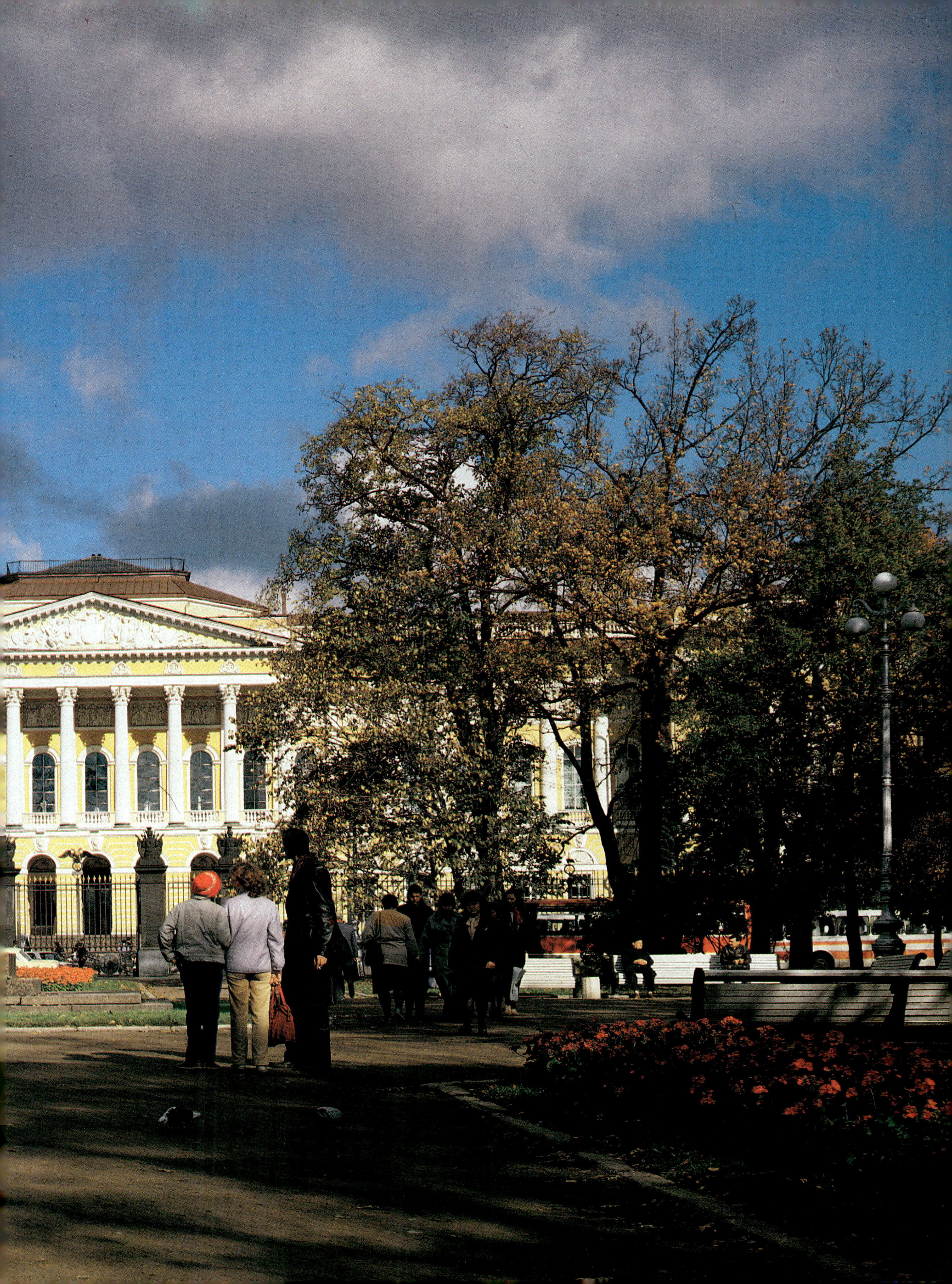

140, 141   Pavilion and pier in the Mikhailovsky
           Gardens
142, 144   Statue of Catherine the Great
    143   Moika. Golden ray
    145   Square of Arts.
           Statue of Alexander Pushkin

146, 147   Russian Museum

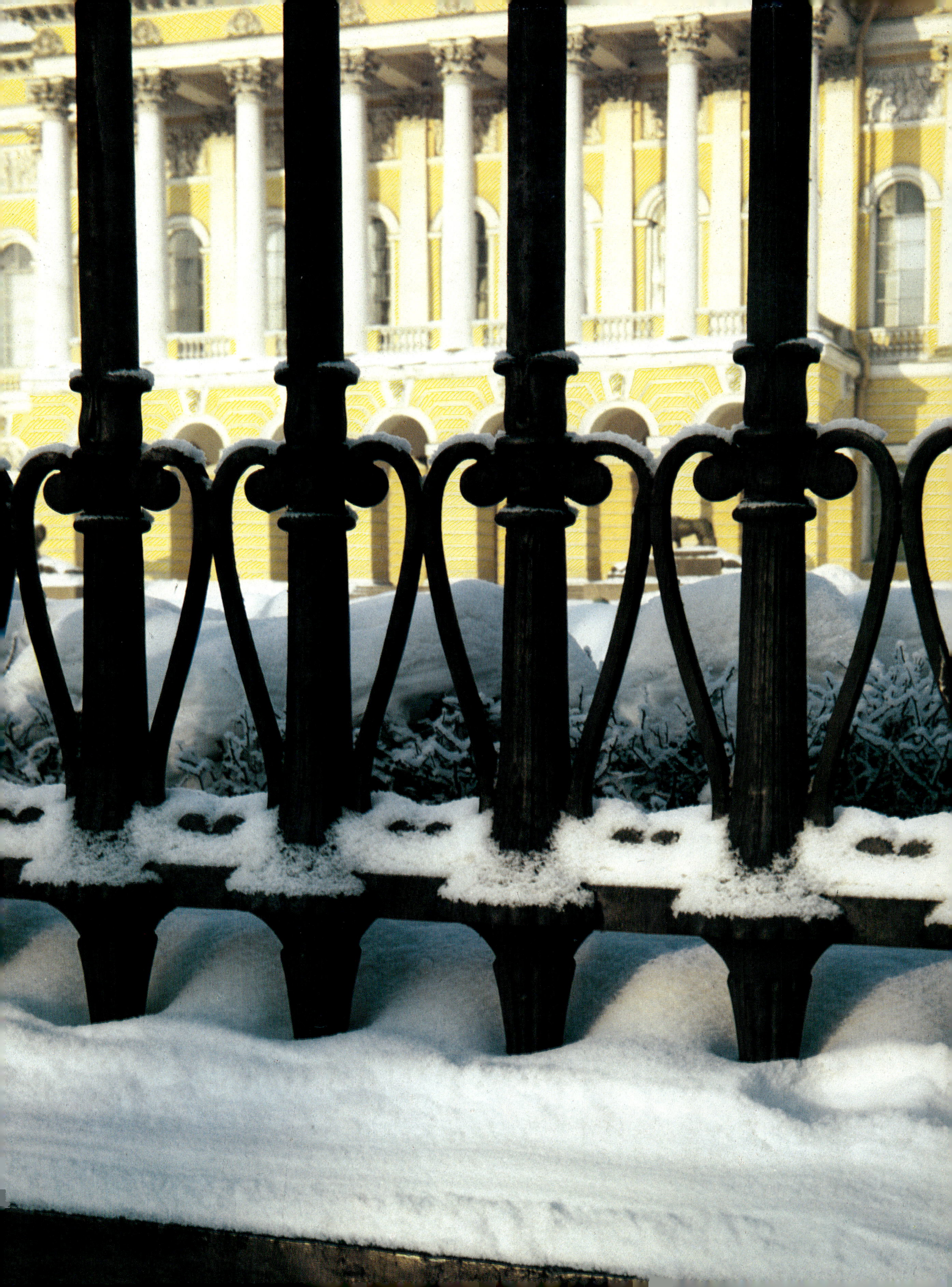

148 *Ethnography Museum*
149 *Moika seen from the Choristers' Bridge*

150, 151 *Yekaterininsky Canal* →

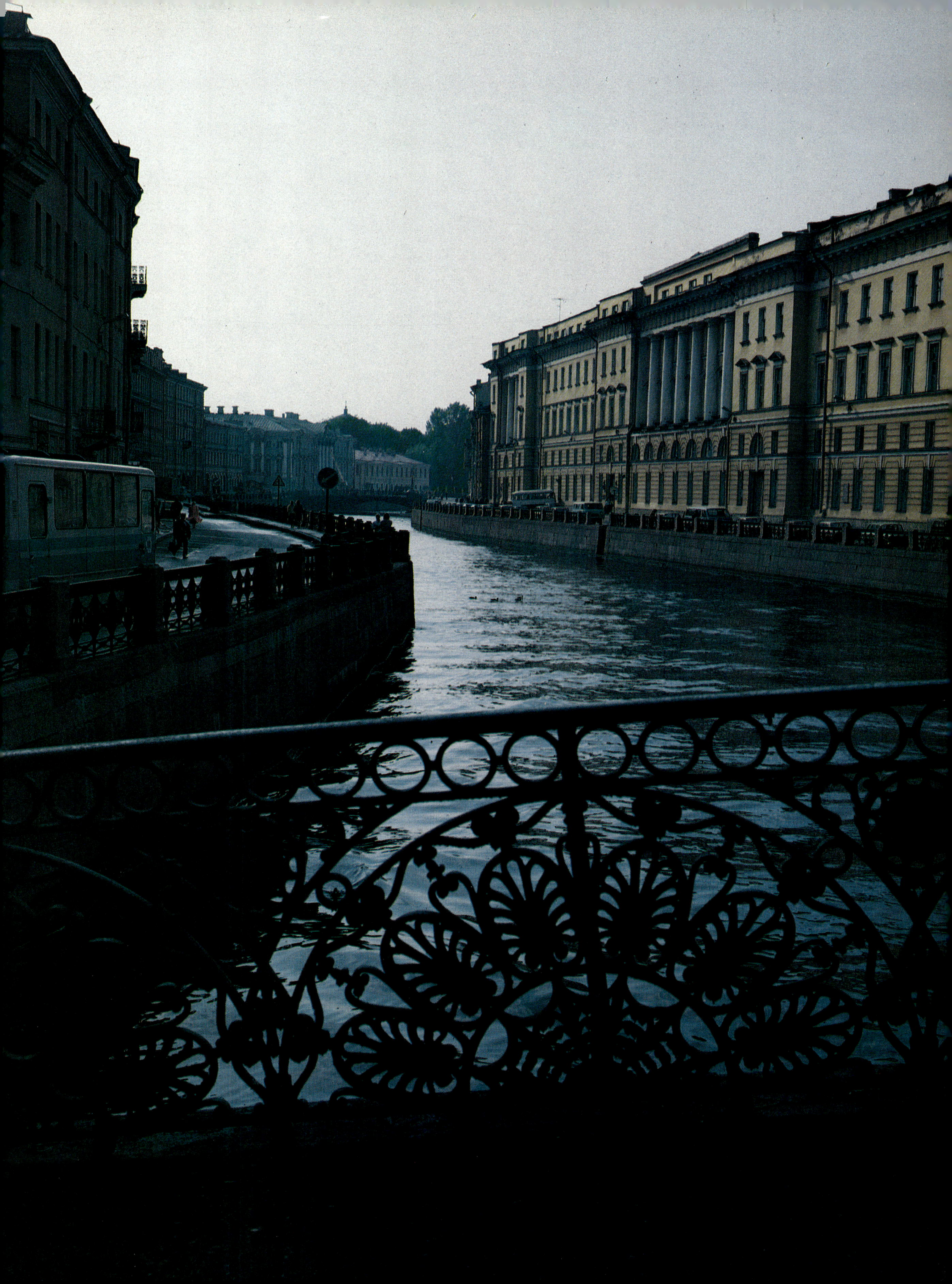

150
→
151

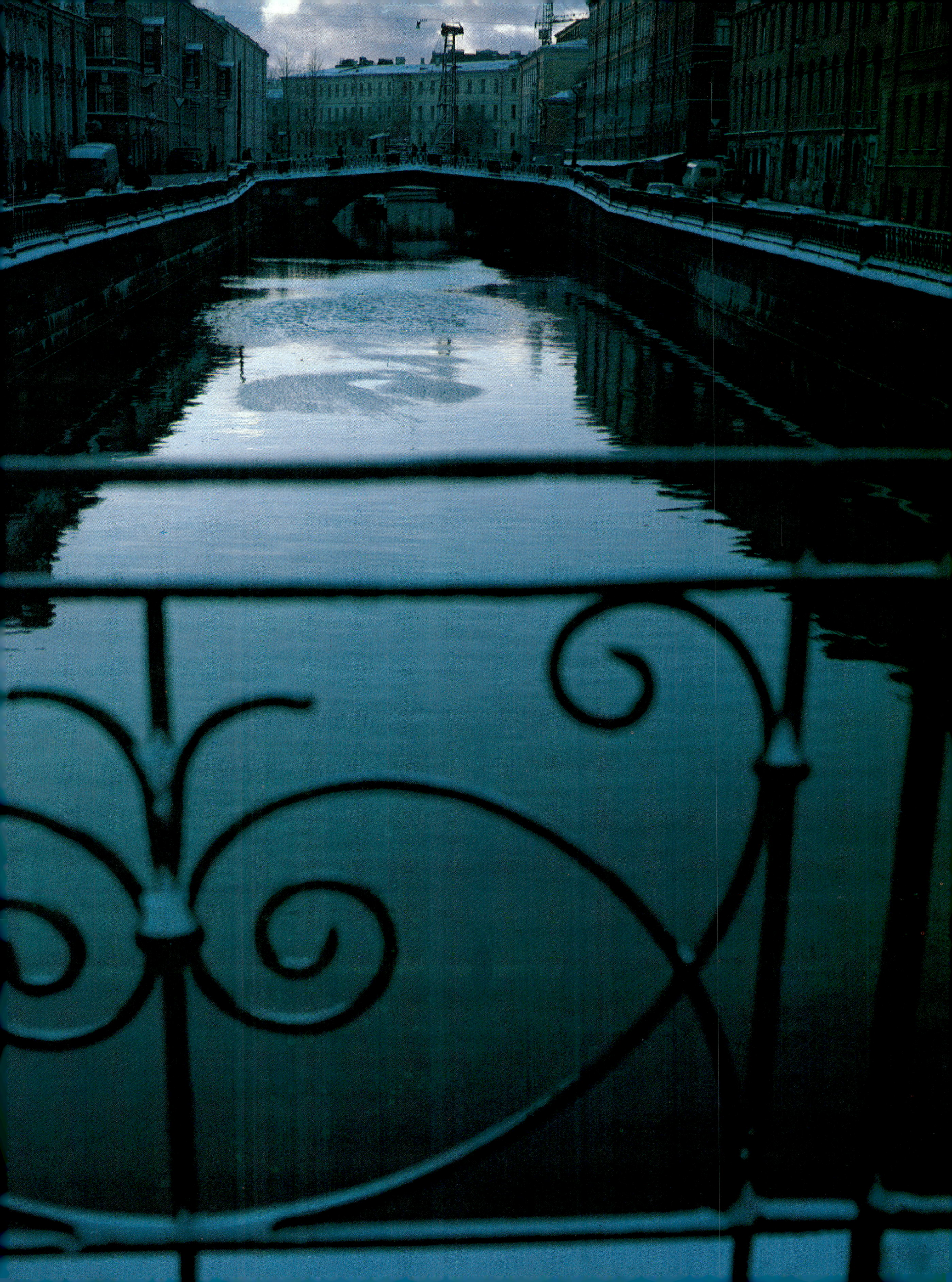

152 Stable yard
153 Memorial Museum of Alexander Pushkin
    {12, Moika Embankment}

154 Nevsky Prospect near Gostiny Dvor →

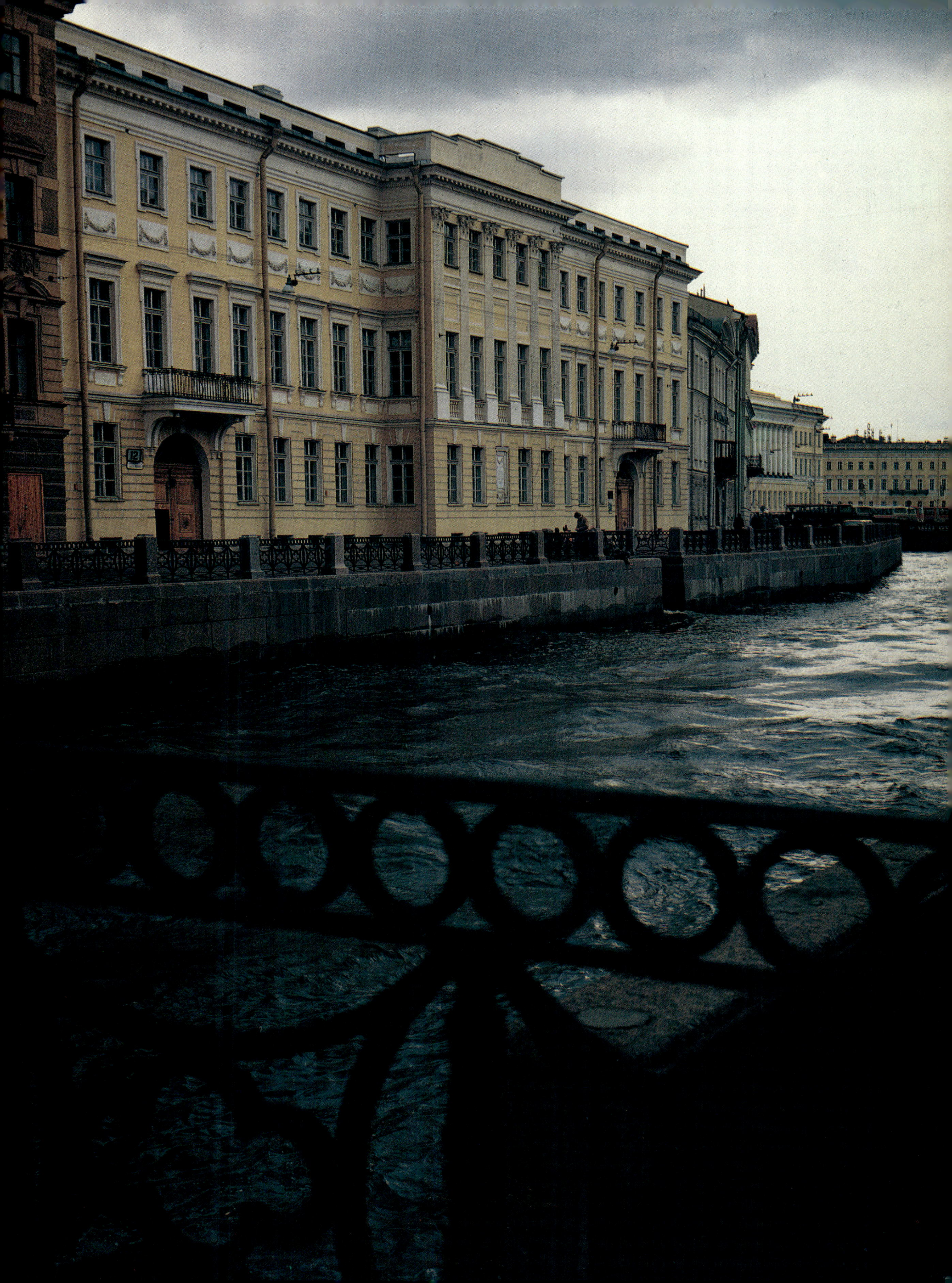
12

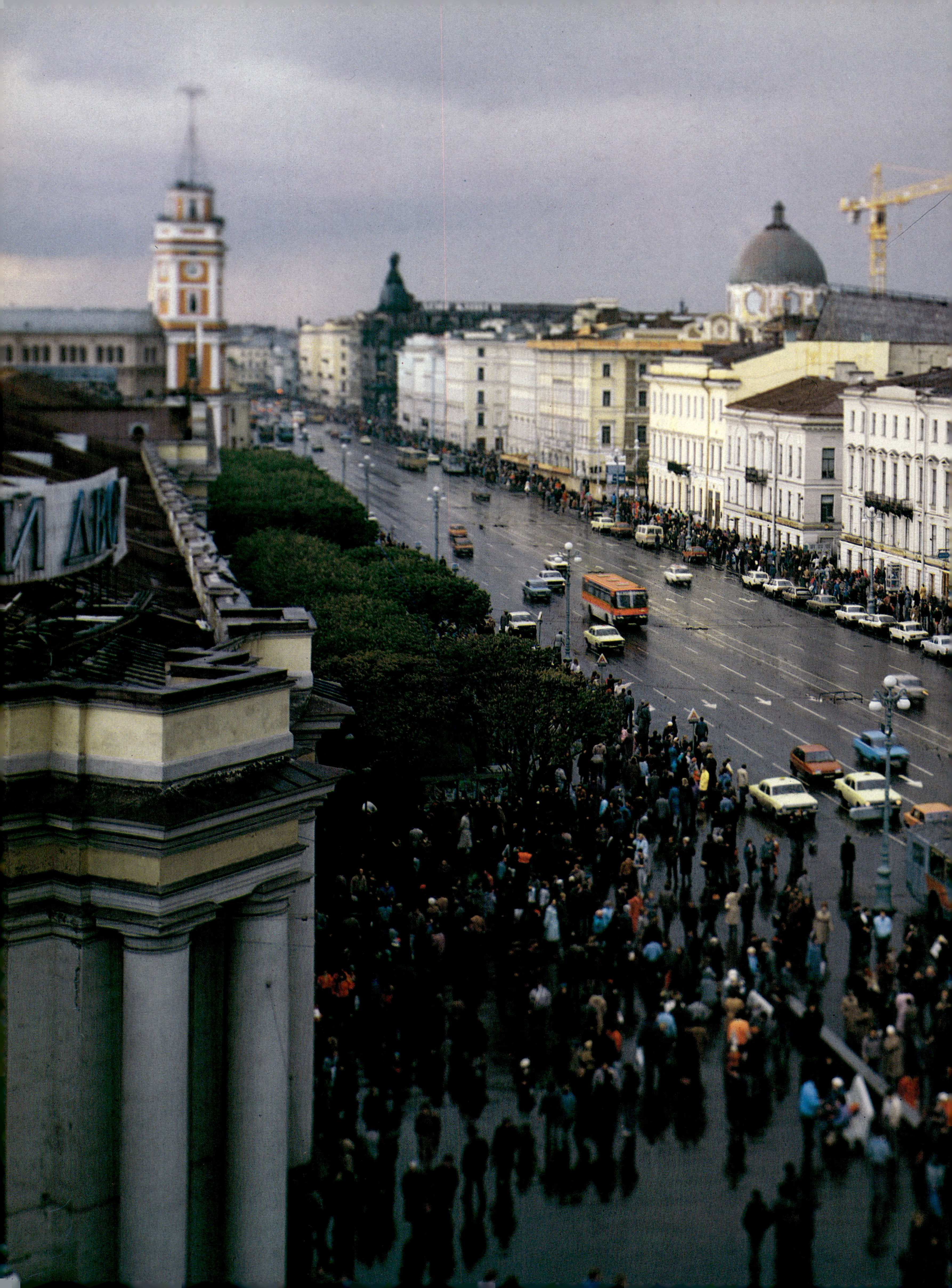

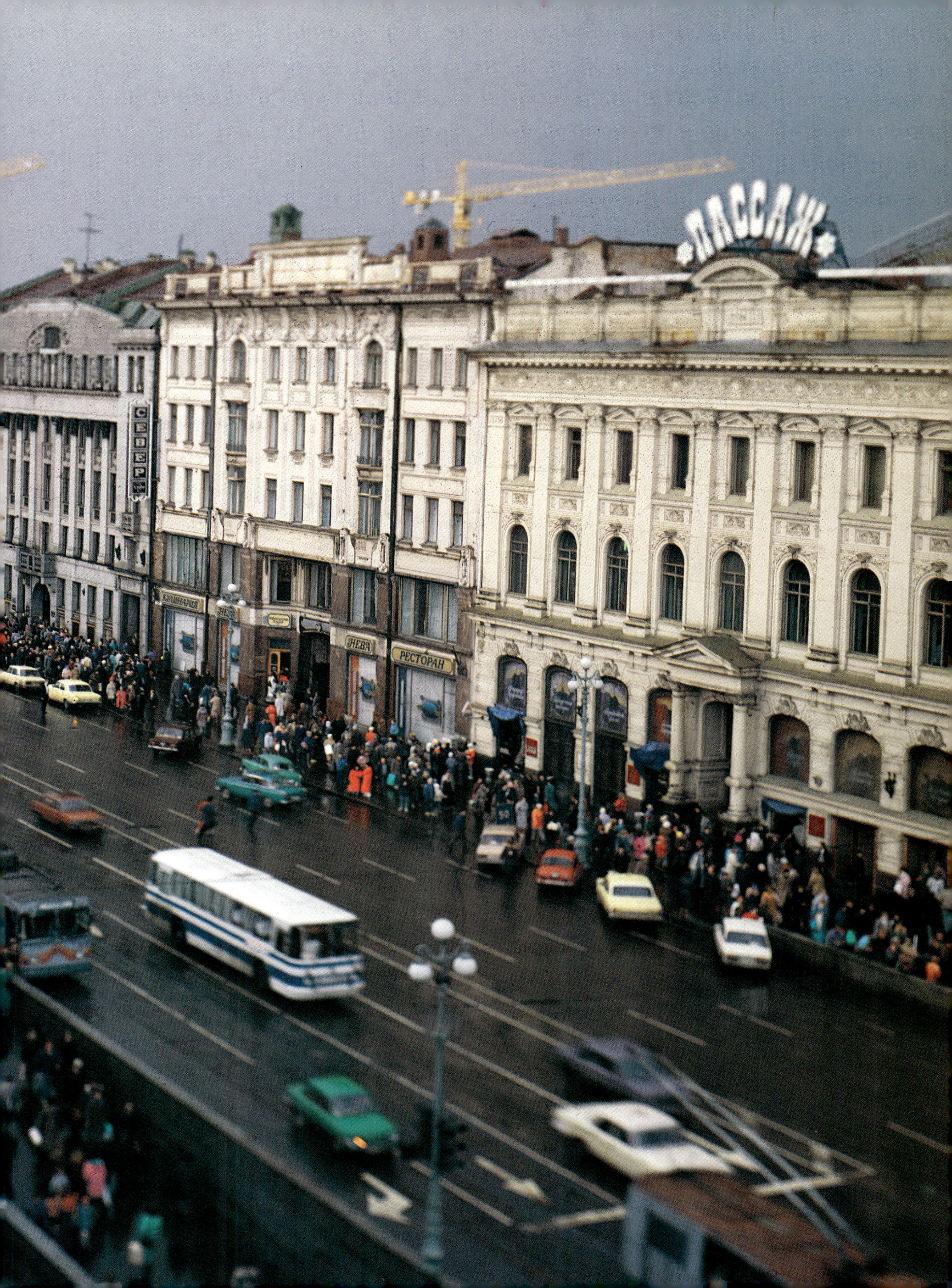

ПАССАЖ
СЕВЕР
НЕВА
РЕСТОРАН

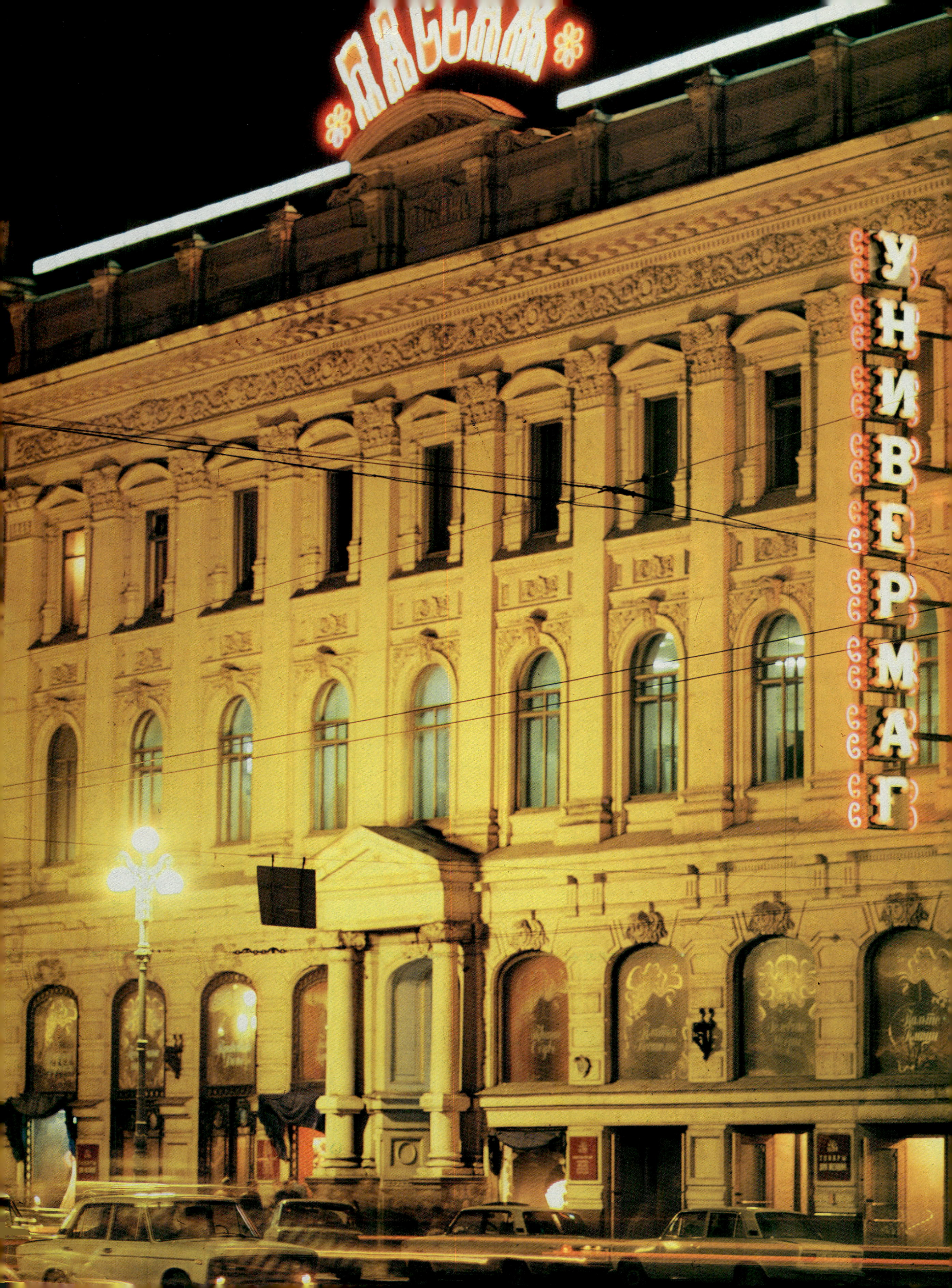
УНИВЕРМАГ

155 Passage
156 Pushkin Drama Theatre
(The Alexandrinsky Theatre)

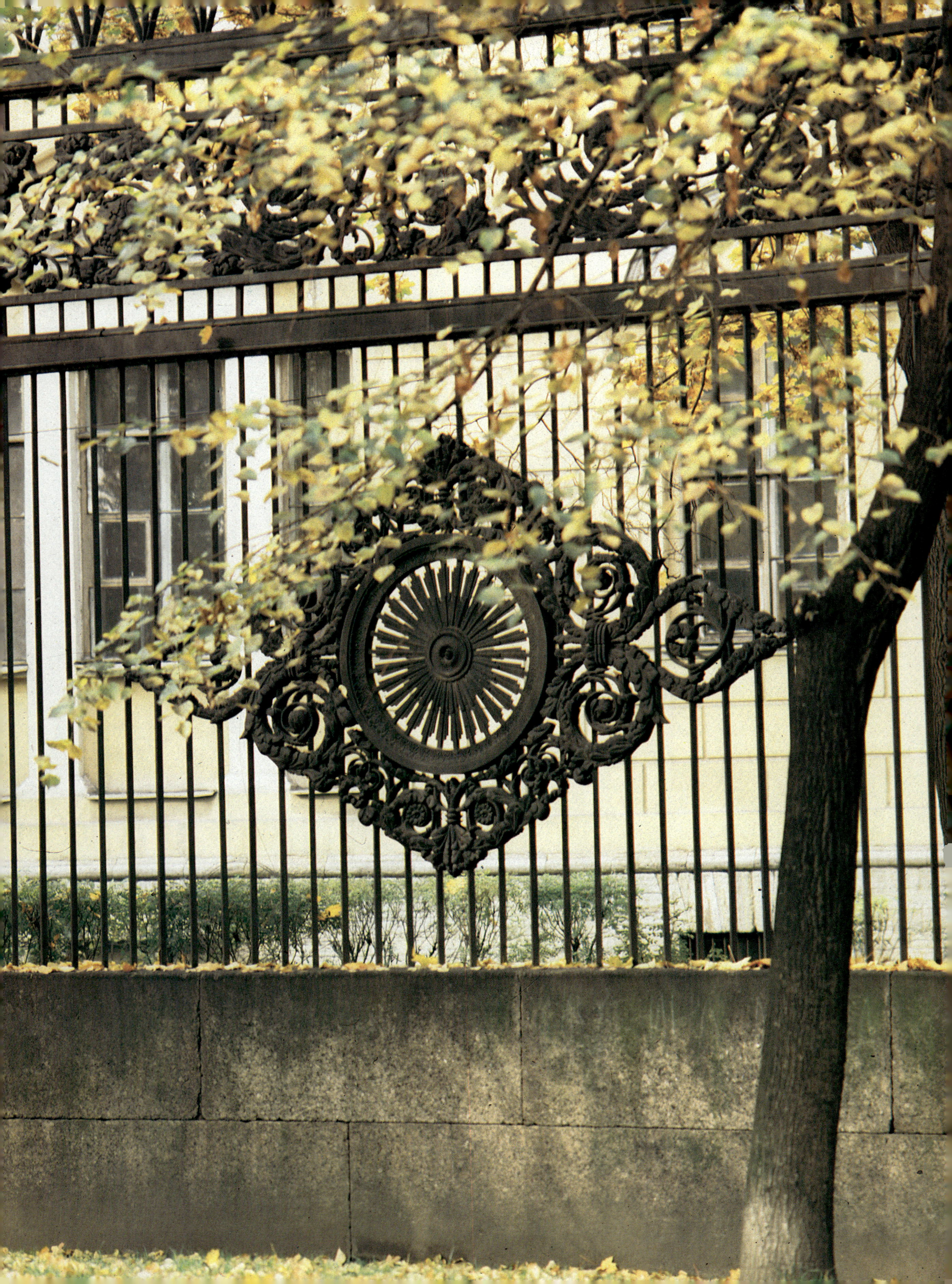

157 *Railing near the Cathedral of Our Lady of Kazan*
158, 159 *Cathedral of Our Lady of Kazan*
160 *Cathedral of Our Lady of Kazan. Mikhail Kutuzov's grave* →
161 *Statue of Mikhail Kutusov near Cathedral of Our Lady of Kazan* →

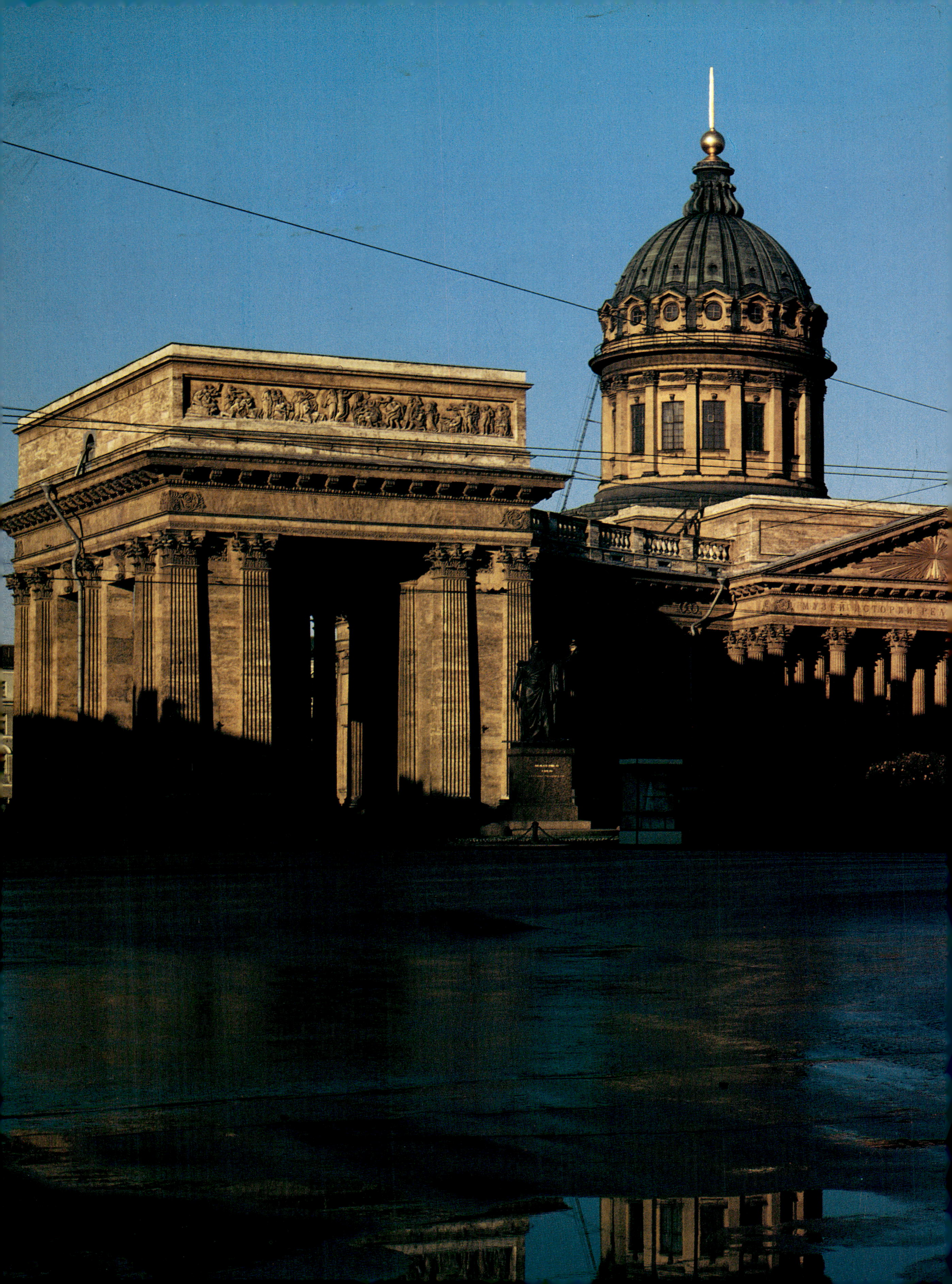
МУЗЕЙ ИСТОРИИ

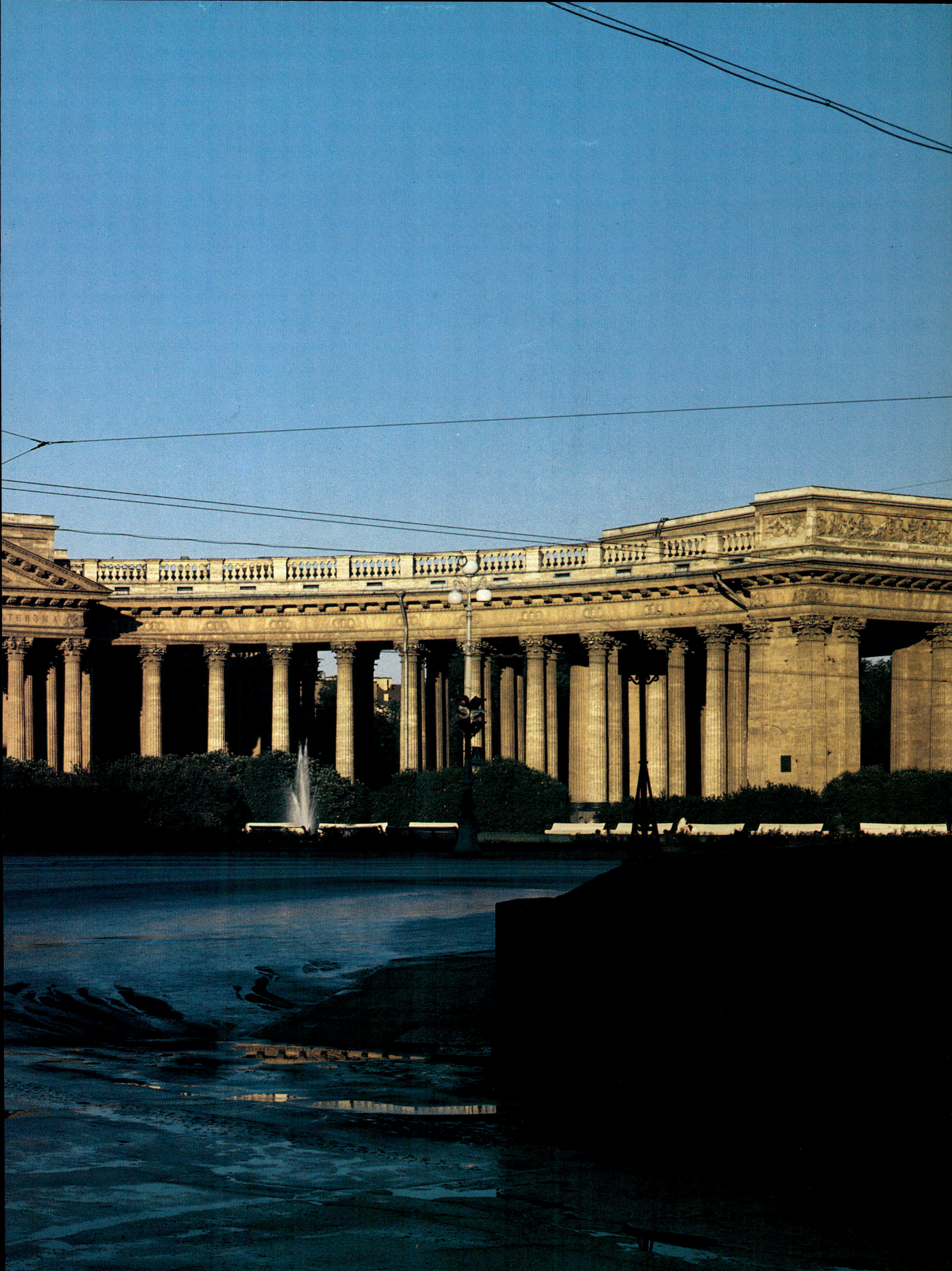

Князь
Михаилъ Иларіоновичъ
Голенищевъ-Кутузовъ
Смоленскій.
родился въ 1745"" году
скончался въ 1813""
въ городѣ Бунцлау.

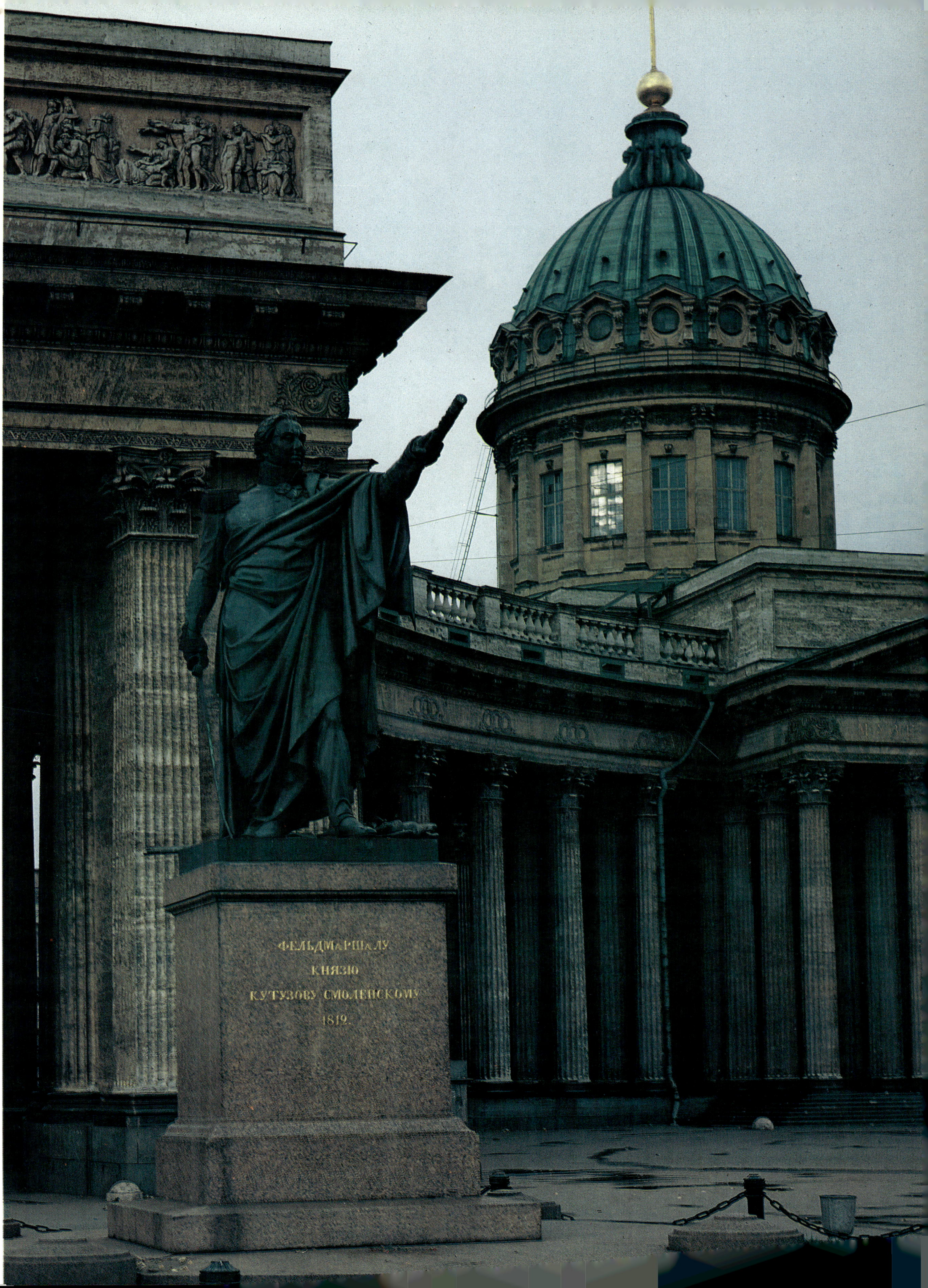

60

61

162, 165   *Pushkin Drama Theatre*
           (The Alexandrinsky Theatre)
163   *Rossi Pavilion*

164   *Zagorodny Prospect and Vladimirskaya*
           Square →

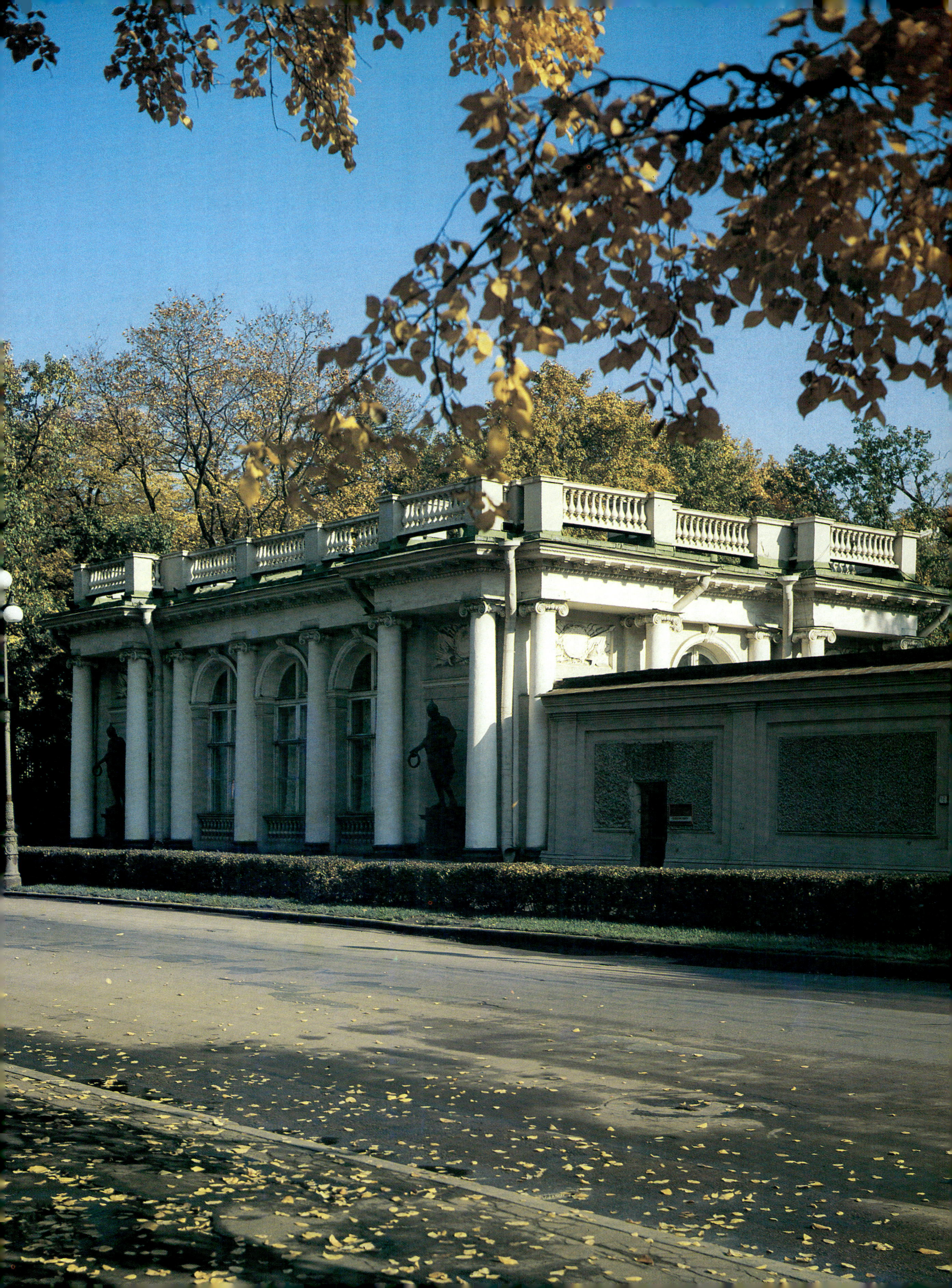

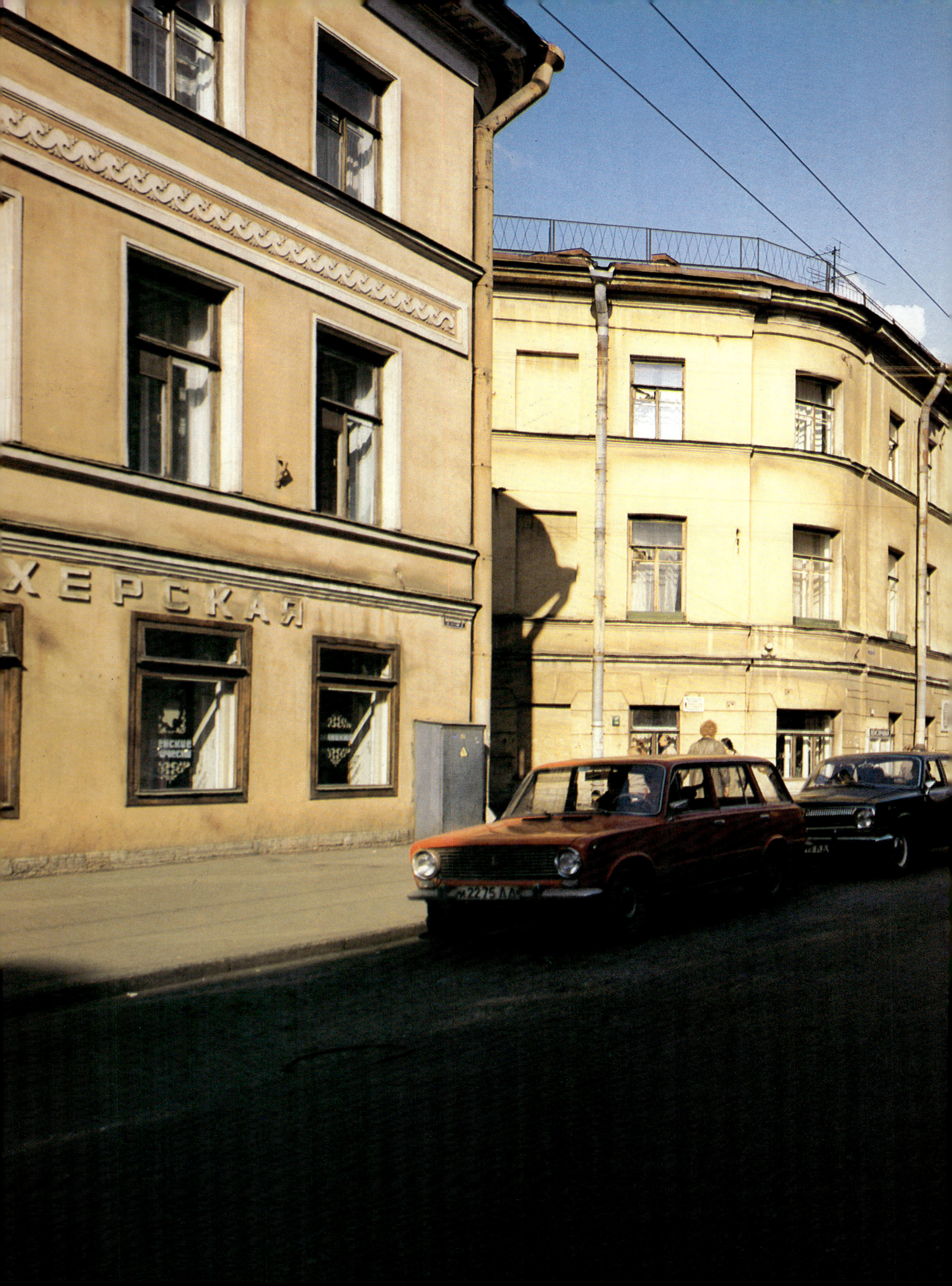
ХЕРСКАЯ

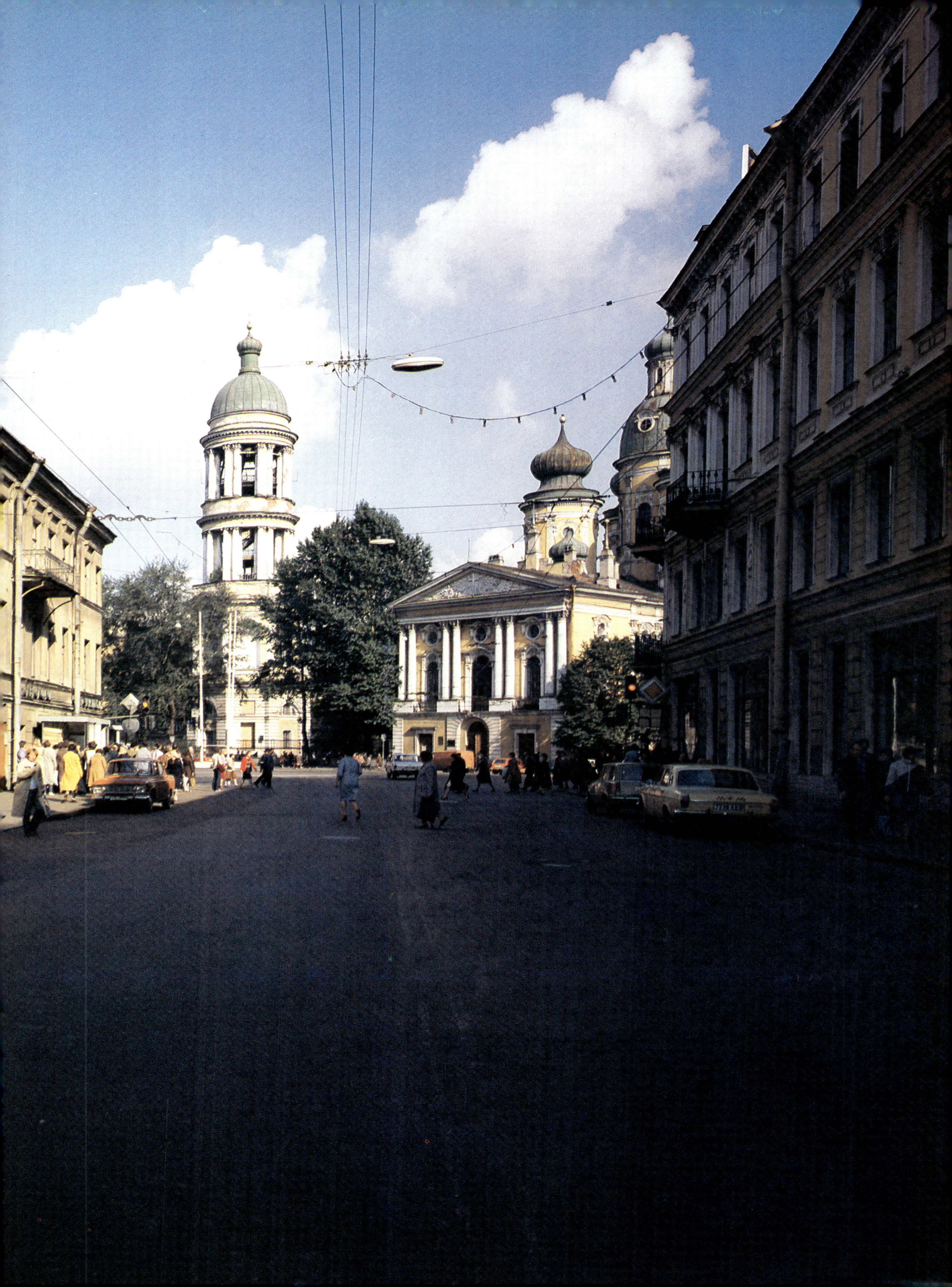

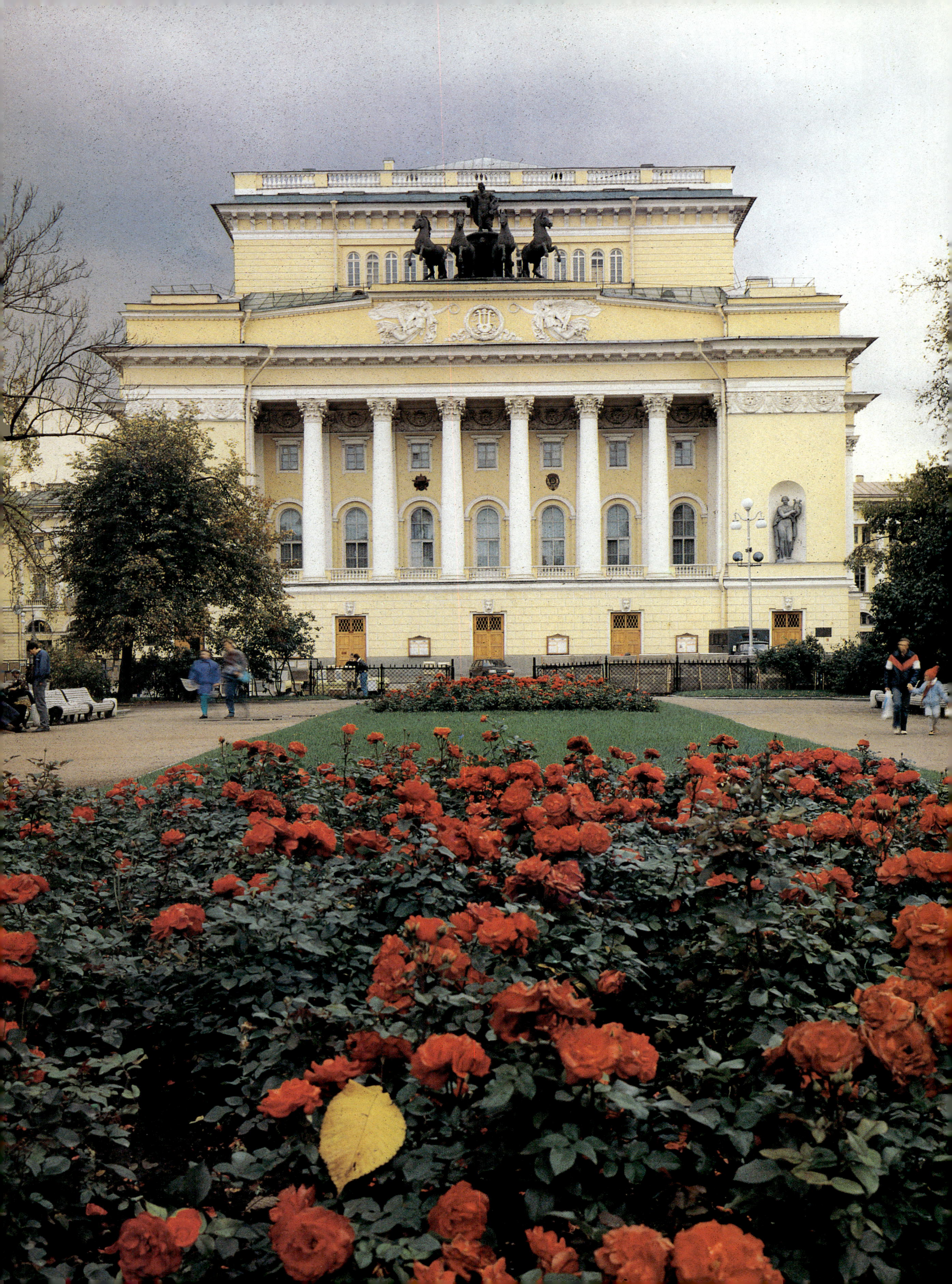

166–168   Russian National Library (The Public Library)

169   Russian National Library. The «Faust Study» →
170   Anichkov Bridge over the Fontanka →

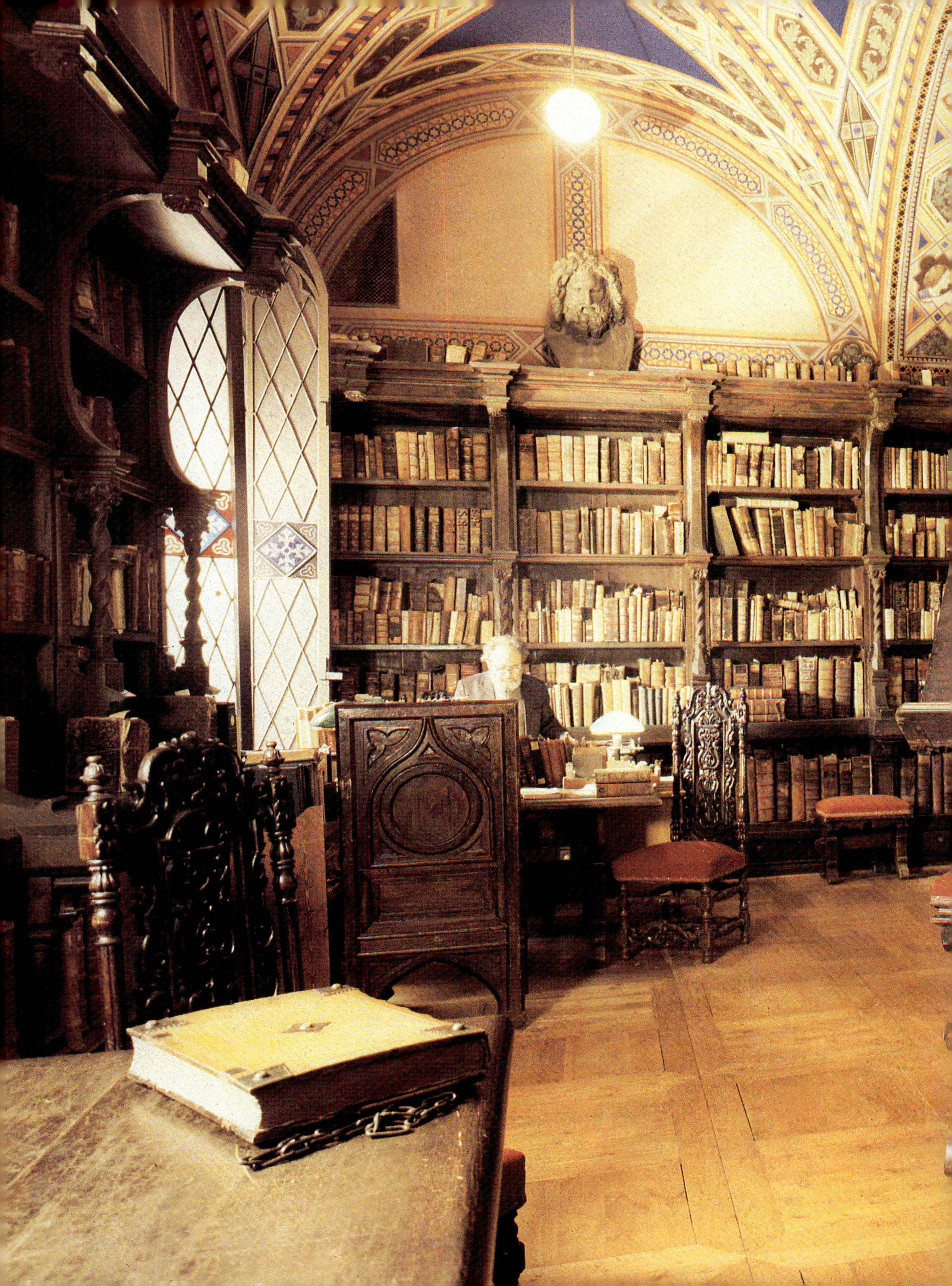

Iohannis Gutembergi Moguntini
inuentoris nomen perire nequit

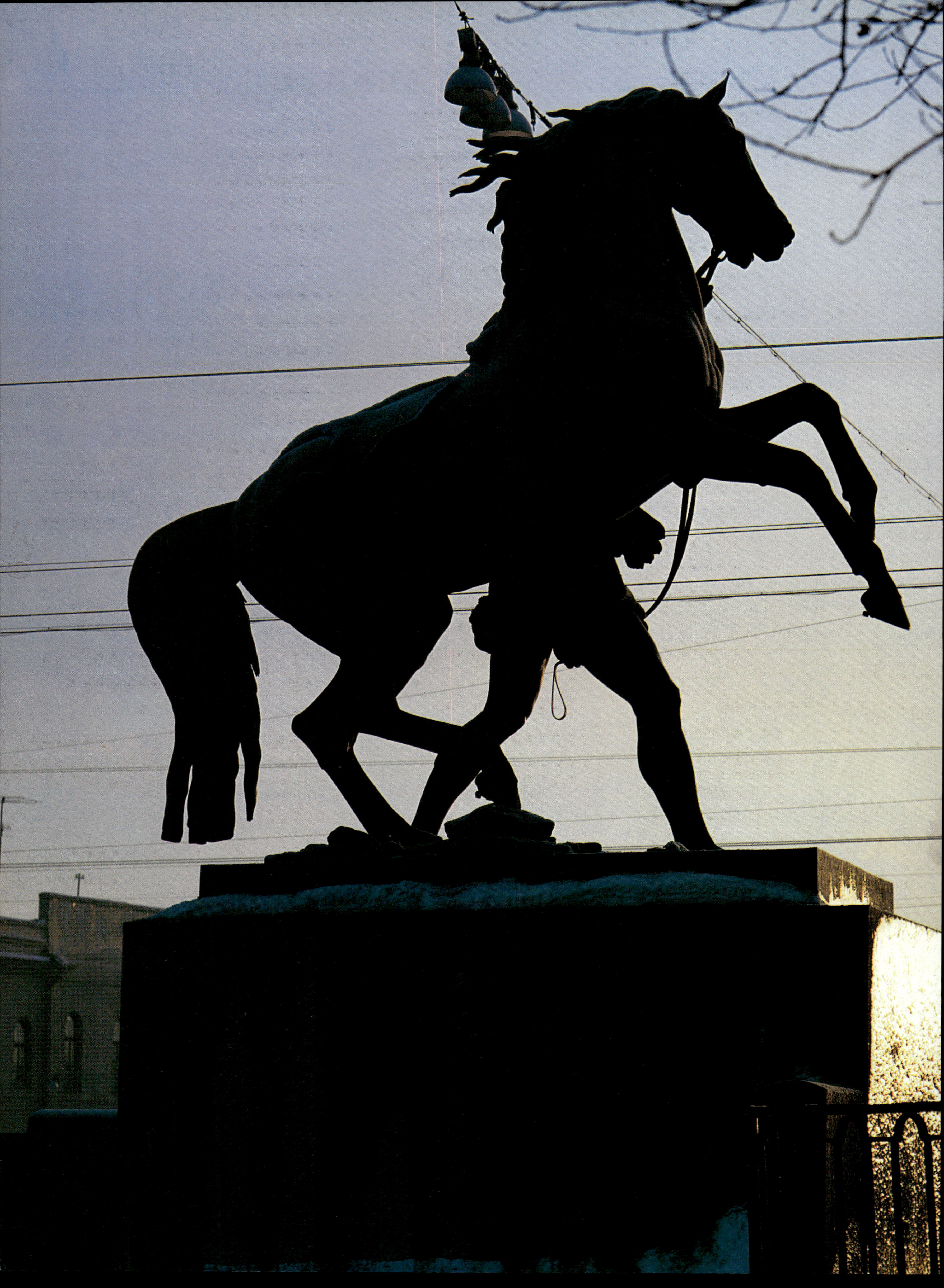

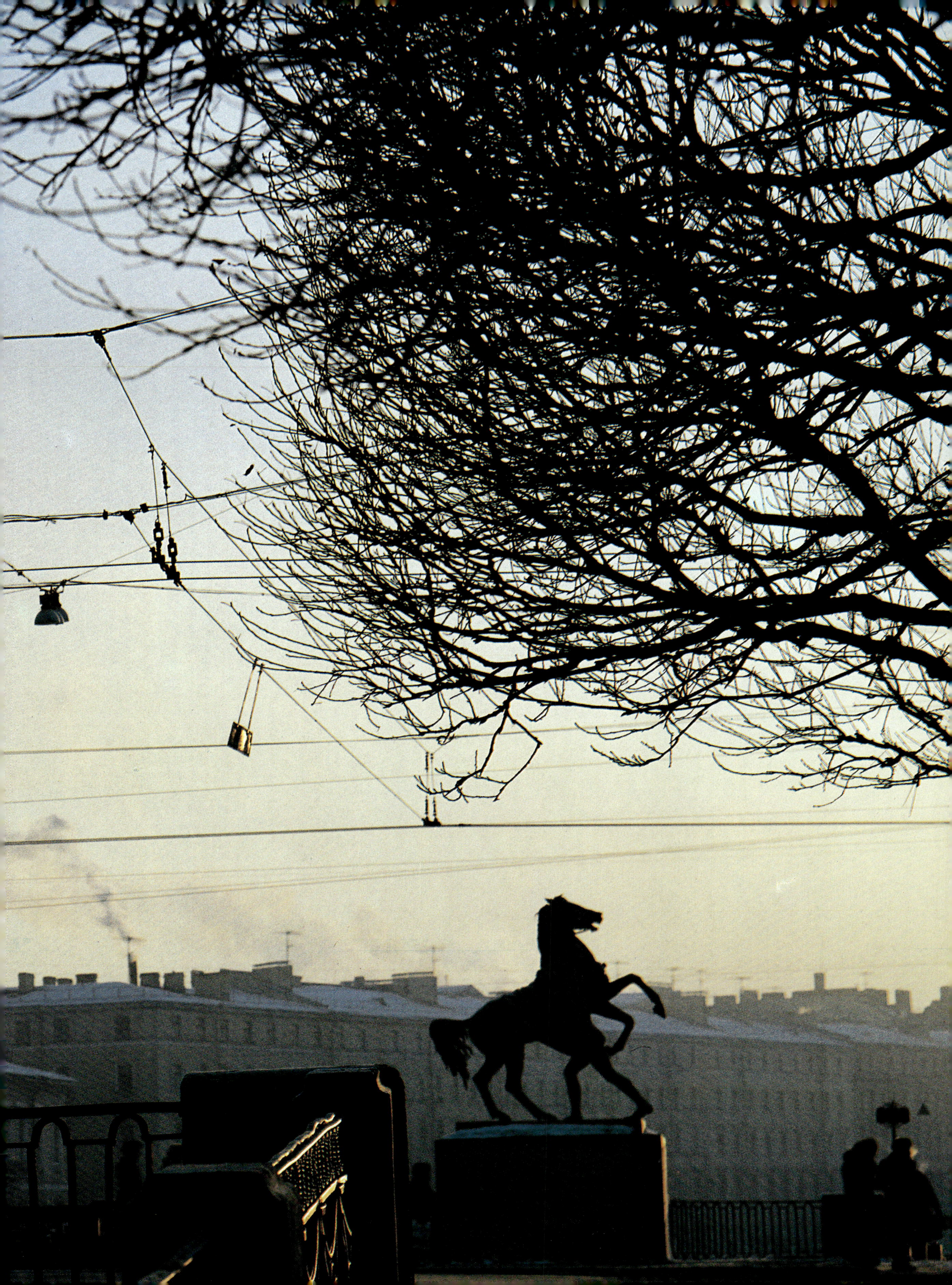

171 Fontanka near Nevsky Prospect
172 Yekaterininsky Institute
173 Anichkov Bridge. Sculptural group
The «Youth with the Horse»

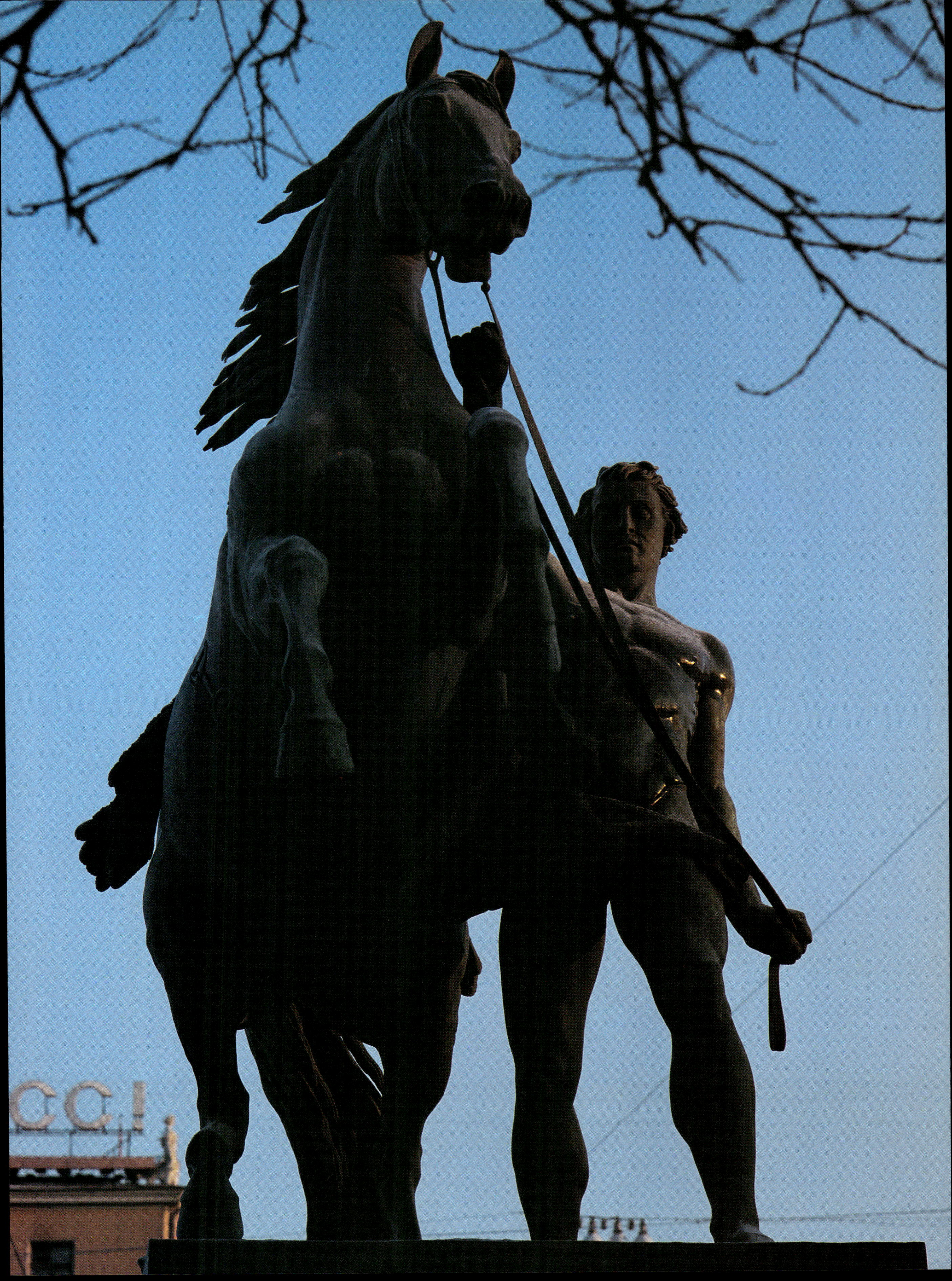

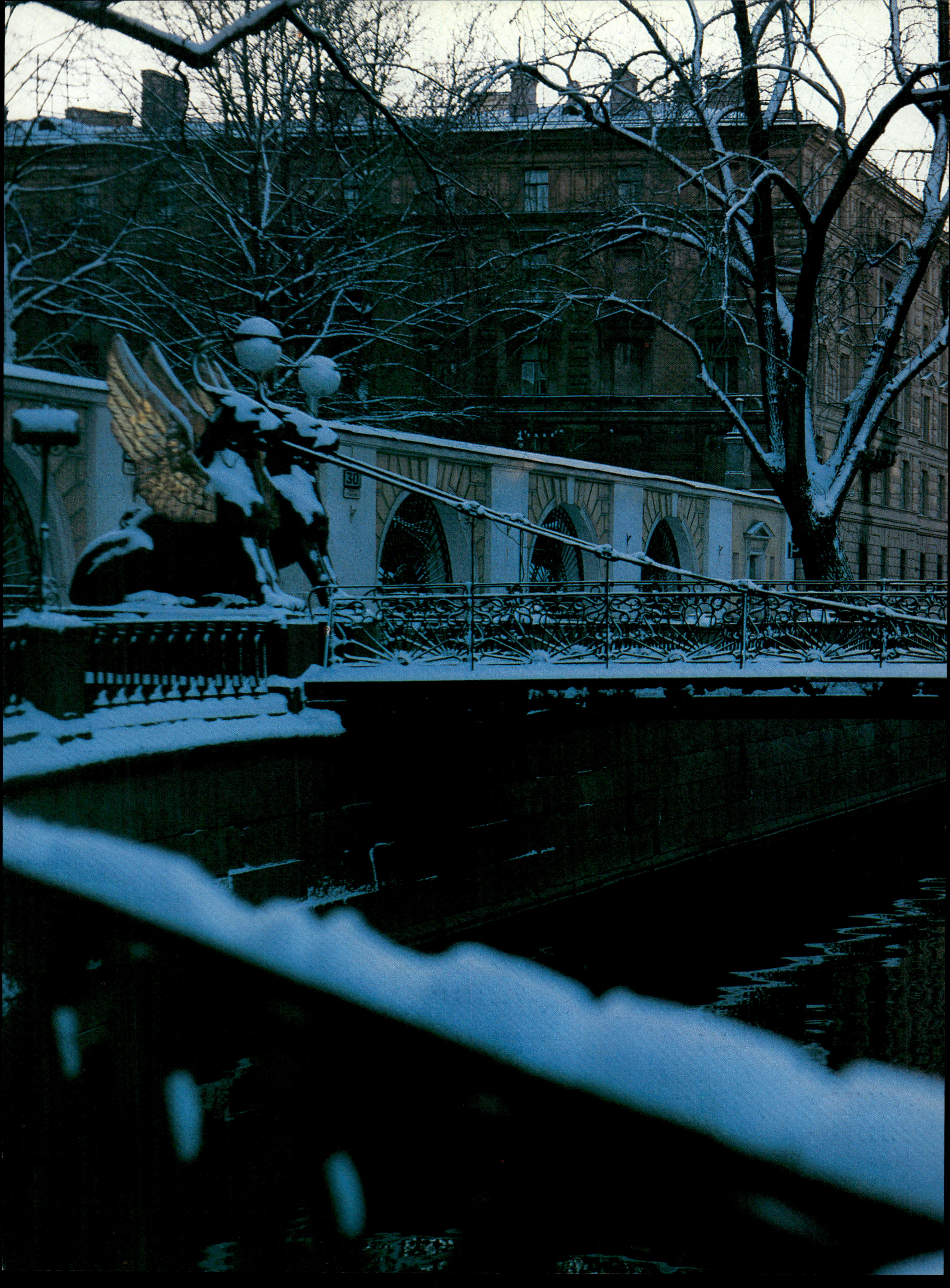

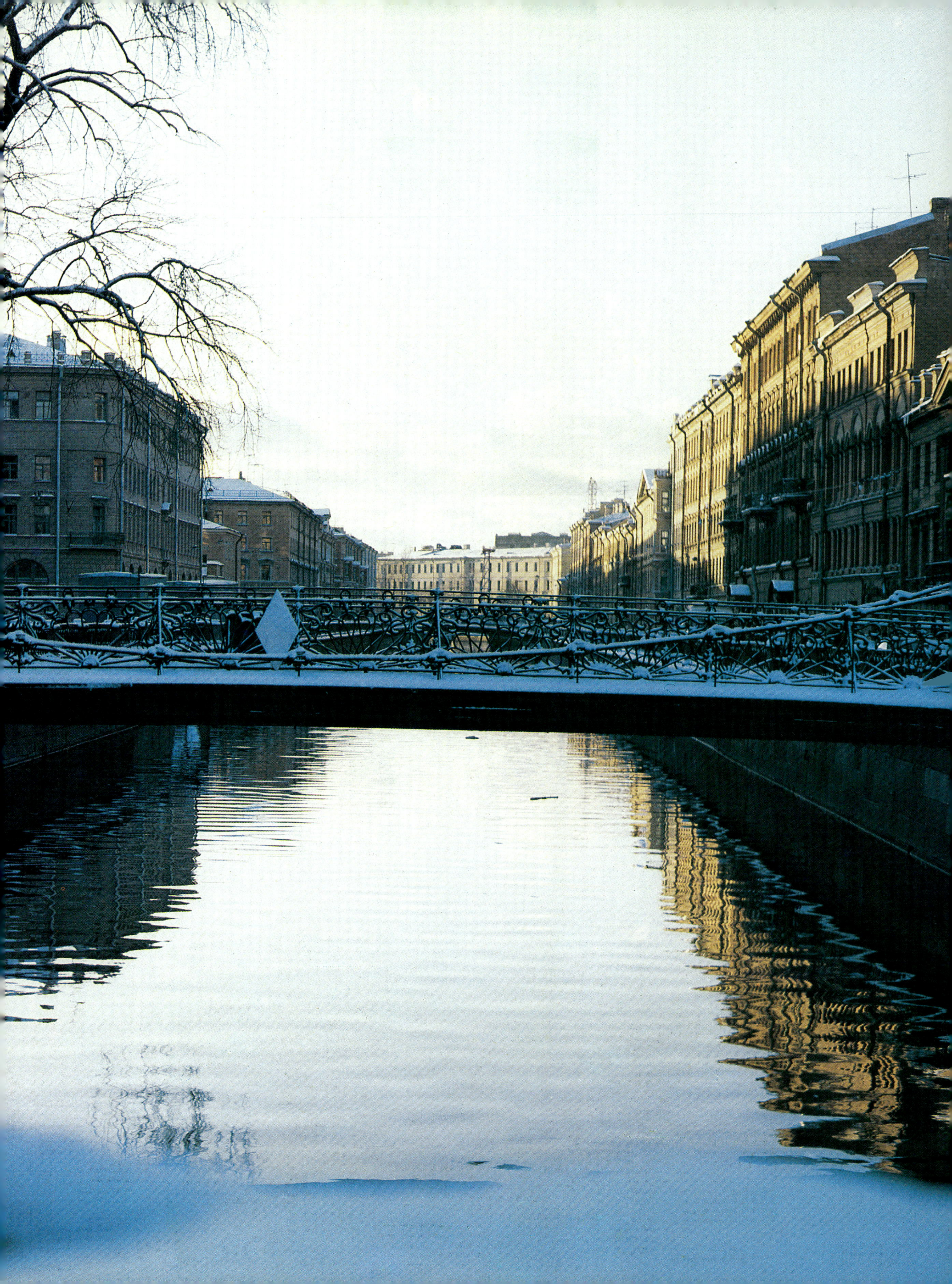

175 →
176

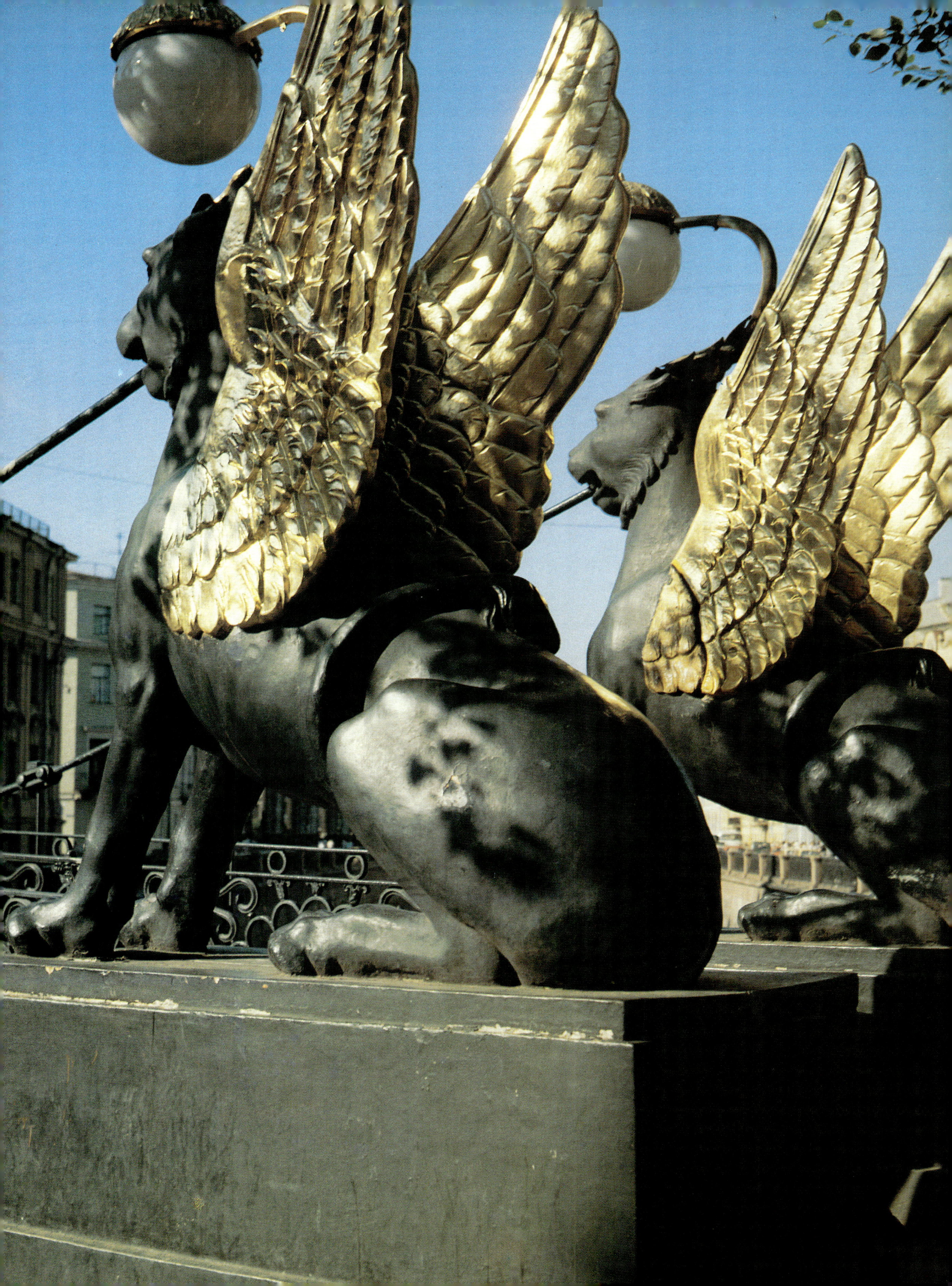

174, 176   Bank Bridge over the Yekaterininsky Canal
175   Building of the Association of Mutual Credit

177, 178   Sheremetev Palace (The «Fontanny House») →

179 Byeloselsky-Byelozersky Palace seen from the Fontanka →
180 Apartment houses on the Karpovka Embankment →
181 Hotel «Europe» →

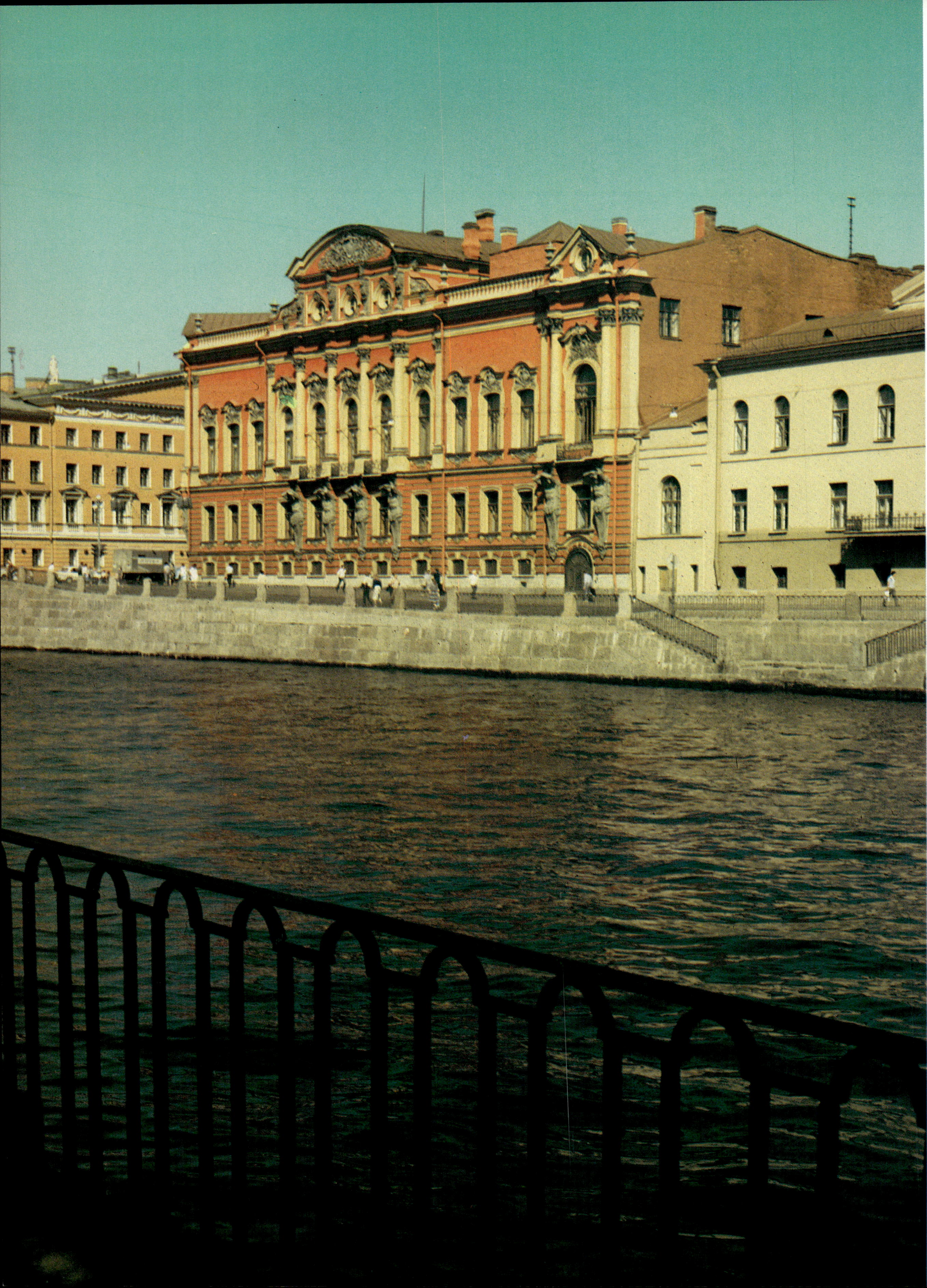

17

→

18

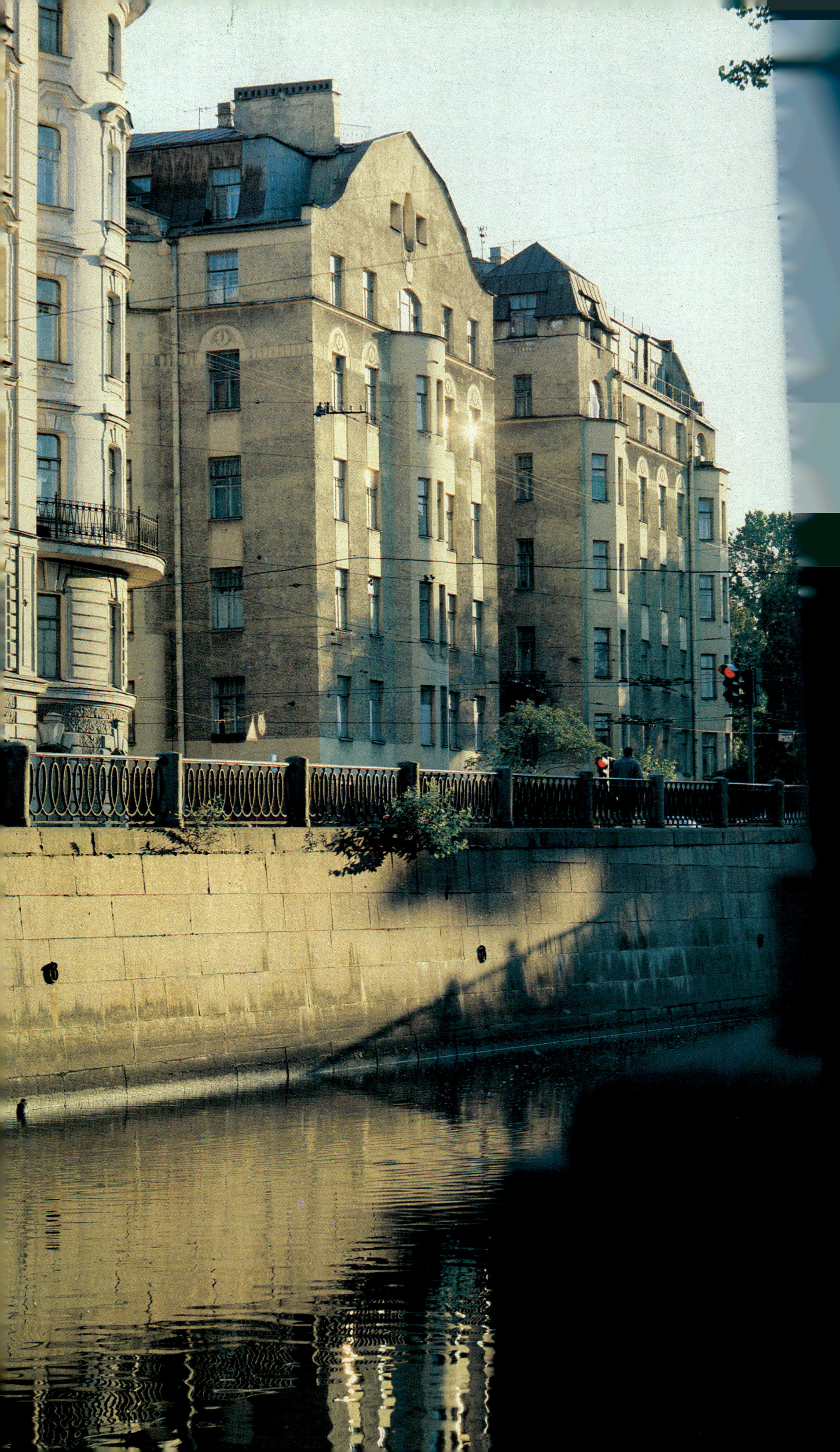

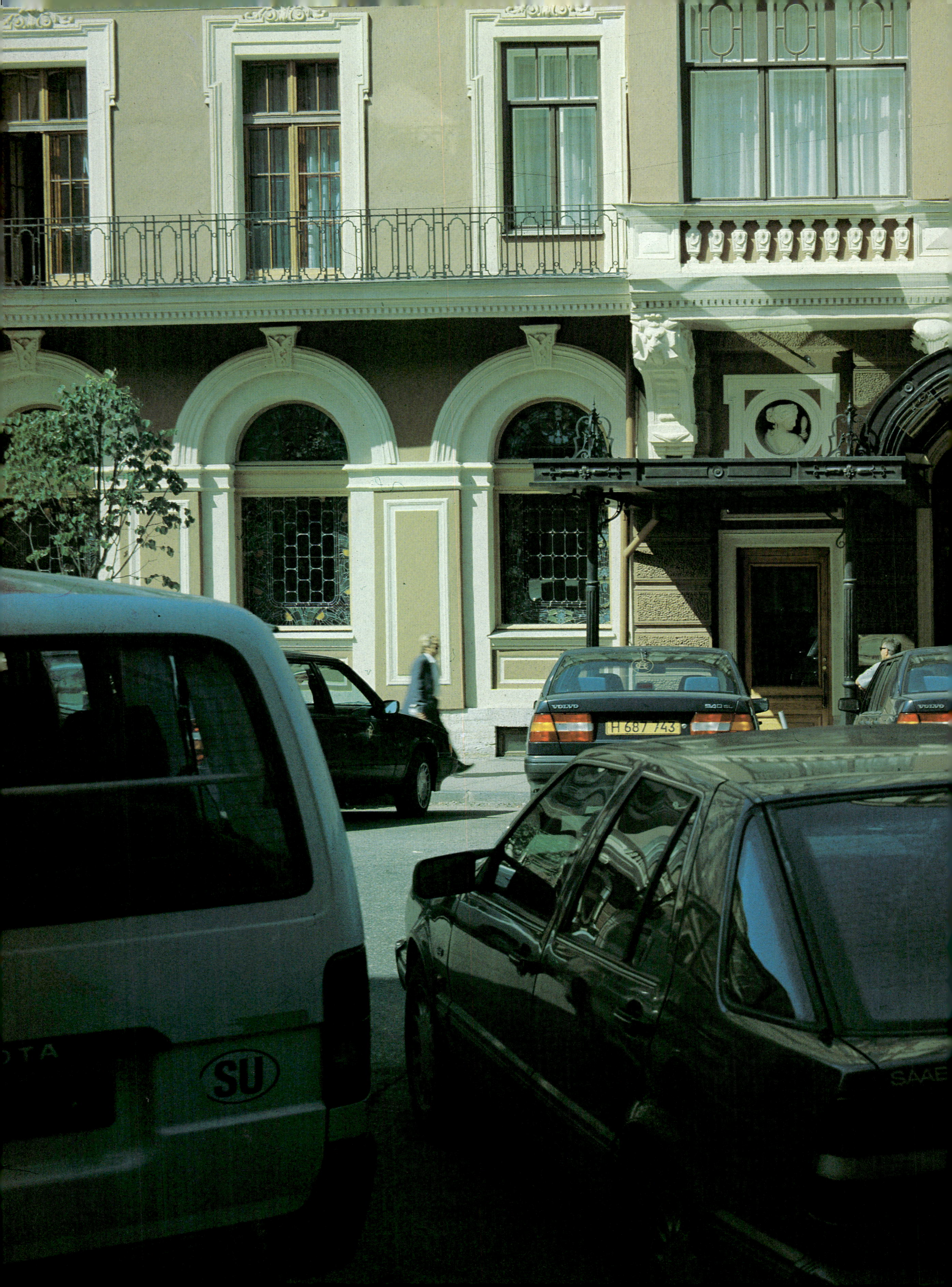
VOLVO
H 687 743
SU
SAAB

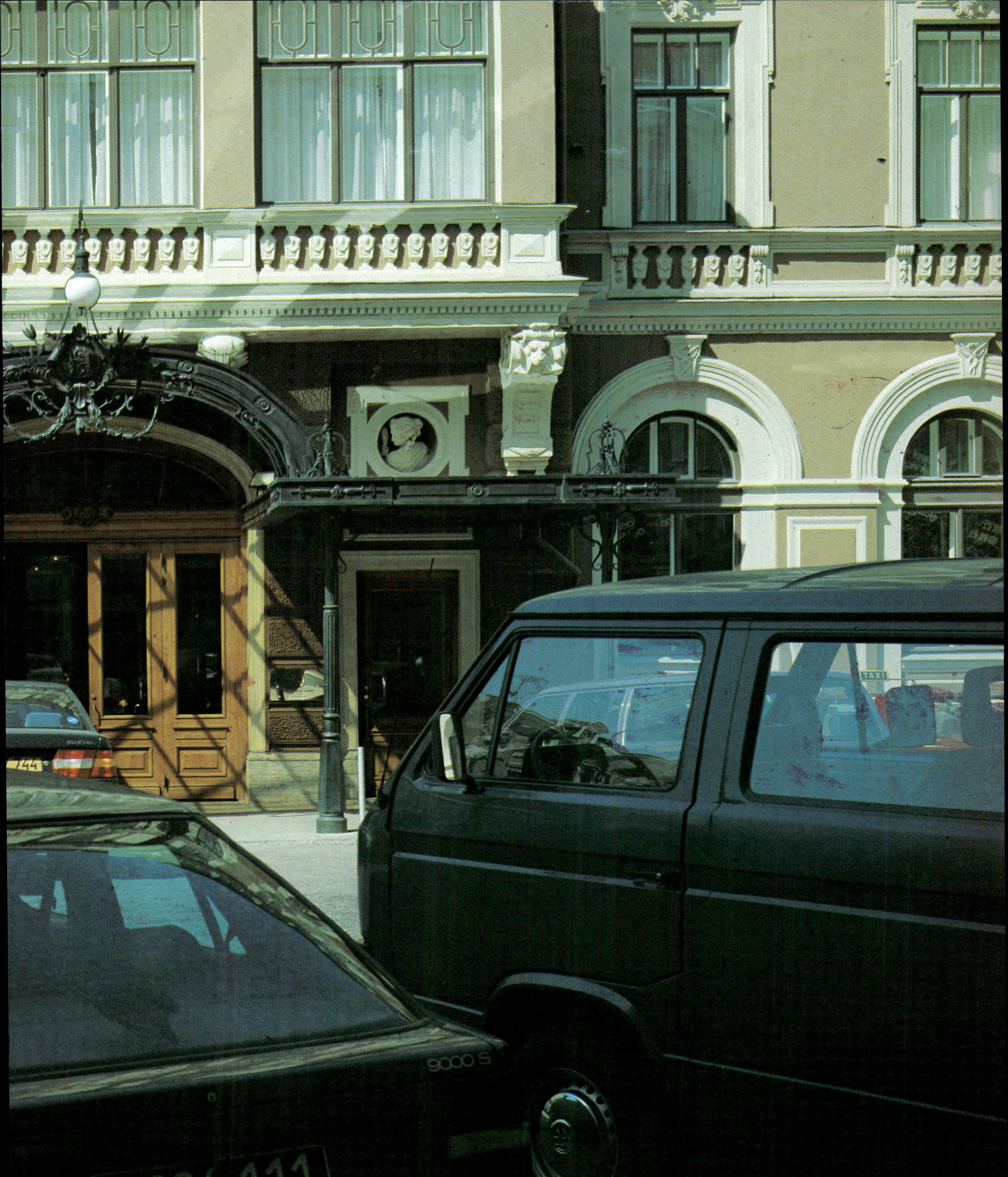
TAXI
9000 S

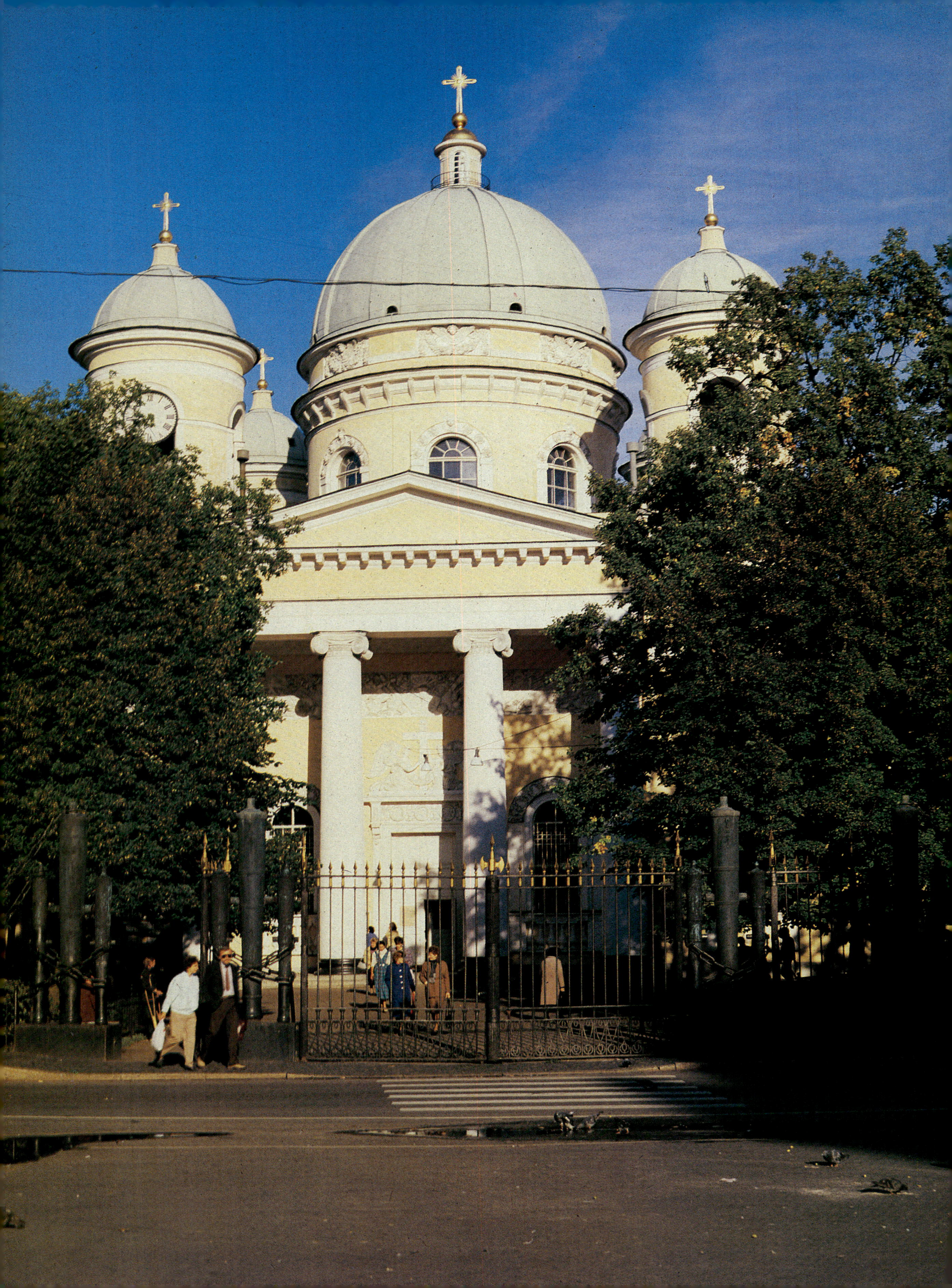

182　　Transfiguration Cathedral
183　　Stroganov Palace seen from the Moika

184—190　　St. Nicholas' Naval Cathedral

185
→
186

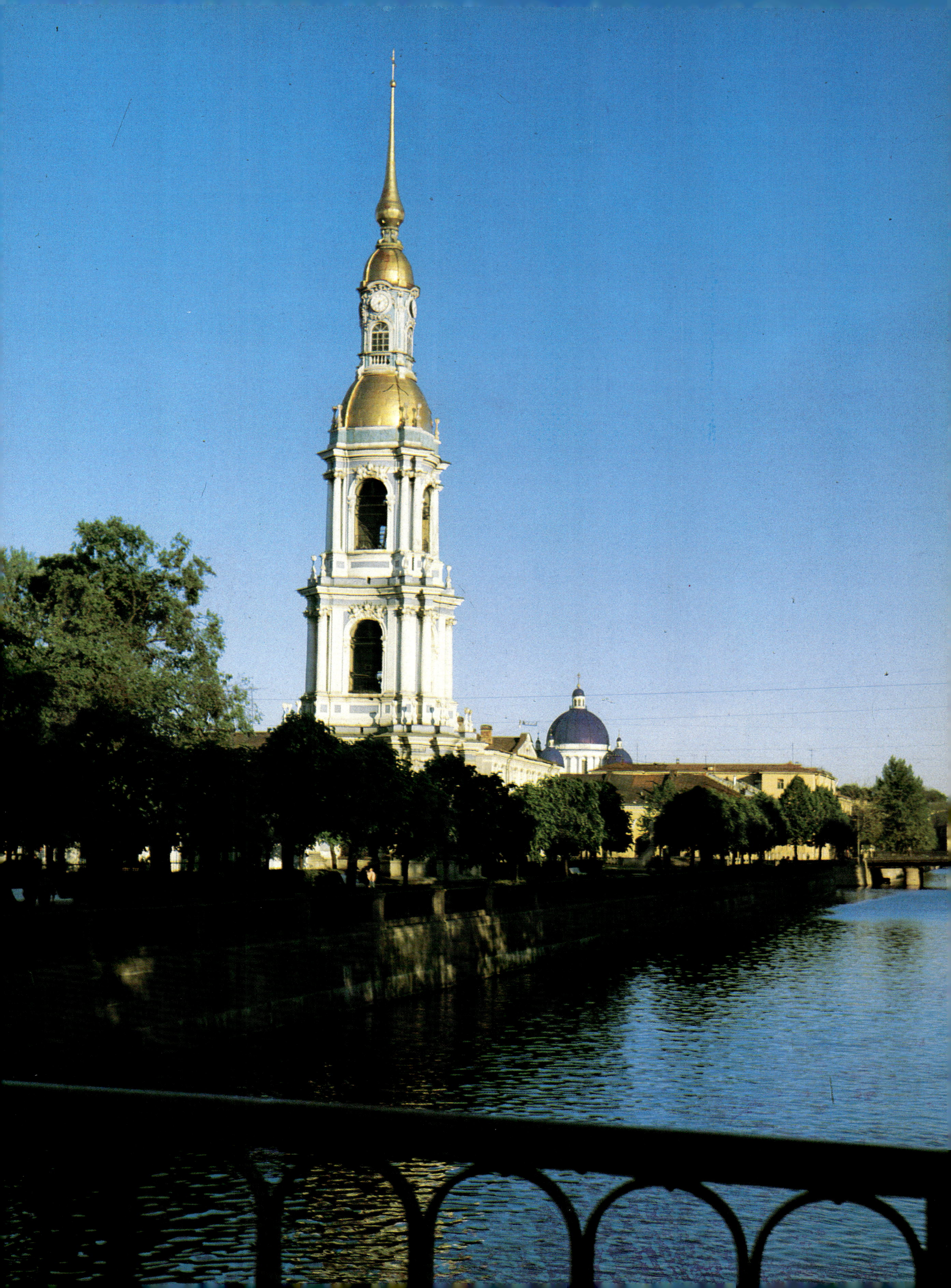

187
→
188

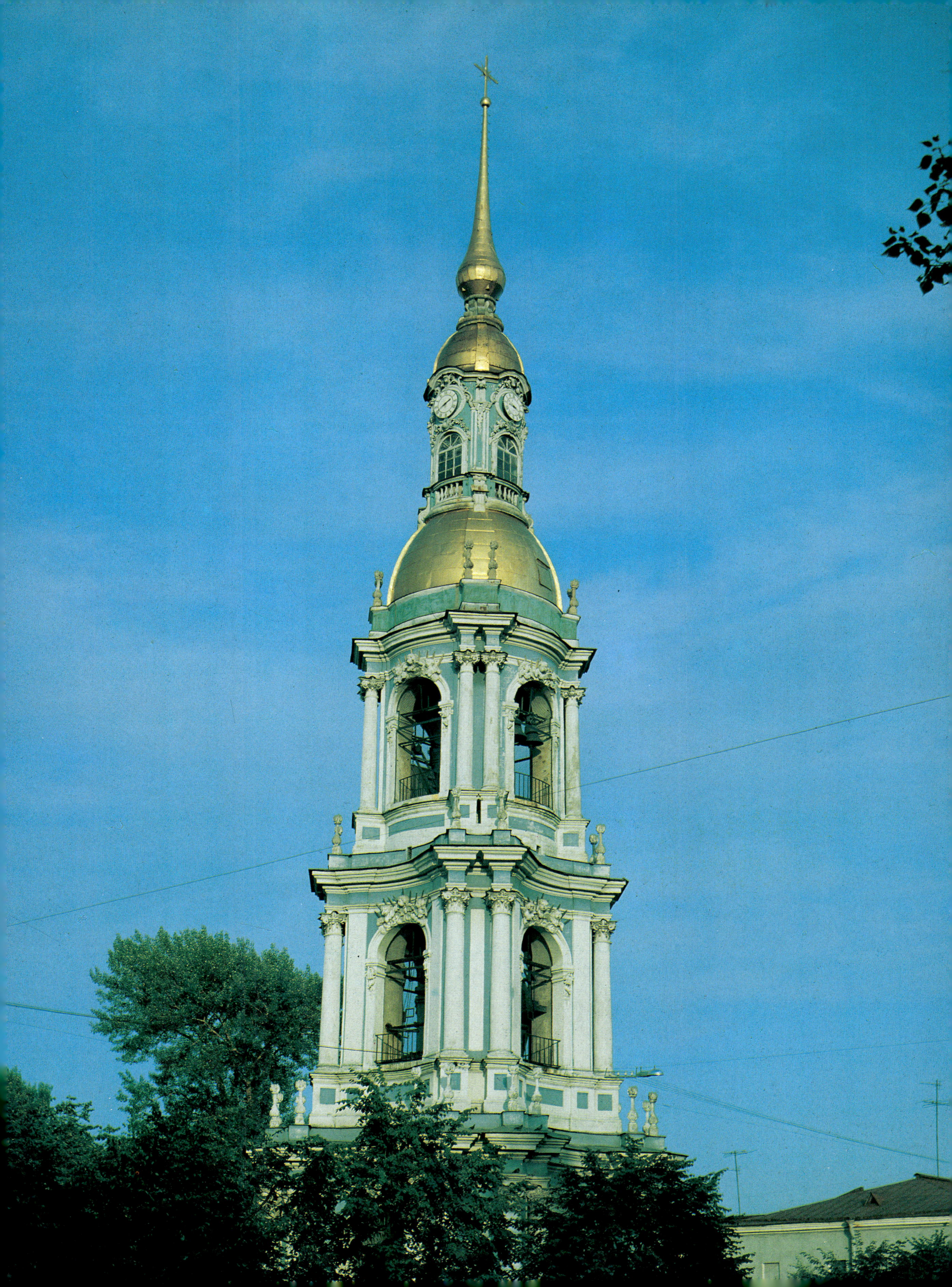

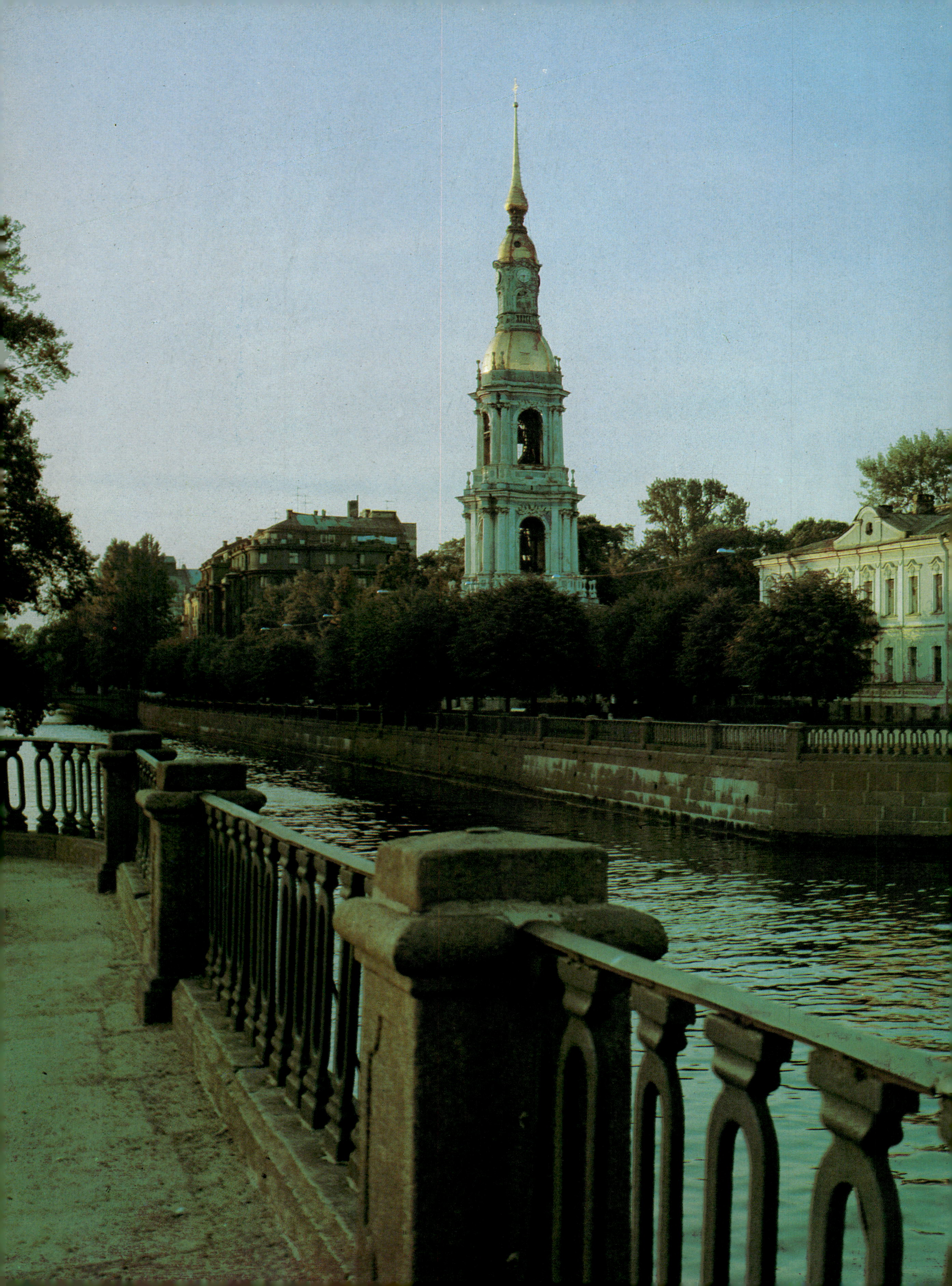

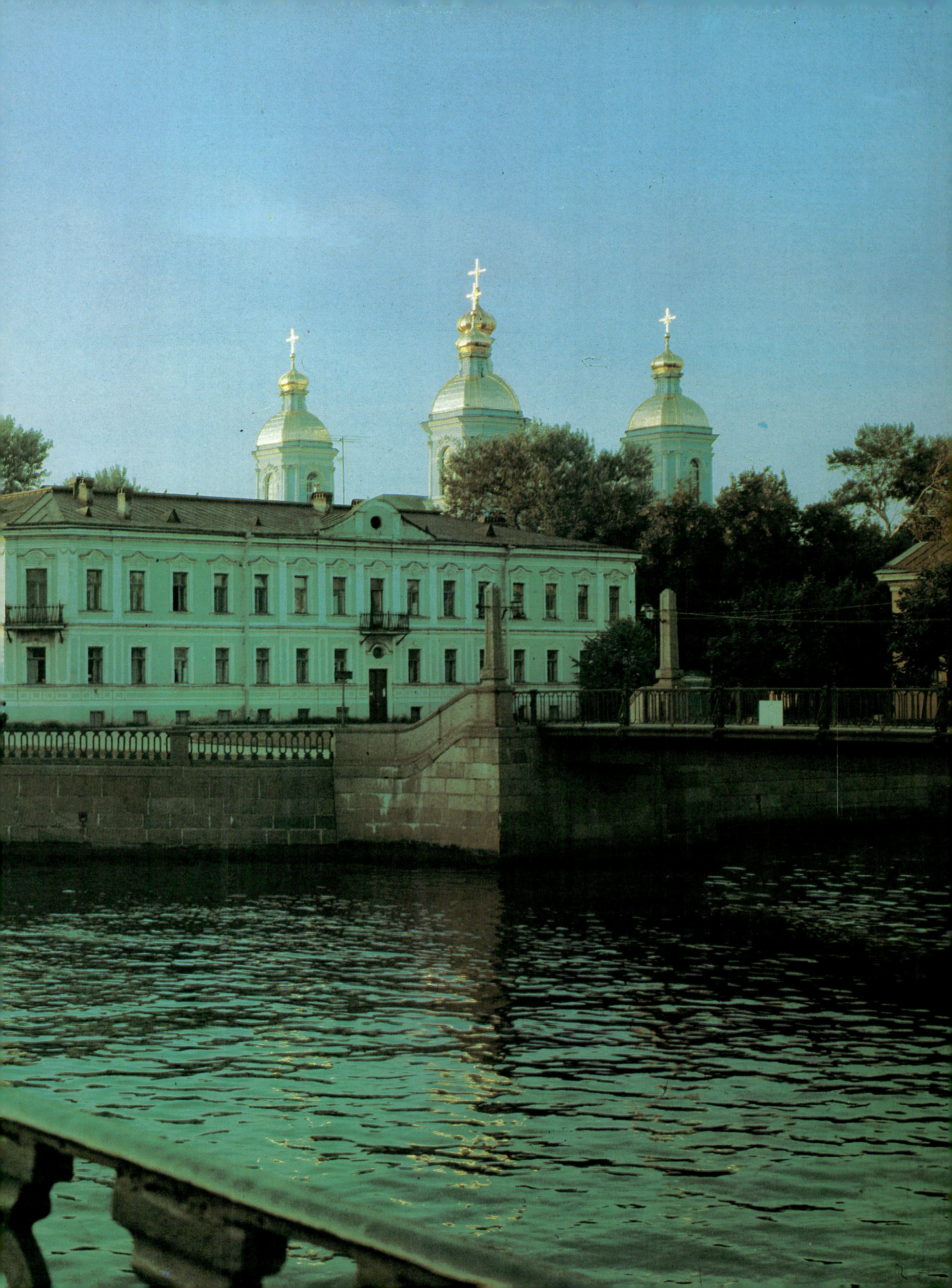

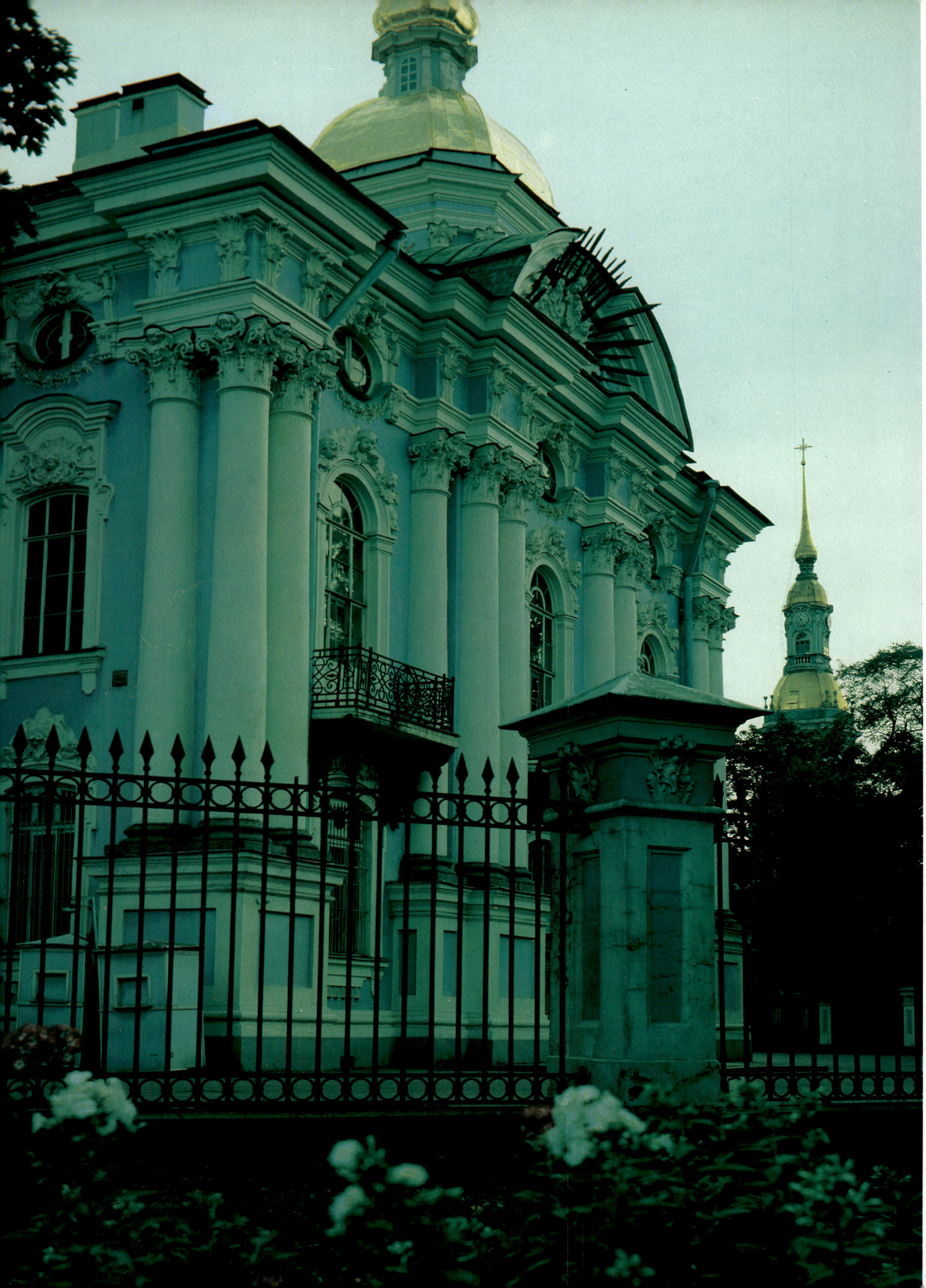

19

→
19

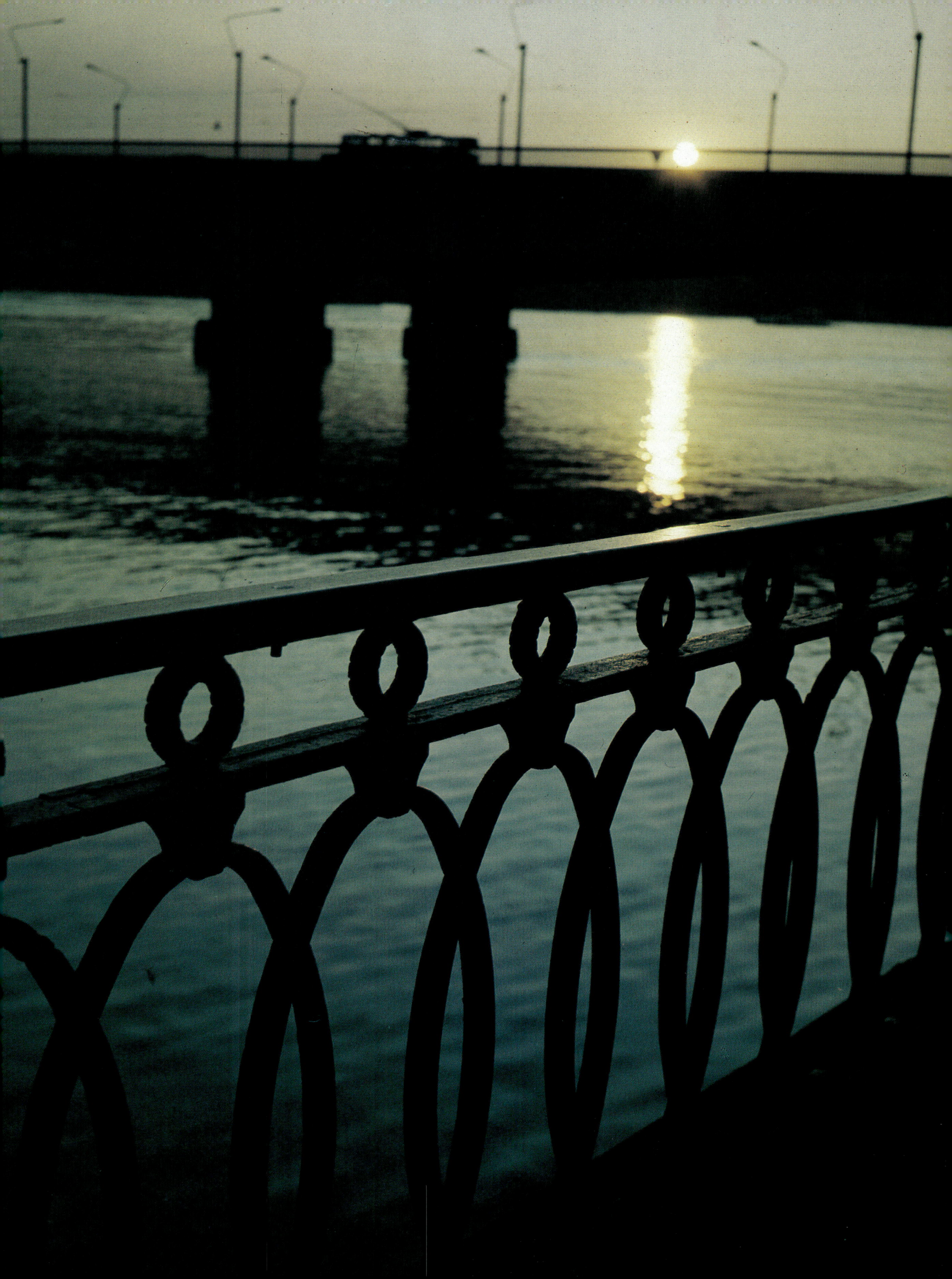

191 Tuchkov Bridge

192 Bolsheokhtinsky Bridge
193—195 Cathedral of Smolny Convent

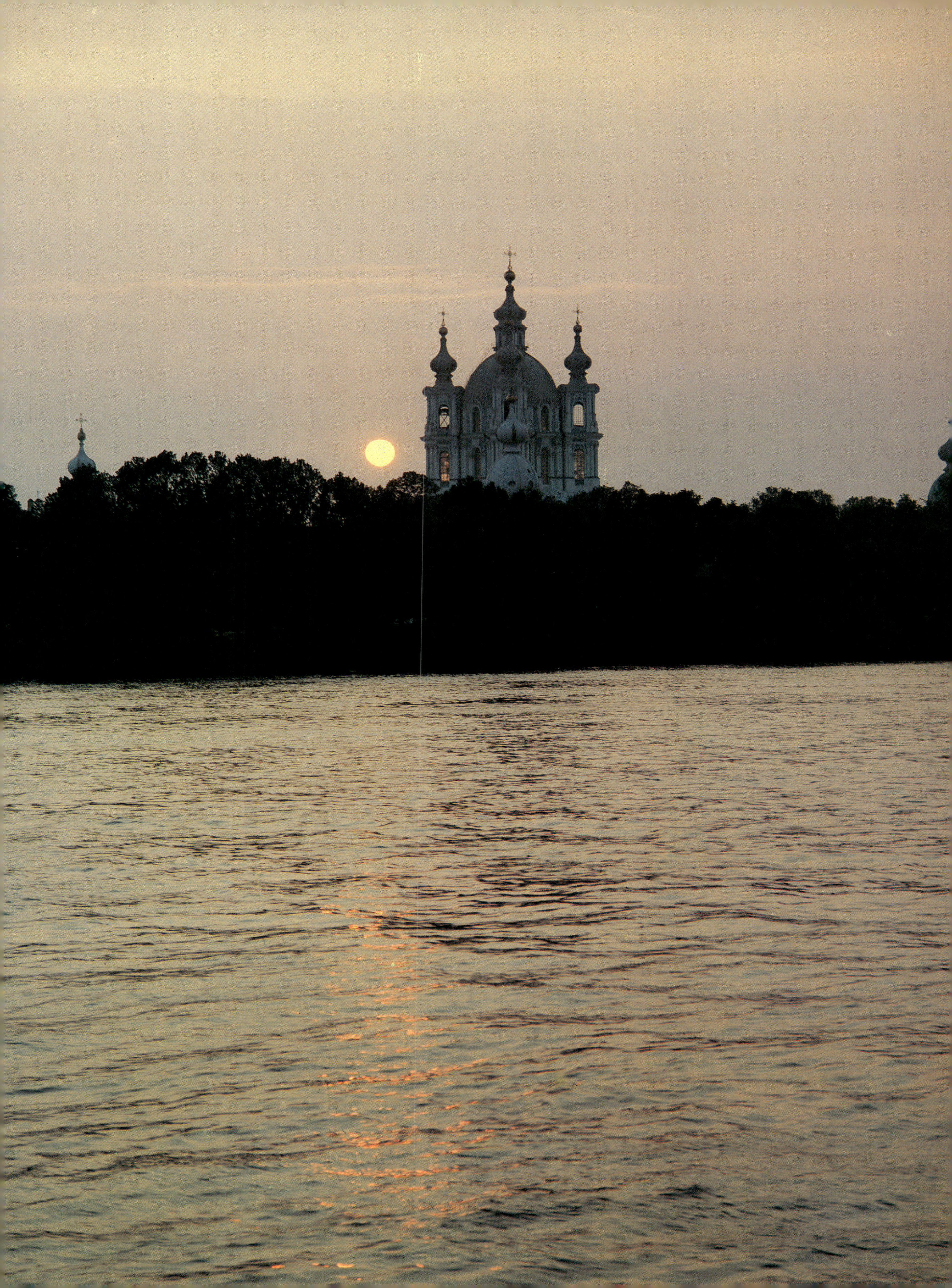

196 Trinity Cathedral

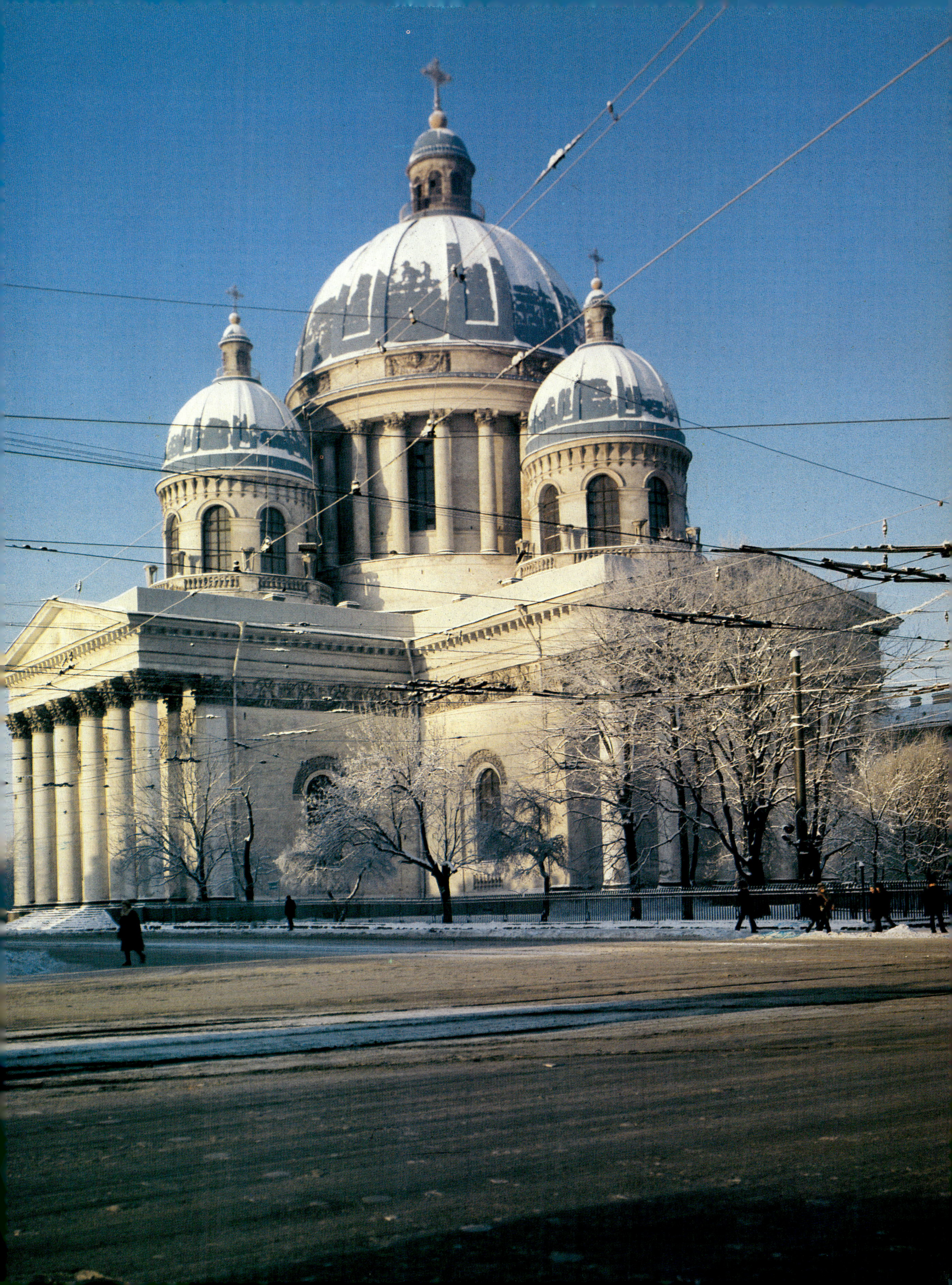

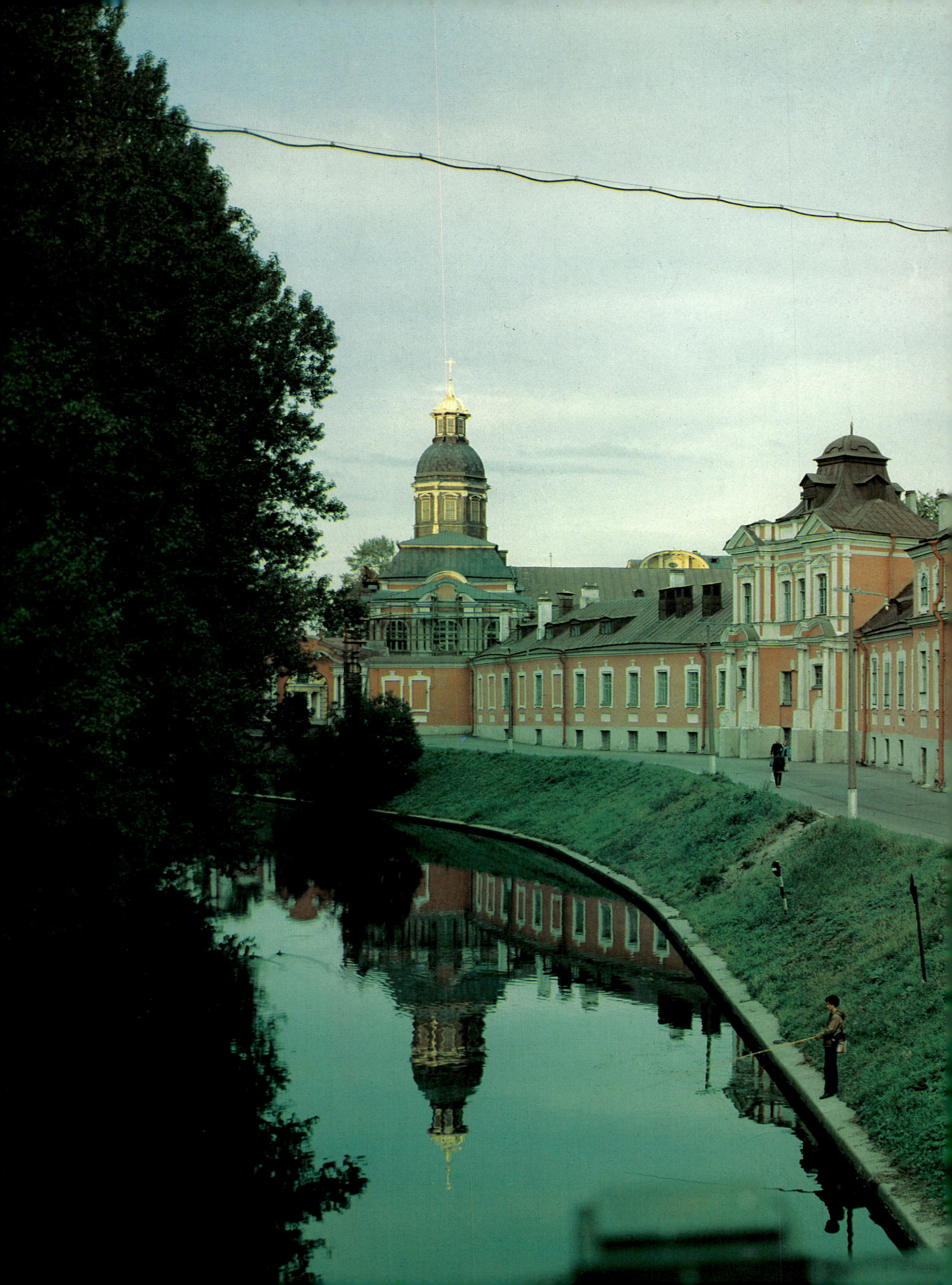

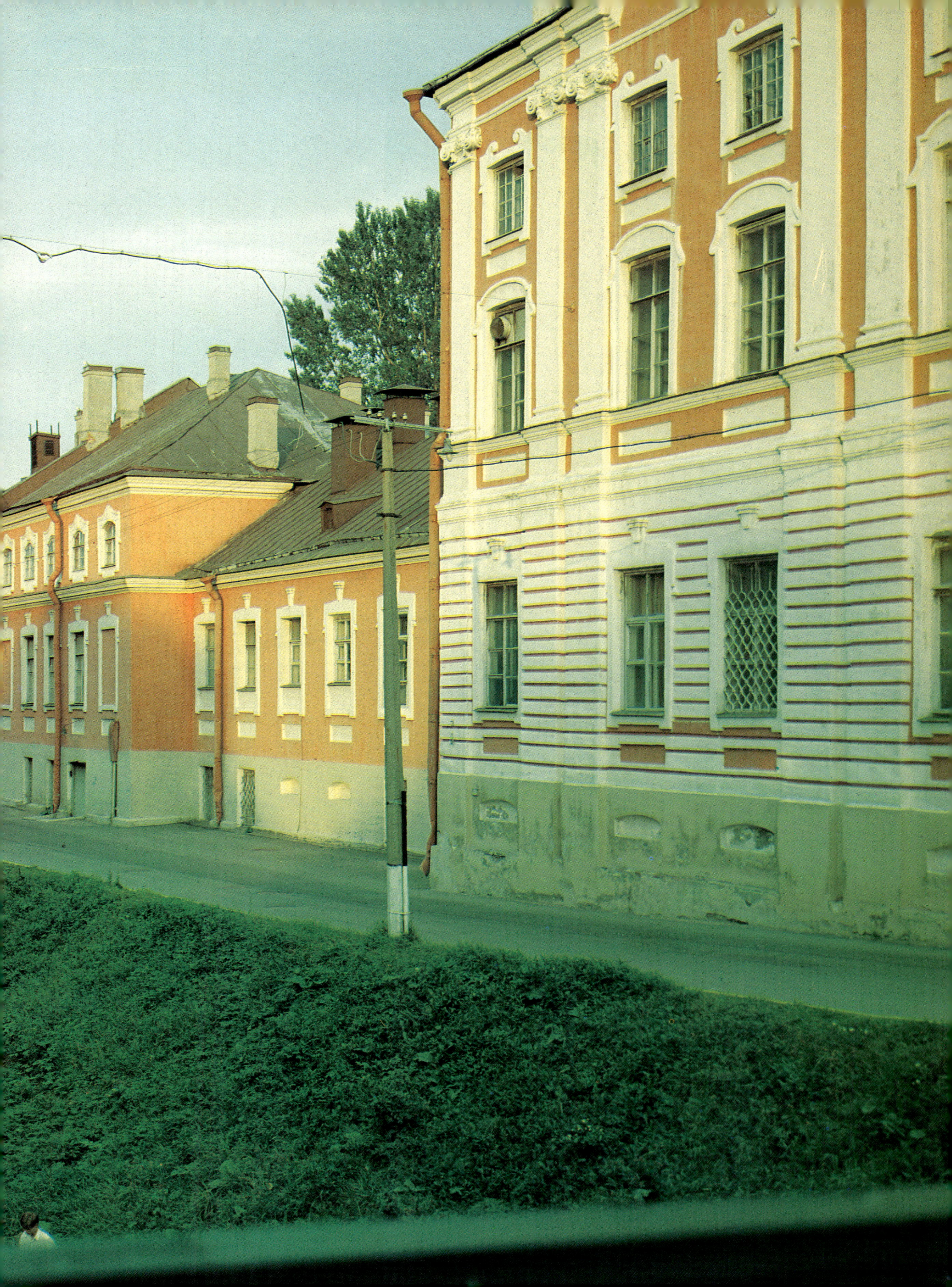

1980
→
199

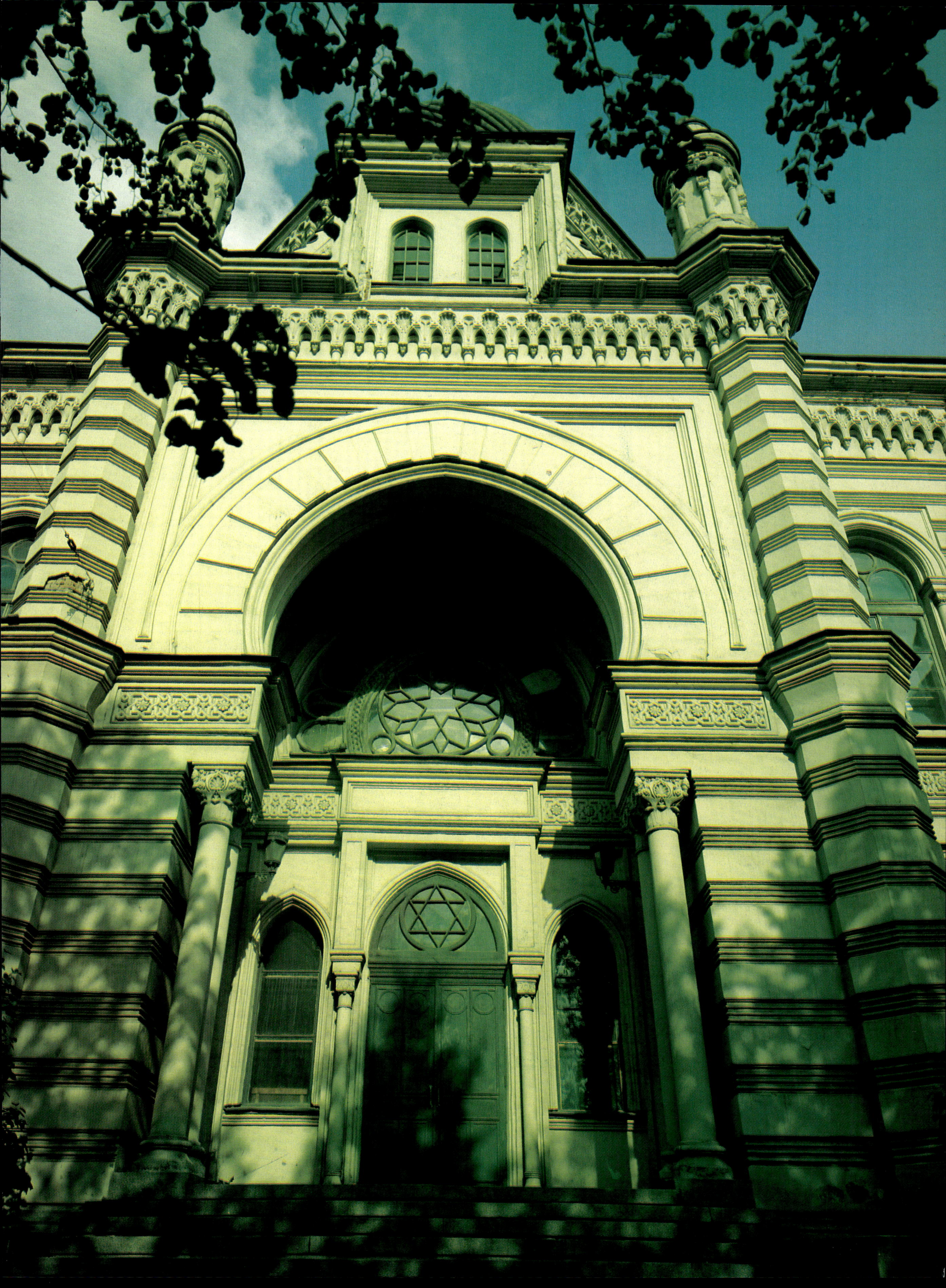

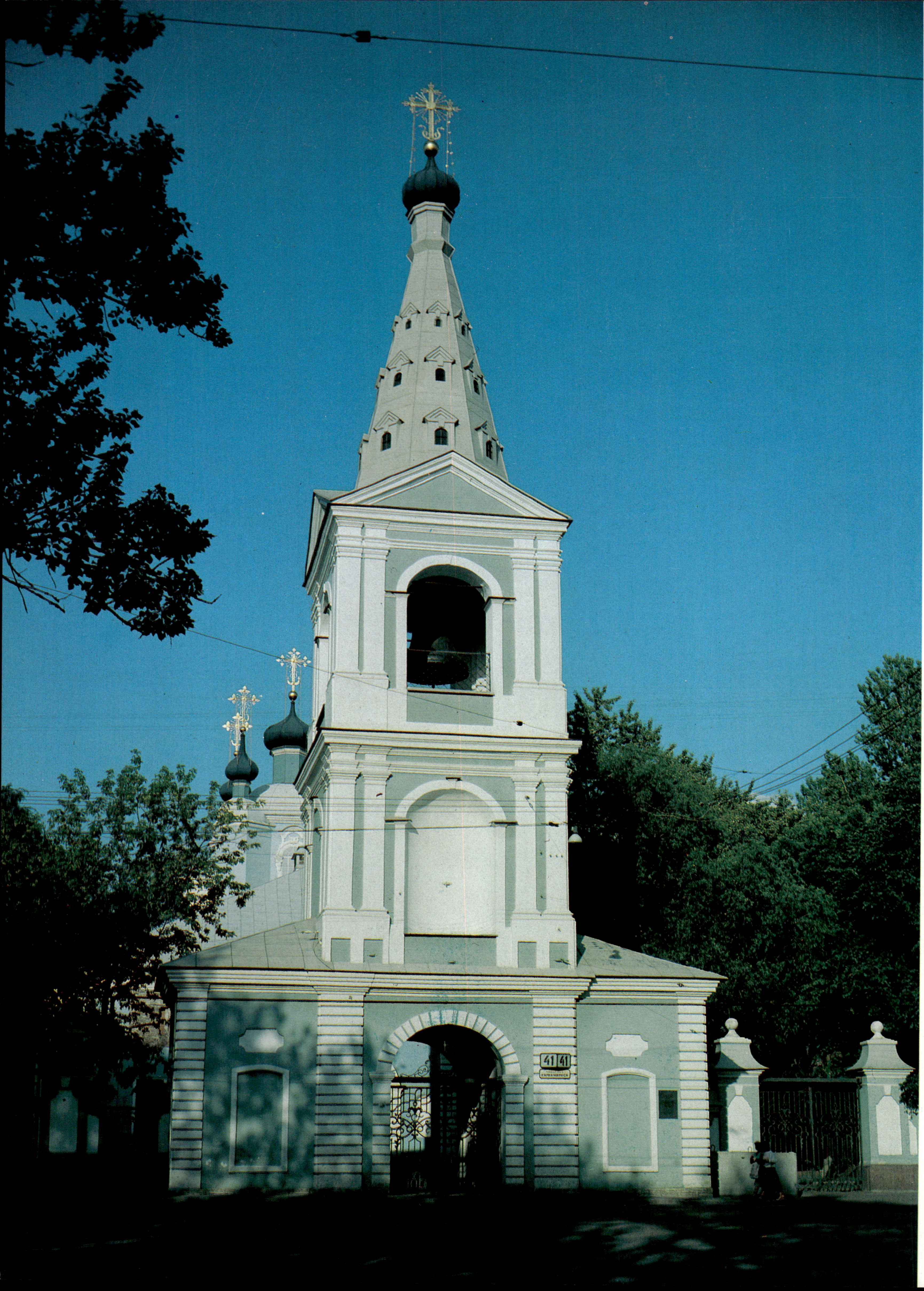
41 41

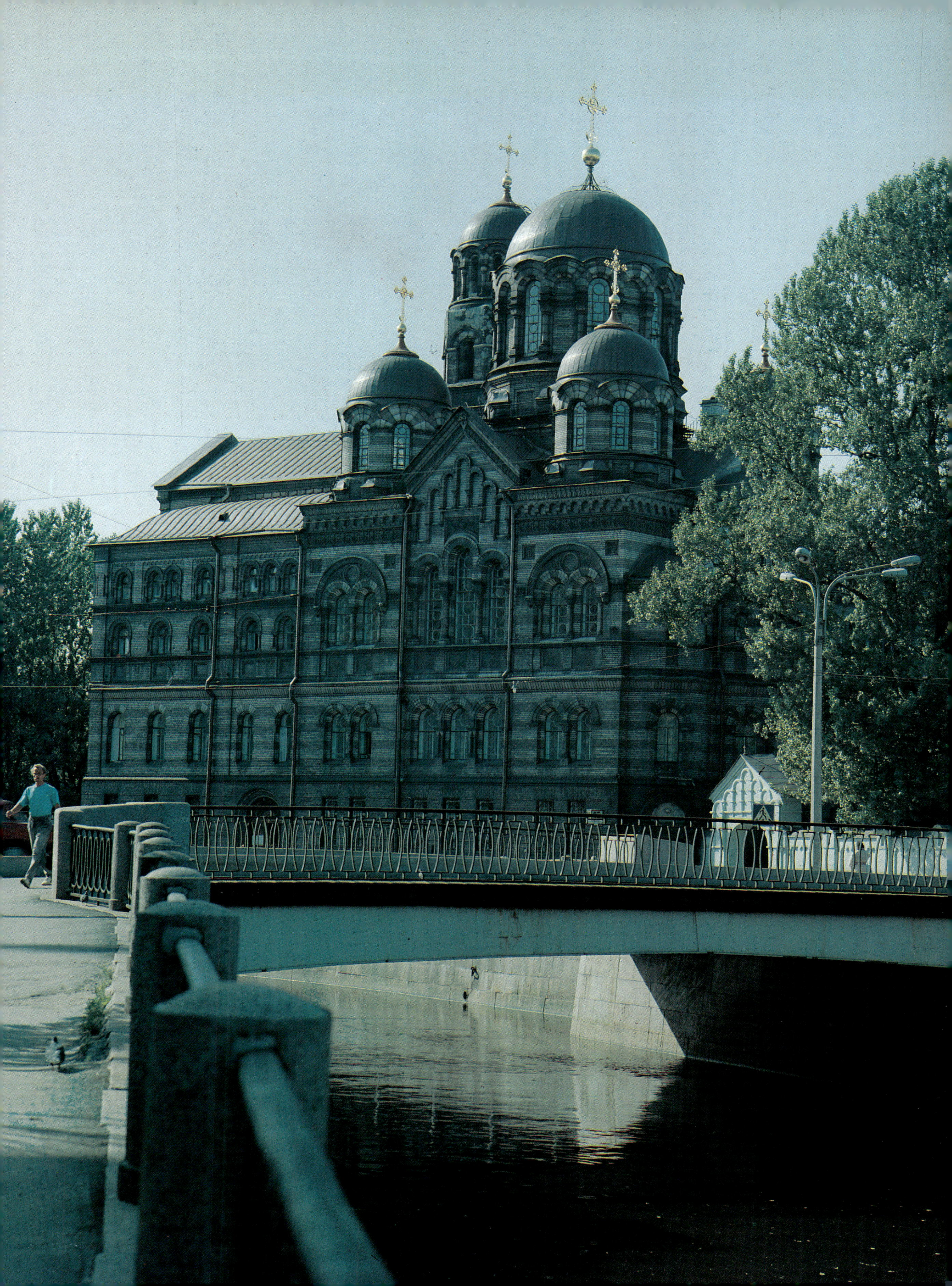

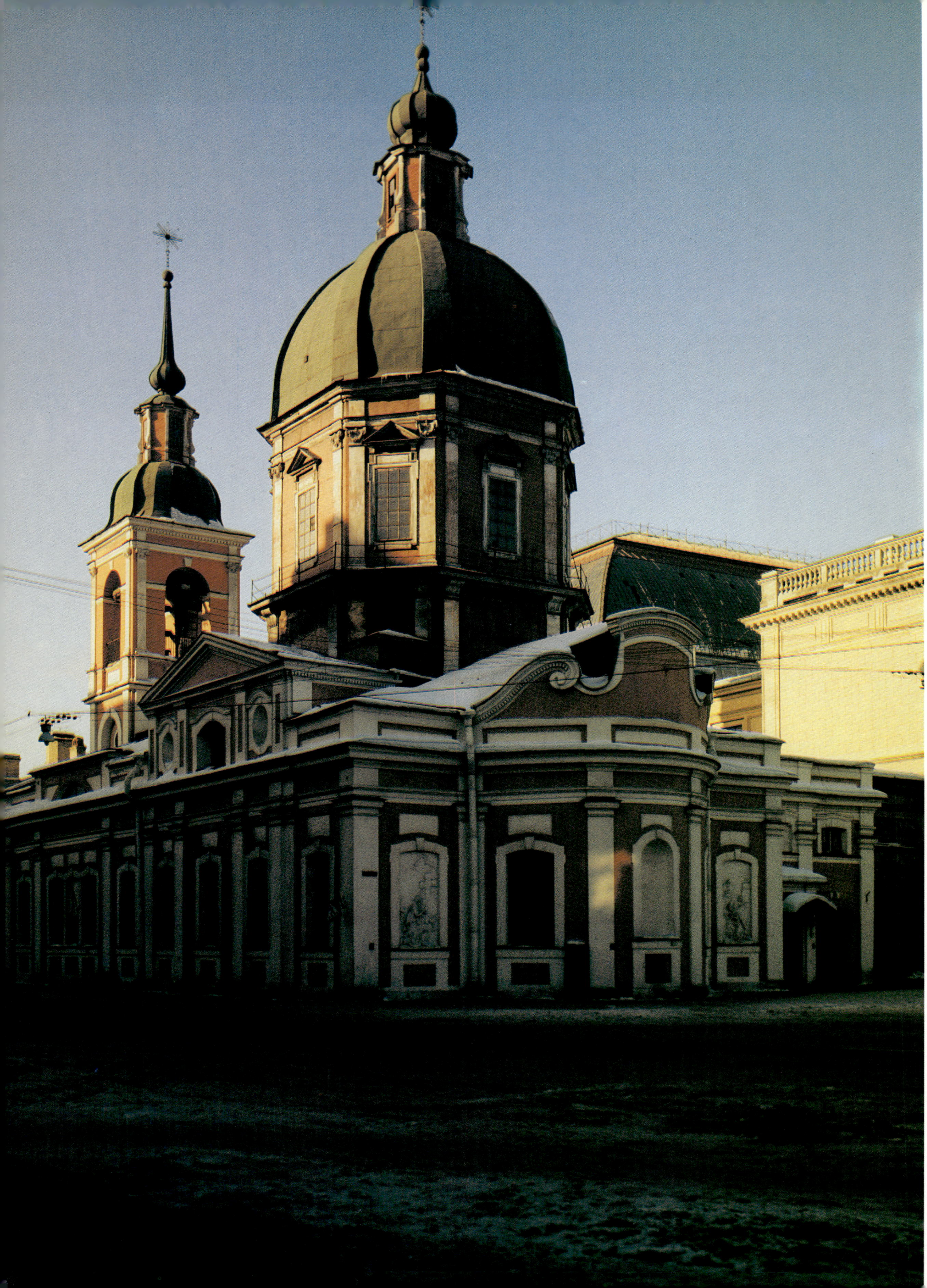

202

→
203

197	St. Alexander Nevsky Monastery
198	Lion's Bridge over the Yekaterininsky Canal
199	Synagogue
200	St. Samson's Cathedral
201	St. John's Monastery on the Karpovka Embankment
202	St. Pantaleon's Church
203	Railing of a garden on the Karpovka Embankment

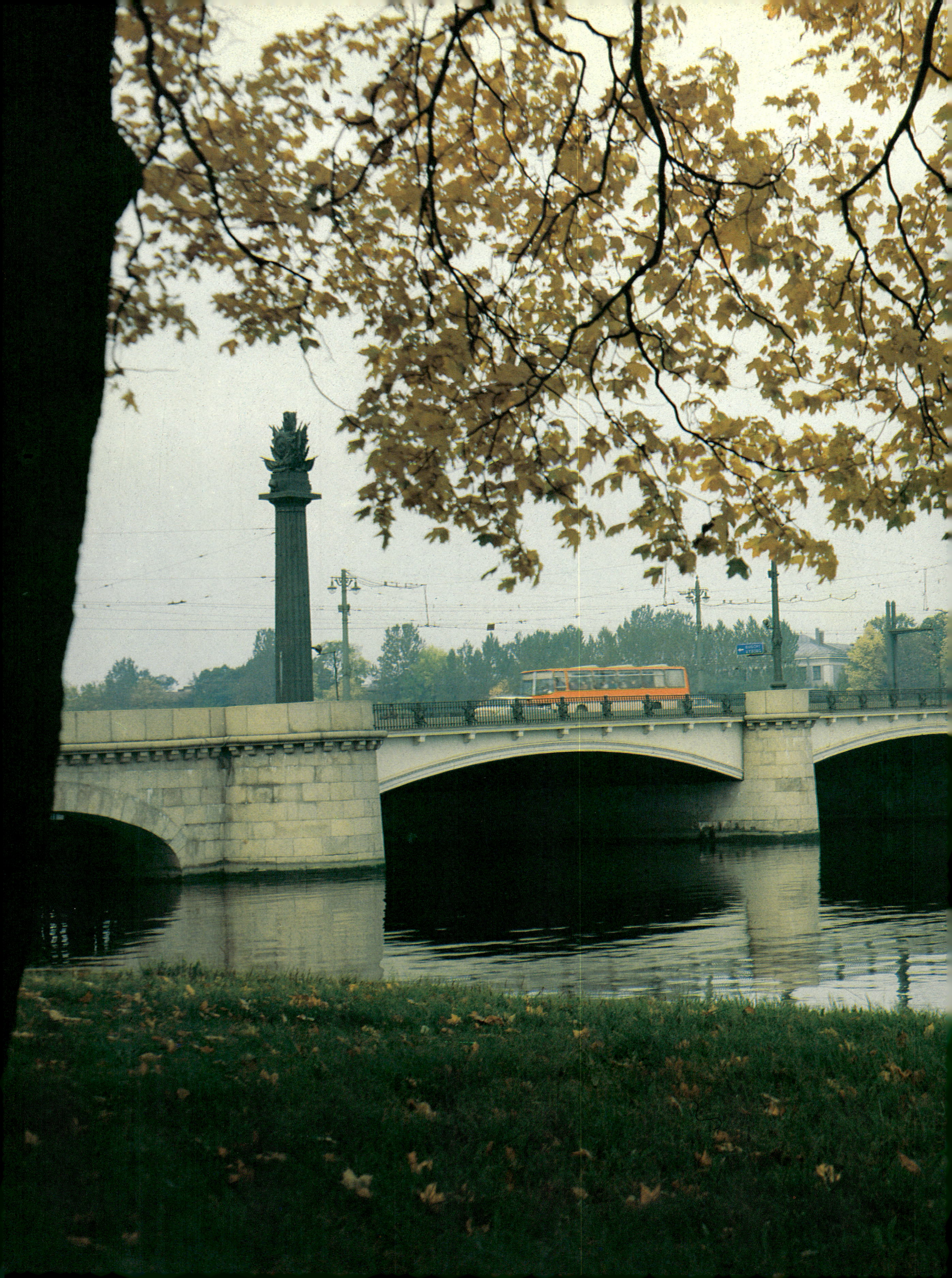

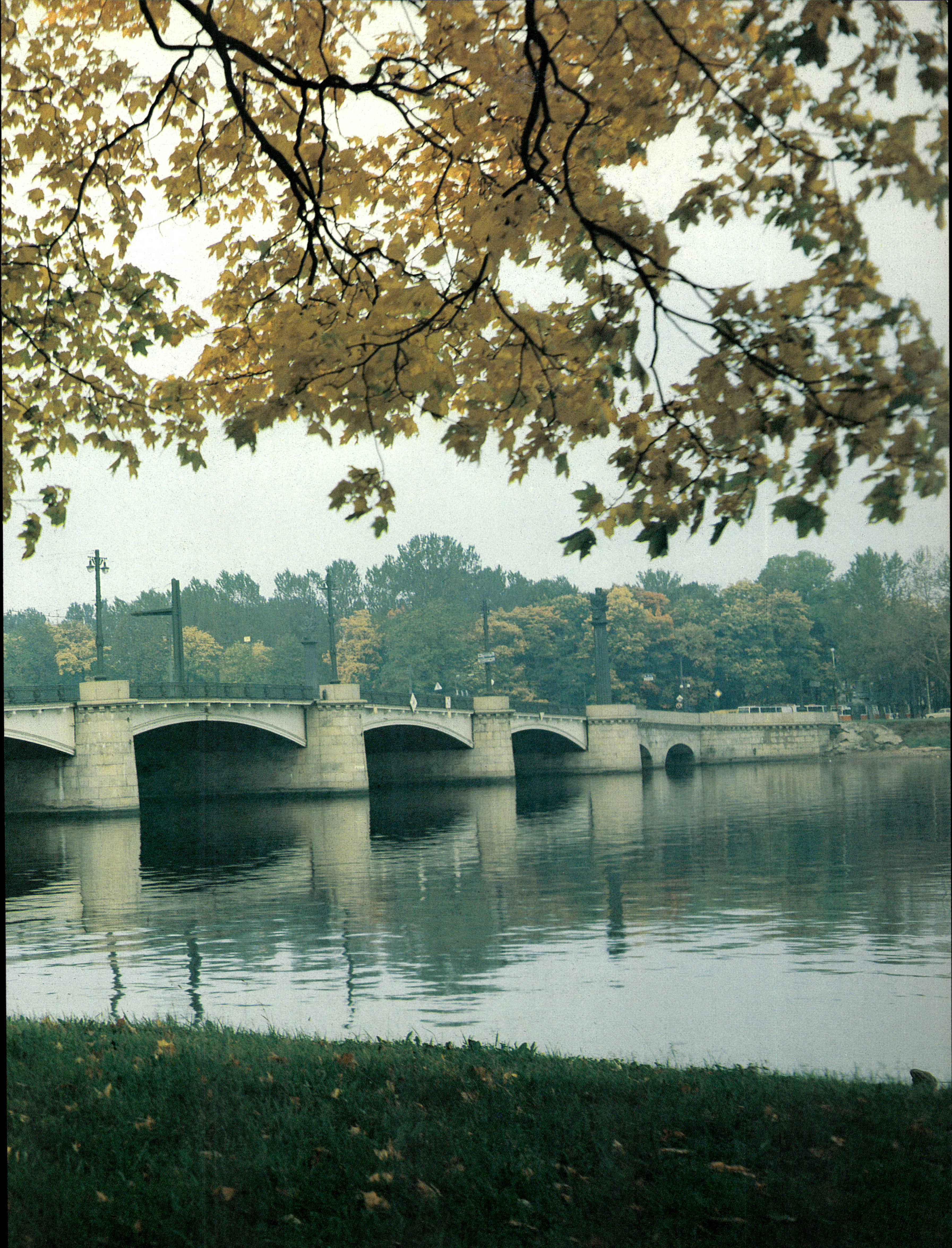

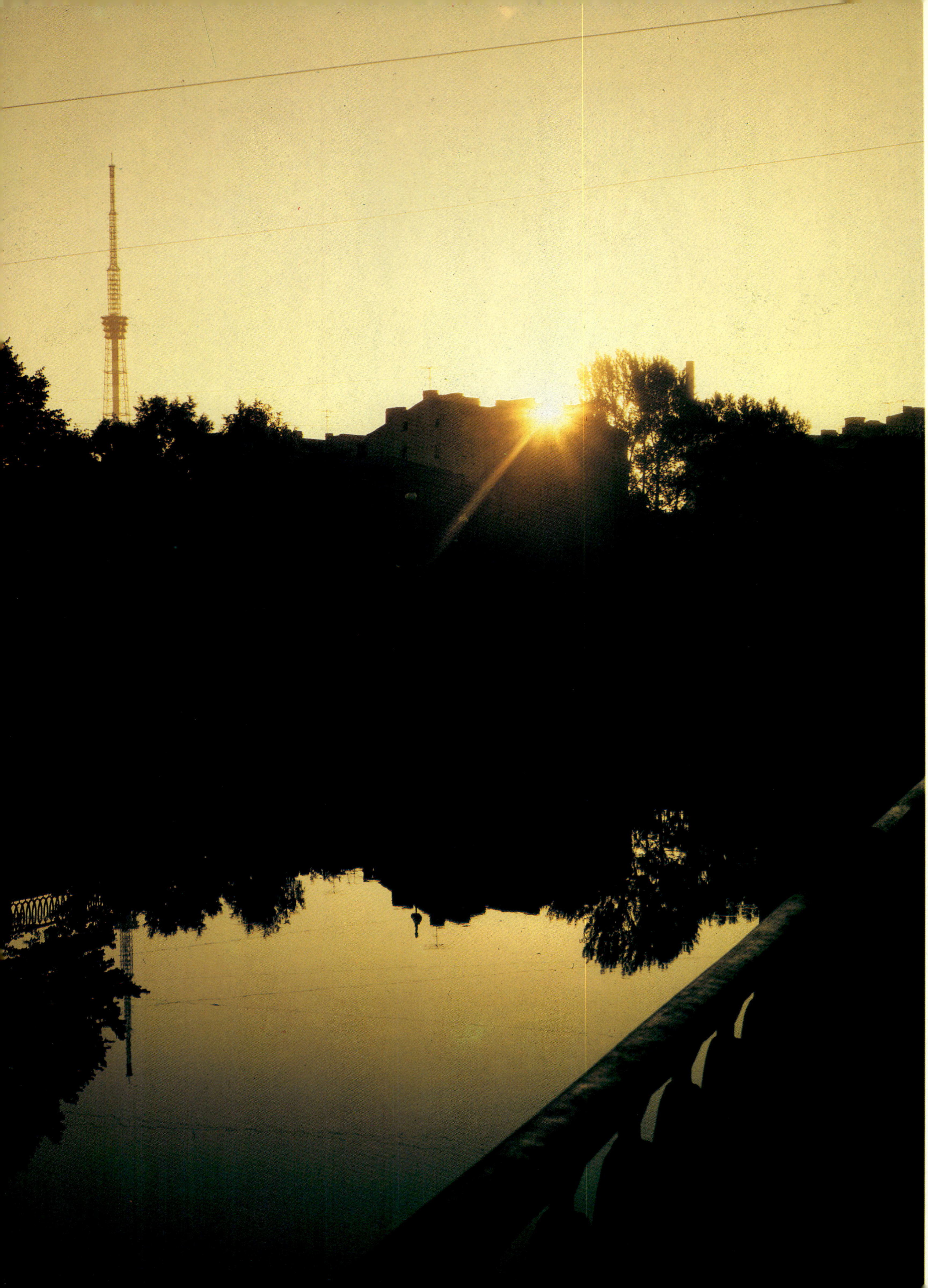

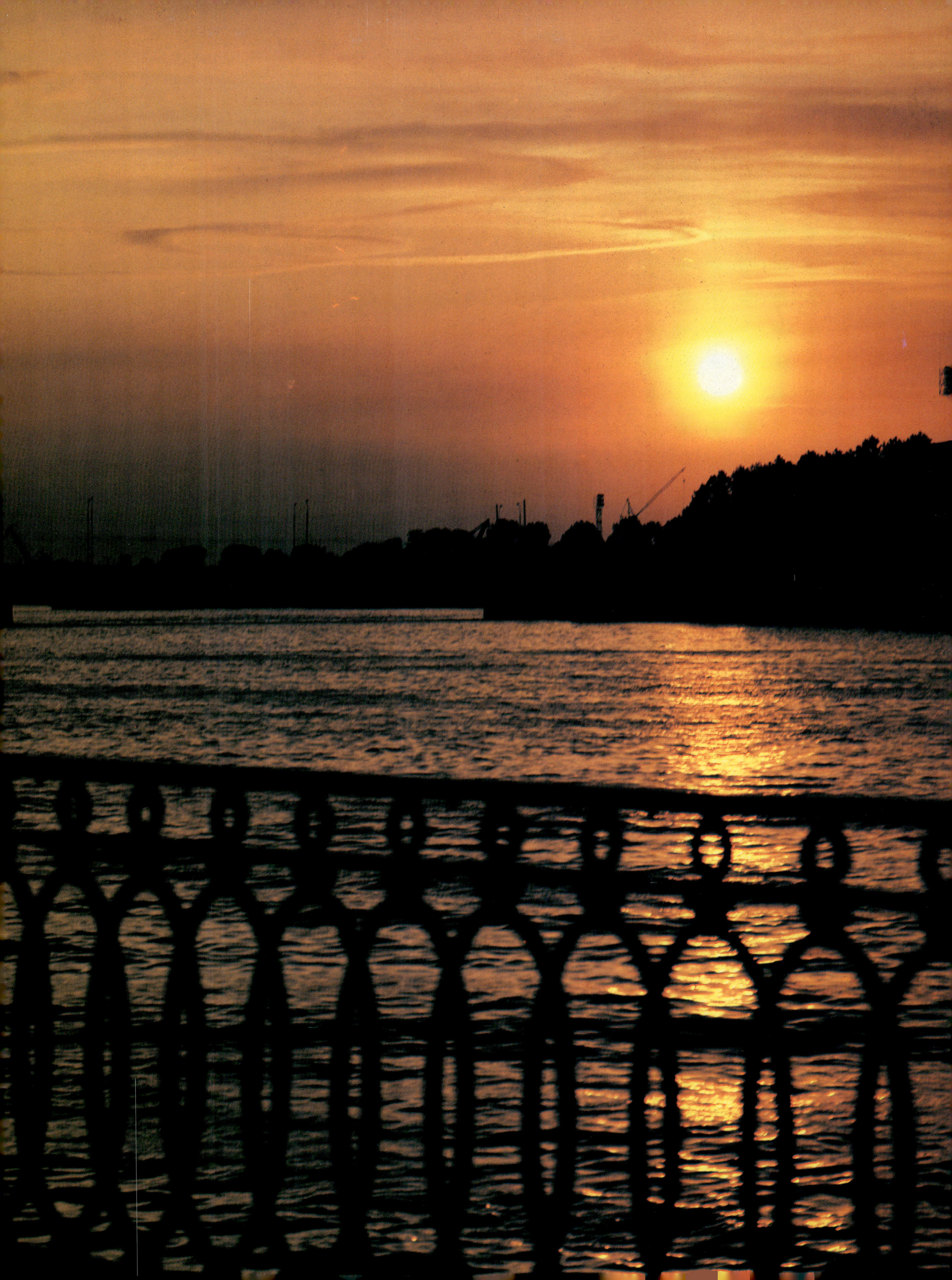

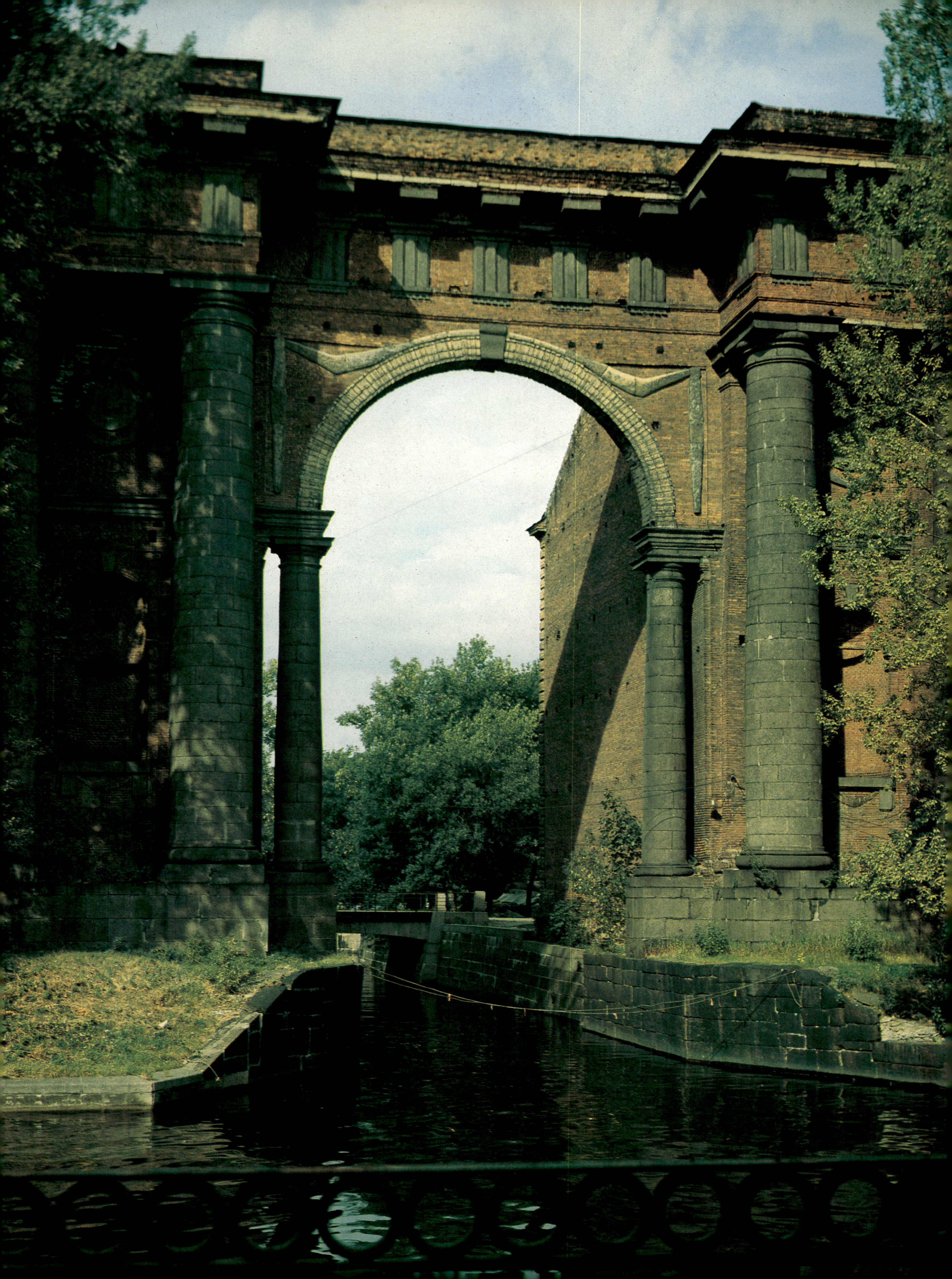

204	Ushakov Bridge
205	Twilight
206	Descends over the water

207, 208	New Holland
209	Moika Embankment. Railing

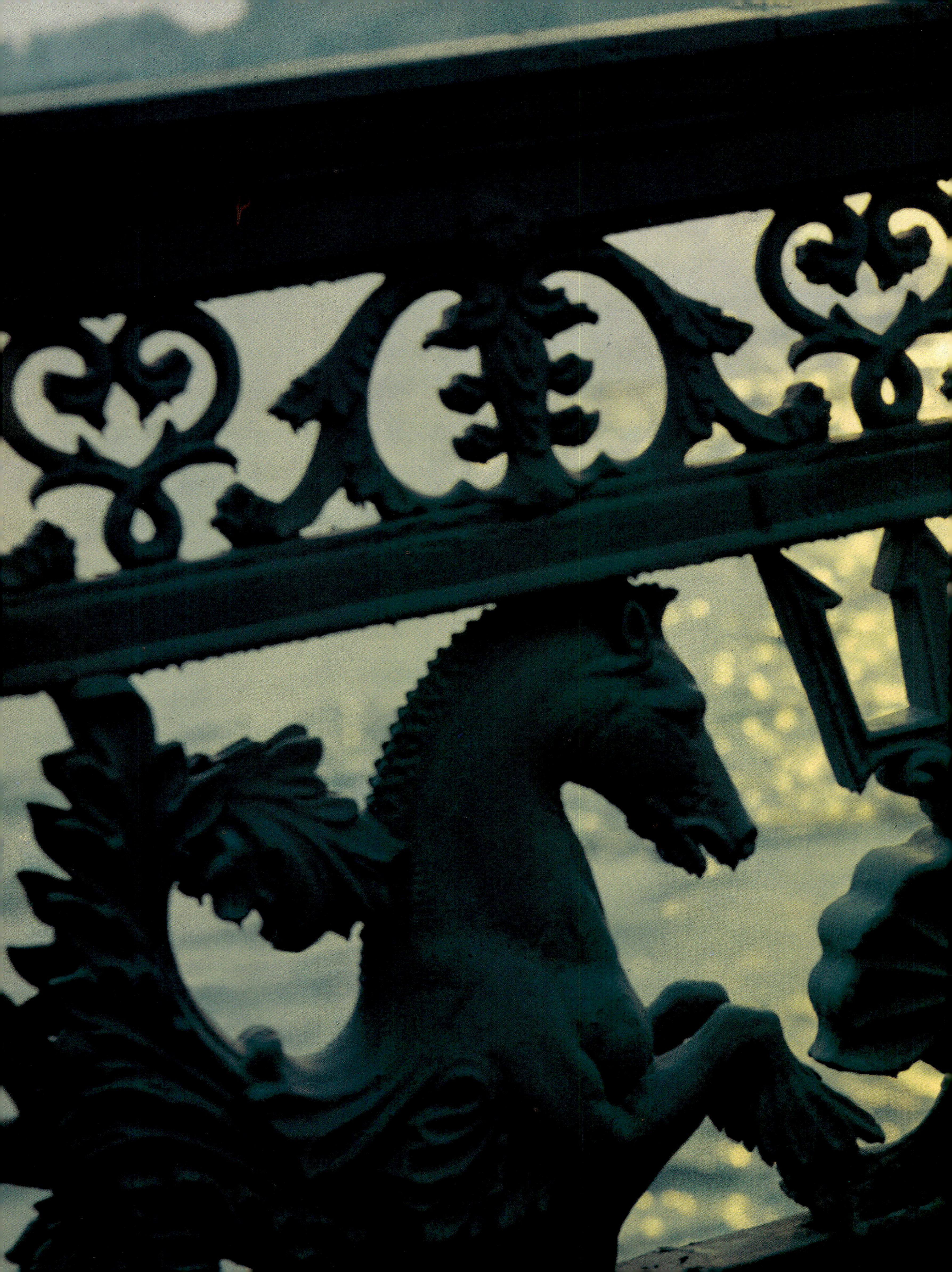

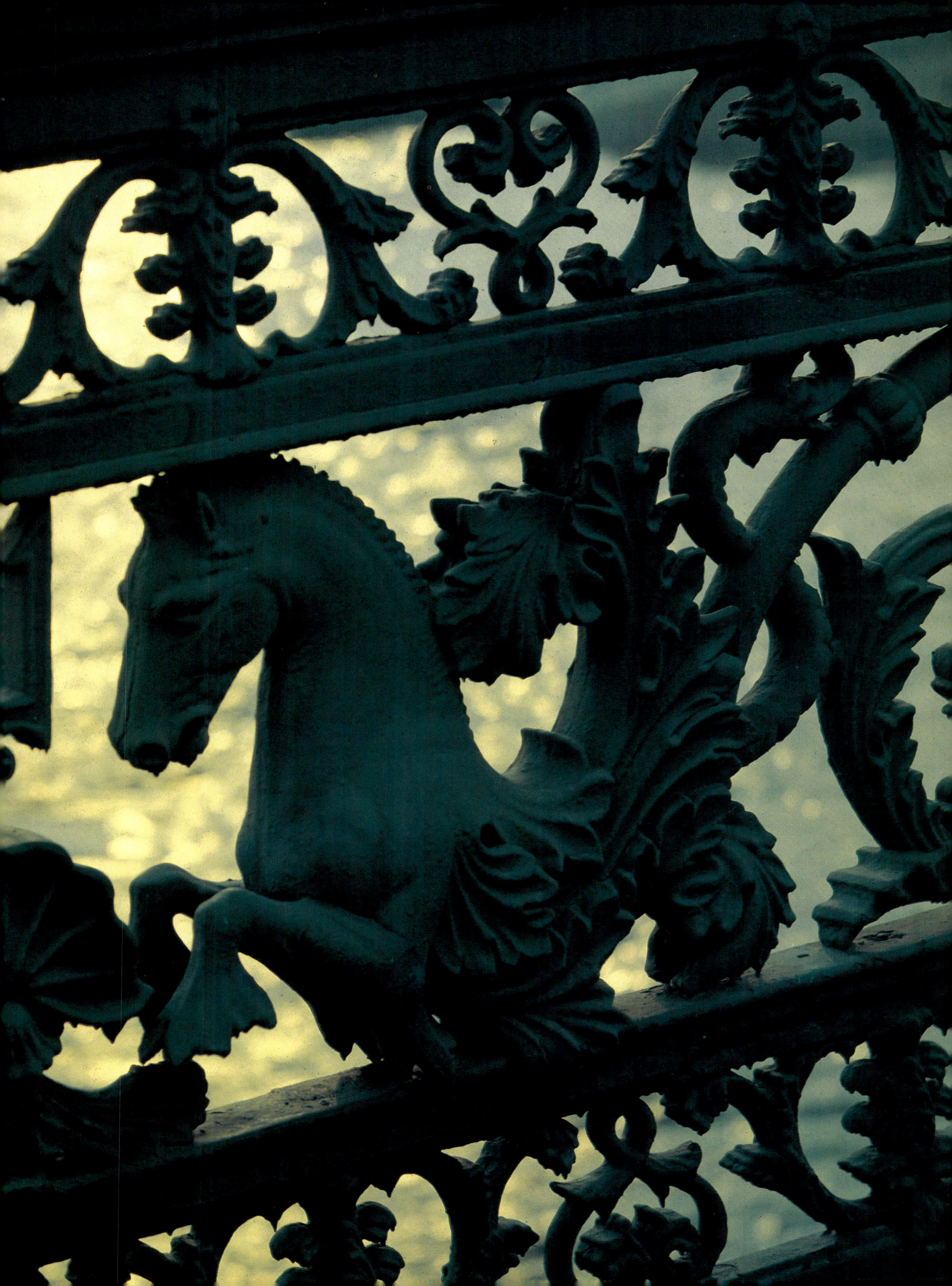

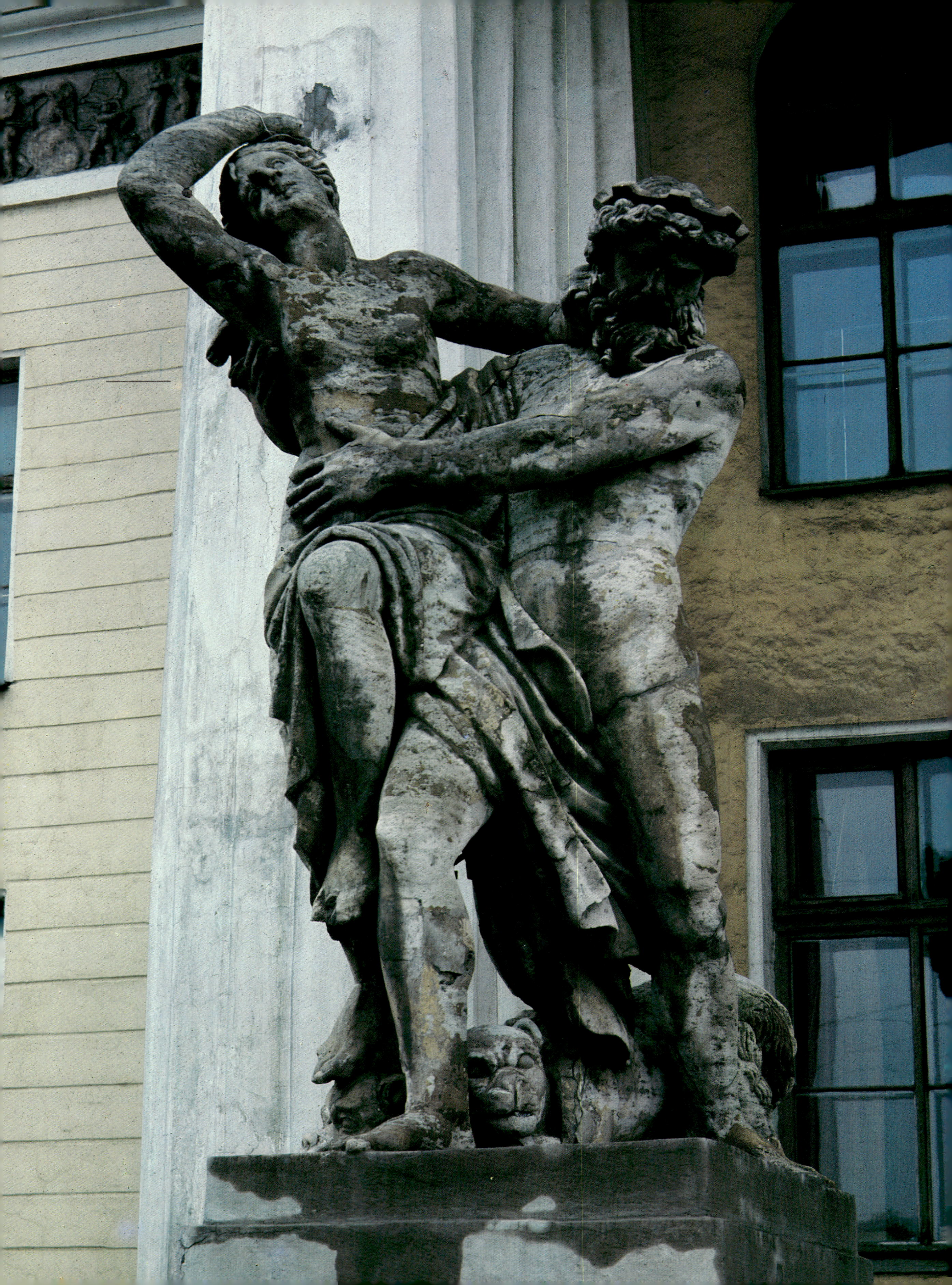

210 St. Nicholas' Bridge. Railing

211, 212 Mining Institute

213 Kshesinsky residence
214 Sphynx on the Sverdlovskaya Embankment
215 Byelogrud House in Leo Tolstoy Square

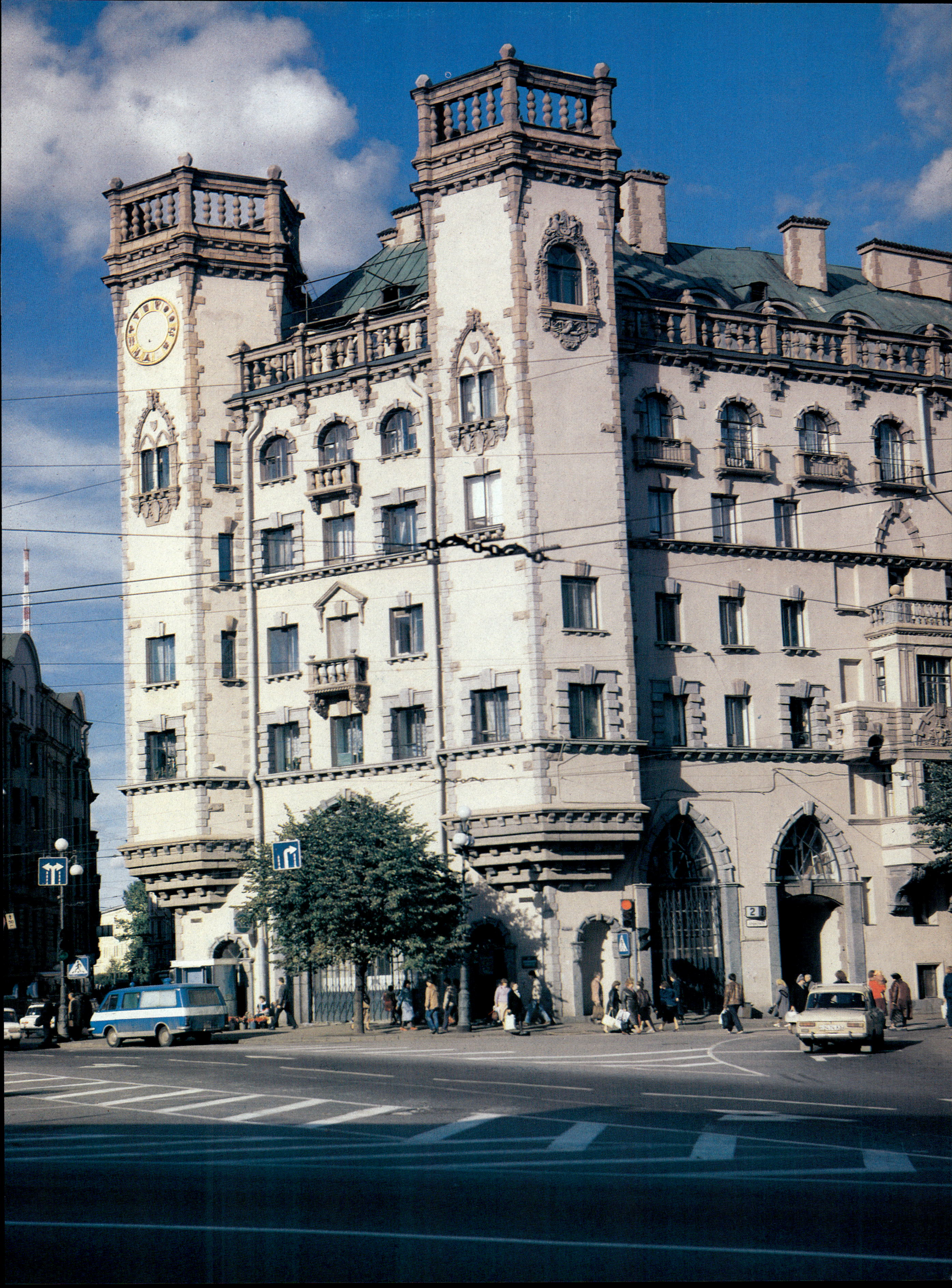
2

216
→
217

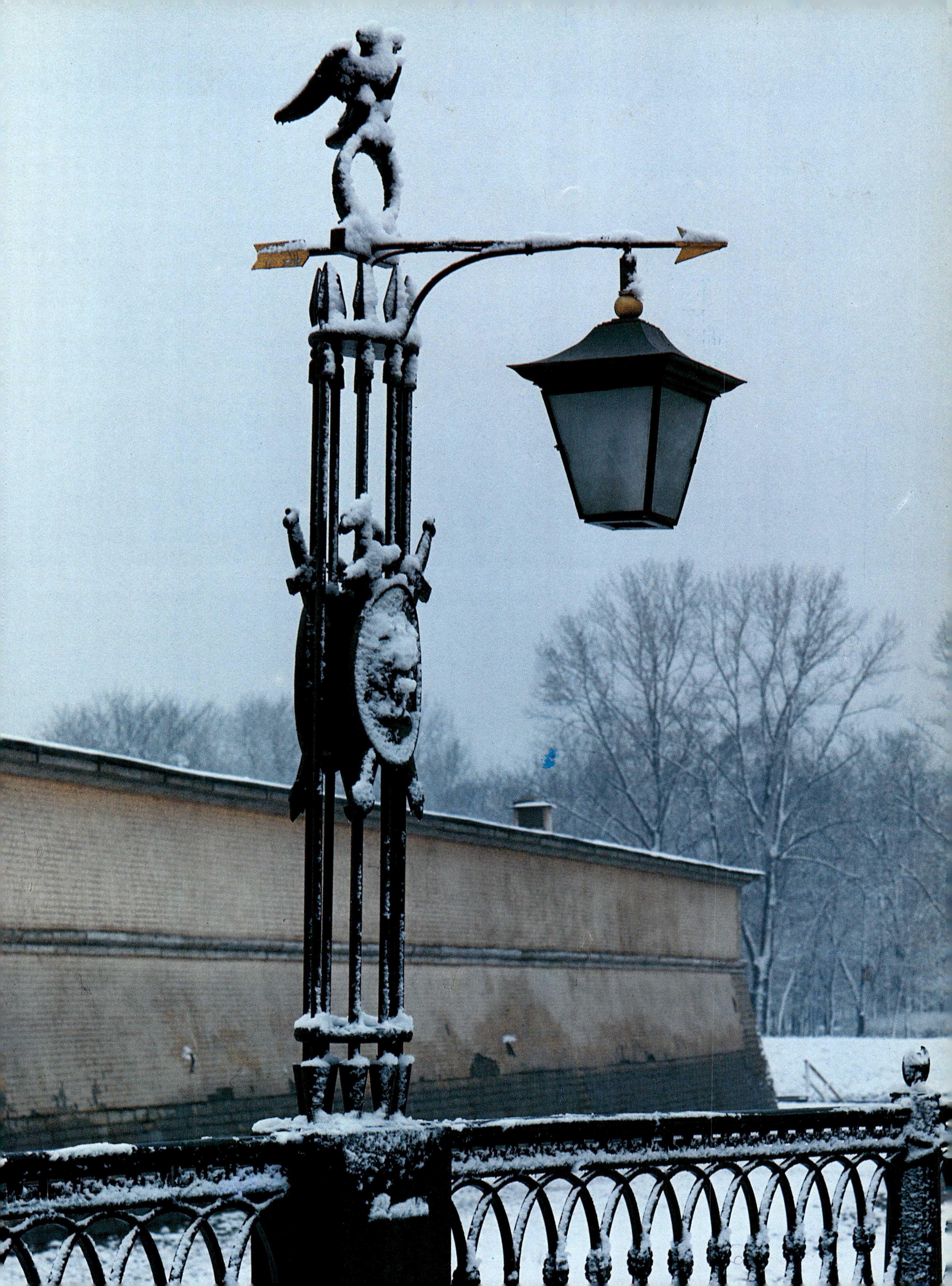

216 Monument of the «Steregushchy» sailors
217 St. John's Bridge. Lamp post
218 Pushkin House (Customs House)
219 Petrogradskaya Embankment
220 Nevsky Prospect near the Admiralty

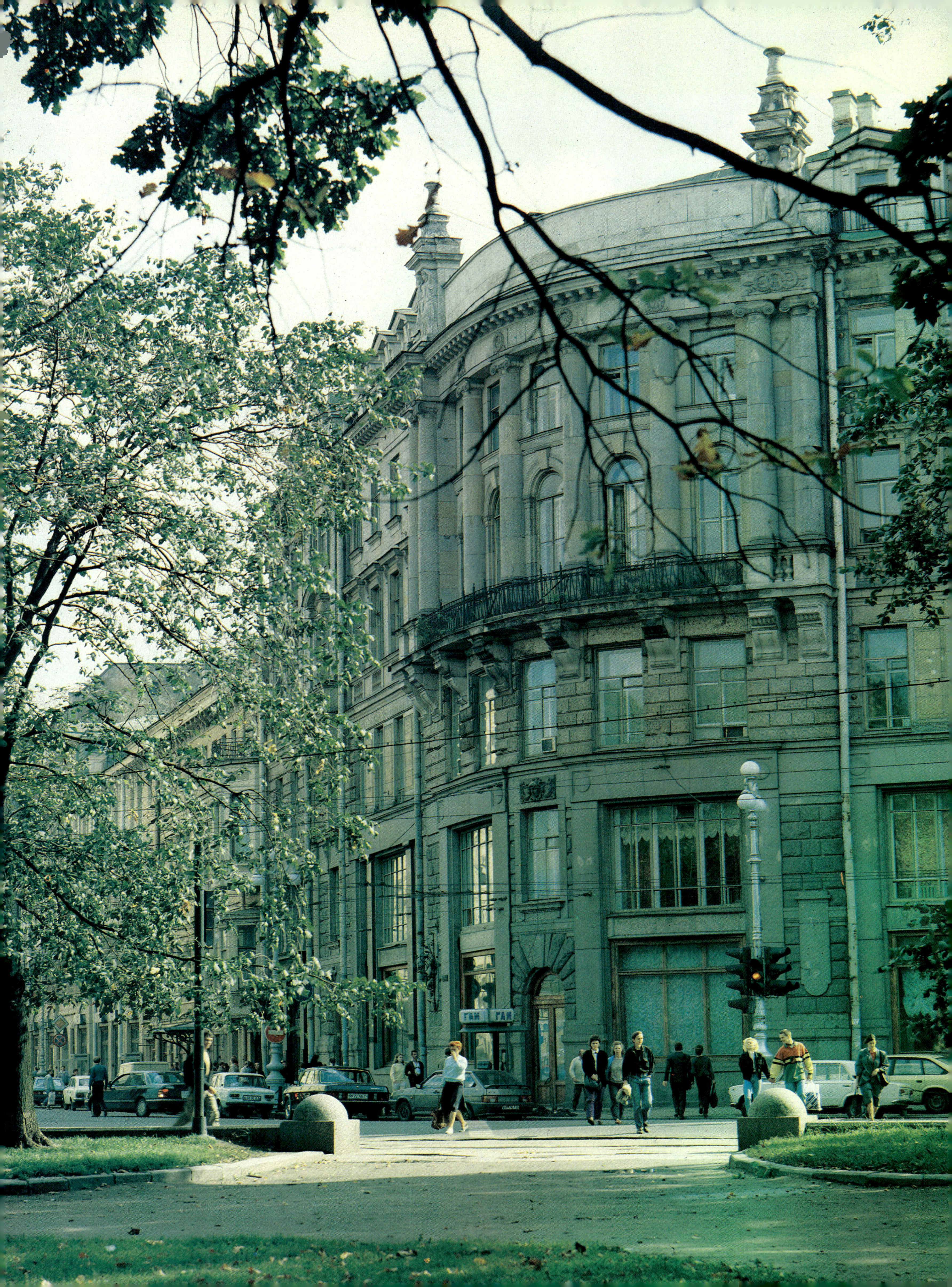
ГАИ ГАИ

221 *Mytninskaya Embankment*
222 *Faberge House*

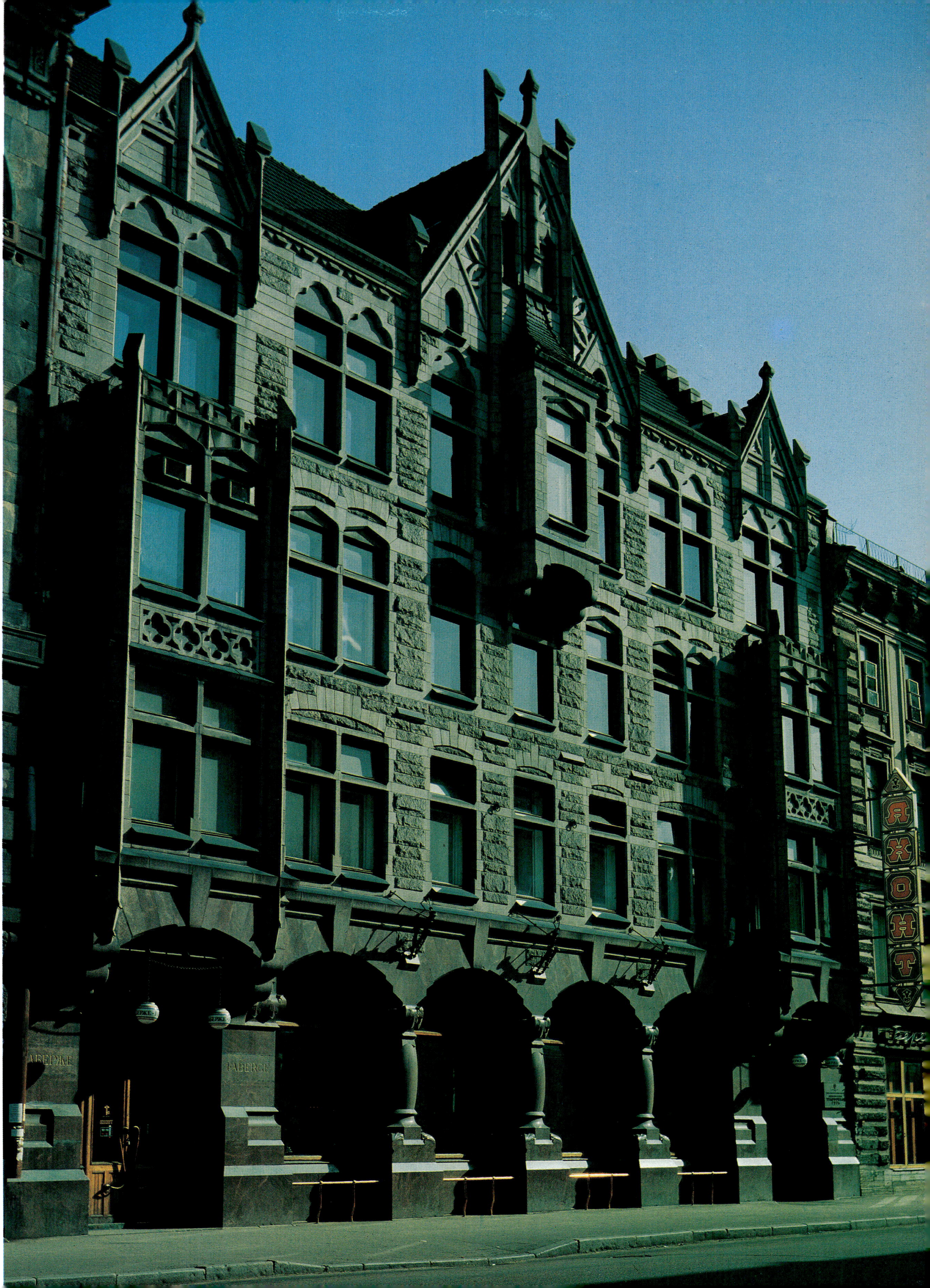
ЯХОНТ
FABERGE

223 *Astoria Hotel*
224 *St. Isaac's Cathedral*

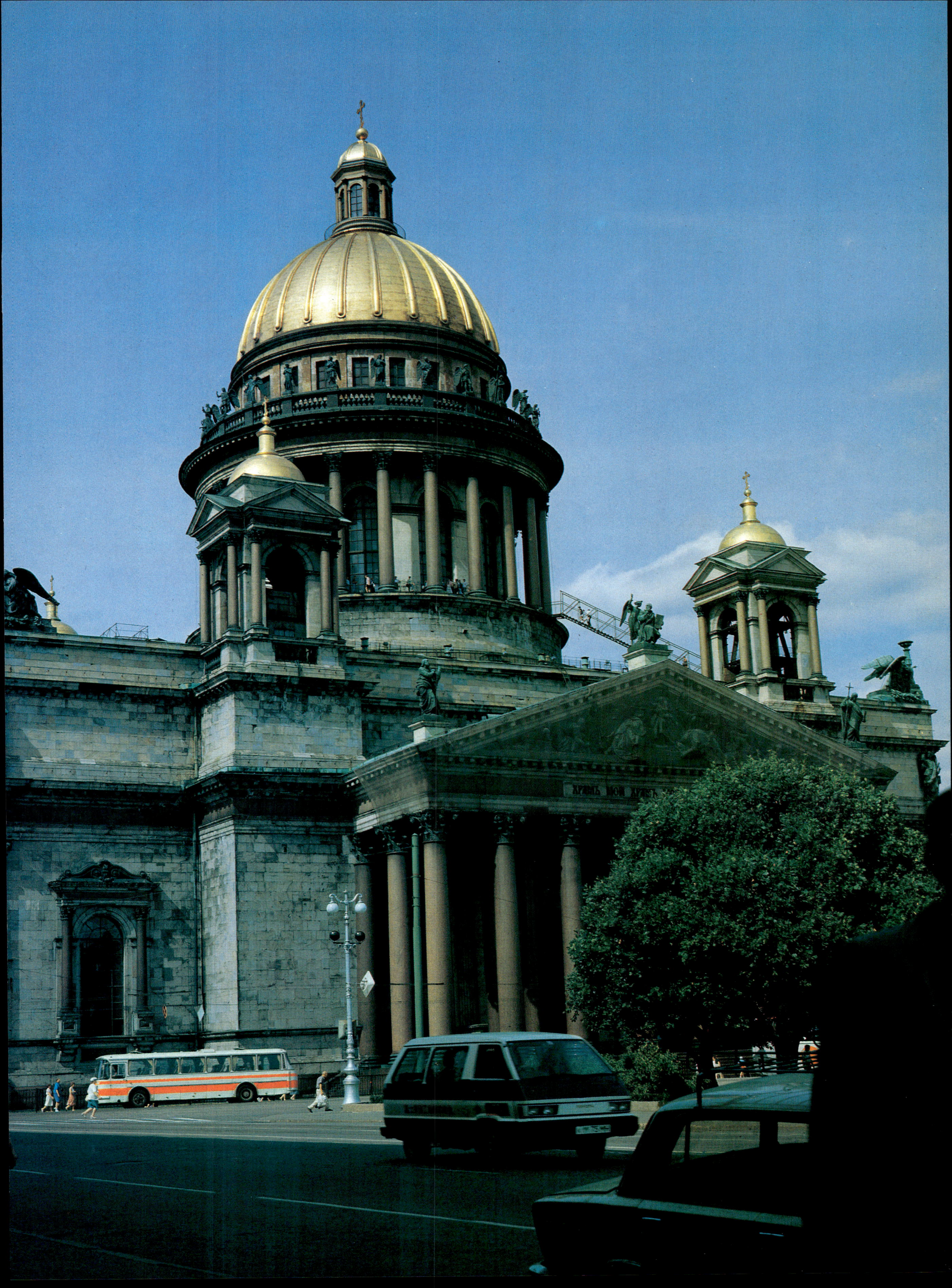

225 Choristers' Capella
226 Marble Palace

227 Trinity Bridge

228 Manege →

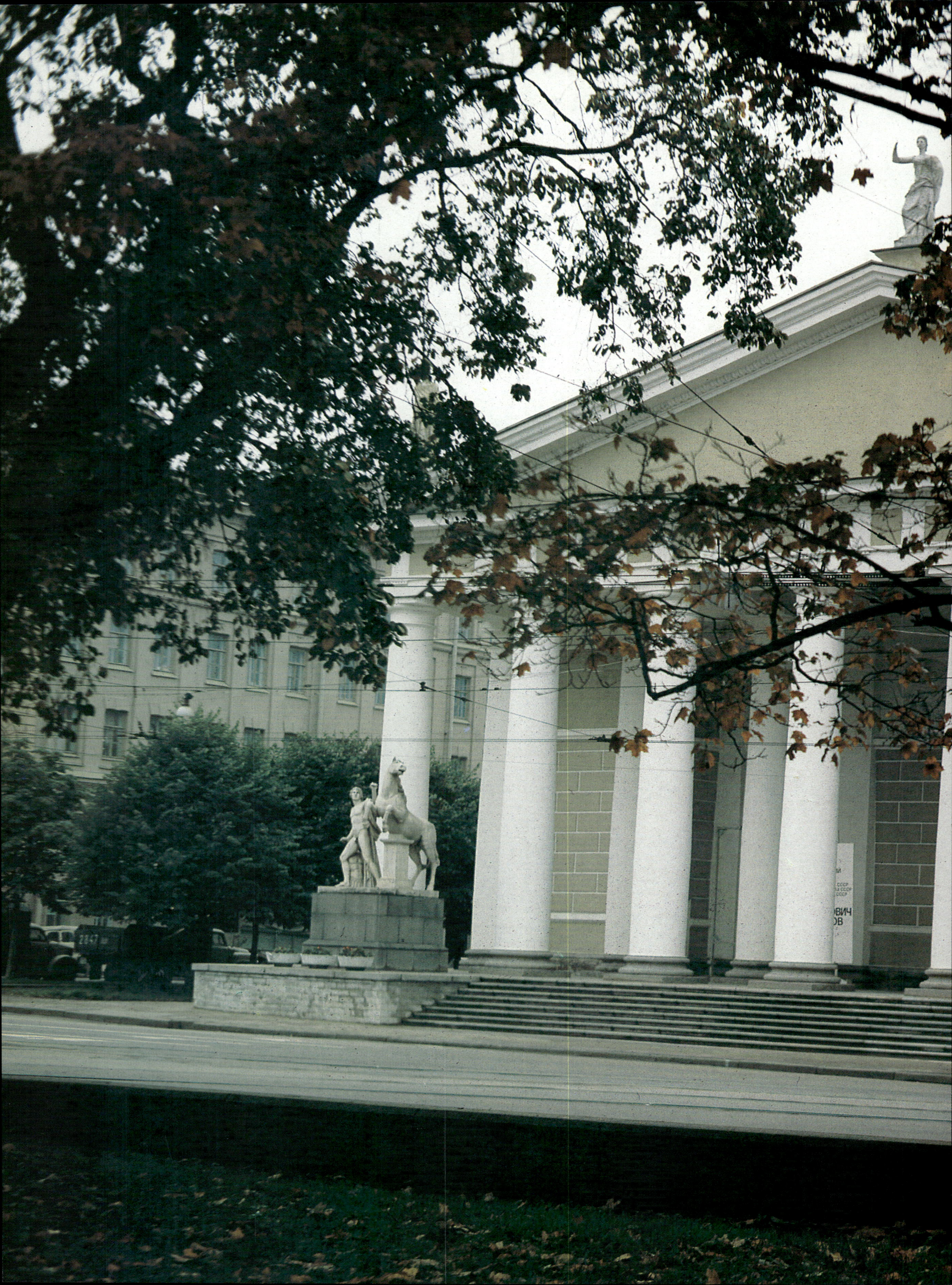

229 Moika Embankment
230 Moscow Triumphal Arch

231 Narva Triumphal Arch

ПОБѢДОНОСНОЙ РОССІЙСКОЙ ИМПЕРАТОРСКОЙ ГВАРДІИ
ПРИЗНАТЕЛЬНОЕ ОТЕЧЕСТВО ВЪ 17 Д. АВГУСТА 1834.
VICTRICIBUS ROSSICIS LEGION. IMP. CORP. CUSTOD.
GRATA PATRIA. D. XVII. M. AUG. AN. MDCCCXXXIV.
КУЛЬМЪ.
ЛЕЙПЦИГЪ.
Ф. ШАМПЕНУАЗЪ.
ПАРИЖЪ.
ПОВЕЛѢНІЕМЪ АЛЕКСАНДРА ПЕРВАГО
ПОЛКИ
ИМПЕРАТОРСКОЙ ГВАРДІИ
КОННИЦА:
КАВАЛЕРГАРДСКІЙ
КОННЫЙ
КИРАСИРСКІЙ
КОННАЯ АРТИЛЛЕРІЯ
ПОЛКИ
ИМПЕРАТОРСКОЙ ГВАРДІИ
КОННИЦА:
ДРАГУНСКІЙ
ГУСАРСКІЙ
УЛАНСКІЙ
КОЗАЧІЙ

232　*Smolny*
233　*Cruiser «Aurora»*

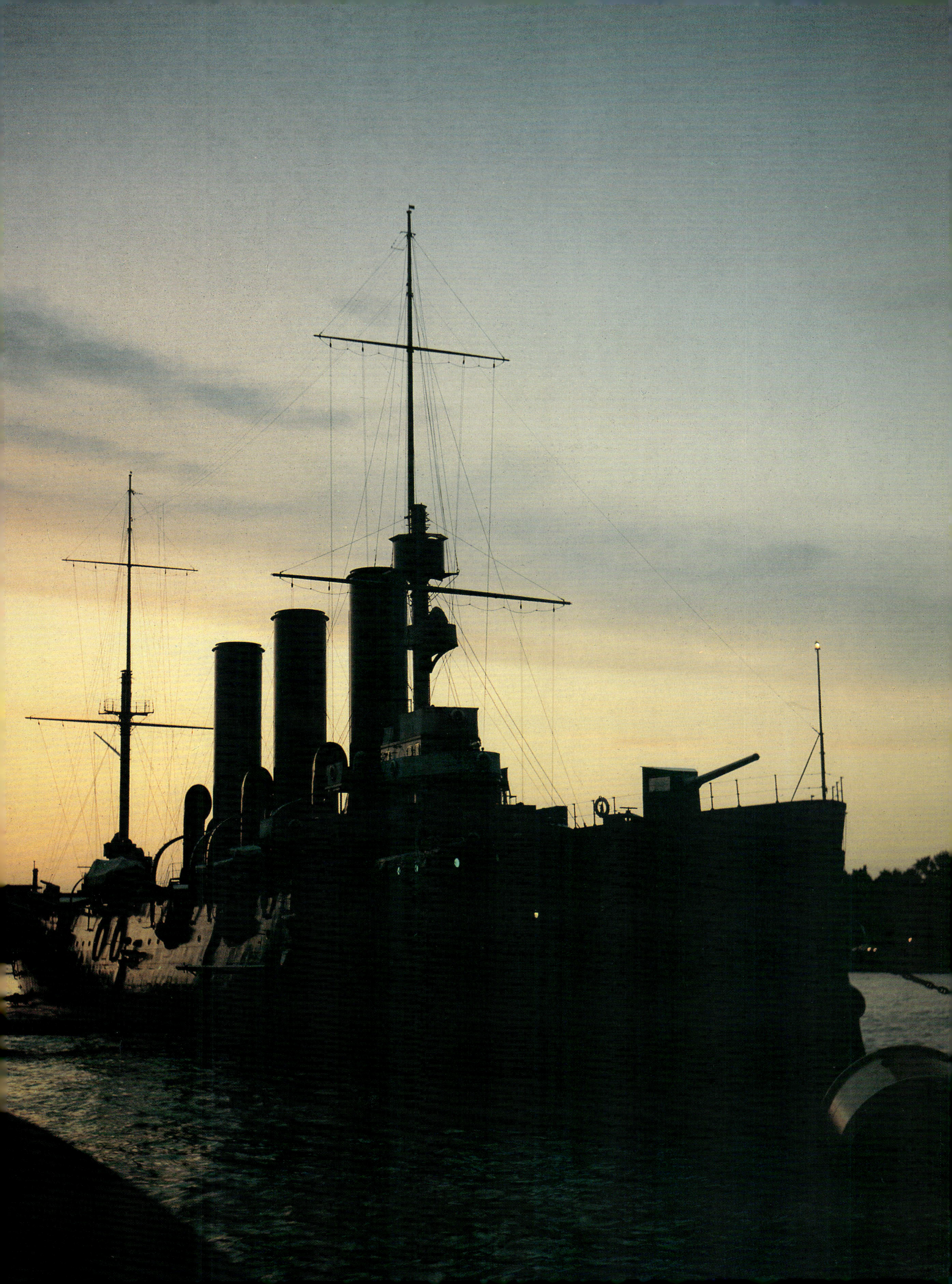

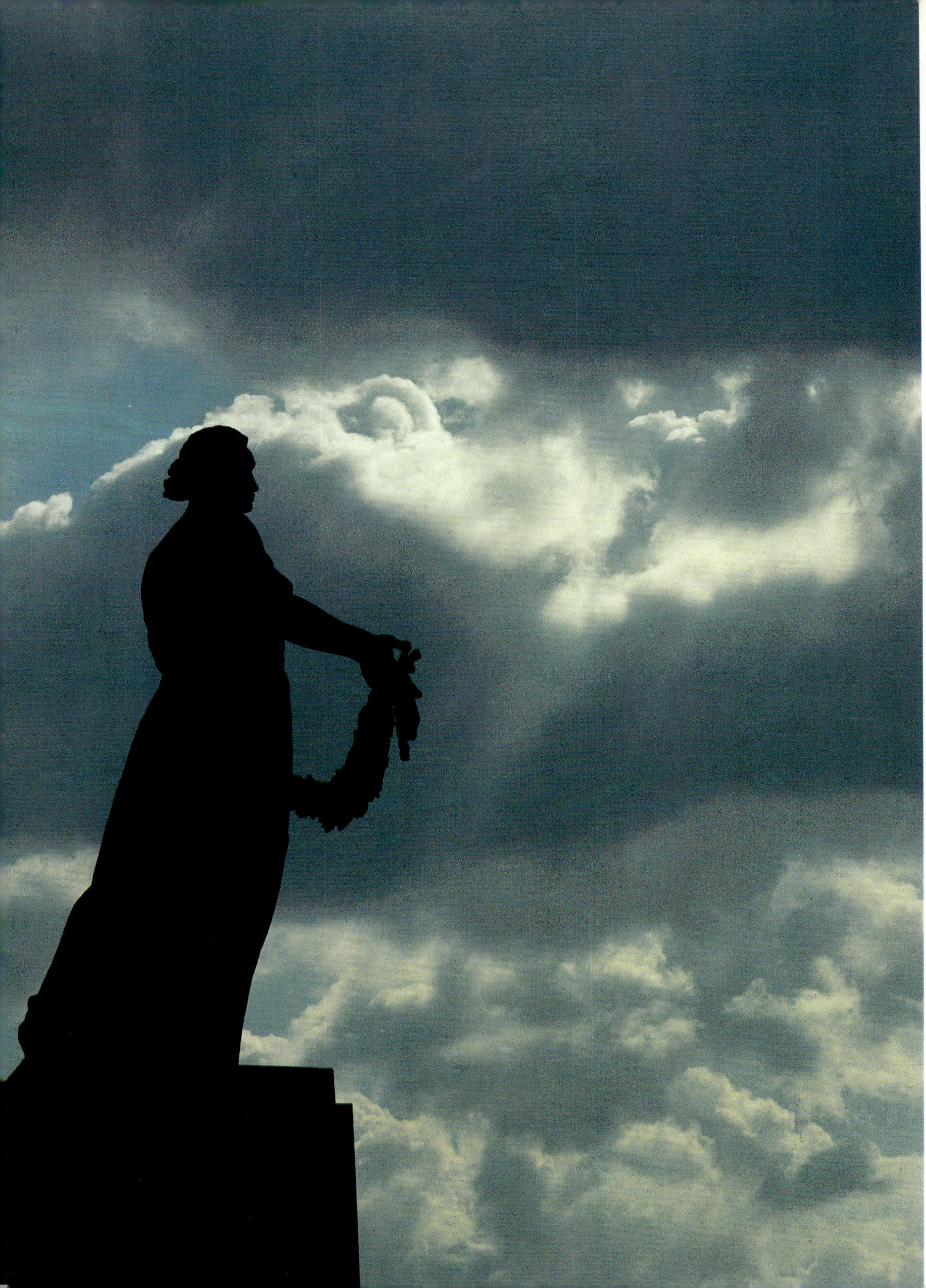

234, 236   *Piscarevsky Memorial Cemetery*
235   *Memorial to the Heroic Defenders of Leningrad*

237 *Naval Parade on the Neva*
238 *Neptune's Trident — a detail of the St. Nicholas' Bridge railing*

239 *St. Alexander Nevsky Bridge* →

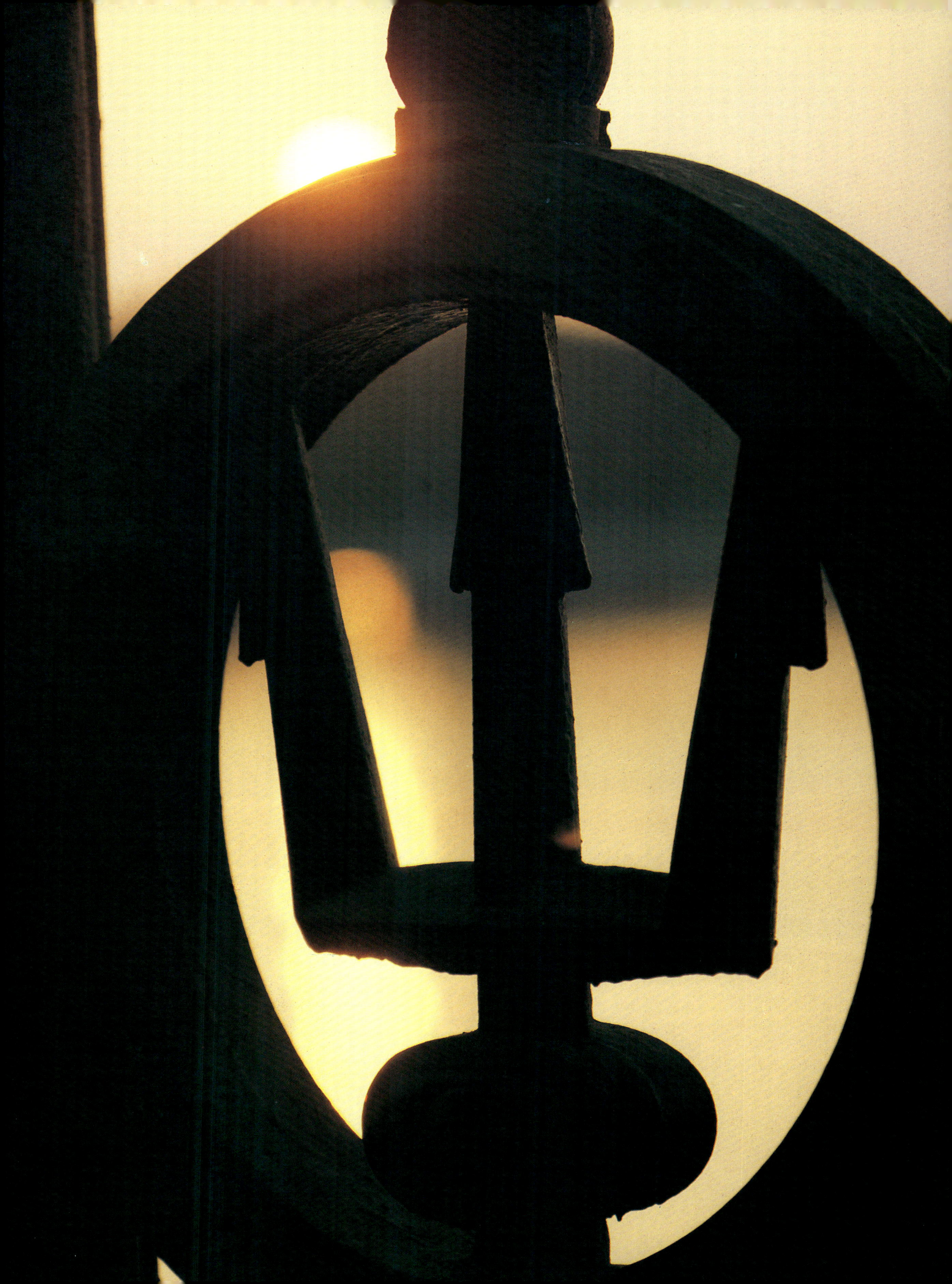

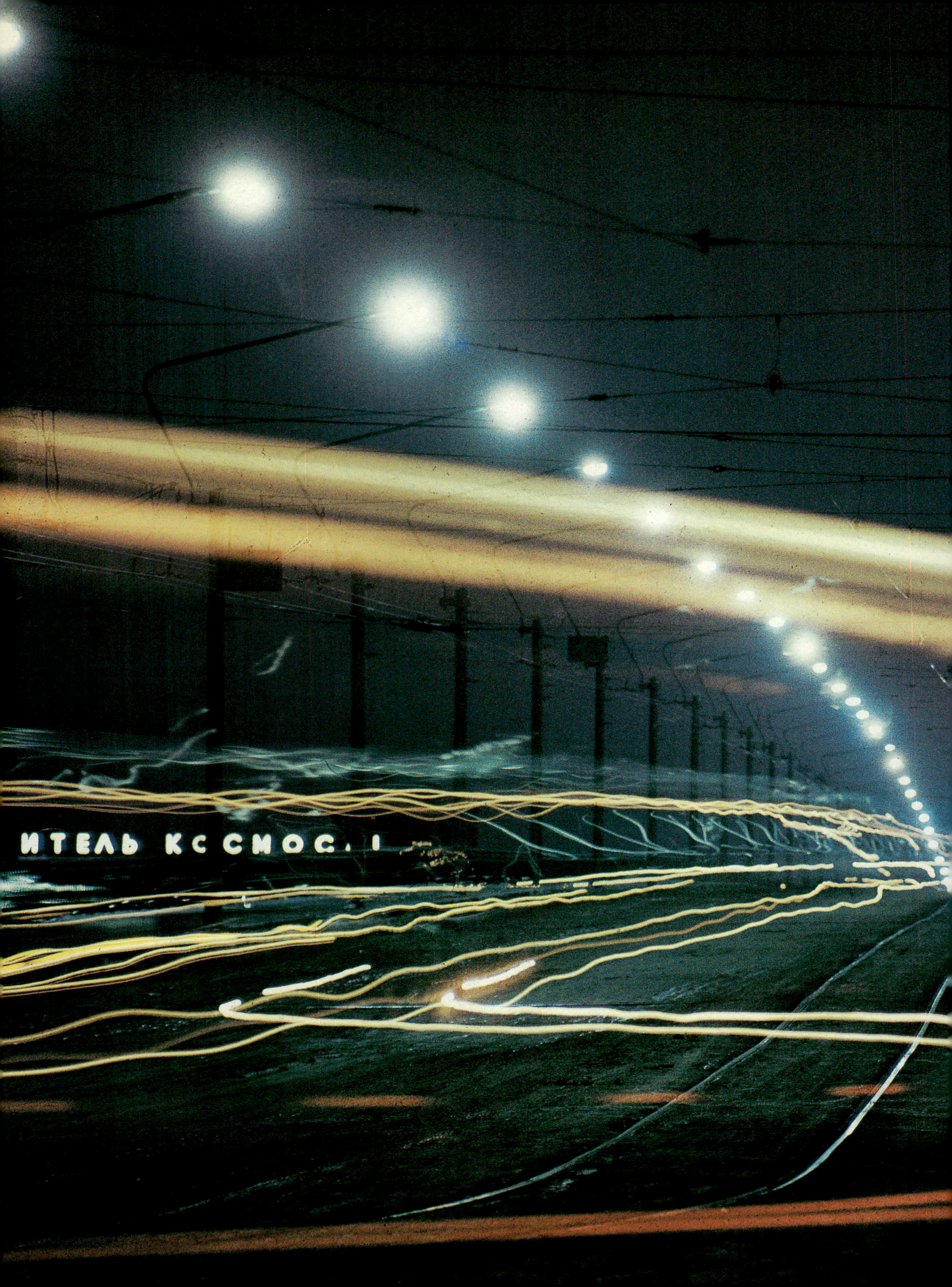
ИТЕЛЬ

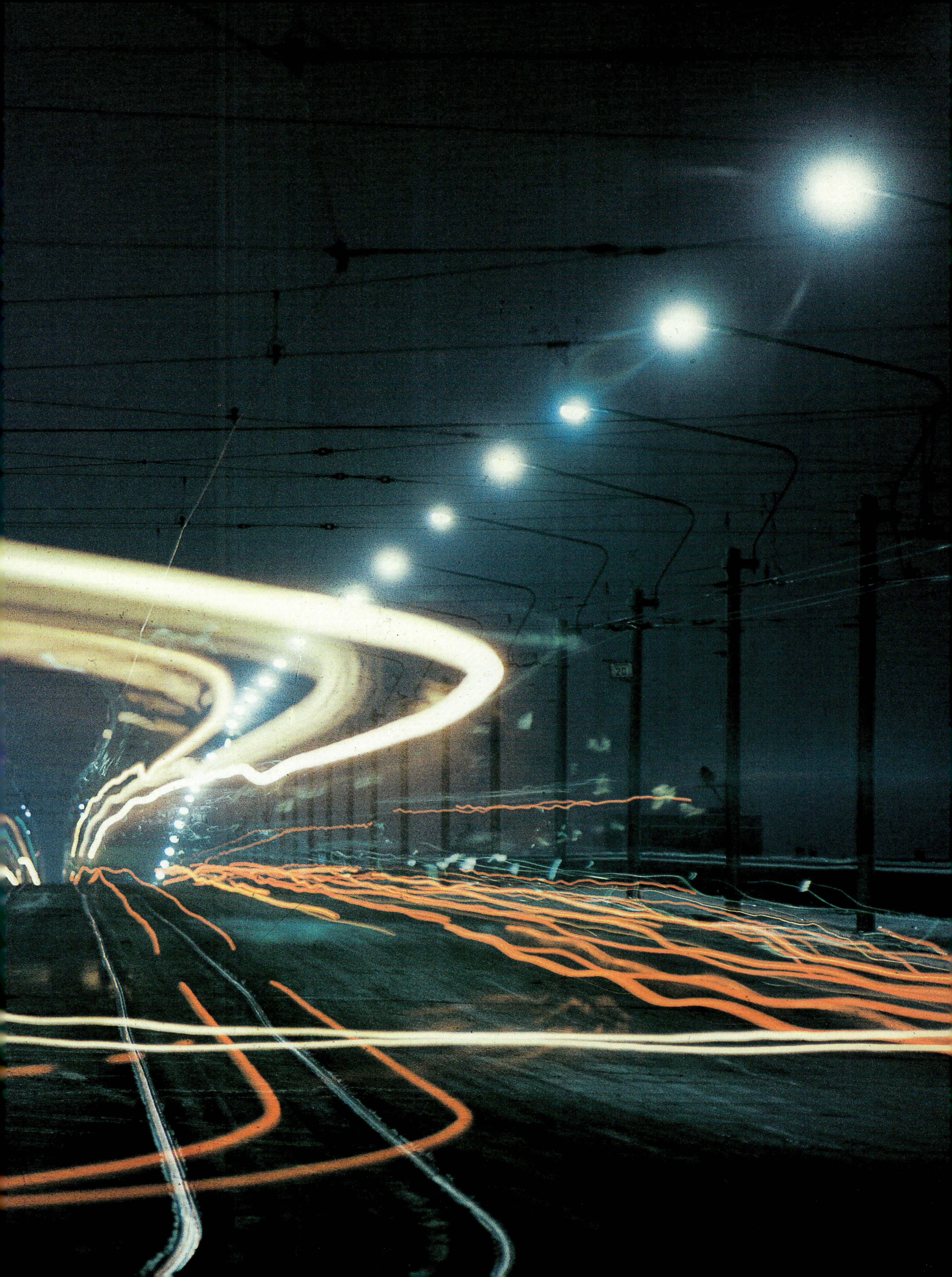

240   St. Petersburg Hotel
241   Moskva Hotel

242   Buddhist Temple

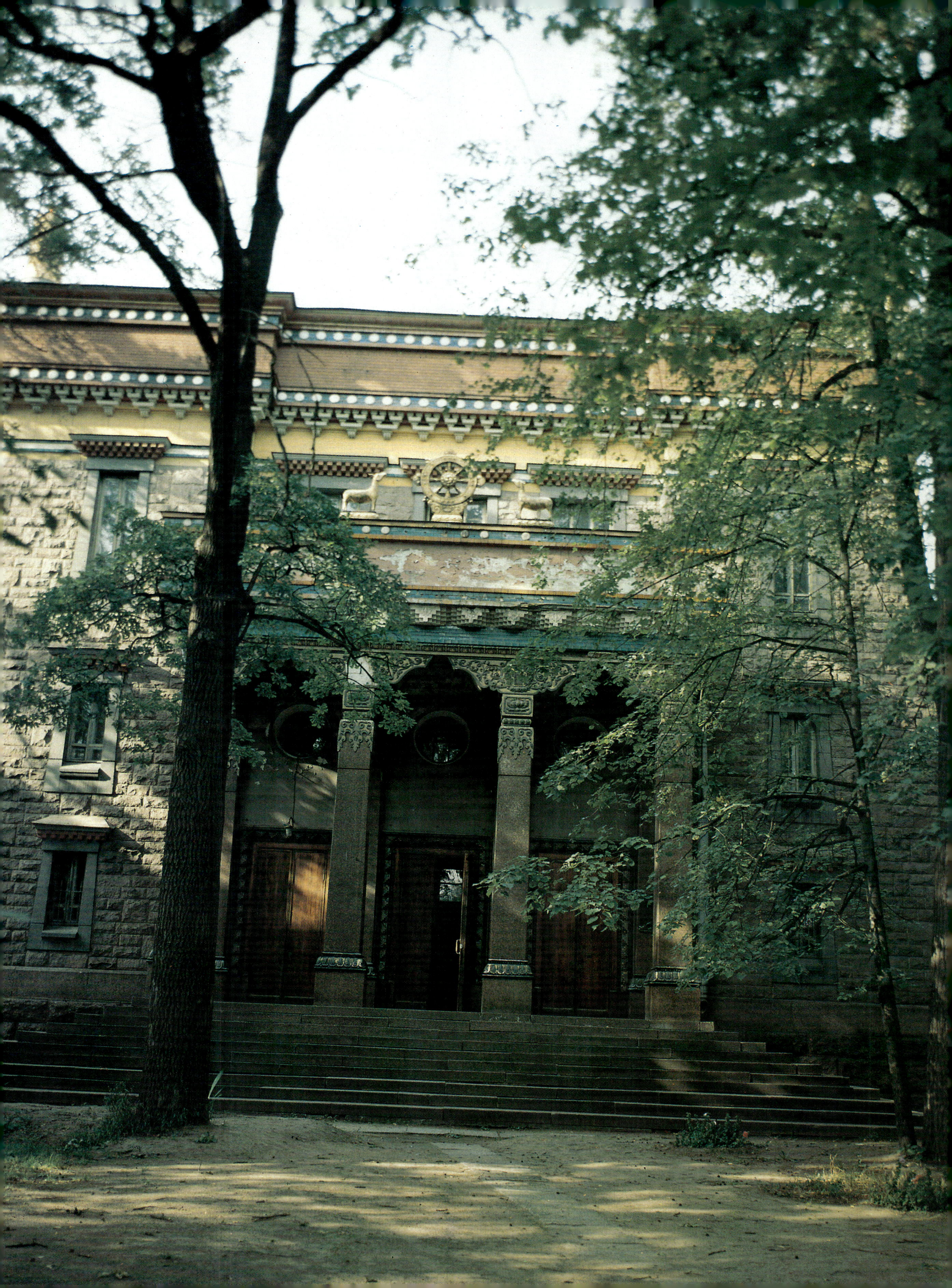

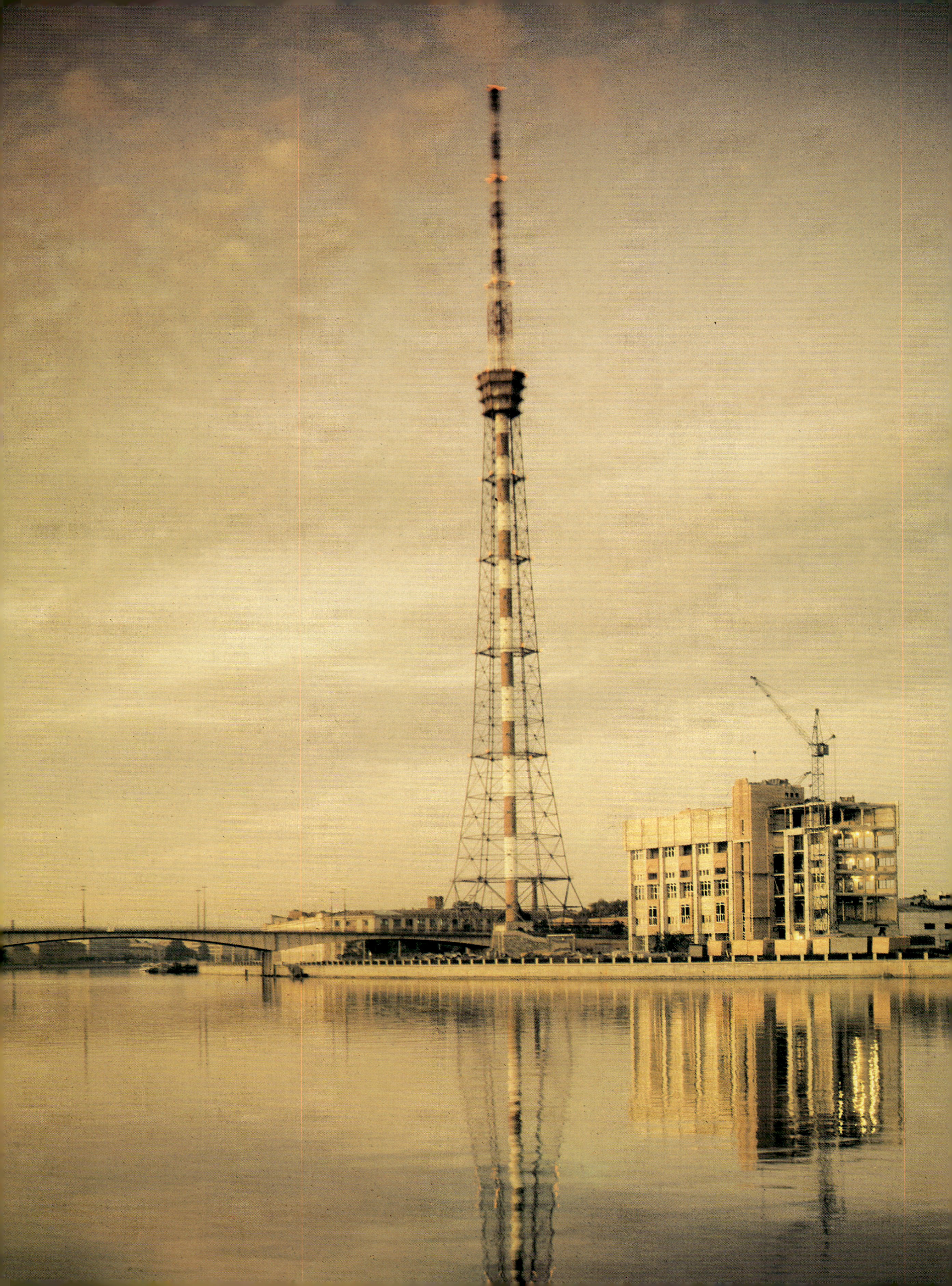

243 Petersburg television tower
244 Sphynx near the Egyptian Bridge
    over the Fontanka

245, 246   *Yelaghin Palace*

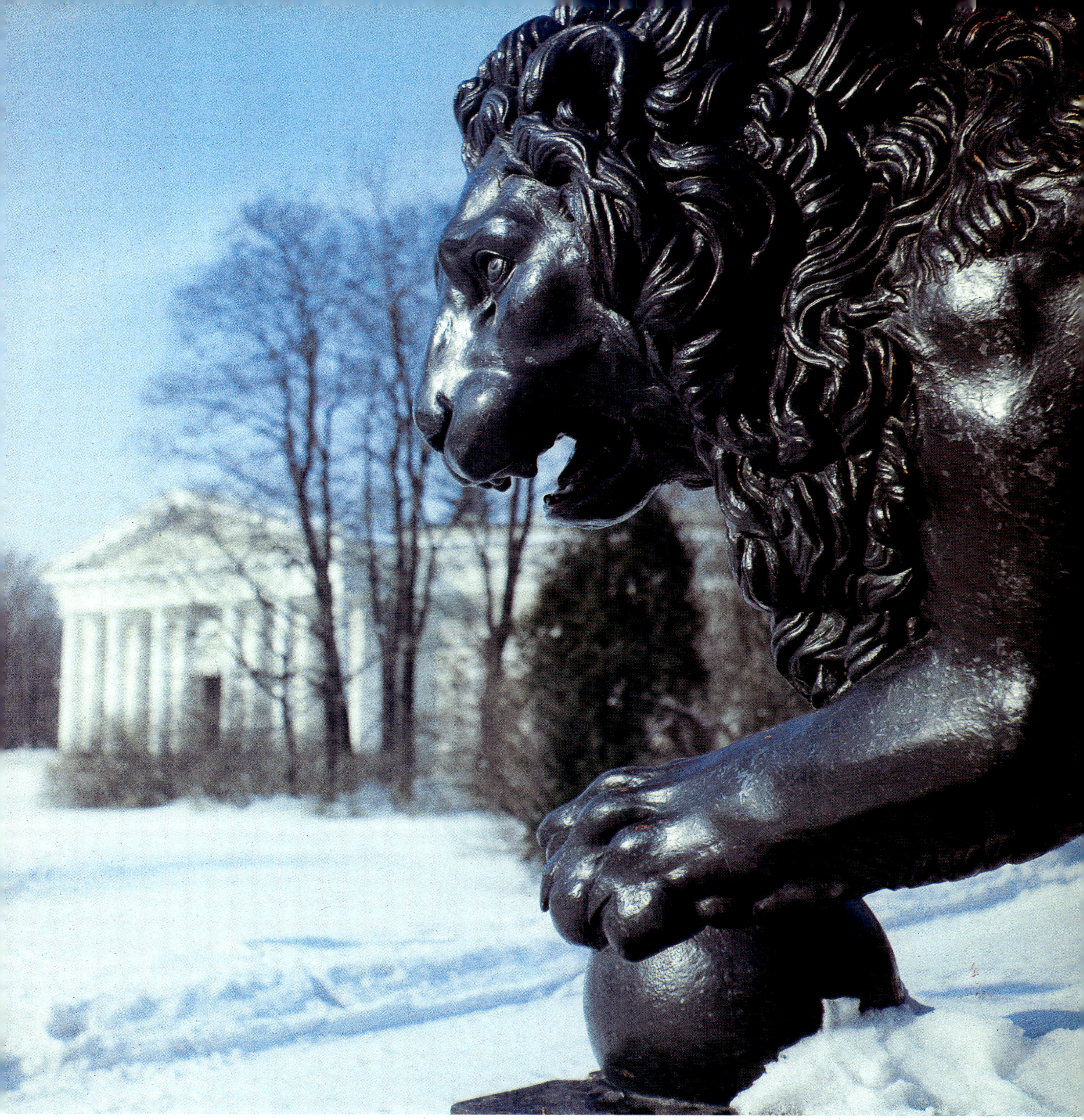

247, 248   *Pribaltiyskaya Hotel*
249   *Fire station in Sadovaya street*

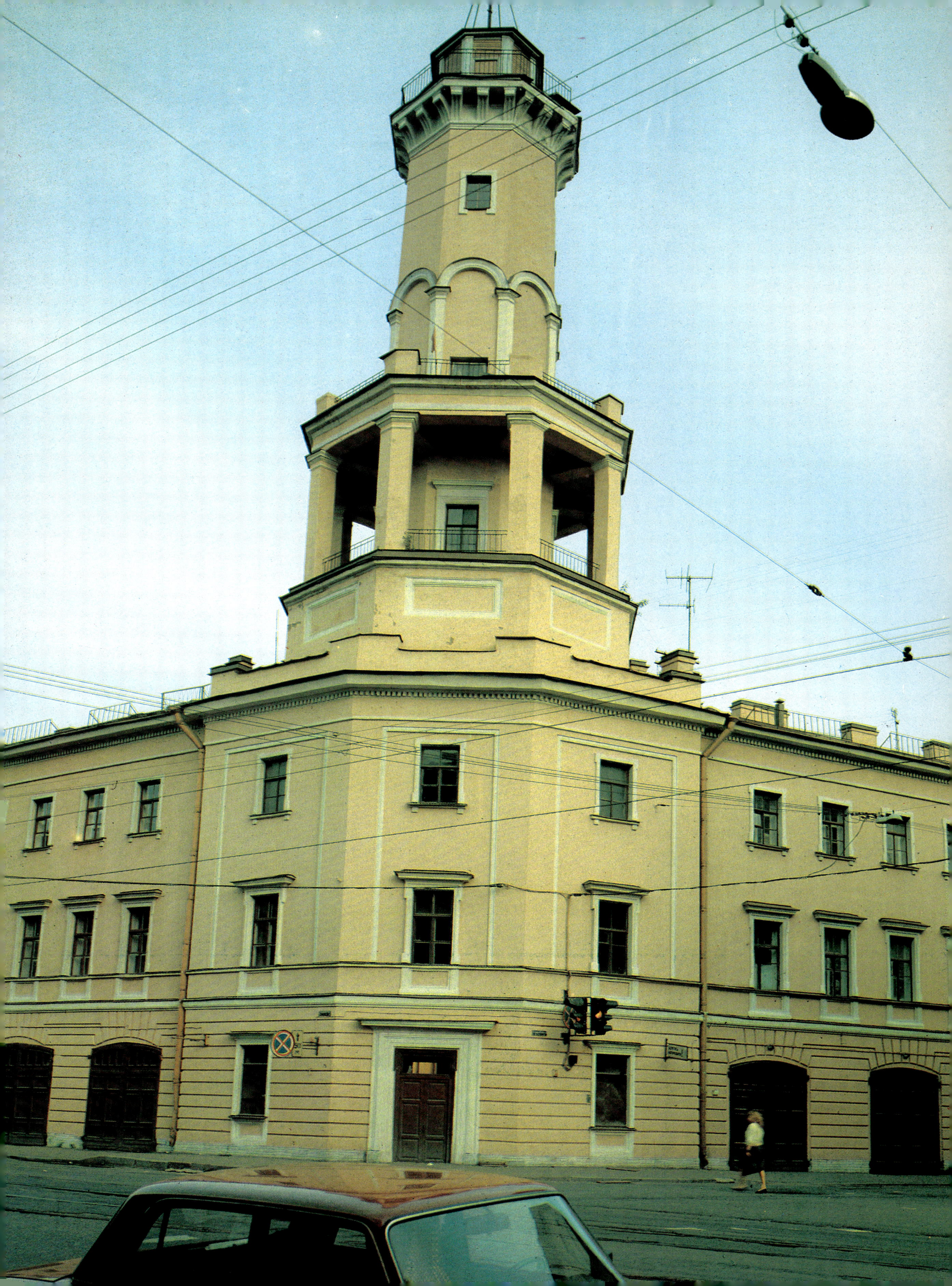

250 Petersburg yacht-club

251 Vitebsky Railway Station
252 Yelaghin Palace

253, 254 Pavlovsk. The Palace →

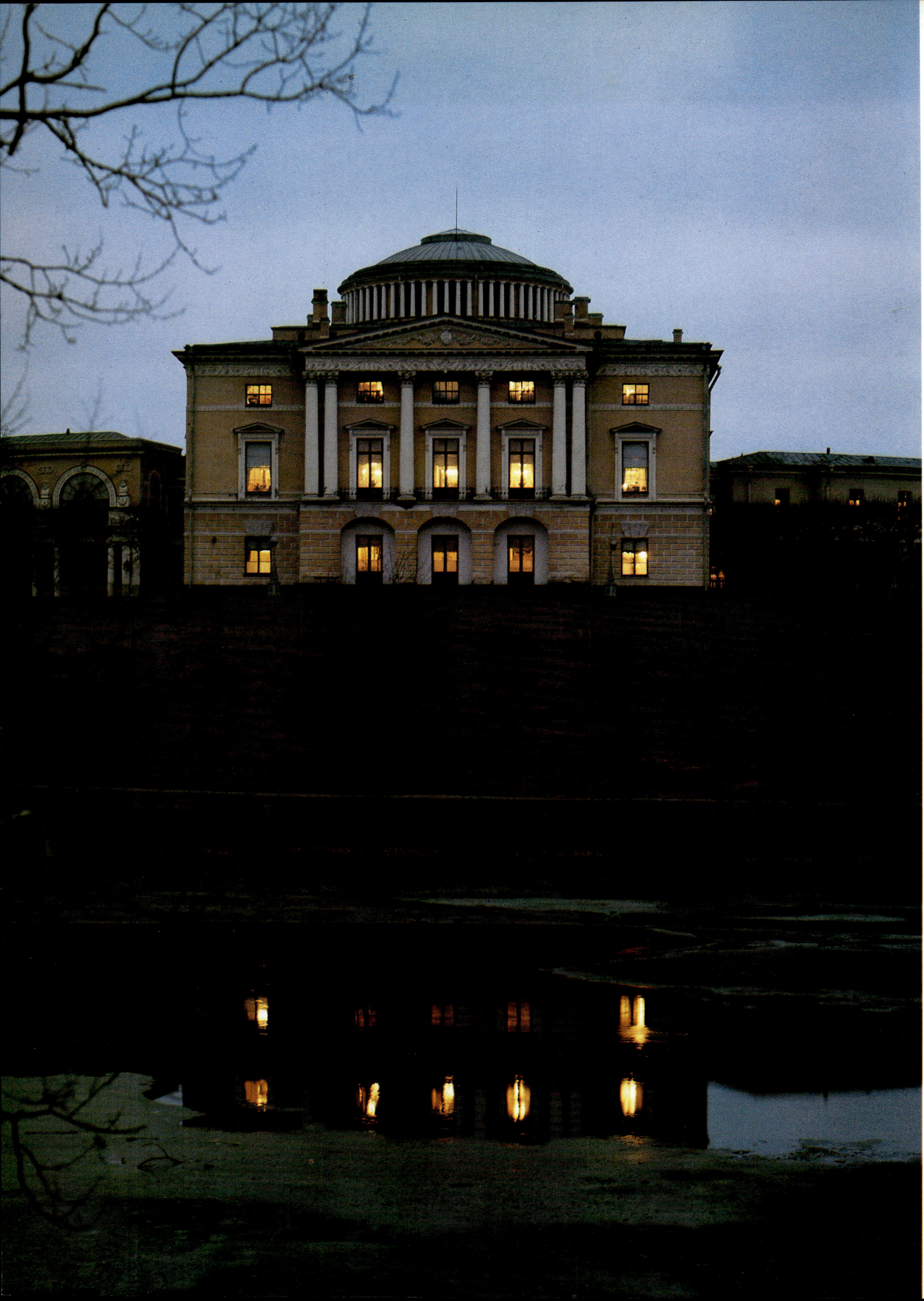

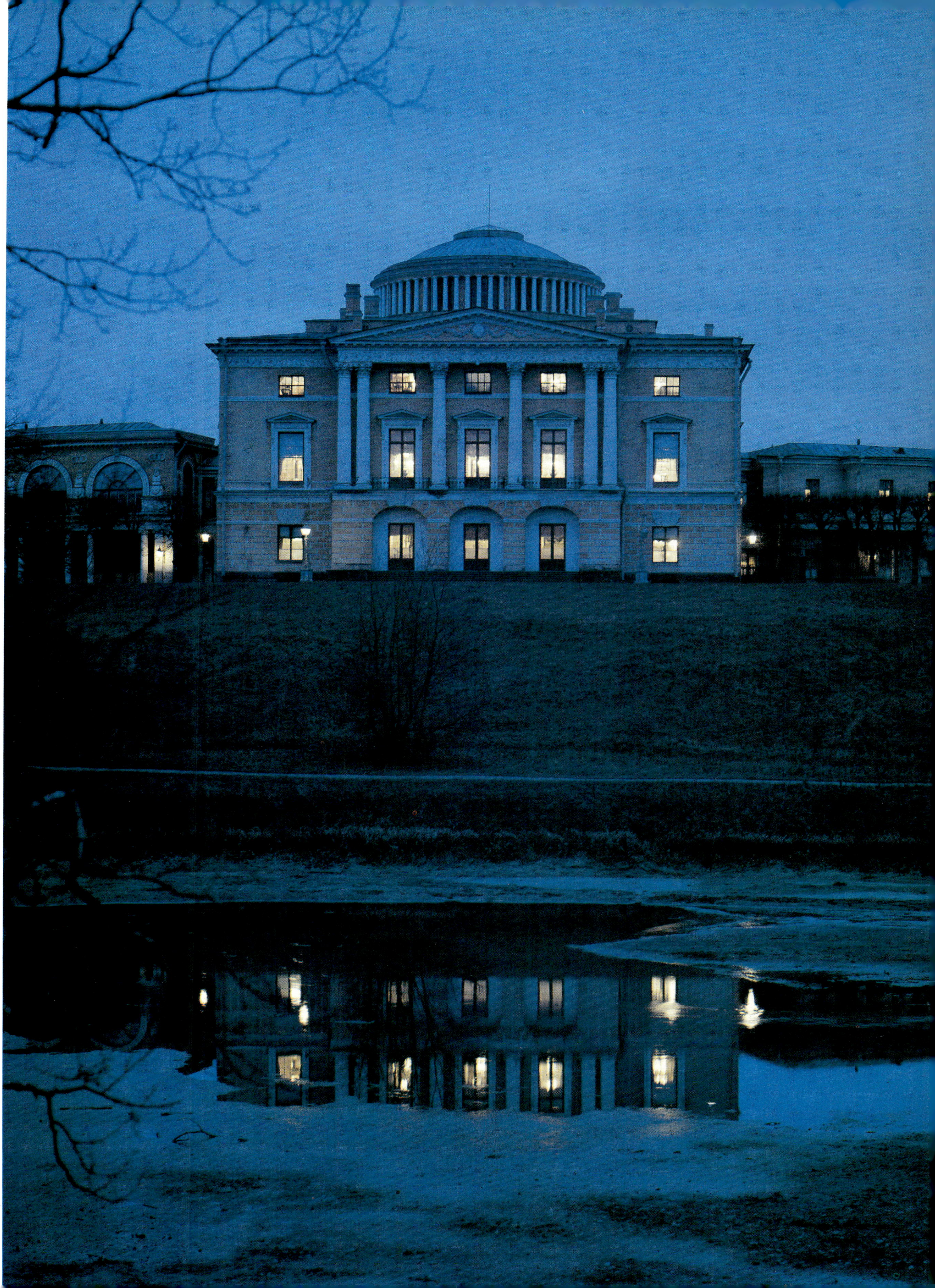

255 *Pavlovsk. The Peel Tower*
256 *Pavlovsk. The Palace. The Little Lantern*

257 *Pavlovsk. The Temple of Friendship* →
258, 259 *Pavlovsk. Apollo's Colonnade* →

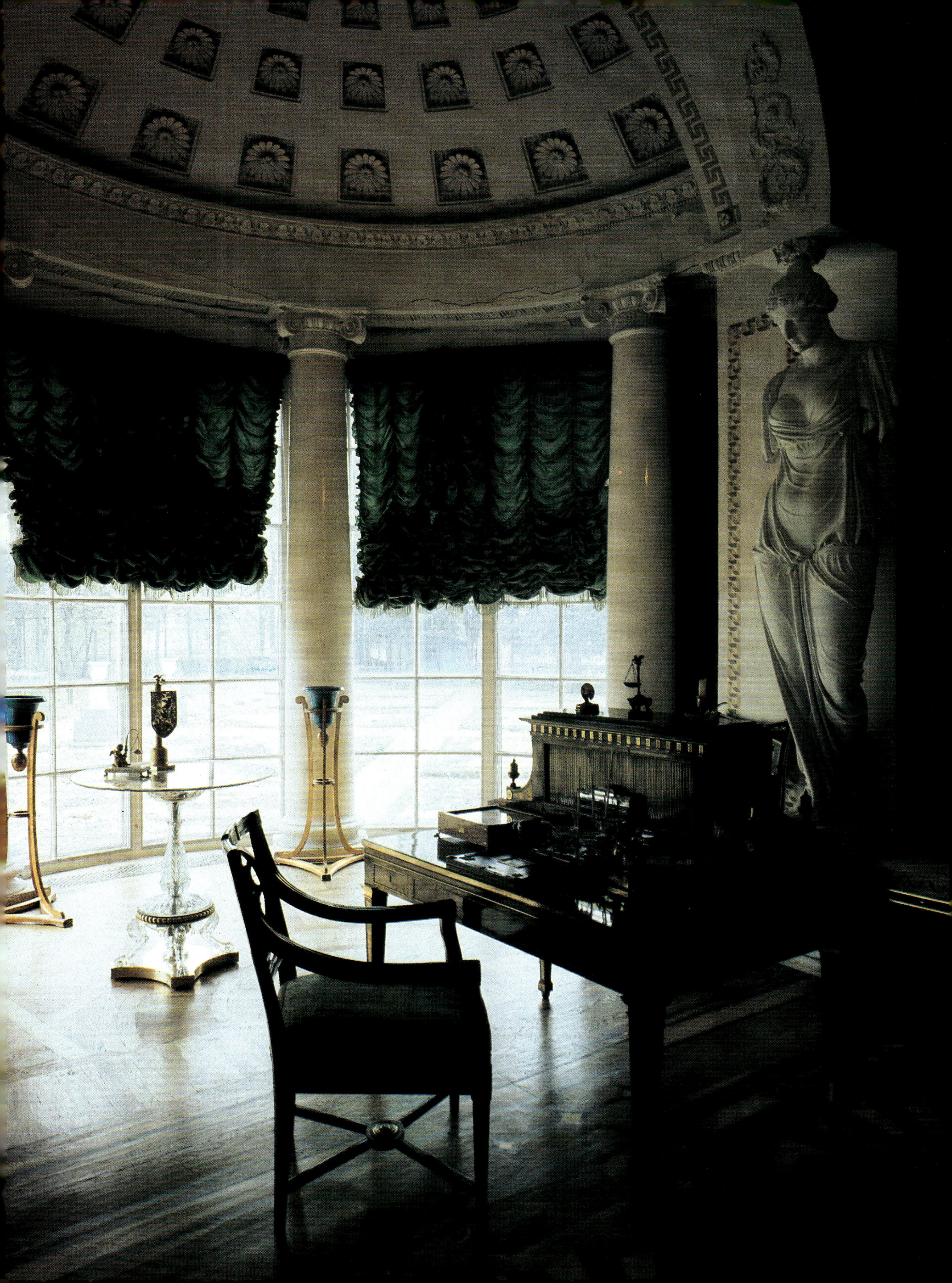

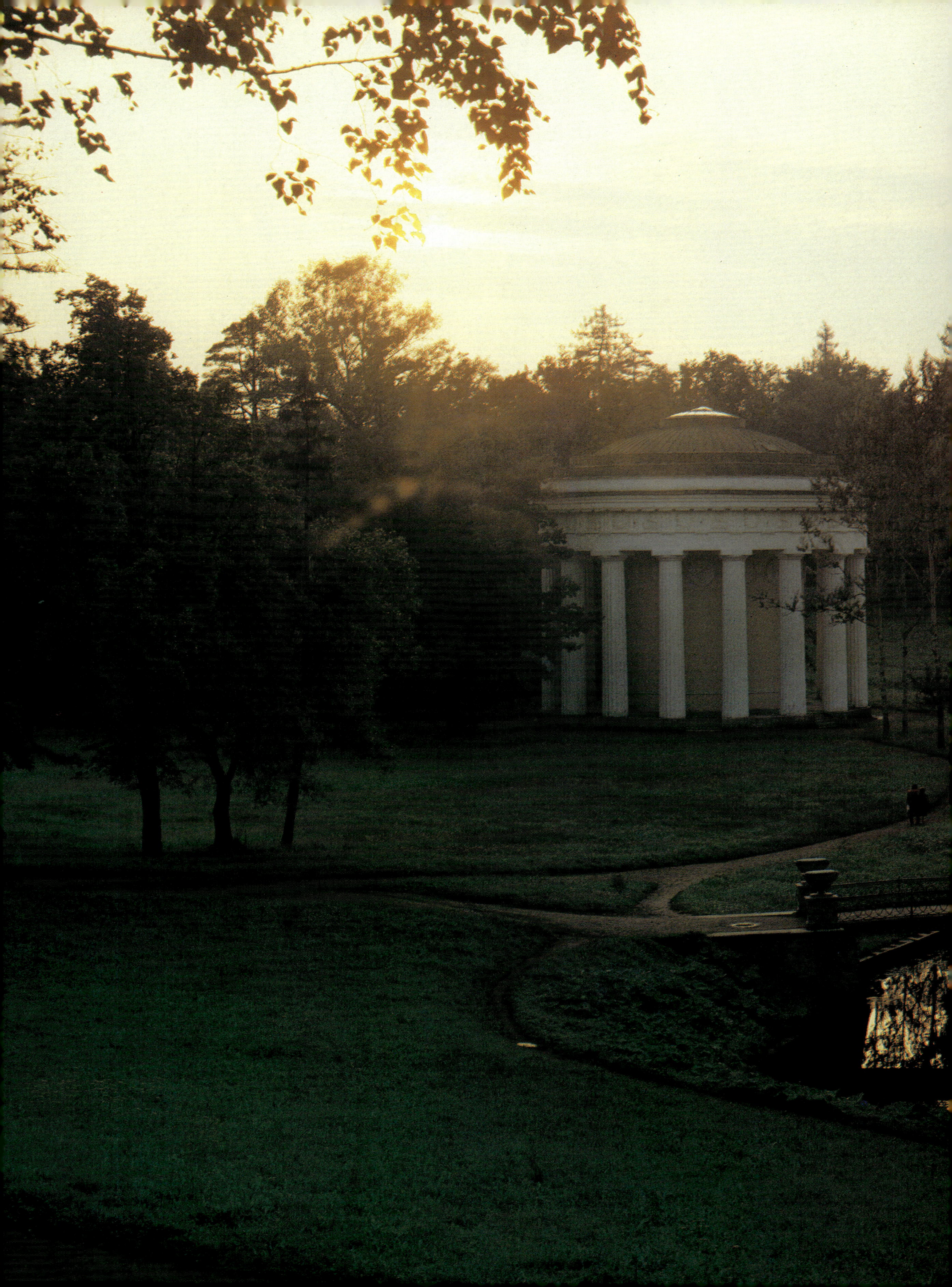

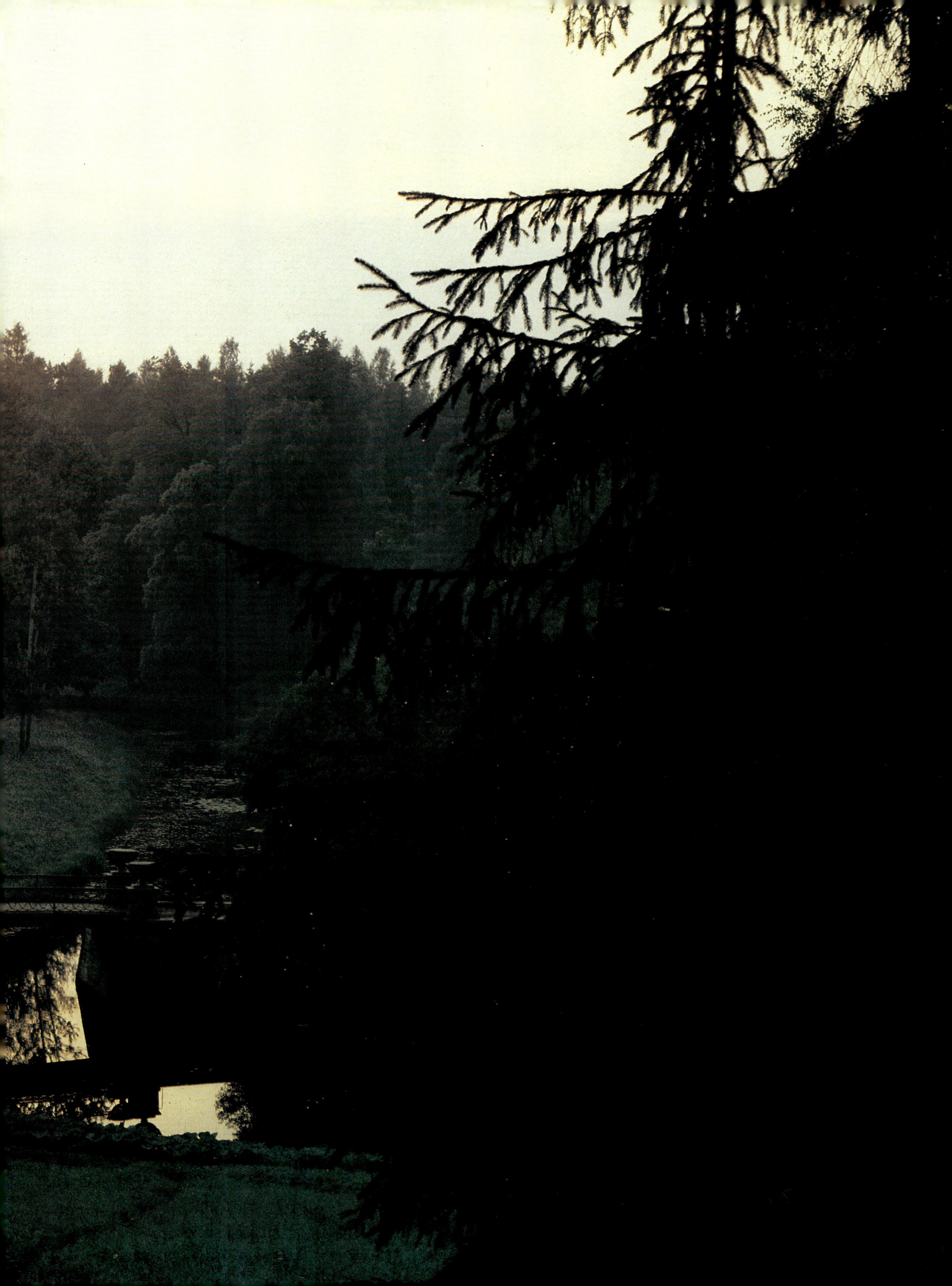

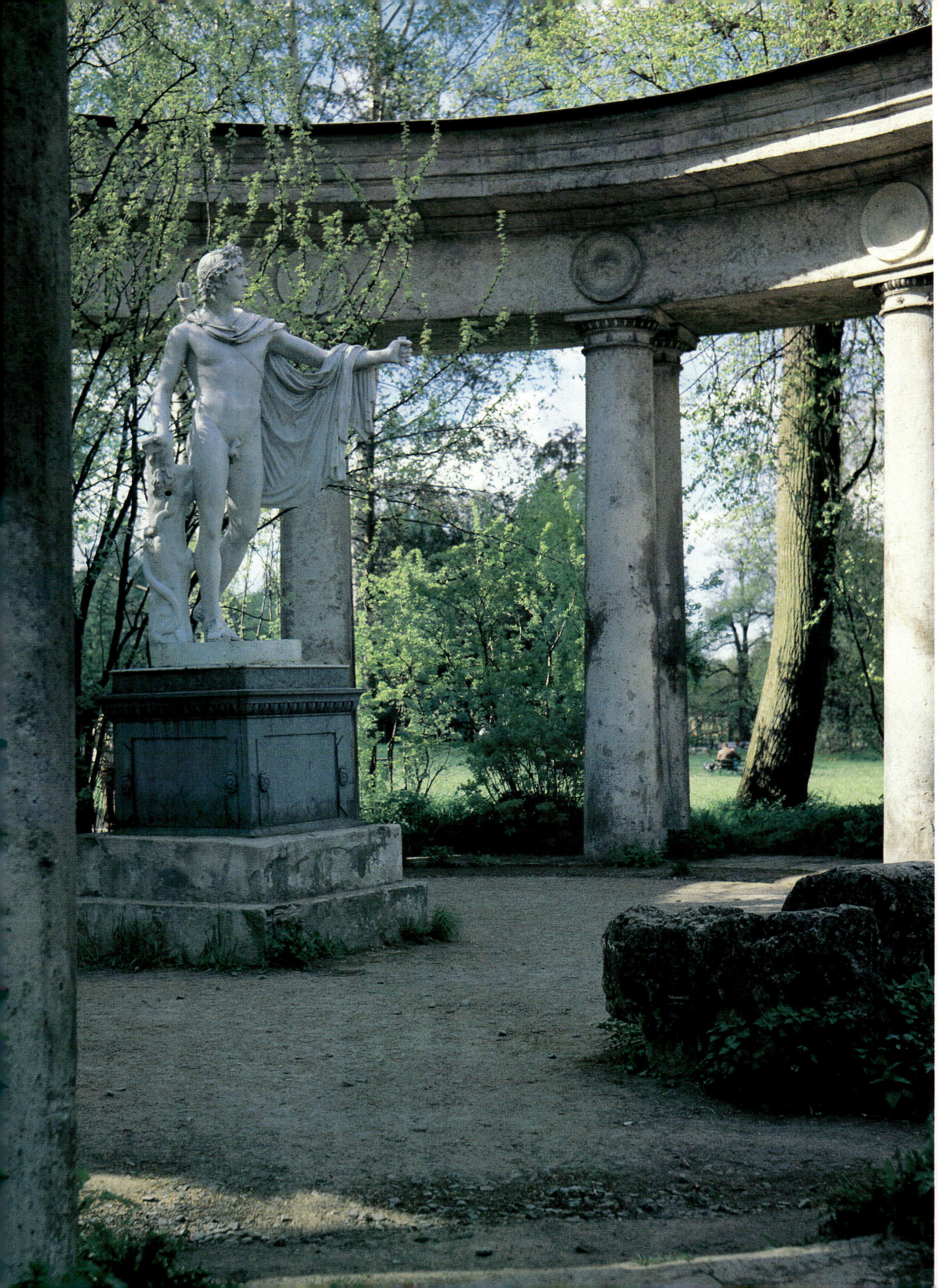

25

→
25

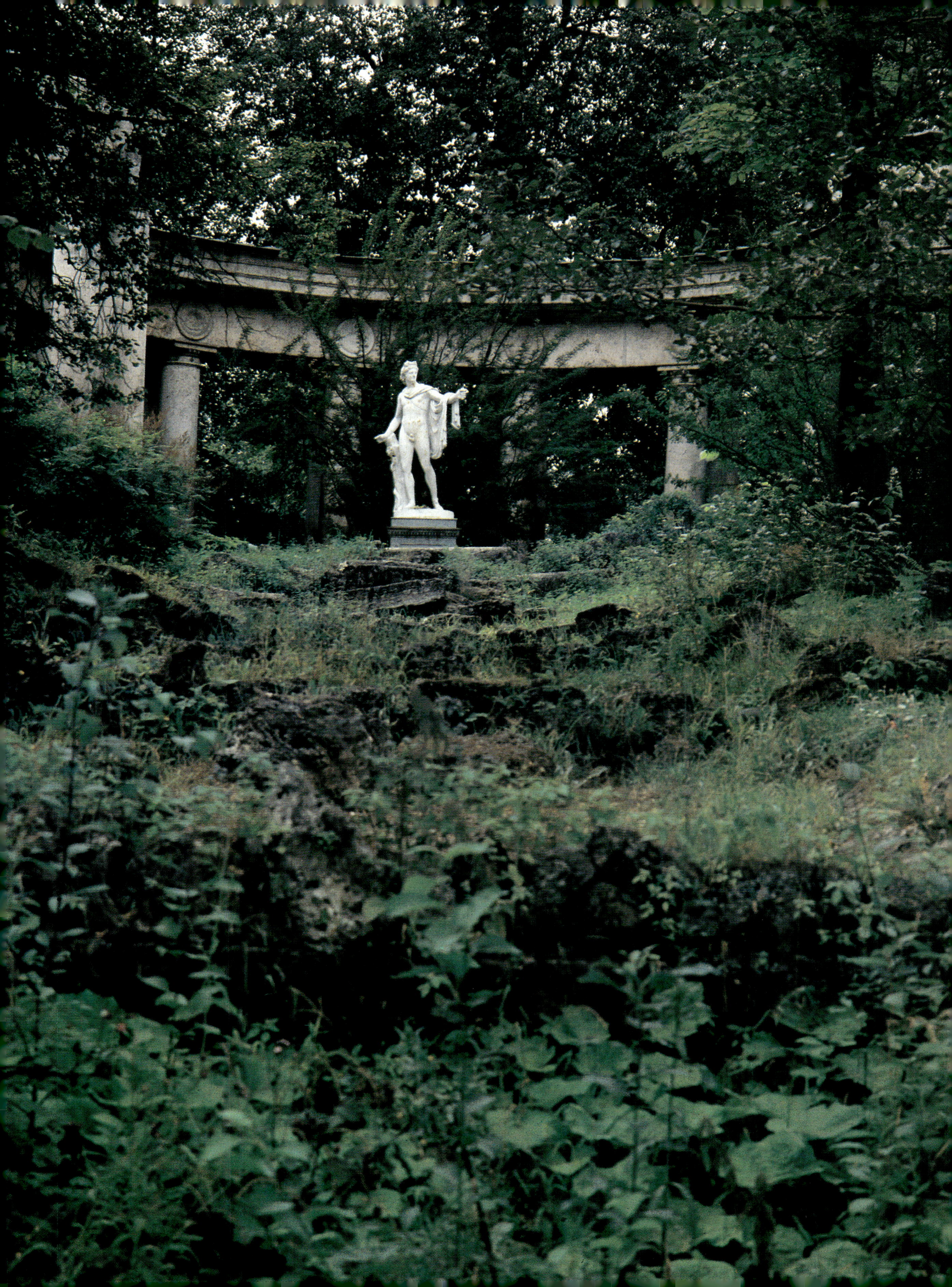

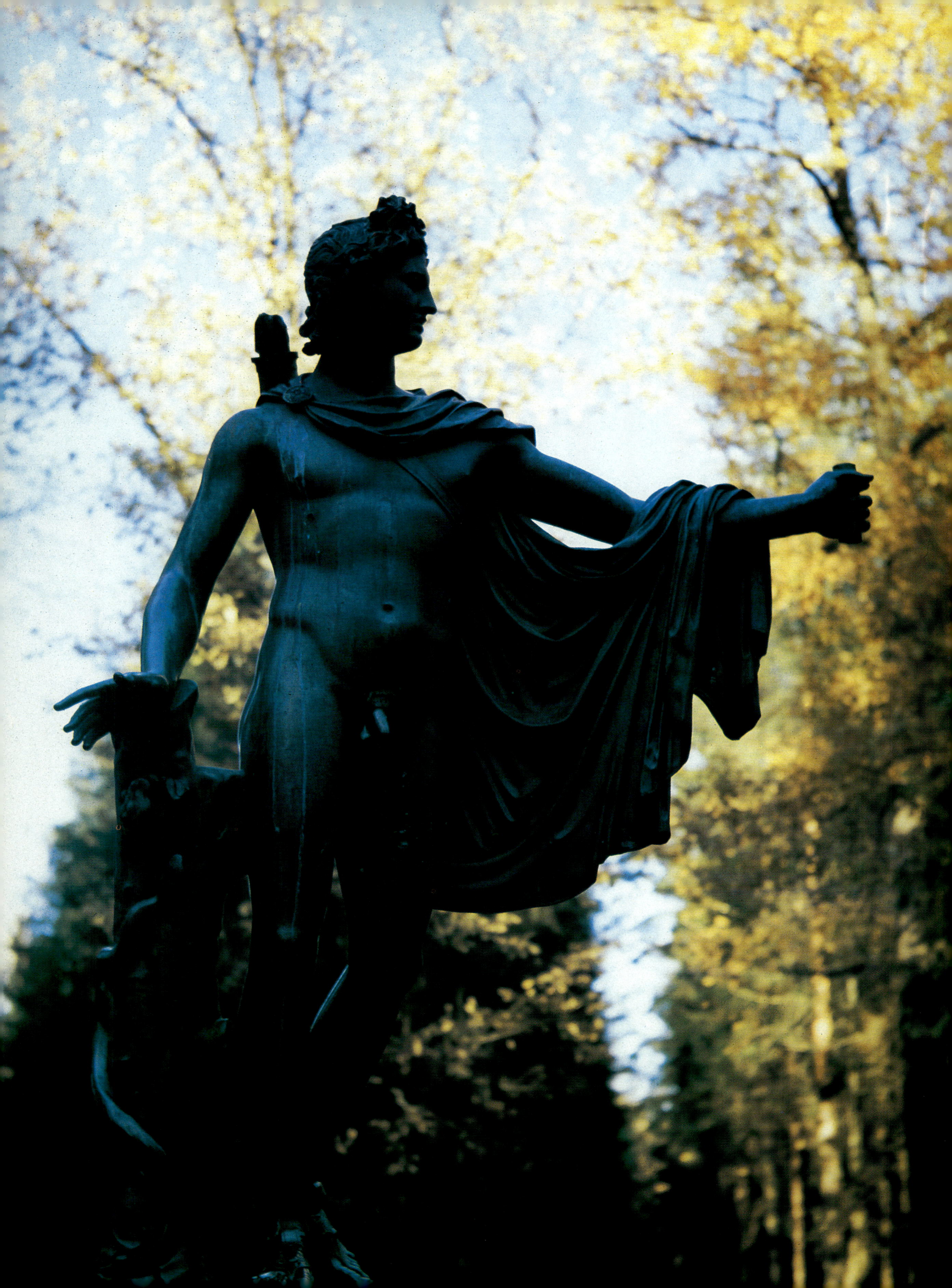

260 Pavlovsk. The Park. Statue of Apollo

261 Pavlovsk. The Park. An old fir-tree
262 Pavlovsk. The Park. The balustrade
of the terrace near the Palace

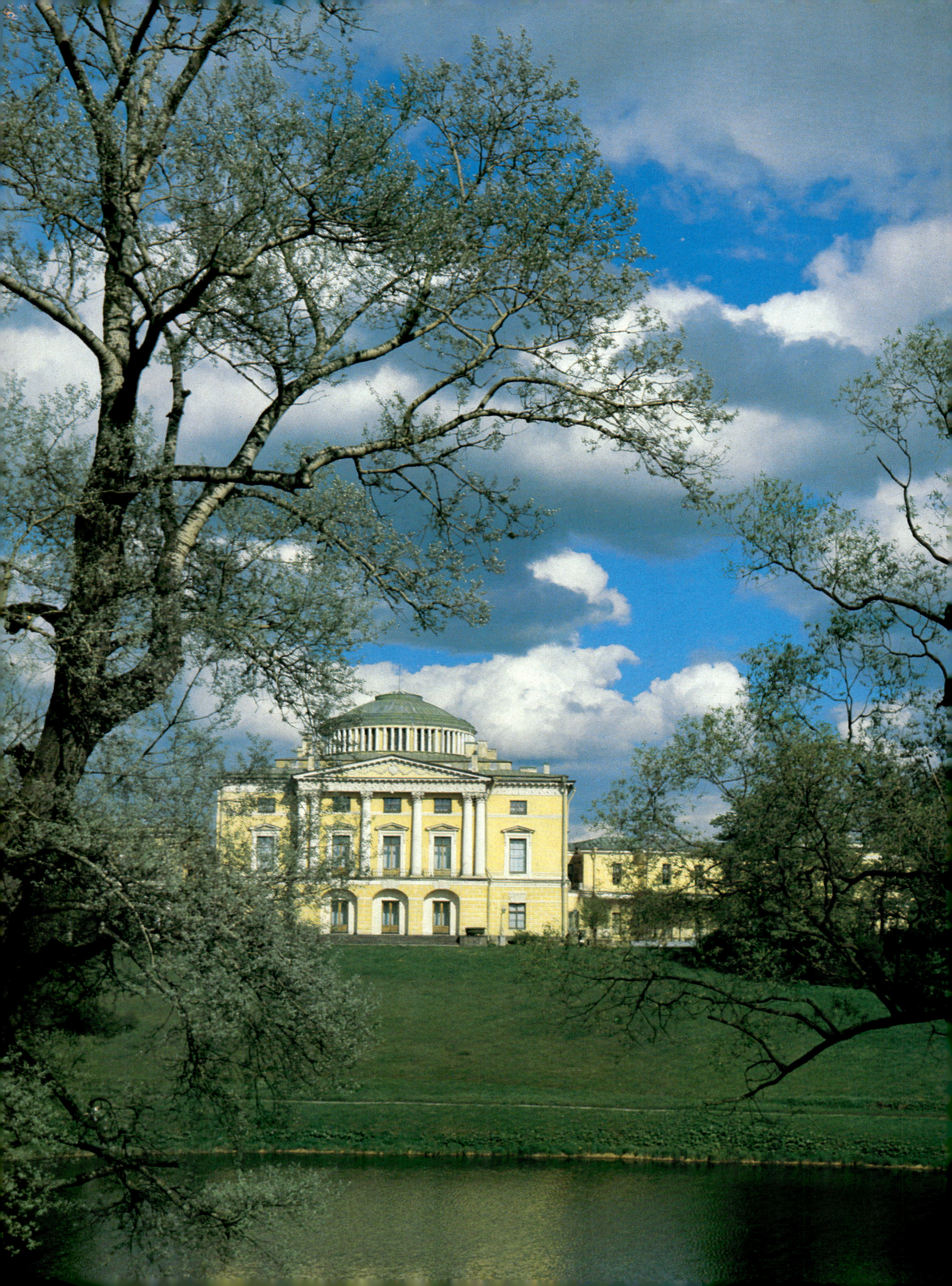

263 Pavlovsk. The Park. The first leaves
264 Pavlovsk. The Park. Haystacks on the bank of the Slavyanka River

265, 267 Pavlovsk. The Park. The lions on the Great Stone Stairway →
266 Pavlovsk. The Park. The Birch Bridge →

26.

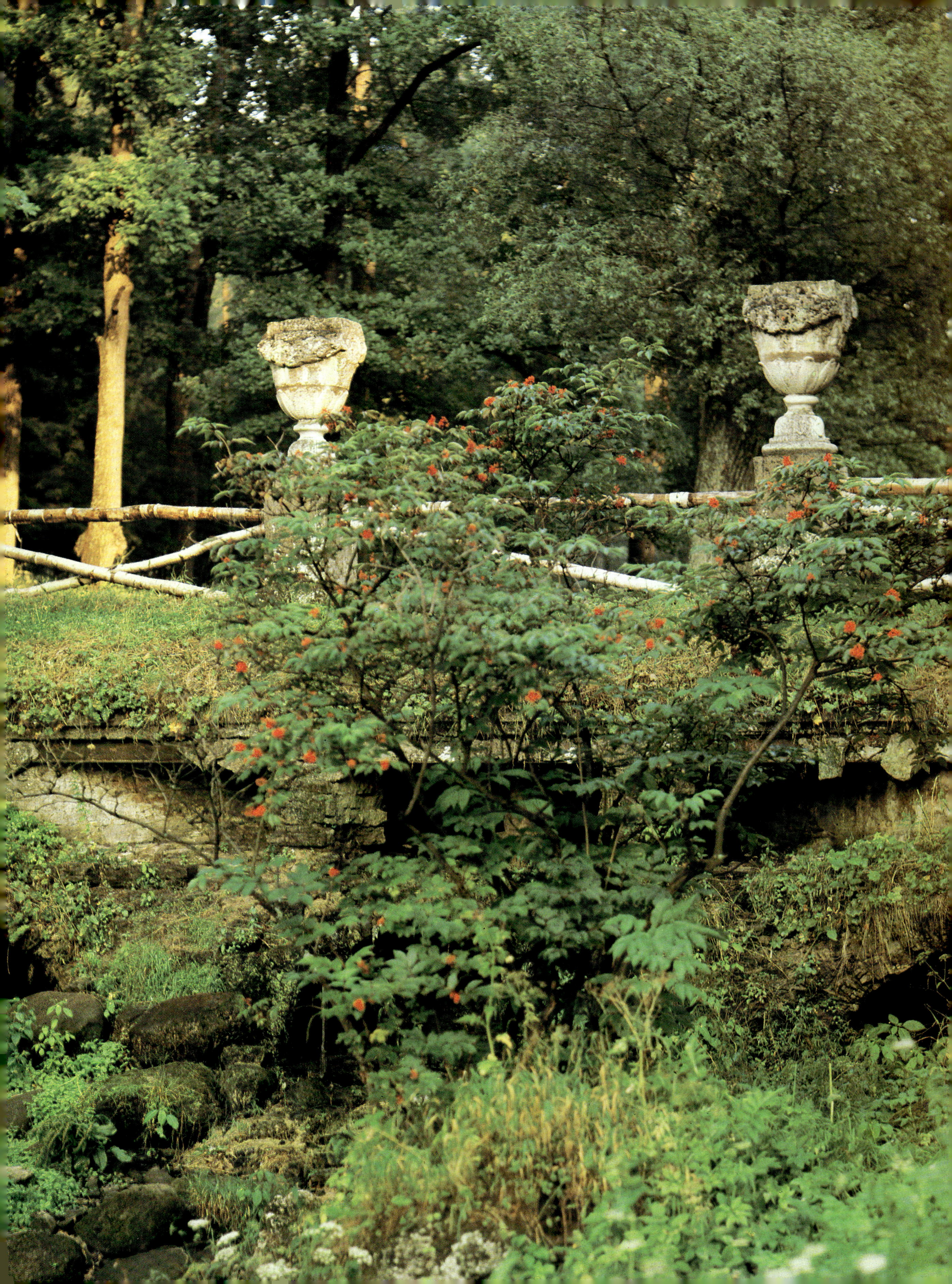

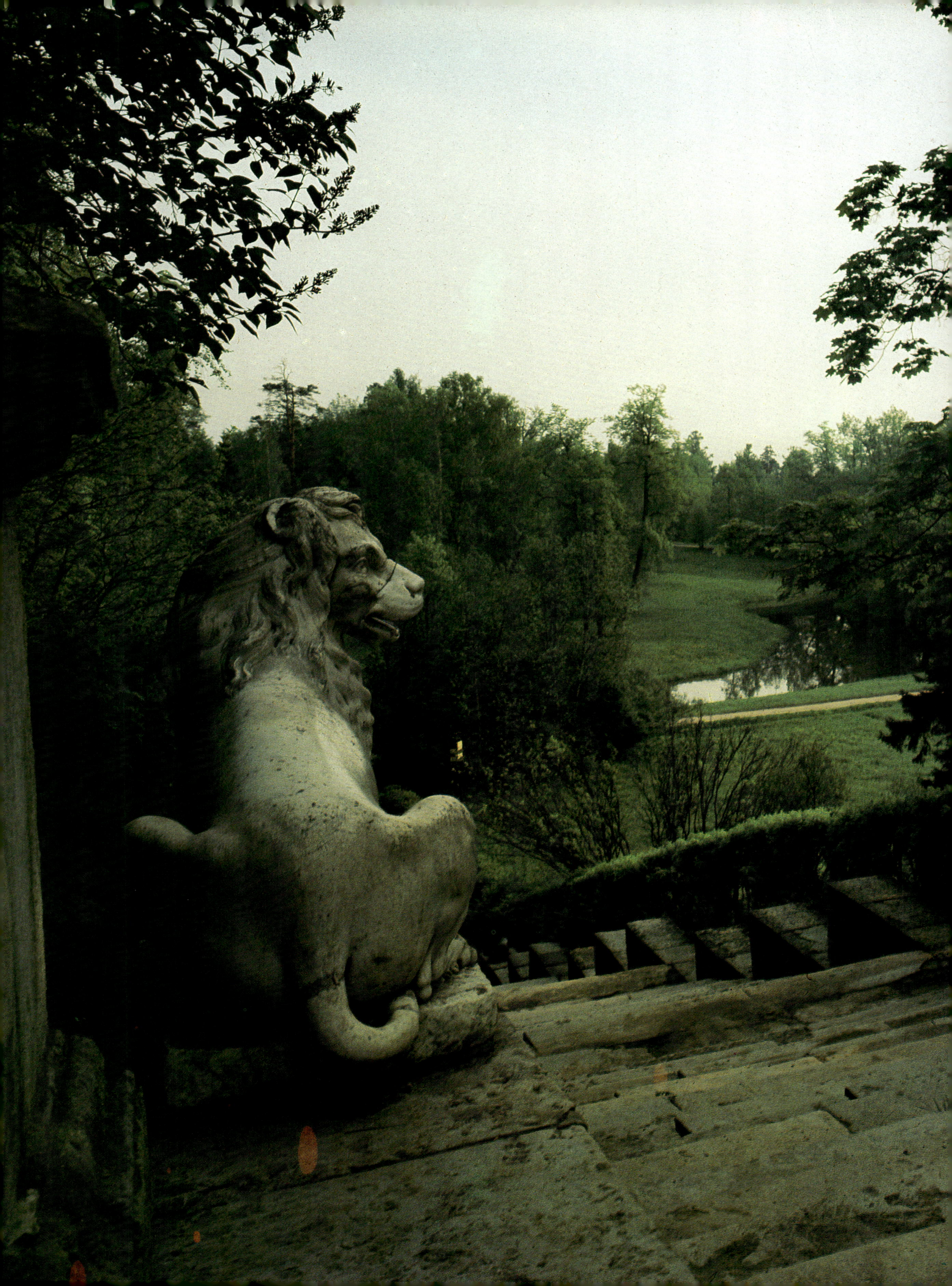

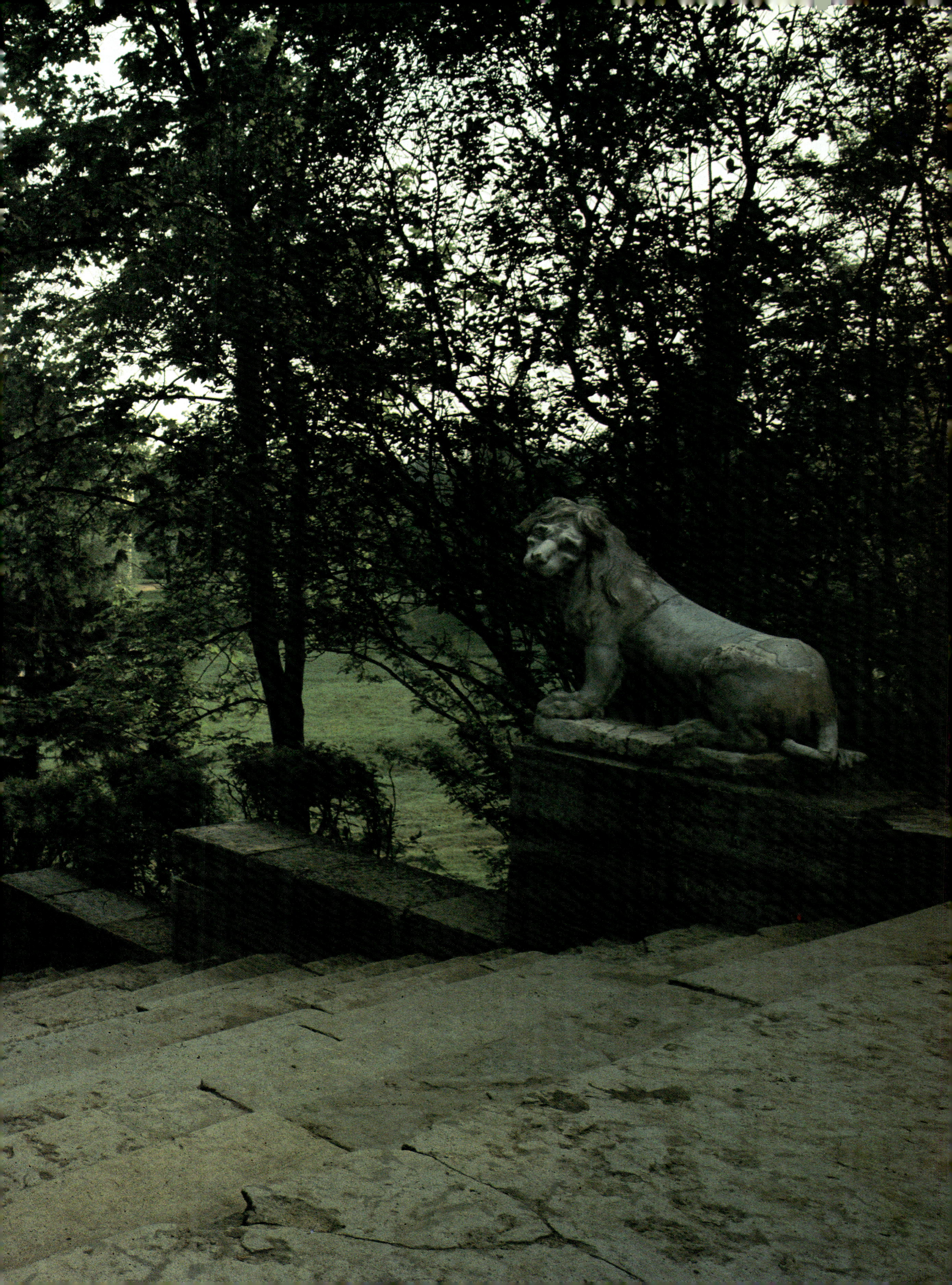

268 *Pavlovsk. The Park. The Ground
   of the Muses*
269 *Pavlovsk. The Park. The frozen river*

270, 271 *Pavlovsk. The Temple of Friendship* →

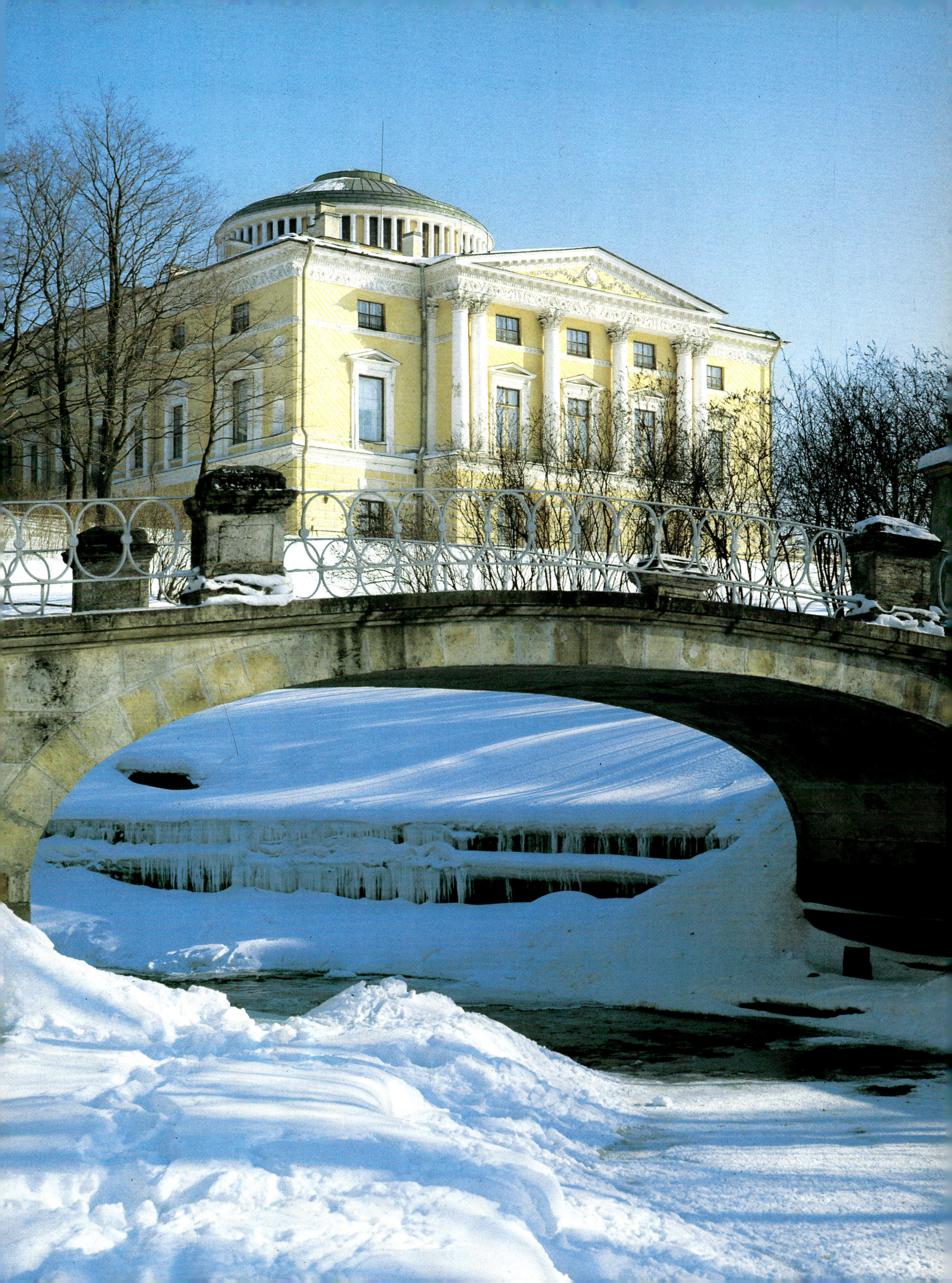

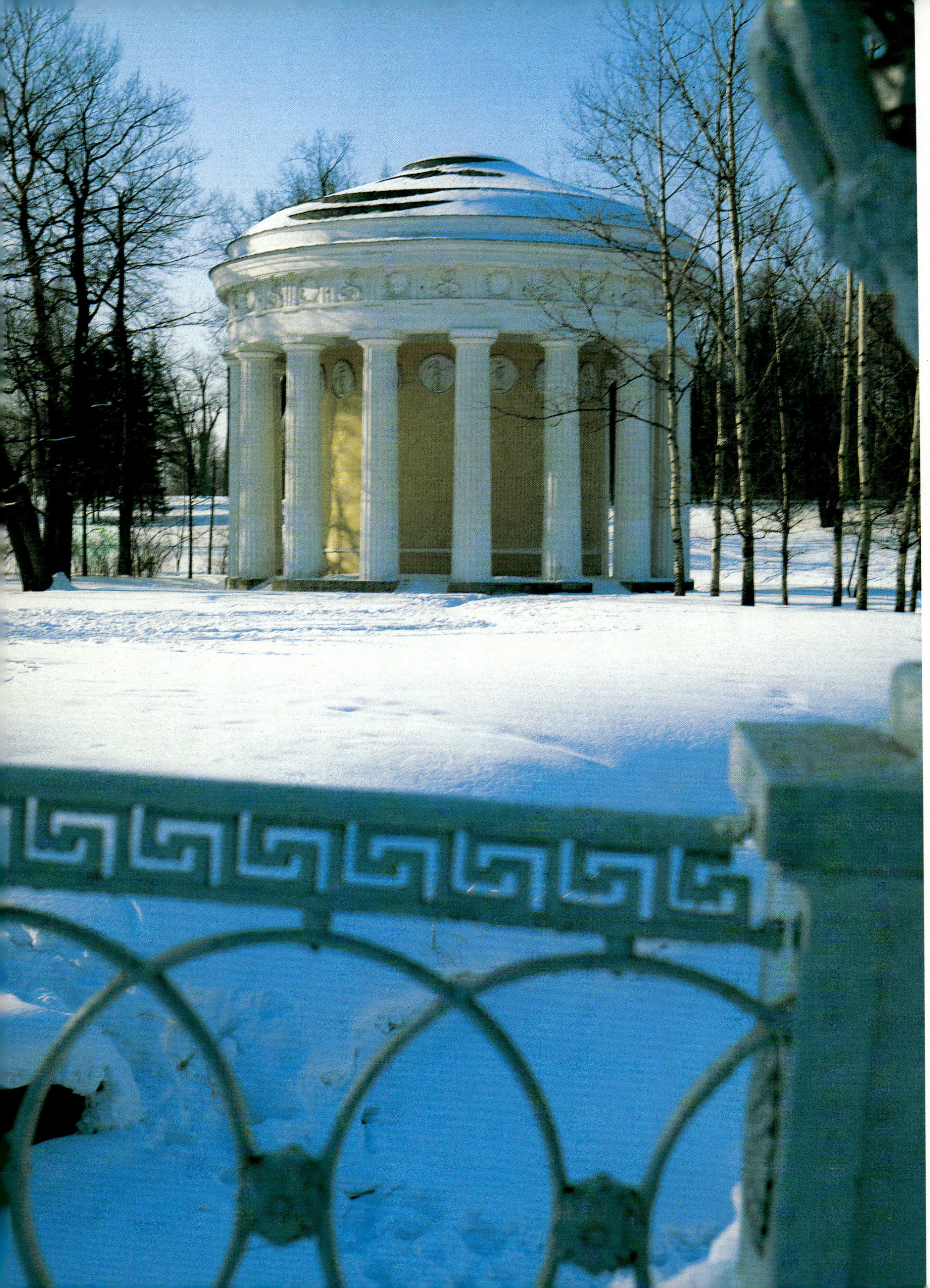

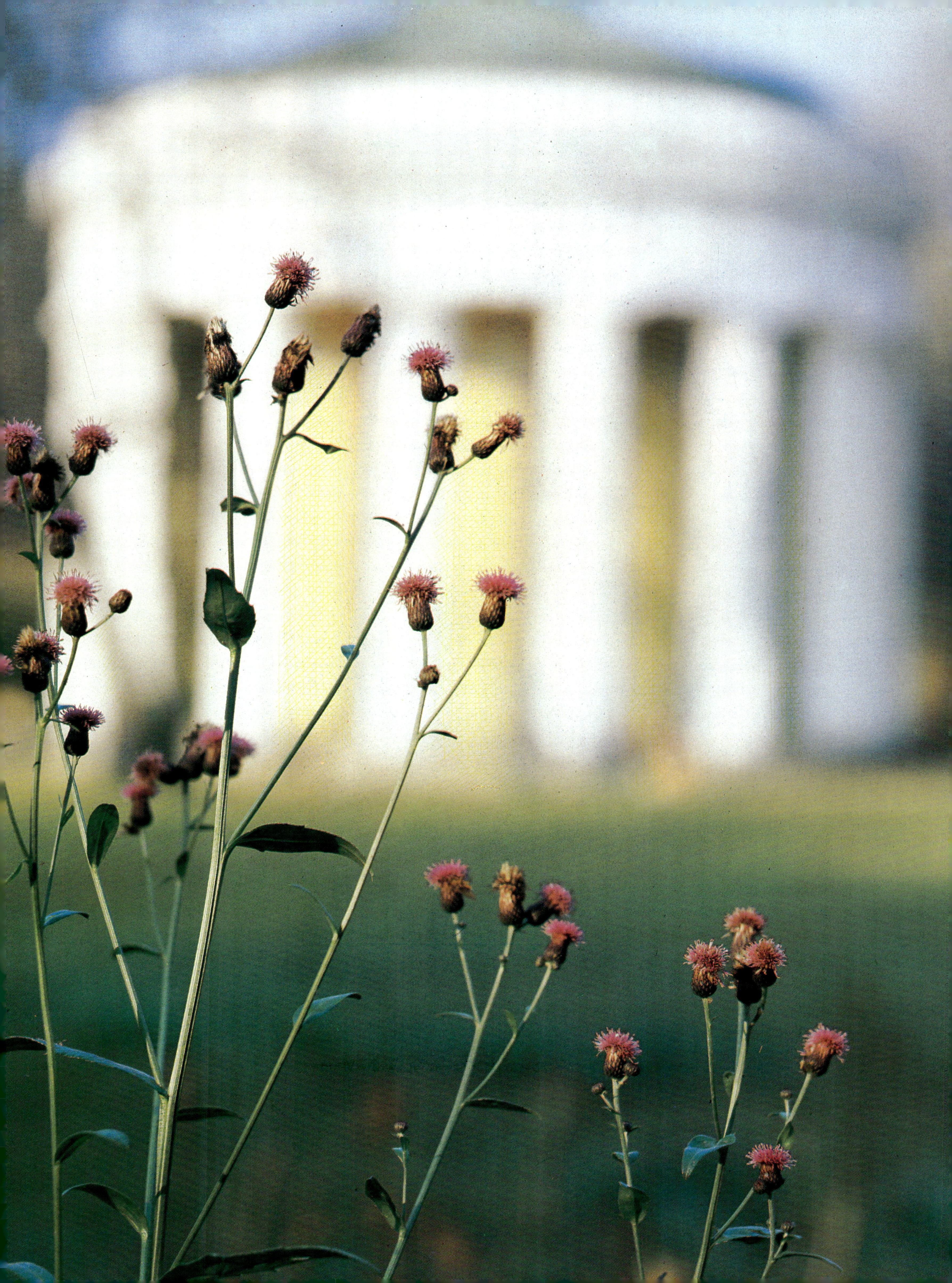

272   *Pavlovsk. The Park. Meadows*
273   *Pavlovsk. The Park. The central alley seen from the Statue of Paul I*

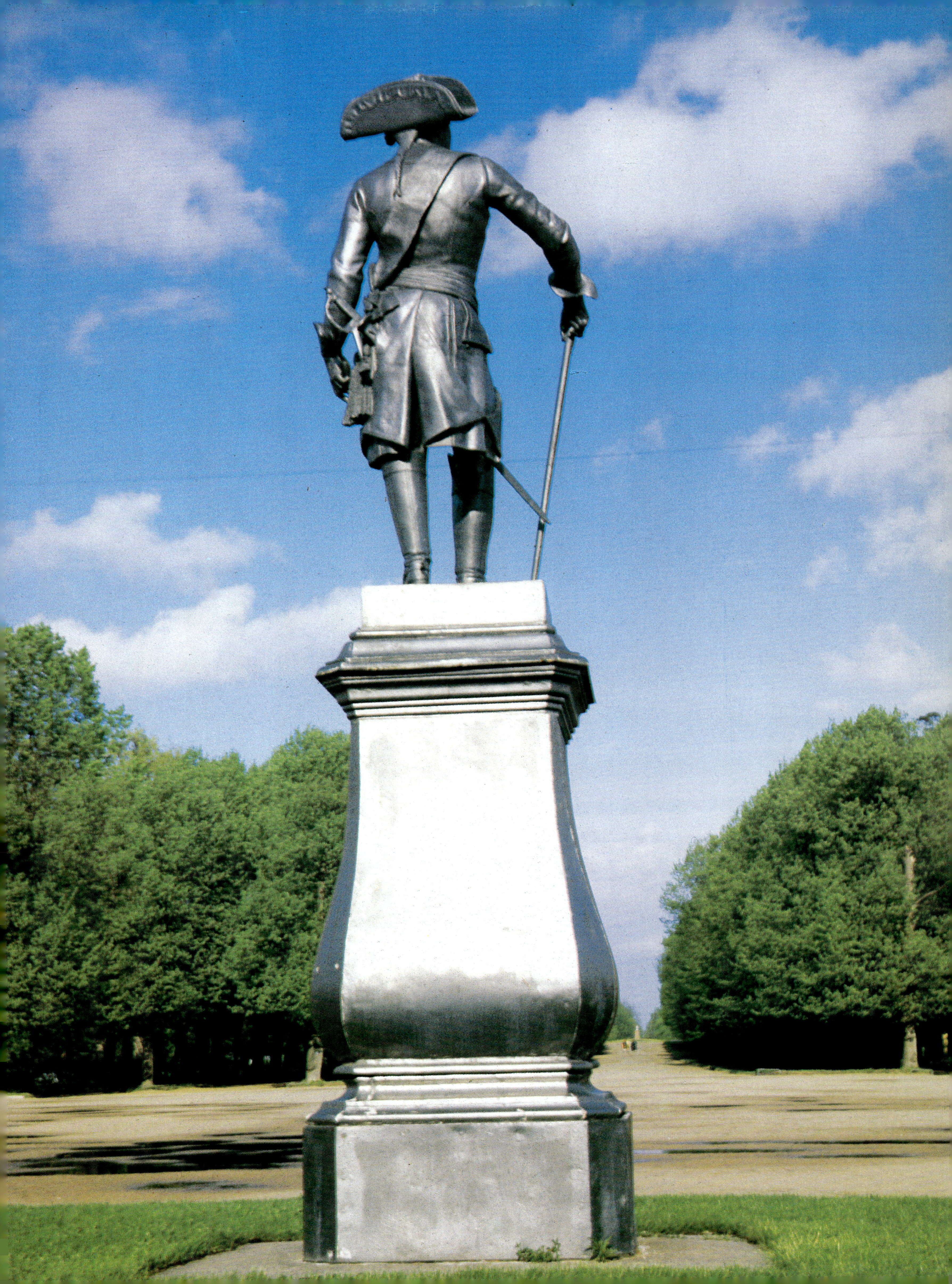

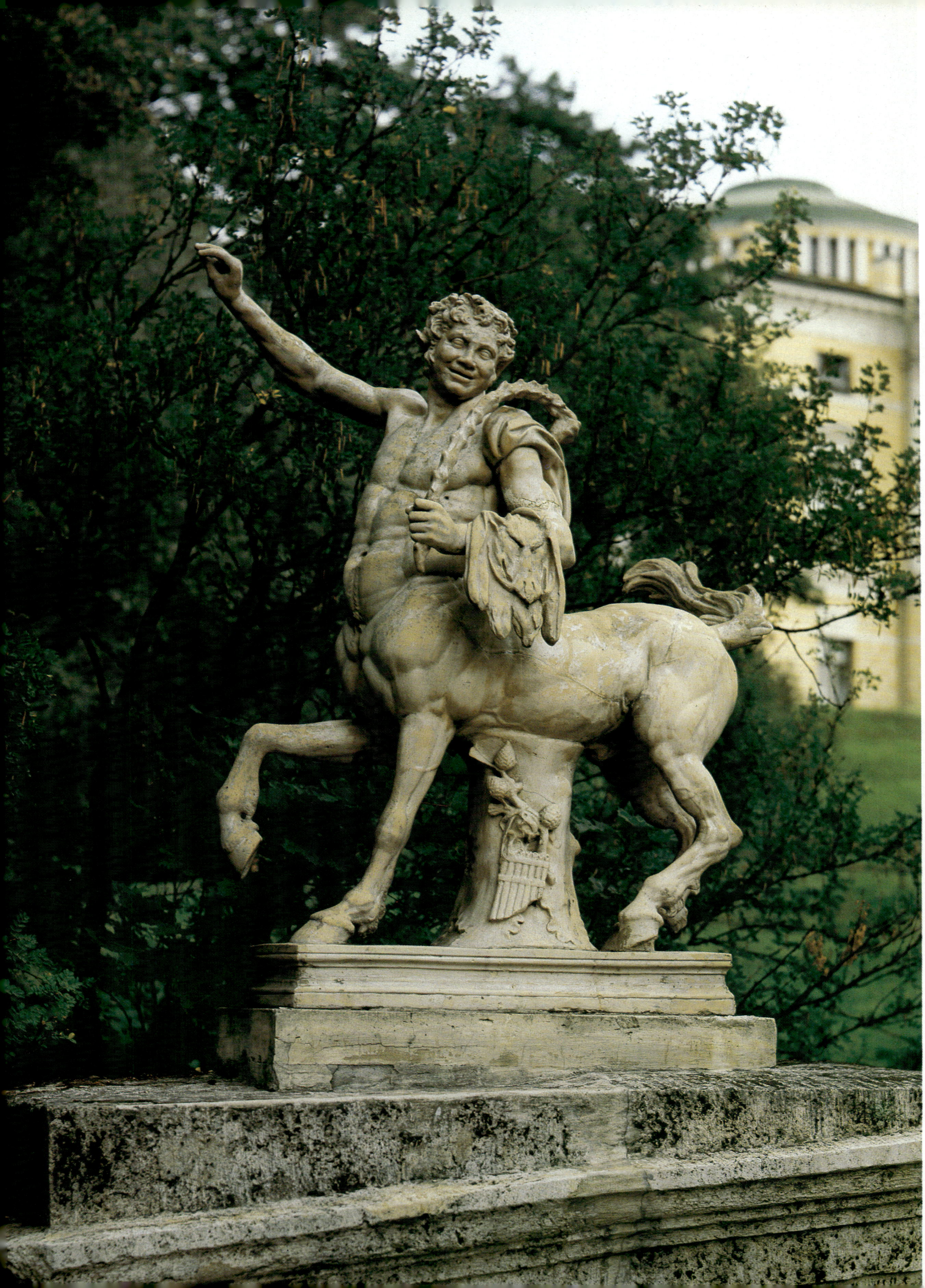

274, 275 Pavlovsk. The Park. The Centaurs' Bridge

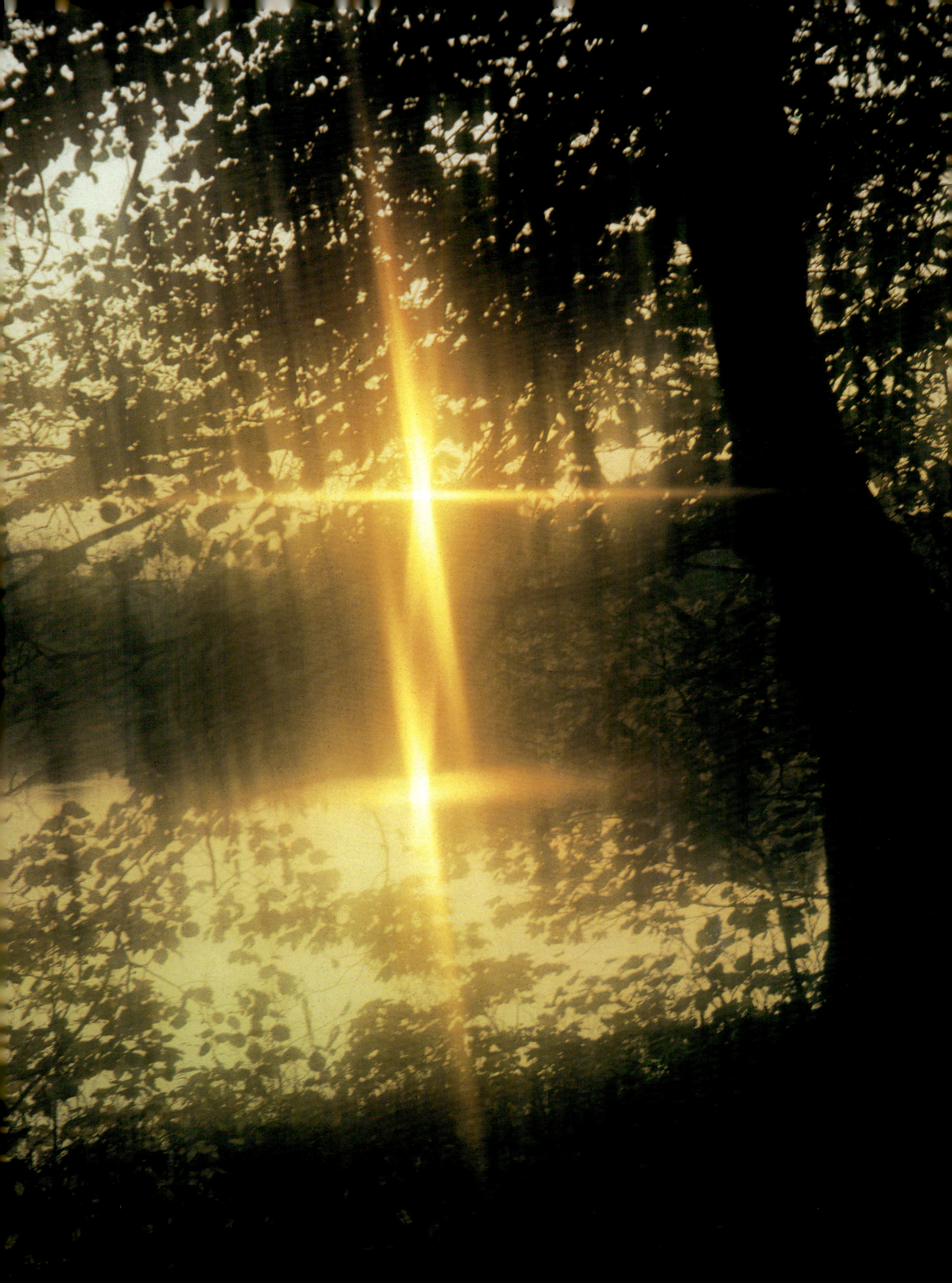

276 Pavlovsk. The Park. Sunrays on the leaves
277 Pavlovsk. The Aviary

278 Pavlovsk. The Three Graces' Pavilion
279 Tsarskoye Selo (Pushkin). The Palace Church and the Lyceum

280 Tsarskoye Selo (Pushkin). The Catherine Palace →
281 Tsarskoye Selo (Pushkin). The pond in the park →
282 Old oak tree →
283 Tsarskoye Selo (Pushkin). The Girl with a pitcher Fountain →
284 Tsarskoye Selo (Pushkin). The Alexander Park. The Greater Chinese Bridge →
285 Tsarskoye Selo (Pushkin). The Terrace →
286 Tsarskoye Selo (Pushkin). The Concert Hall →
287 Golden autumn →

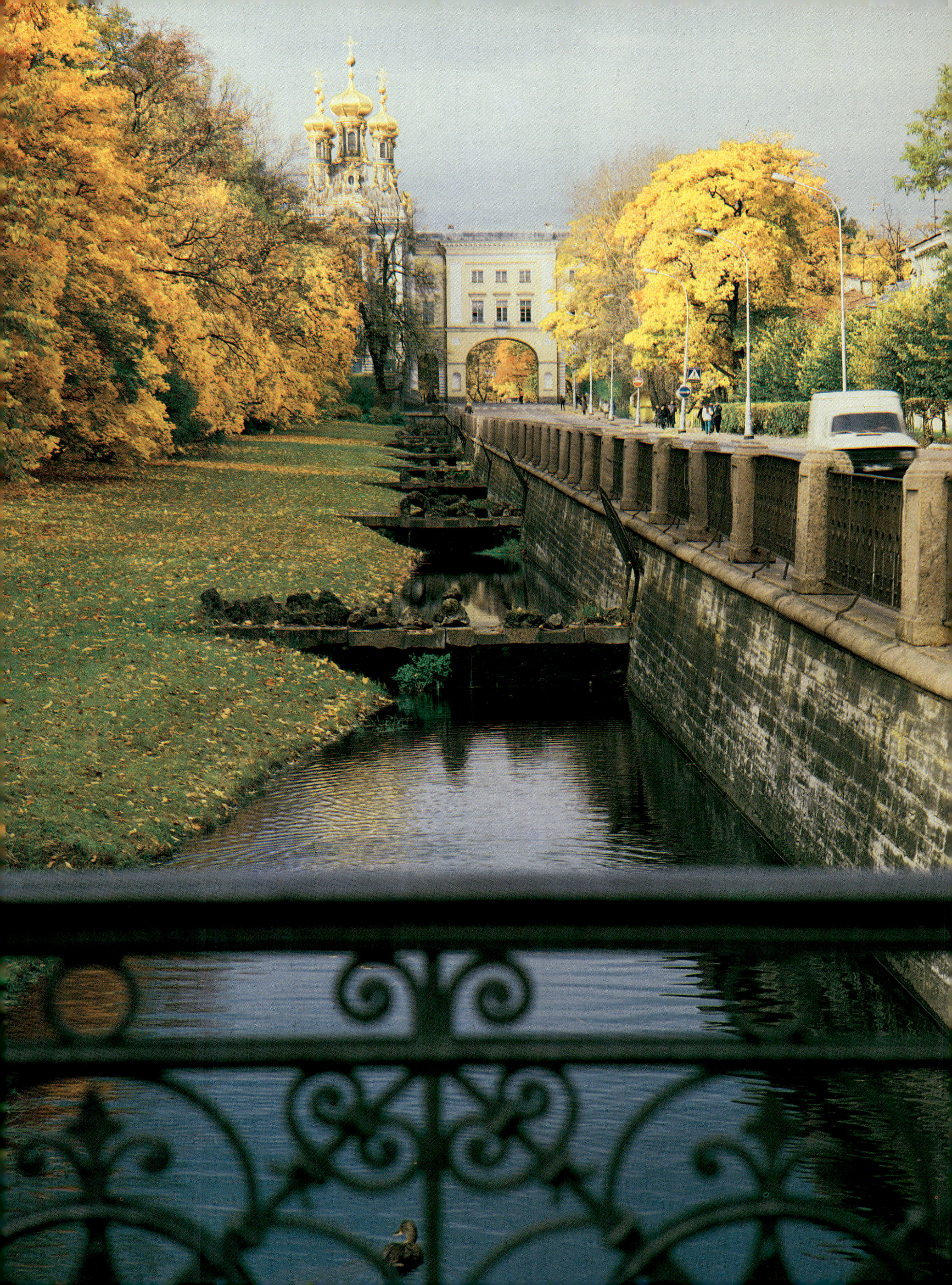

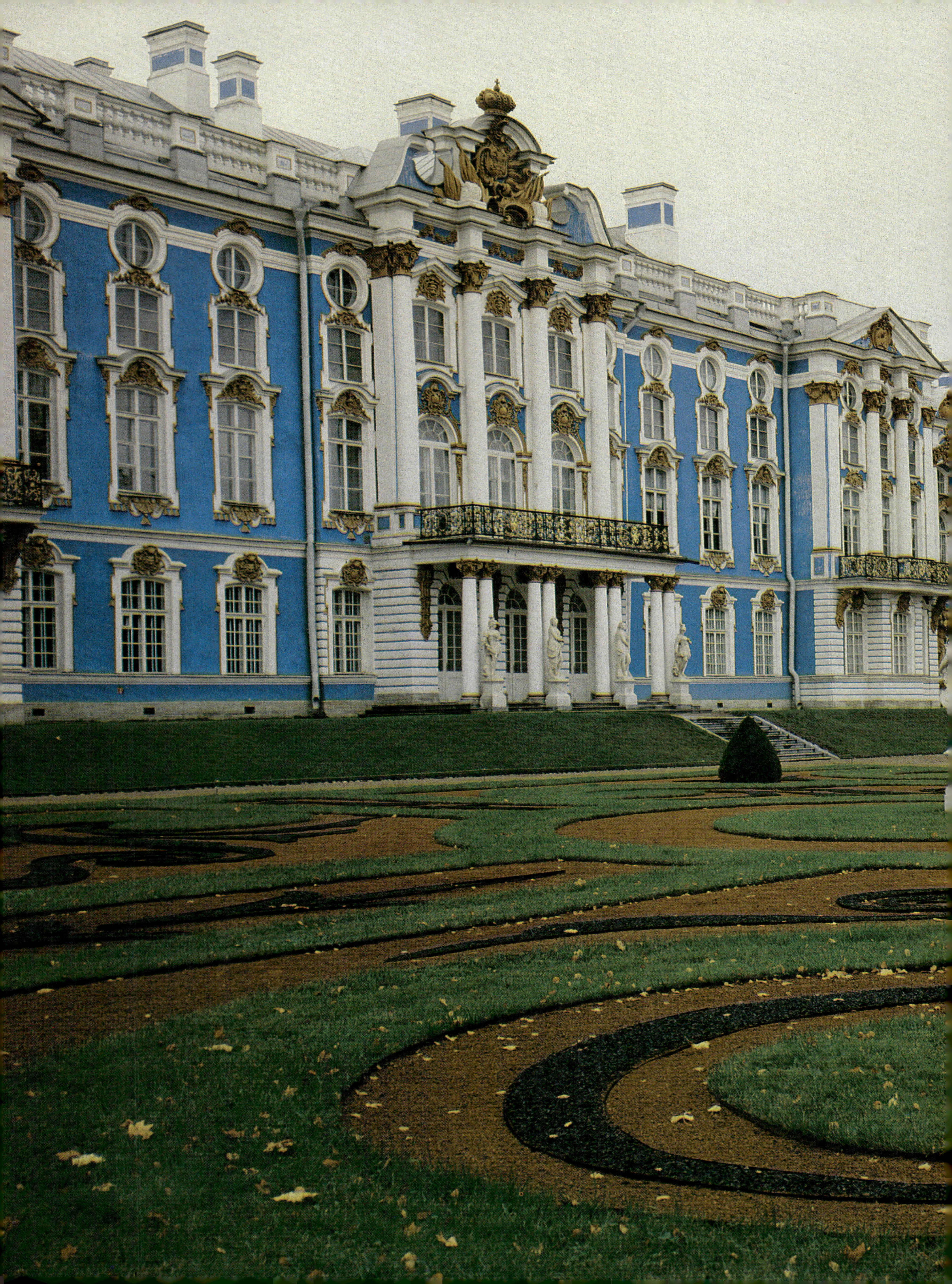

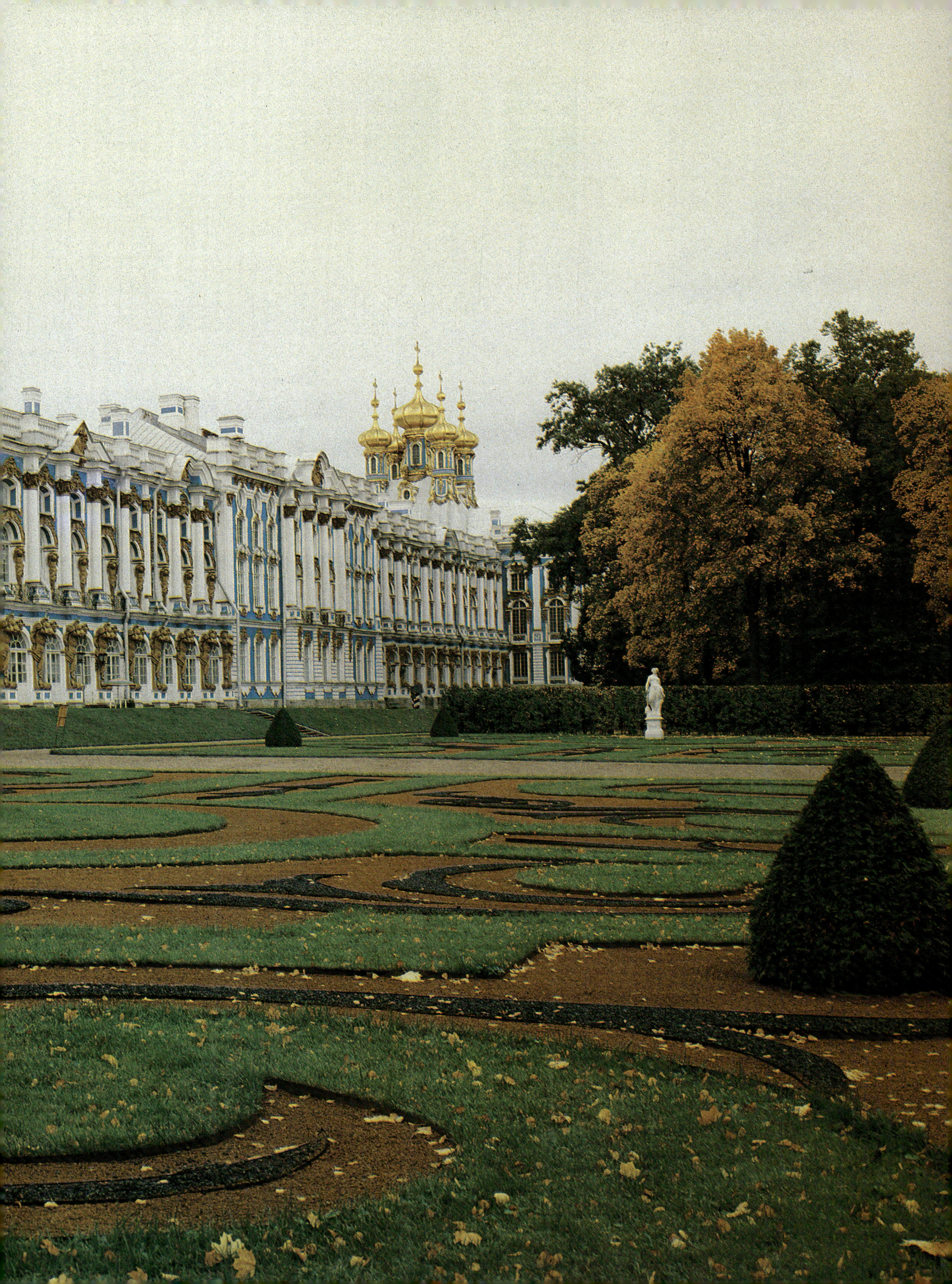

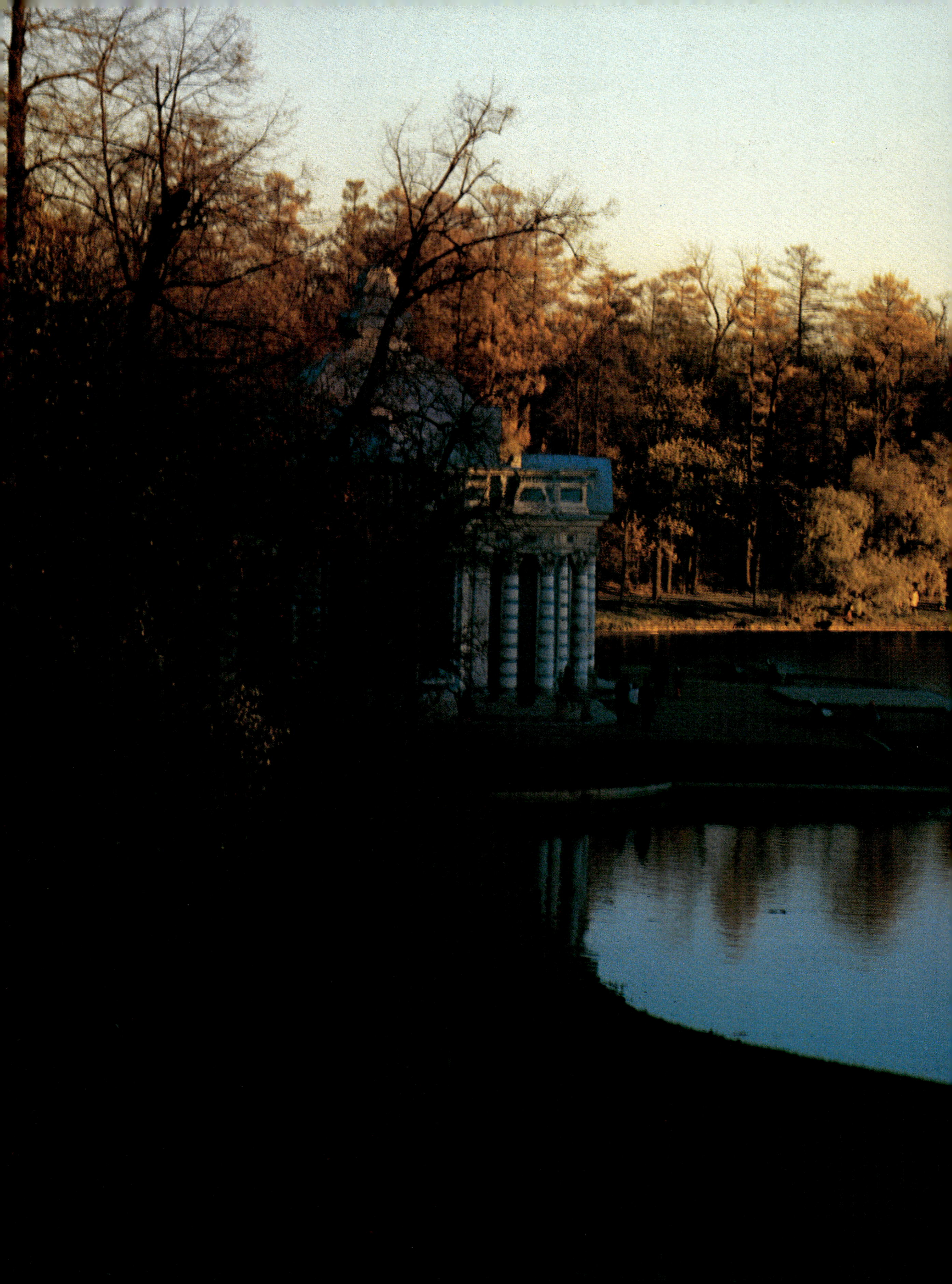

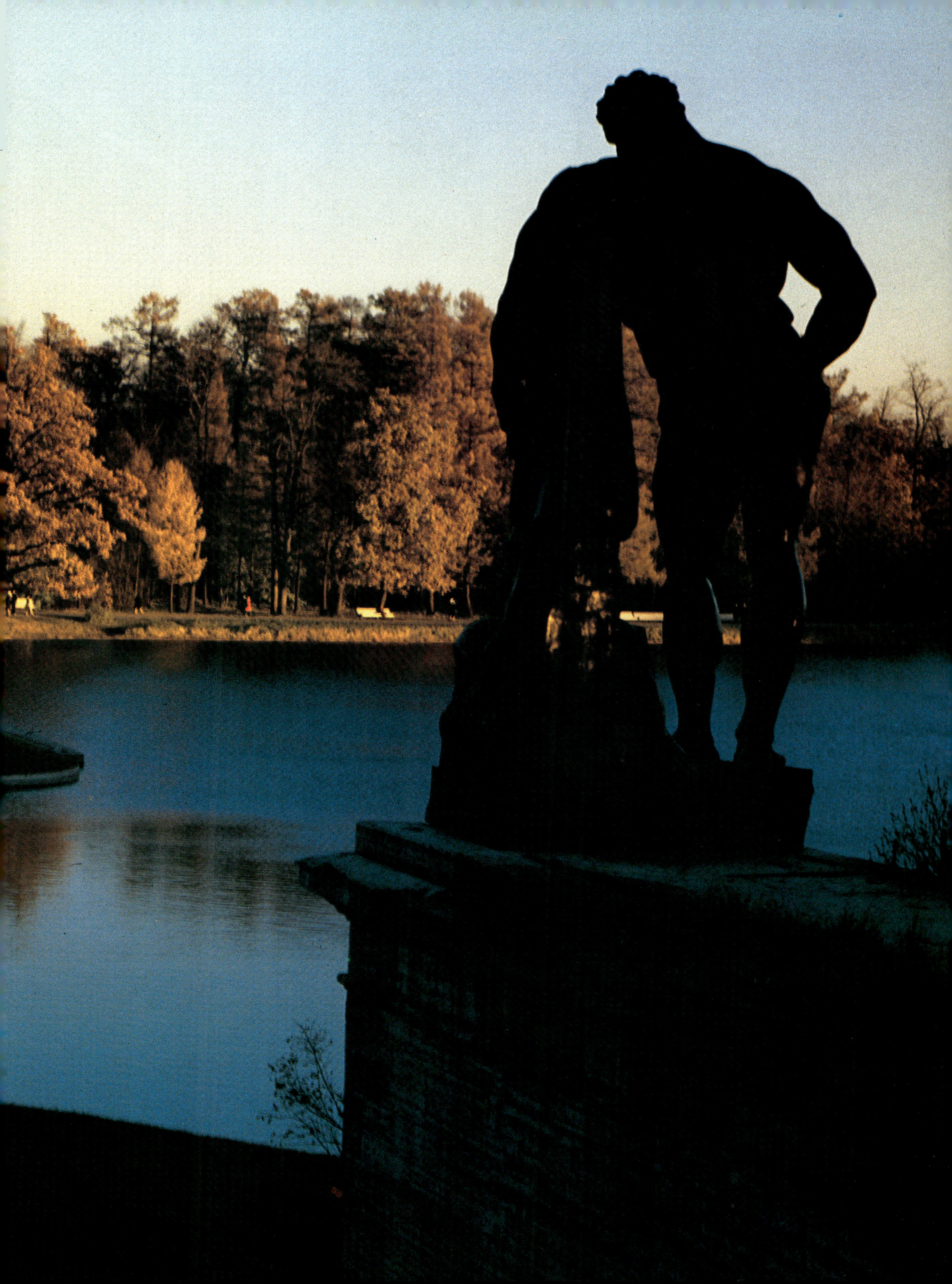

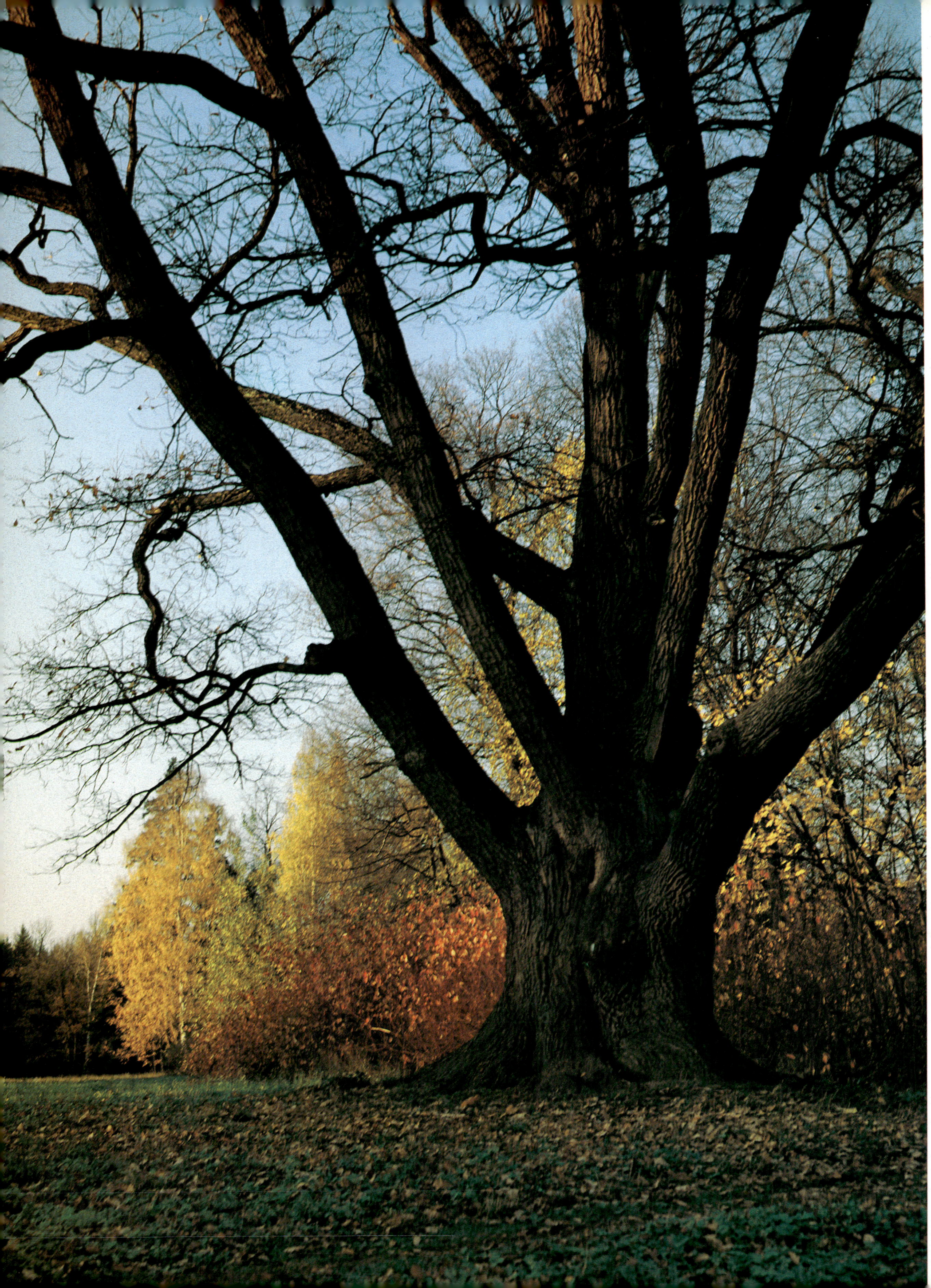

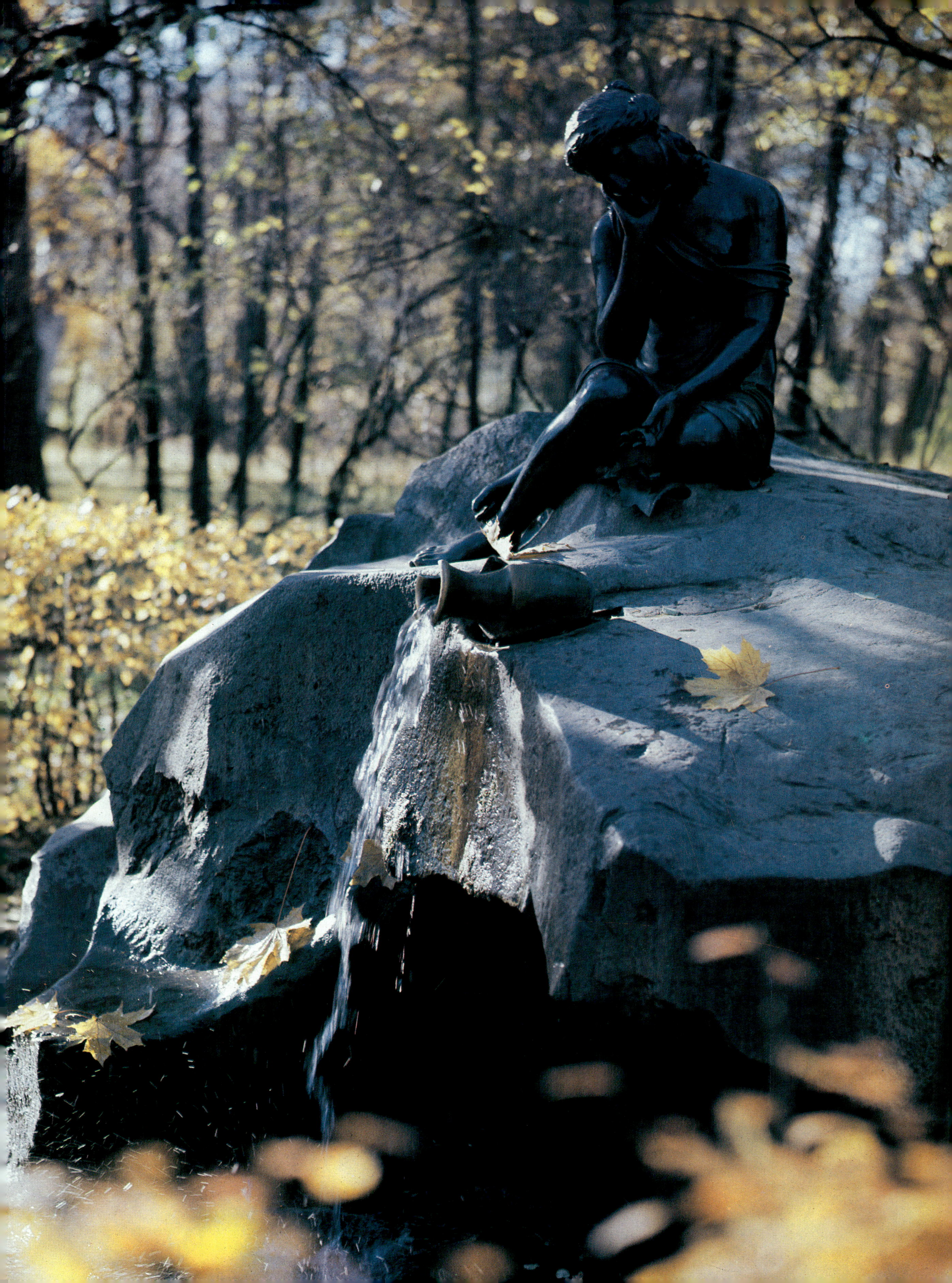

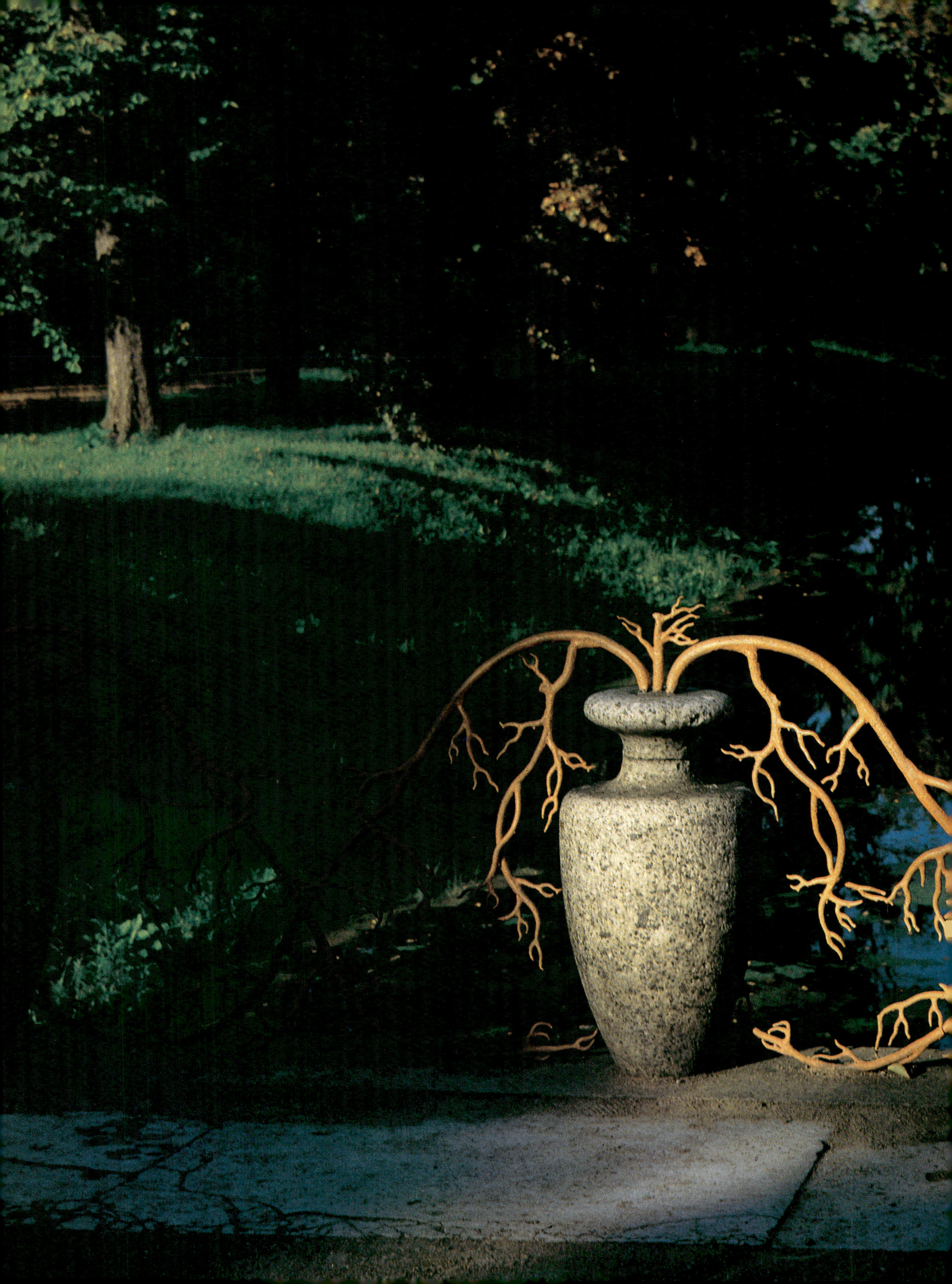

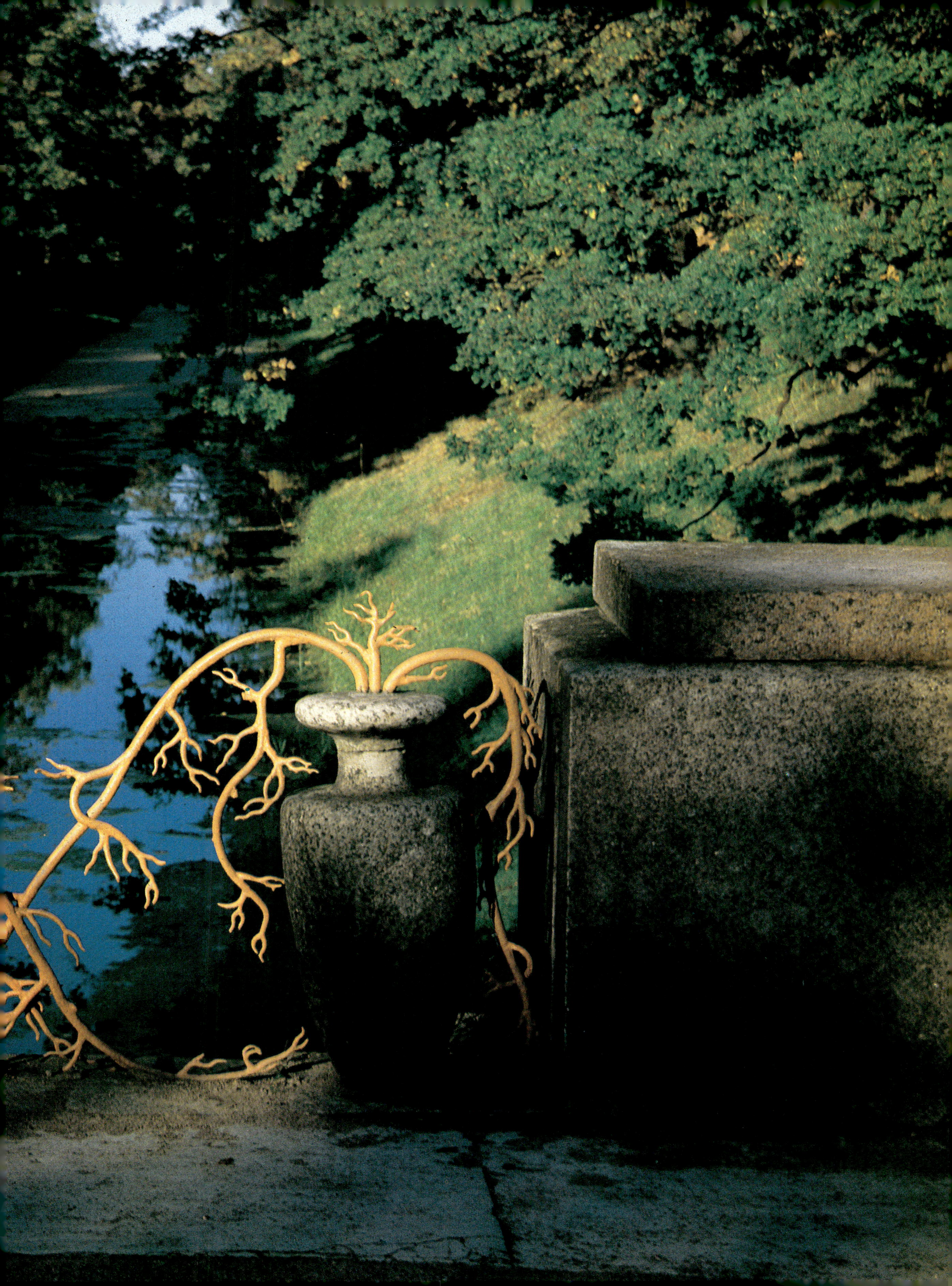

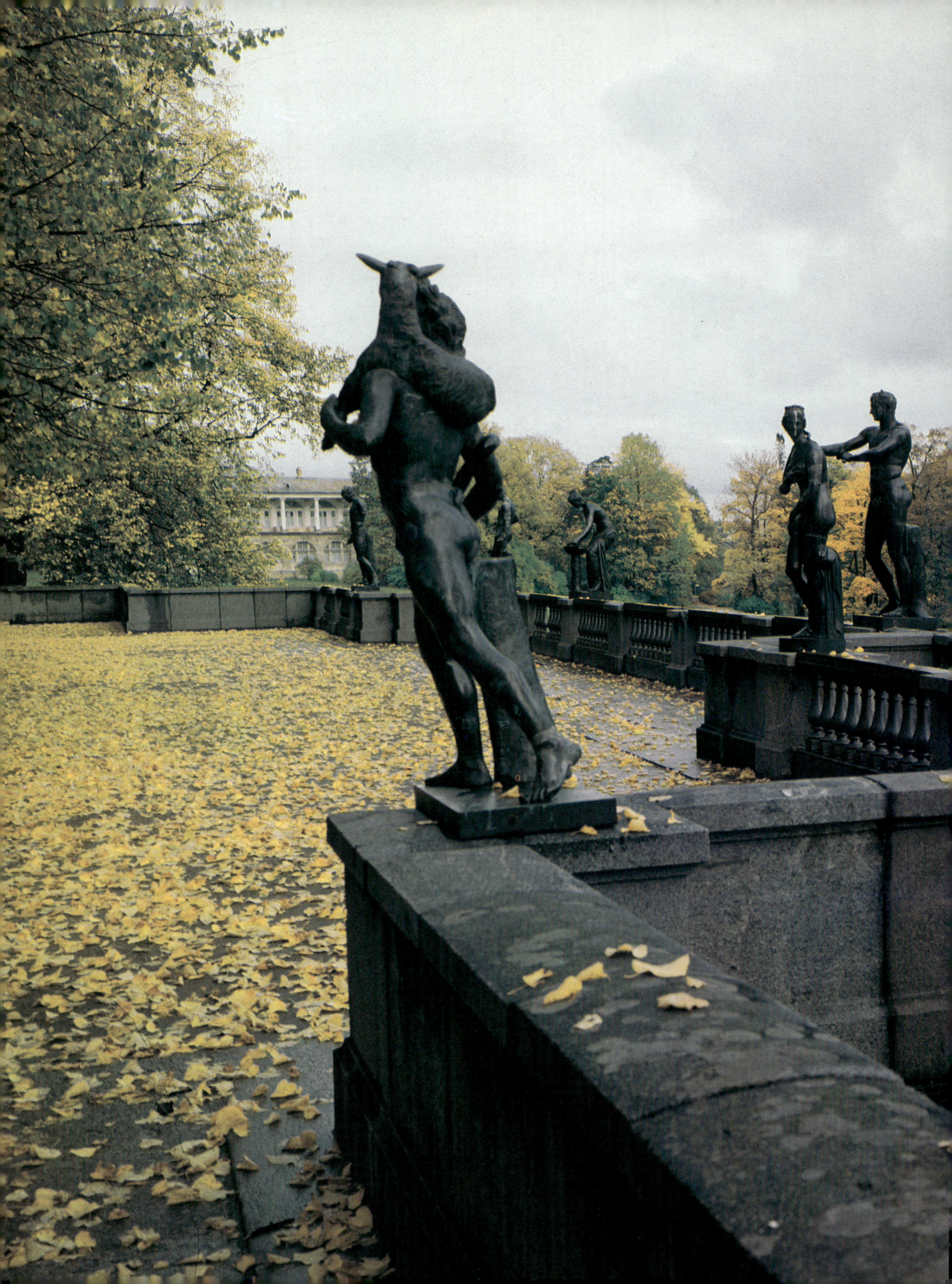

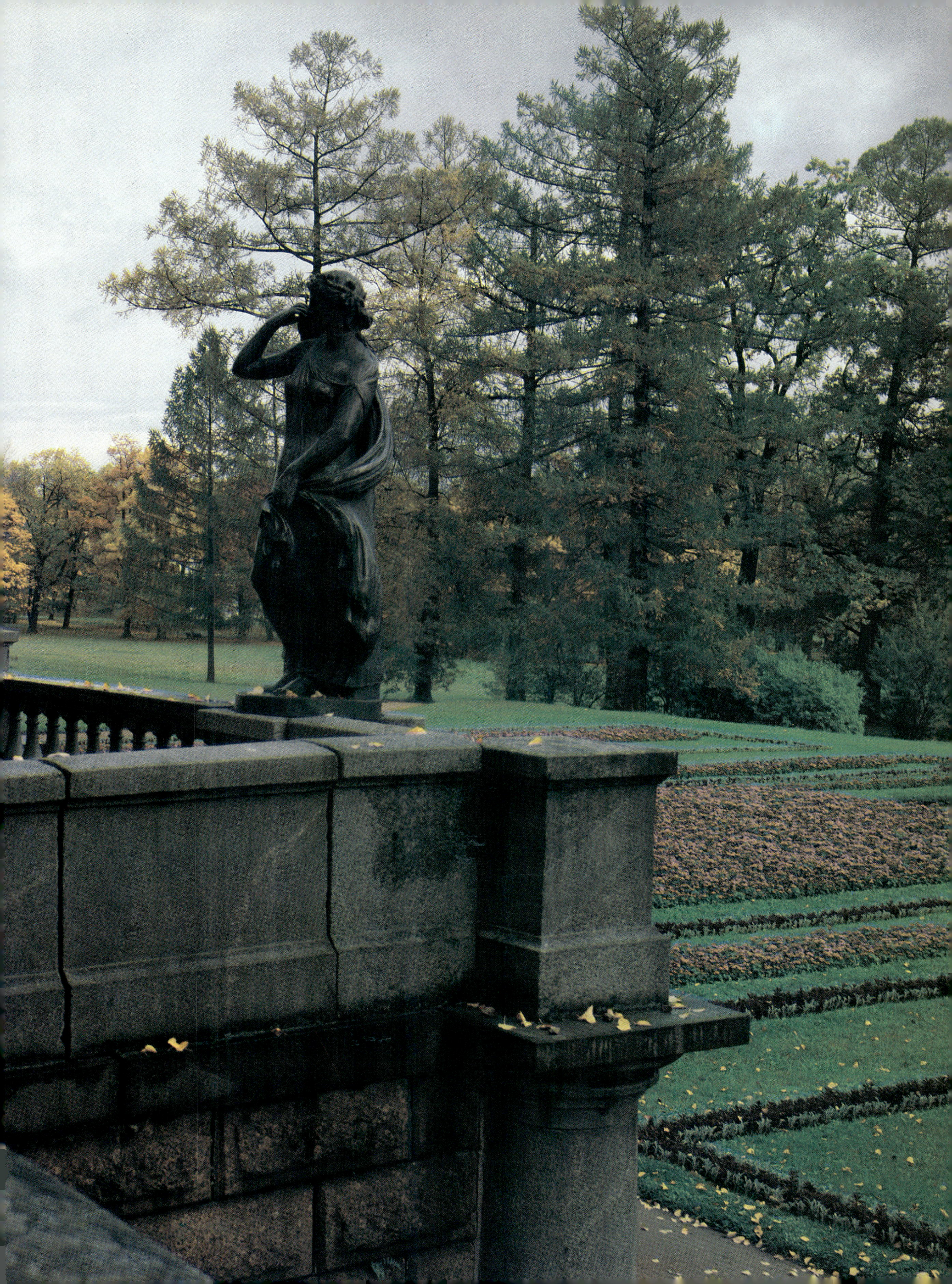

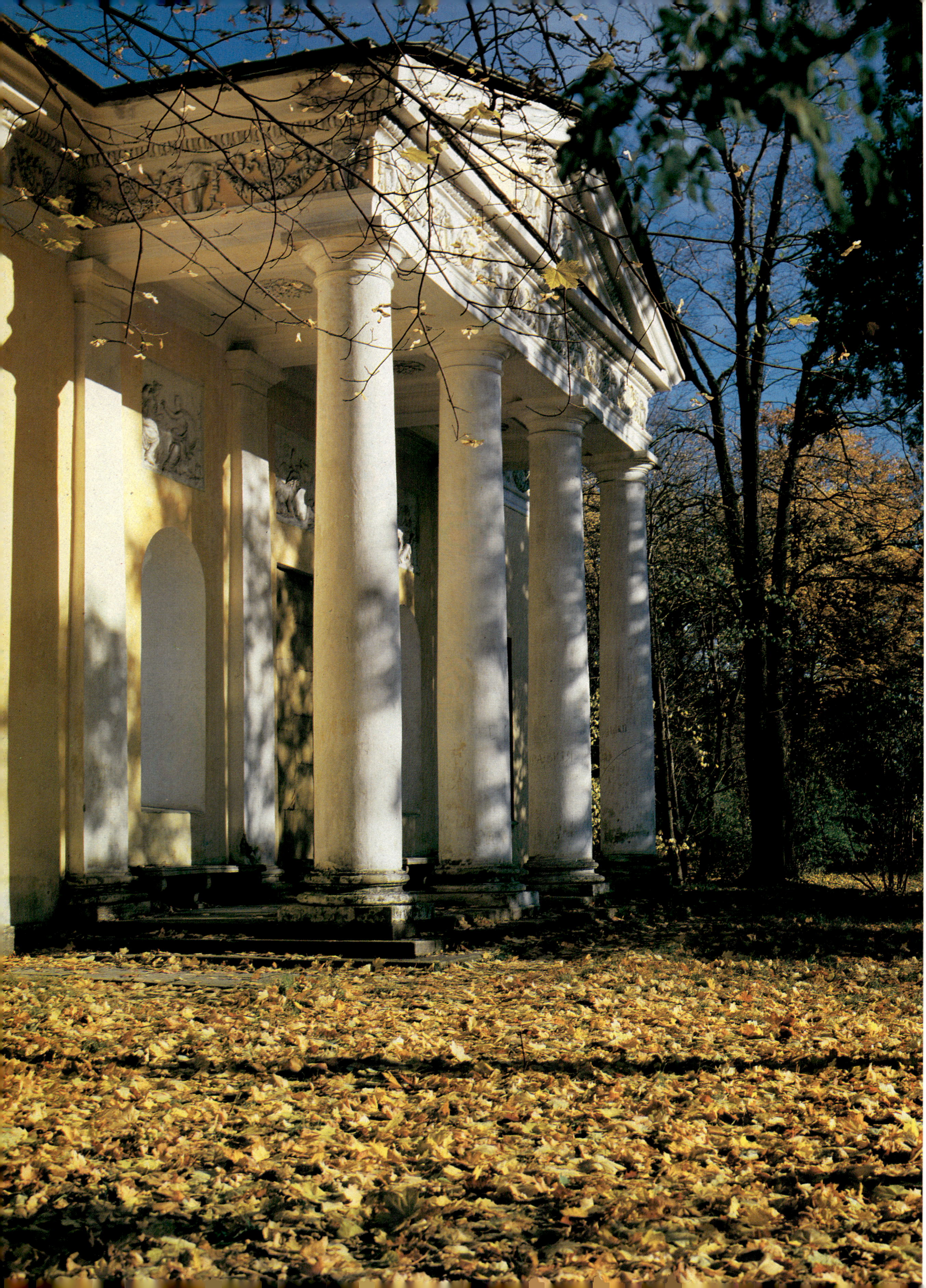

286
→
287

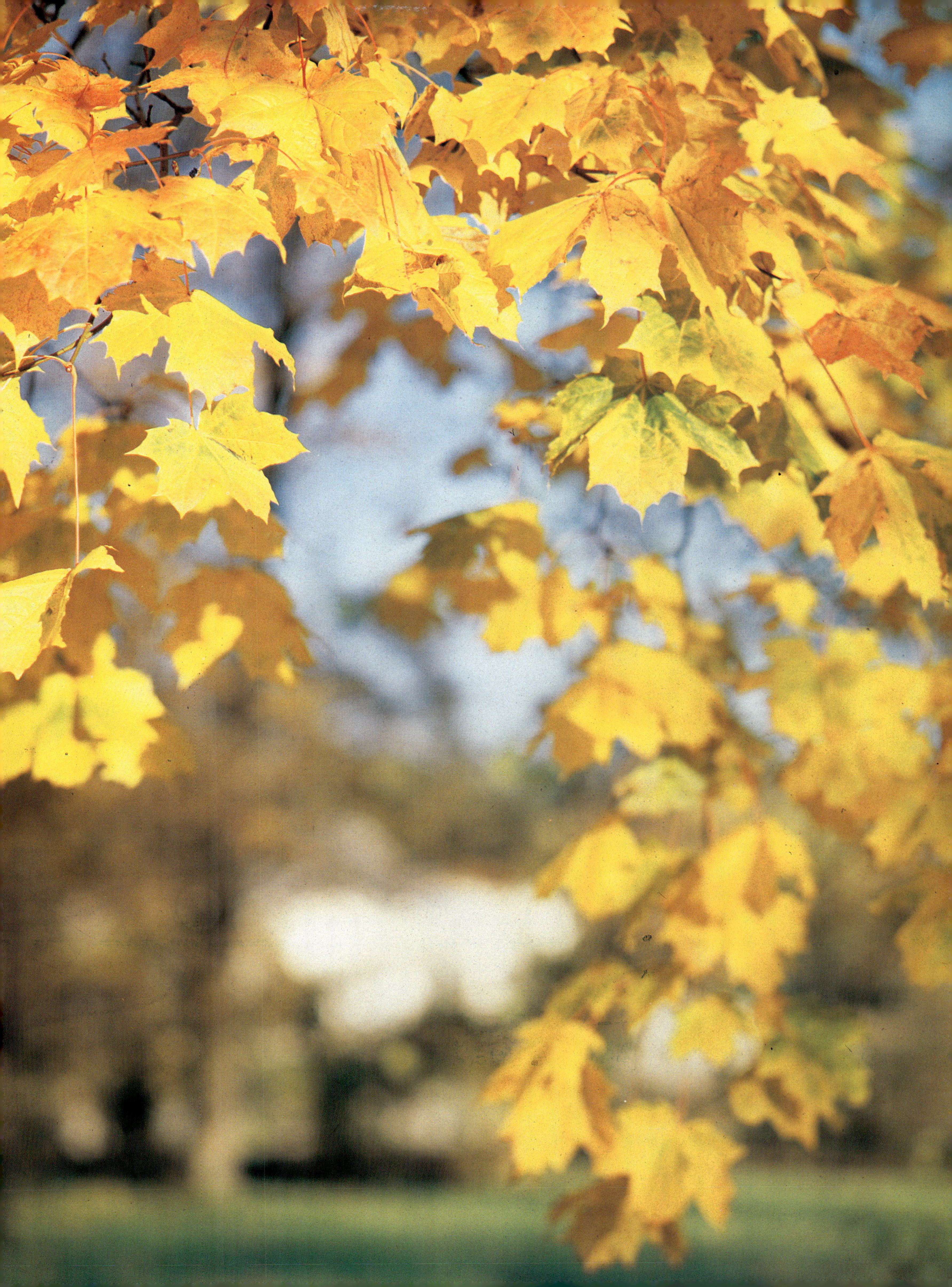

288, 289 Tsarskoye Selo (Pushkin). The Cameron Gallery

290 *Peterhof. The Lower Park. The Grand Cascade*

291 *Peterhof. The Lower Park. The Samson Fountain*

292 *Peterhof. The Lower Park seen from the terrace of the Great Palace* →

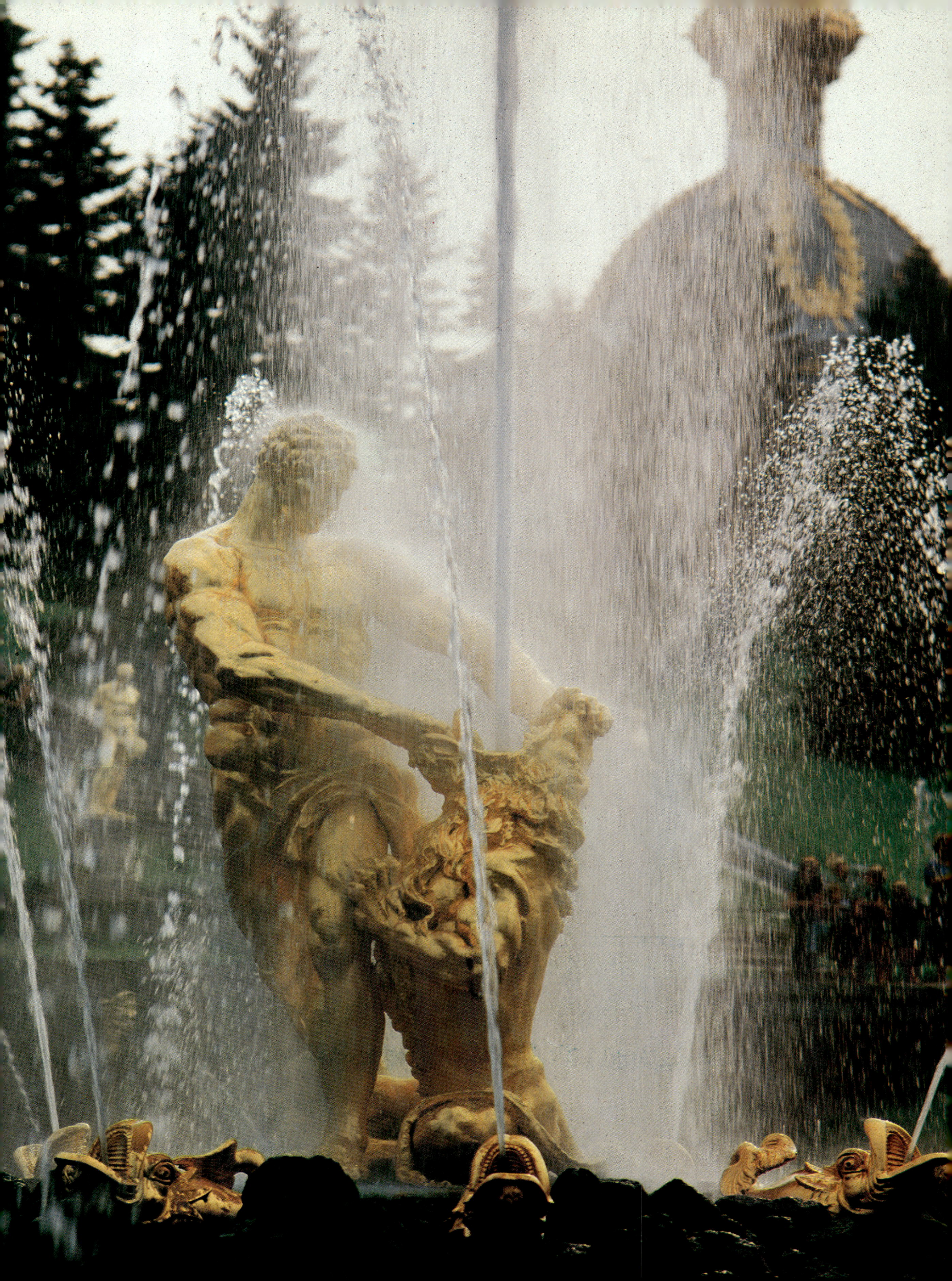

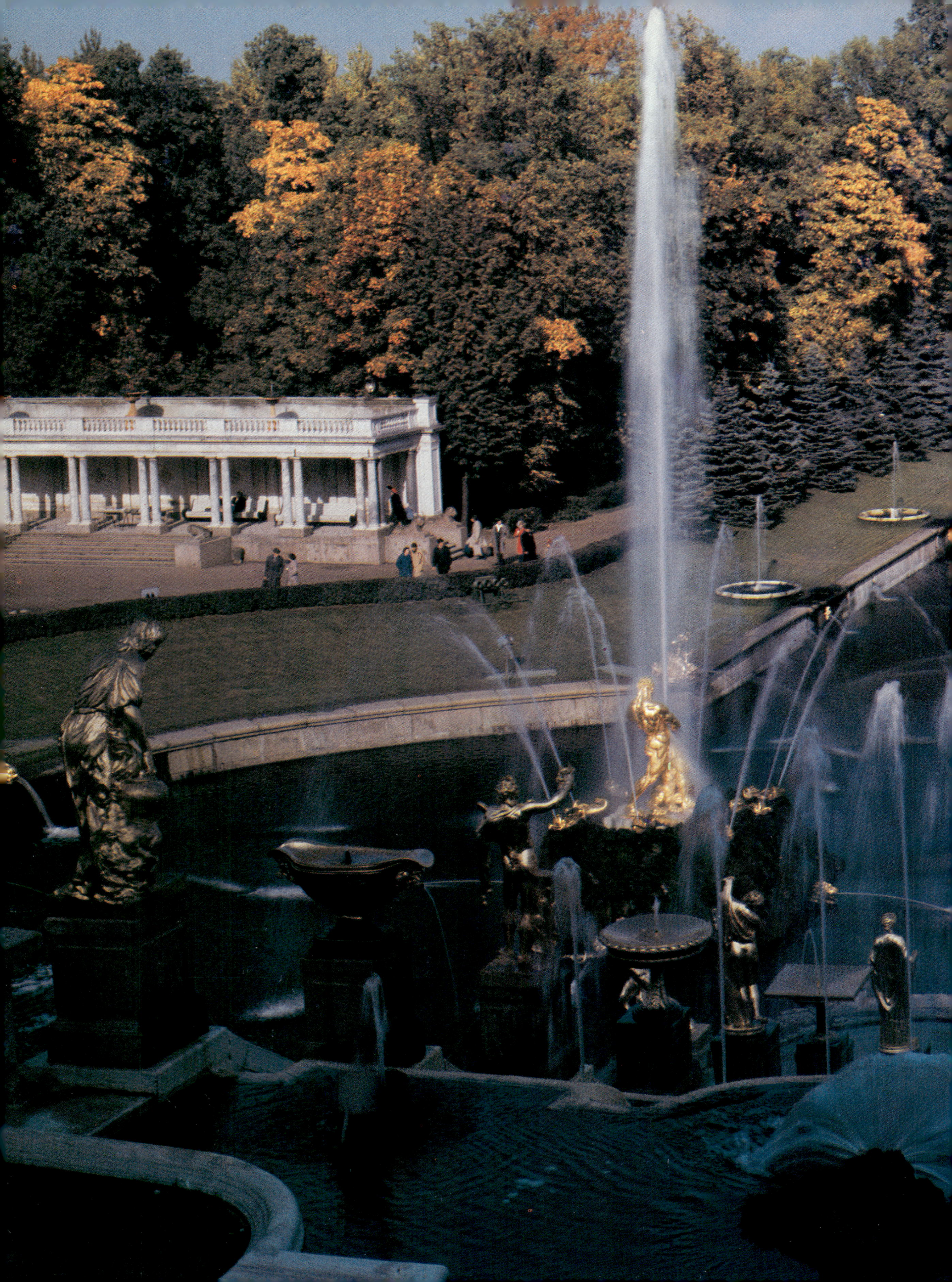

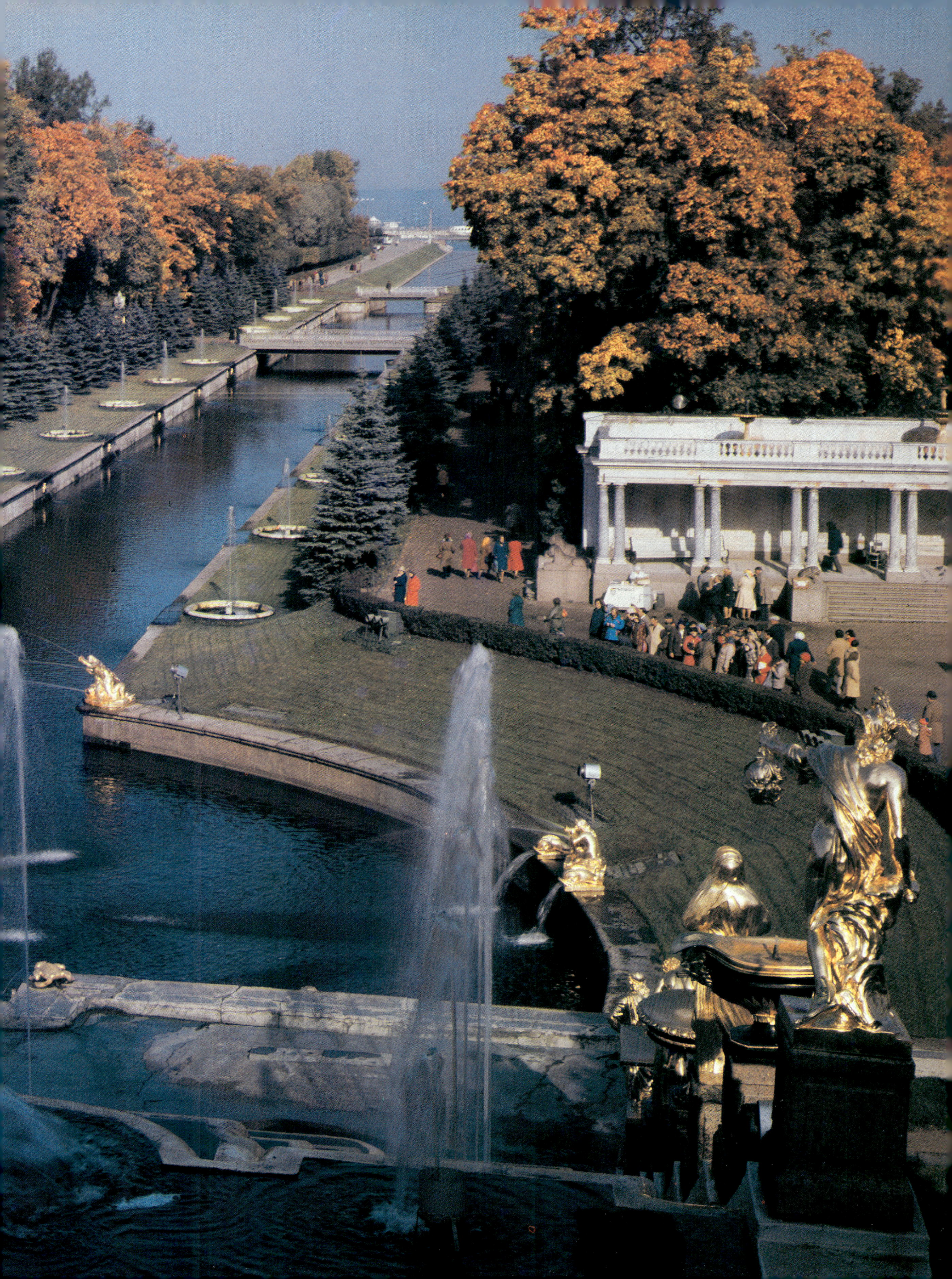

293 Peterhof. The Lower Park. The Marly Palace
294 Peterhof. The Lower Park. The Roman Fountain

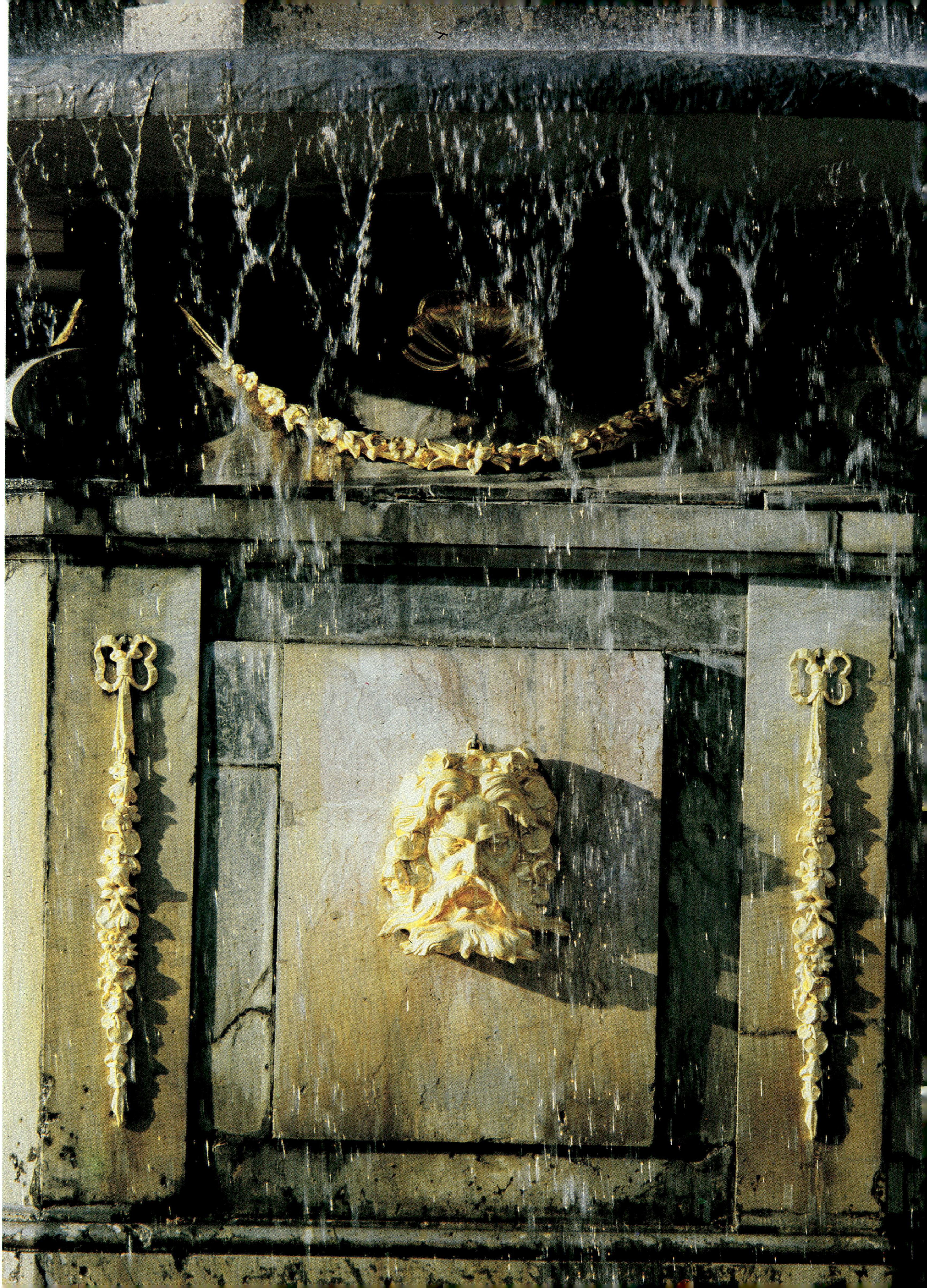

295, 296 Peterhof. The Lower Park. The Great Palace

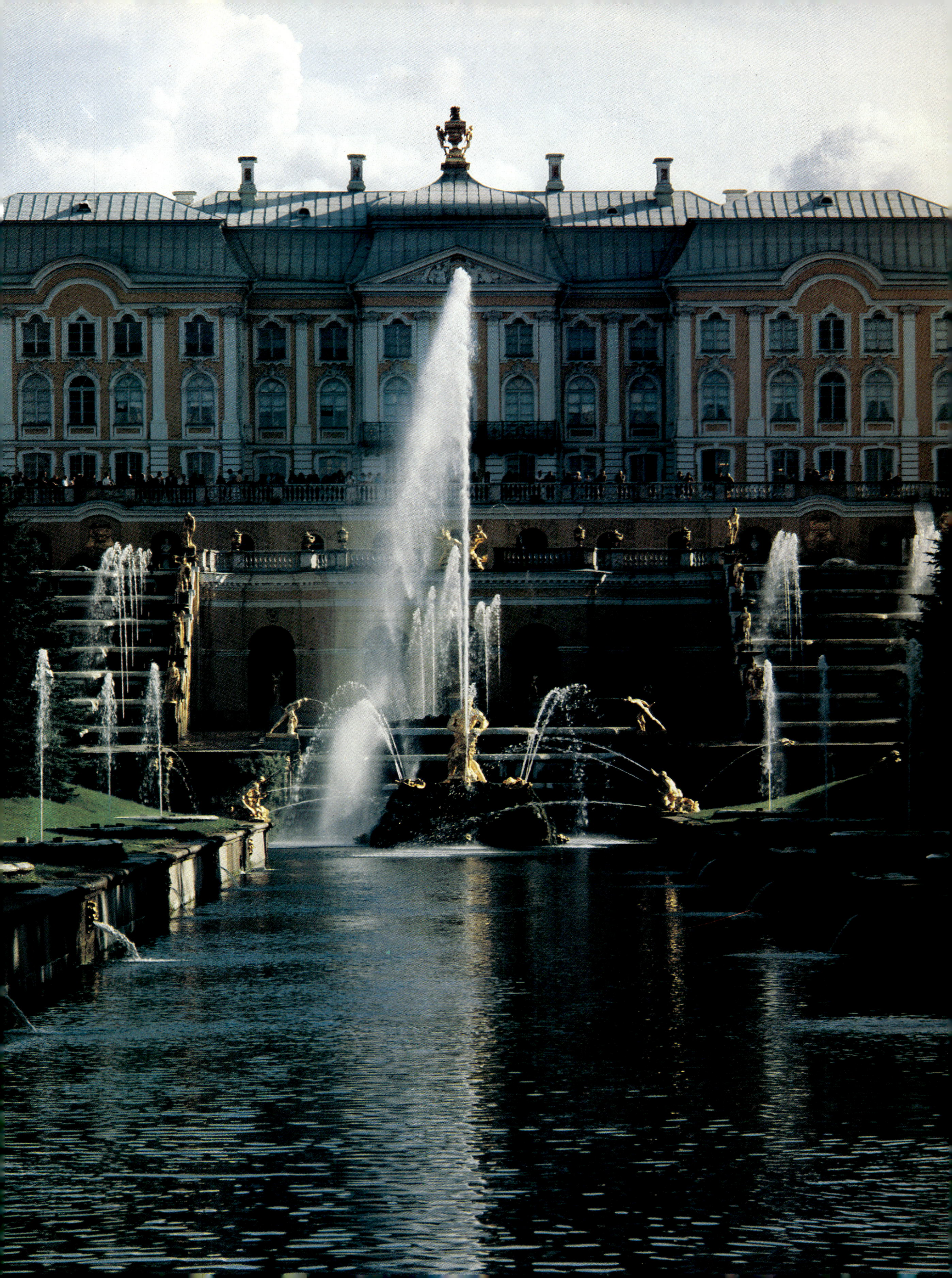

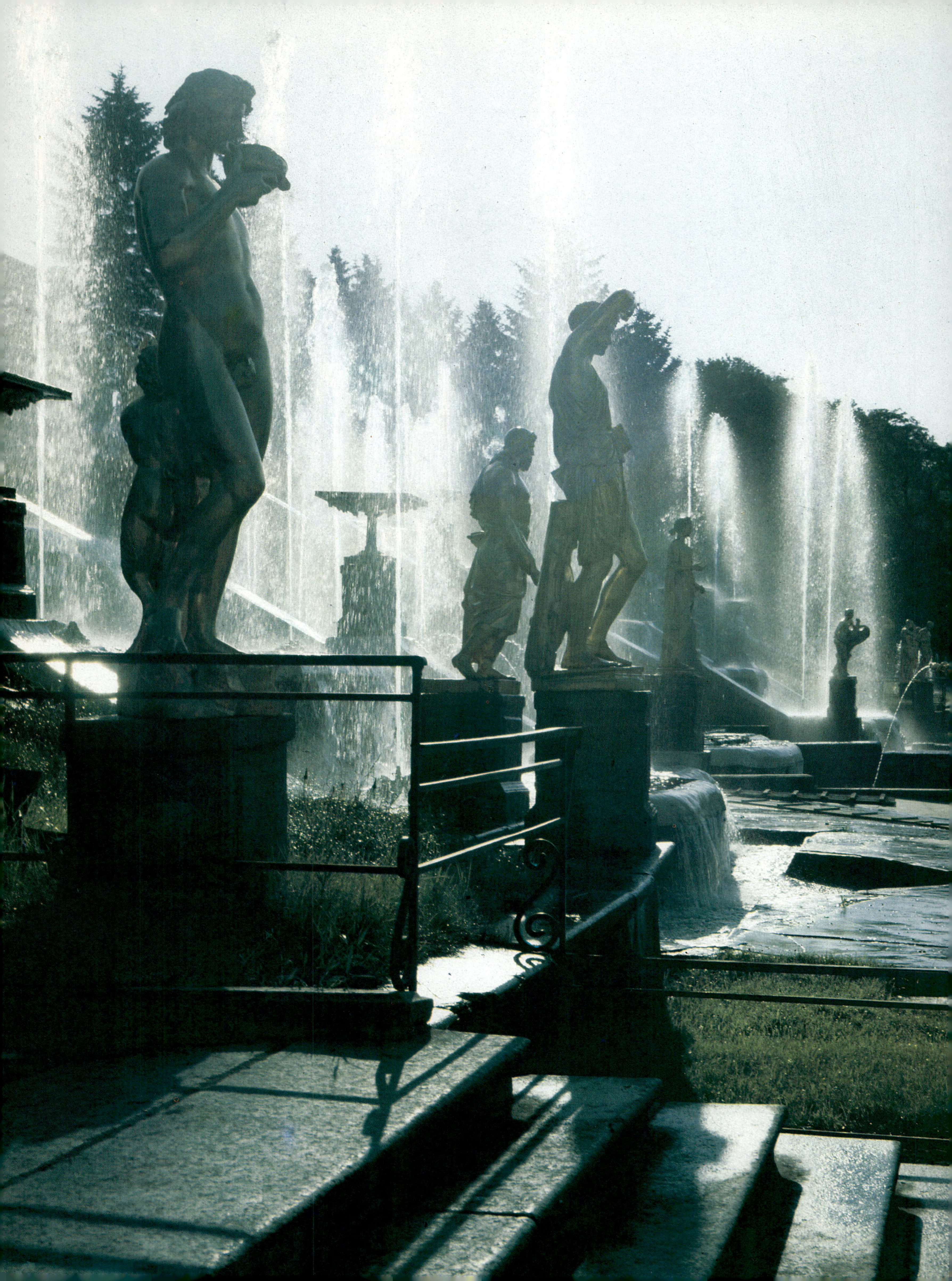

297, 299 *Peterhof. The Lower Park. The Grand Cascade sculpture*
298 *Peterhof. The Lower Park. The Hermitage Pavilion*

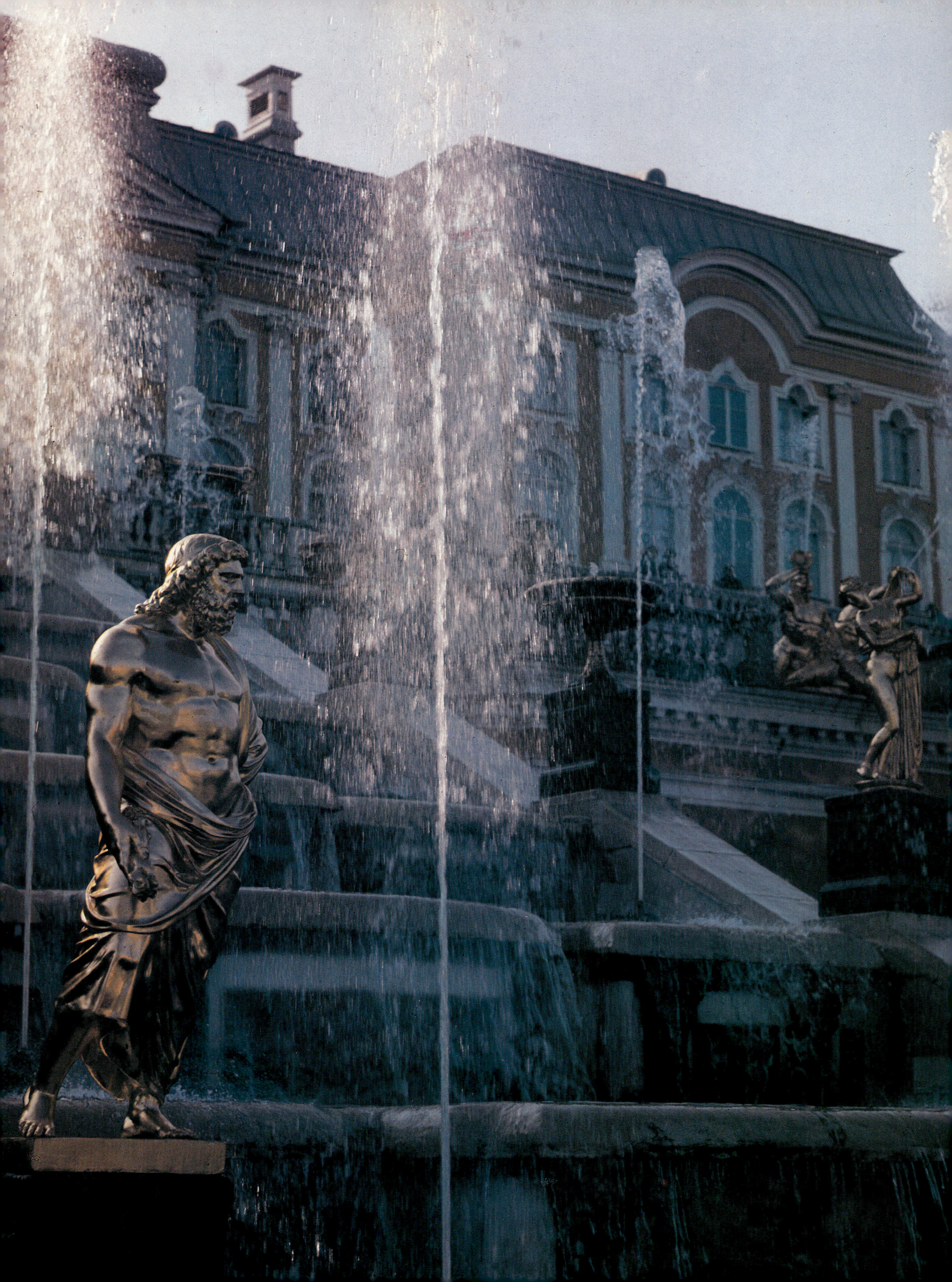

300   Peterhof. The Lower Park. The Chess
      Mountain Cascade

A Brief Notice about Architectural Monuments Illustrated in the Book

THE ACADEMY OF FINE ARTS
One of the earliest constructions of Russian classicism, the building was erected in 1764-88 after the design by A.F. Kokorinov and J.-B. Vallin de La Mothe. It has a rectangular section with a circular court in the centre and four small rectangular courts in the corners. The main facade facing the Neva is decorated with a portico having columns of the Tuscan order and a triangular pediment — a motif characteristic for the baroque style.

From the time of its foundation the Academy of Fine Arts became the focus of the Russian artistic life. Many of the outstanding artists, sculptors and architects were its students.

The pier on the Neva Embankment in front of the Academy of Fine Arts was constructed in 1830s, after the design by the architect K.A. Thon. The two decorating Sphynxes were found in 1830s during excavation in Egypt. Their heads portray the Pharaon Amenkhotep III (thirteenth century B.C.). Bought by the Russian government, the Sphynxes were brought to Petersburg in 1832 and installed on granite monolithic blocks which flank the descent towards the Neva. There are also two lamps and figures of four griffins.

THE ADMIRALTY
The Admiralty was laid in 1704 to be a fortress-shipyard. The first wooden building was constructed after the conception and designs made by Peter the Great. From the central gate of the shipyard, diverging like three rays, three roads of the growing city lay (Nevsky Prospect, Gorokhovaya Street and Voznesensky Prospect), forming the «*Trident of Petersburg*» as it is called.

In 1727-38 I.K. Korobov changed wooden constructions for the stone ones, preserving the original plan of the building and the tower over the main entrance. The present building, which is the third one, was constructed in 1806-23 after the design by the architect A.D. Zakharov. It became a major achievement of the Russian classicism, a masterpiece of Russian national architecture.

The building comprises two П-shaped constructions; their ends facing the Neva are connected by pavilions. Over the centre of the main facade there rises a tower decorated with columns, with a spire crowned by a boat-shaped weathercock.

The best sculptors of the time headed by F.F. Shtchedrin worked toghether with Zakharov; the building of the Admiralty is decorated with the haut-relief *Starting the Navy in Russia* (the sculptor I.I. Terebenev), on the sides of the main arch sculptural groups are placed *The Nymphs Carrying the Globe*; over the upper colonnade of the tower there are twenty-eight statues (the seasons, the elements, the main winds, the goddess Isis, the patroness of shipbuilding, and Urania, the Muse of astronomy).

THE ALEXANDER COLUMN
The column was erected by the architect Auguste Montferrand in 1830-34 in the centre of the Palace Square to commemorate the victory of Russia over Napoleon during the 1812-14 war.

The column is hewn out of a granite monolith. The facets of the base are decorated with bas-reliefs made by P.V. Svintsov, I. Leppe, D. Scotti. The column is crowned with the figure of an Angel made by the sculptor B.I. Orlovsky.

THE ALLEGORICAL STATUE OF A.V. SUVOROV
The allegorical monument is placed to commemorate the great Russian general, the hero of Russian-Turkish and Napoleonic wars, Generalissimo Alexander Vasilyevitch Suvorov-Rymniksky. It is cast after the model by the sculptor M.I. Kozlovsky.

The monument was inaugurated on May 5, 1801, in the first anniversary of Suvorov's death.

On the pedestal there are figures of Glory (cast after the model by the sculptor F.G. Gordeyev) which support the bronze shield with the legend, «*Prince of Italy, Count Suvorov-Rymniksky. 1801*».

Originally the monument was installed in the Field of Mars, on the bank of the Moika. In 1818 C.I. Rossi transferred it to the square between the house of the Saltykovs and the outbuilding of the Marble Palace.

THE ANICHKOV BRIDGE
The three-spanned stone bridge in Nevsky Prospect over the Fontanka built after the design by the engineer A.D. Gotman and the drawing by the architect K.F. Schenkel was inaugurated in 1841. The bridge is famous for its sculpture groups created by P.K. Klodt. The four groups symbolize the four stages of taming the wild horse by the man: in the first one the man is thrown down, in the last one he is the victor and leads the tame animal.

THE ASTORIA HOTEL
The six-storey building of the hotel with a garret storey was constructed in 1911-12 after the design by the architect F.I. Lidval in the modernist style. The reconstruction which took place in the late 1980s preserved the exterior of the hotel completely and restored many of the original interiors.

THE BANK BRIDGE
The suspension foot-bridge over the Yekaterininsky Canal was constructed by the engineer G. Tretter and inaugurated for pedestrians in 1826.

The griffin figures were cast at the Alexandrovsky iron foundry after the models made by the sculptor P.P. Sokolov.

The massive griffin figures contrast with the delicate construction of the bridge span.

THE BELOSELSKY-BELOZERSKY PALACE
In 1846 the architect A.I. Stackenschneider rebuilt the constructions of the Palace that had faced Nevsky Prospect and the Fontanka, to the order of the Prince K.E. Beloselsky-Belozersky and had utterly changed their exterior and interior decoration. In his design he used some methods of the Russian baroque architects. The palace interior remained completely unchanged till this day. Since 1884 the palace belonged to a brother of the Tsar Alexander III — the Great Duke Sergey Alexandrovich.

THE BRIDGES AND EMBANKMENTS OF PETERSBURG
The Neva estuary chosen by Peter the Great to lay down the city abounded in channels, rivers and streams. Petersburg is a city spreading on the islands (there are over 40 islands), many

of them are formed by canals dug to drain swampy parts of the ground. From the first years of the existence of the city it was necessary to fortify low swampy banks by ramming piles and building artificial embankments.

The Neva embankments originally were wooden (sometimes painted to imitate bricks), but as early as the second half of the eighteenth century after the design by Yu. Veldten they were covered with granite, and cast-iron gratings were placed. Descents to the water, piers for boats and ships were decorated with sculpture, vases and lamp-posts.

The first bridges to appear in the city were those over canals and small rivers; first they were wooden, later changed for the stone ones (they are still functioning), during the time of Pushkin cast-iron bridges were built, delicate and easy to assemble.

The first permanent bridge across the Neva — the Annunciation, later named the St. Nicholas' Bridge, was built in 1842-50 (before that the bridges were floating ones). Today there are eight bridges over the Neva within the city boundaries, all of them are the drawbridges; there are over five hundred bridges in Petersburg altogether, each of them being not only a complicate engineering structures, but a striking piece of art.

THE BUDDHIST TEMPLE
A unique building constructed by the architect G.V. Baranovsky in 1909-15. Some motifs of the Medieval Tibetan architecture are used in the design. A special committee took part in the work at the project, which included the most prominent Orientalists and painters: S.F. Oldenburg, V.V. Radlow, N.K. Roerich, F.I. Sherbatsky.

THE CASTLE OF ENGINEERS (MIKHAILOVSKY CASTLE)
The palace was built to be the residence of the Emperor Paul I in 1797-1800 after the design by V.I. Bazhenov and V. Brenna. Of a square section, with an interior octagonal yard, the palace forms a closed space which reminds one of a medieval castle. The main south-eastern facade with the gala entrance into the interior court is characterized, despite the richness of the decor, by a deliberate severity. The opposite facade, which faces the Summer Gardens, with a columned portico bearing the balcony, the caryatides and statues on the wide stairs descending into the garden, are characteristic of an estate palace.

Since 1819 the building housed the Main Engineering School and the palace started to be called the Engineers. Castle of Some interiors were destroyed. Part of the rooms remained unchanged till this day: the gala staircase, the Throne Hall, the Raphael Gallery, the Oval Hall, and the chapel.

THE CATHEDRAL OF OUR LADY OF KAZAN
In 1799 a competition was held to work out a design of a new cathedral. In 1800 the design made by the architect Andrey Voronikhin was approved. The building was laid down in August 27, 1801. The construction lasted for a whole decade.

The section of the cathedral has the shape of a Latin cross. The altar part traditionally faces the East. The northern facade faces the Nevsky Prospect; it is adjoined with a grand colonnade of ninety-six Corinthian columns standing in four rows, hewn in Pudost stone monoliths.

Voronikhin had planned a colonnade on the southern facade as well, but the plan was never carried out.

In the exterior decoration of the cathedral sculpture plays a major part. A panneau in relief over the eastern passage *Moses Extracting Water in the Desert* is made by I.P. Martos, the one over the western passage *Erecting the Copper Serpent* by I.P. Prokofiev. On the attic of the church apse *Jesus Entering Jerusalem* is made by D. Rachette. Four bronze statues in the niches, St. Vladimir and St. Alexander Nevsky, are cast by the model of S.S. Pimenov; St. Andrew is made by V.I. Demuth-Malinovsky, St. John the Baptist is made by I.P. Martos.

In 1805-06 the northern door folds were cast in bronze, reproducing the *Paradise door* of the Florence Baptistery.

There are fifty-six Corinthian monolithic columns in rose Finland granite in the interior.

In 1813 the hero of the 1812 Patriotic war, Field Marchal M.I. Kutuzov was buried in the Cathedral. Numerous trophies of the Patriotic war were placed in the cathedral: one hundred and seven banners and standards, keys of eight fortresses and seventeen towns, and the Marshal Davou's sceptre. The cathedral became the pantheon of Russian military glory.

The significance of the Cathedral of Our Lady of Kazan as the Patriotic war memorial increased after the monuments to the Field Marchals M.I. Kutuzov and M.B. Barclay de Tolli were installed in 1837. The monuments are made after the sketches of the sculptor B.I. Orlovsky and architect V.P. Stasov.

THE CATHEDRAL OF THE RESSURECTION (THE «SAVIOR ON THE BLOOD»)
March 1, 1881, the Emperor Alexander II was assassinated. That very year the government decided to build a church at the spot of the assault. The design of I.V. Makarov and A.A. Parland got approved. In their conception they used compositional methods and forms of the monument of ancient Russian architecture — the Intercession-at-the Ditch (the Cathedral of St. Basil the Beatific) in the Red Square in Moscow.

The construction lasted for over twenty years and was finished in 1907.

The Cathedral of the Ressurection has one altar and three apses. In the decoration of the facades and interiors an important role is played by mosaic. The pediments of the porches are decorated with mosaic panels created after the drawings by V.M. Vasnetsov, — *Christ Bearing the Cross, Crucifixion, Deposition from the Cross, Descent to Hell*. A.P. Ryabushkin, N.A. Bruni, V.V. Belyaev, etc., worked at drawings of mosaic for interior decoration of the cathedral. The mosaics were made in A.A. Frolov's shop.

THE CATHEDRAL OF THE SMOLNY CONVENT
One of the finest F.B. Rastrelli's works, a brilliant example of the eighteenth century Russian architecture, the cathedral was laid in 1748 and finished in the rough in 1764. However, the interior decoration was not made. The construction of the cathedral was completed by V.P. Stasov in 1832-35.

THE CATHEDRAL OF ST. NICHOLAS-ON-THE SEAS
The two-storey five-domed cathedral built in 1753-62 by S.I. Tchevakinsky is an outstanding monument of the Russian baroque architecture. Light elegant volumes, abounding stucco works, a capricious rhythm of the columns, the striking broad girdle of the entablement accords with the principles of the ancient Russian architecture. The fourtier campanile placed on the bank of the channel is particularly expressive.

THE CATHEDRAL OF THE TRANSFIGURATION
The cathedral was built in 1743-54 after the design by M.G. Zemtsov to be the church of the oldest regiment of the Guards — the Preobrazhensky Regiment. In 1825 the cathedral burned down. In 1828-29 it was restored after the design by V.P. Stasov.

In 1829-32 around the cathedral a railing was made after the design by V.P. Stasov, of Turkish guns and chains, — the trophies of the 1828 Russian-Turkish war.

The carved wooden iconostasis of the cathedral is of a great artistic significance.

THE CHORISTERS' CAPELLA

The complex of the buildings of the Choristers' Capella was erected in 1887-89 after the design by the architect L.N. Benois on the bank of the Moika near the Palace Square. The main building is removed into the interior of the main court, three-storey outbuildings face the embankment opposite the Choristers' Bridge.

THE CRUISER AURORA

The man-of-war built in 1897-1900 at the Petersburg shipbuilding yard took part in the Tsushima Battle during the 1905 Russian-Japanese war. In October 1917 the crew of the cruiser passed over to the people revolted against the Provisional Government. The signal shot was made from its board which announced the start of the assault of the Winter Palace, the residence of the government. A monument to the October revolution, the cruiser is put at her eternal mooring in the Greater Nevka near the Nakhimov Naval School.

THE ETHNOGRAPHY MUSEUM

The Museum is built after the design by the architect V.F. Svinyin in 1900-11 to replace the outbuildings of the Mikhailovsky Palace.

Architectural methods and forms of Russian classicism are used in the compositional concept. The architect tried to achieve accord of the building with the Mikhailovsky Palace, but did not fully succeed.

Olonets marble is used for interior decoration. The three walls of the main hall are surrounded with the frieze by M.Ya. Kharlamov *The Peoples of Russia*.

THE EUROPE HOTEL

The comfortable hotel appeared in 1873-75 as the result of reconstructing the old houses at the corner of Mikhailovsky Square and Mikhailovsky Street after the design by the architect L.F. Fontana. The facades of the building are richly decorated in the eclectical style. The interiors are reconstructed in 1905-14 after the designs by K.E. Mackenzen and F.I. Lidval.

THE FIELD OF MARS

The history of forming one of the largest park and architectural ensembles of Petersburg started in 1710s, when, after joining the rivers Moika and Fontanka and digging the Swan Canal, the borders of the Summer Gardens were defined. The vast meadow to the west of the Summer Gardens which was first called the Great, and late, Tsaritsin Meadow, was never occupied. Reviews of the Guards' regiment were held in the meadow.

After the revolution, the Field of Mars lost its meaning of a military parade ground.

On the 23 of March 1917, the participants of the February revolution killed during the armed conflicts with the police were buried here. After the design of the architect L.V. Rudnev, in 1917-19 an immense monument to the deceased was erected over the fraternal graves.

In 1920-23 a parterre garden was planned on the territory of the Field of Mars after the design by the architect I.A. Fomin.

THE GOSTINY DVOR

In 1752 the architect F.B. Rastrelli was commissioned to create the disign of a two-storey building. The construction began in 1757, but was stopped soon. In 1761 the design was revized. On the whole, the general manner of the compositional solution remained, although the facades were changed after the design by the architect J.-B. Vallin de La Mothe. The construction of the building was finished only in 1784-85.

The repeated reiteration of the arcades and the solemn porticoes, the simplicity and expressiveness of the architectural forms define the features of the real grandeur of the building.

At present it houses a major department store of the city.

THE HEADQUARTERS

In 1918-29 Carl Rossi reconstructed several houses in the Palace Square and created a single immense building of the Headquarters. It comprises two constructions connected in the centre of a bow-shaped facade with monumental arches.

The western part housed the Headquarters, the eastern one was left to the Ministry of Foreign Affairs and the Ministry of Finance.

The central Triumphal Arch crowned with the chariot of Glory and decorated with statues of soldiers was conceived by Rossi to be a memorial to the 1812 Patriotic war.

THE HERMITAGE

The complex of buildings of the Hermitage, a major world collection of art, is situated in the very centre of Petersburg.

In the second half of the eighteenth century several buildings were erected on the Neva Embankment near the Winter Palace, where the growing collections of the prospective museum were housed.

In 1764-65 J.-B. Vallin de La Mothe built the Small Hermitage, one of the most attractive and harmonious constructions of the early classical period. The interiors of the «La Mothe's Pavilion», as it was called by contemporaries, did not remain; the present Pavilion Hall of the Small Hermitage was created by A.I. Stackenschneider.

In 1771-87 Yu.M. Veldten built the Old Hermitage, a strickt and quiet building of perfect proportions which brings the line of the Hermitage buildings up to the Winter Canal.

Almost at the same time G. Quarenghi created his masterpiece, the Hermitage Theatre, connecting it with the other buildings by the means of an archway and making in this way a most poetical spot in Petersburg.

The fourth building of the Hermitage, the New Hermitage, was erected in the mid-nineteenth century by V.P. Stasov after the design by the Munich architect L. von Klenze, who had adjusted the design to the existing conditions. The New Hermitage facade which faces Millionnaya Street running parallel to the Neva Embankment, is decorated with the famous portico with the giant Atlantes figures hewn out of monolithic granite blocks (the sculptor A.I. Terebenev).

After the revolution of 1917 the Winter Palace was transferred to the Hermitage, the fifth and the earliest building of the museum complex to have been constructed.

THE HOUSE WITH TOWERS
(THE BYELOGRUD HOUSE)

The construction of the multy-storey dwelling house in the Leo Tolstoy Square began in 1913 after the design of the owner, K.I. Rosenstein, and finished in 1916 by the architect A.E. Byelogrud.

THE KUNSTKAMMER

One of the few well preserved monuments of the early eighteenth century Russian architecture, in whose construction (1718-34) N.F. Gerbel, G.I. Mattarnovi and M.G. Zemtsov took part. The building was to house the library and collections.

In 1747 the Kunstkammer was greatly damaged by the fire. It was restored by S.I. Tchevakinsky in 1754-58 (except the burned turcet which only reappeared after the restoration works of 1947-48). At present collections of Peter the Great Ethnography and Antropology Museum the Russian Academy of Sciences are exposed here.

THE KSESINSKY MANSION
The mansion which belonged to the famous ballerina M.F. Ksesinsky was built in 1904 after the design by A.I. Gaugin — a famous architect of the 1900s, a representative of the modernist style.

THE LION BRIDGE
The foot-bridge over the Yekaterininsky Canal was constructed after the design by the engineer G. Tretter in 1825-26. The lion figures on the cast-iron bases are made after the model by the sculptor P.P. Sokolov. When reconstructing the bridge in 1954, the lamps and the cast-iron grating have been restored according to the original conception.

THE MANEGE
The building constructed in 1804-07 after the design by G. Quarenghi was a part of the barrack complex which was intended for Horse Guards Regiment. In front of the portico there are twin marble statues of Dioscuroi made in Italy by the sculptor P. Triscorni.

In 1930s the building was refashioned by N.E. Lanceray to become a garage. In 1967 it was transferred to the Union of Artists to serve as an exhibition hall.

THE MARBLE PALACE
The palace was erected in 1768-85 after the design by A. Rinaldi.

Marble and granite of different colours were used to face the building, which was why it was named the Marble Palace. This is a most outstanding architectural monument of the early Russian classicism.

The two statues on the attic and compositions of military armours are made by the sculptor F.I. Shubin.

In 1937 a branch of the Central Museum of V.I. Lenin was opened in the Marble Palace. At present the palace is a branch of the Russian Museum.

THE MEMORIAL MUSEUM
OF ALEXANDER PUSHKIN
(12, MOIKA EMBANKMENT)
On the first floor of the house there is a ten-room flat occupied by A.S. Pushkin since October 1836, where he died on January 29, 1837 as a result of the duel wound. The interior of the flat is restored on the basis of archive documents and recollections of the contemporaries; personal belongings of Pushkin and his family are preserved here. Here he worked at the *History of Peter the Great*, finished *A Captain's Daughter*; here many poets and writers, Pushkin's friends, used to come. The hands of the clock on the wall of his study were stopped at the moment of the poet's death.

THE MEMORIAL TO THE HEROIC DEFENDERS
OF LENINGRAD
The sculptural and architectural ensemble that glorifies the fortitude and heroism of the defenders of Leningrad during the Great Patriotic war of 1941-45 is created by the famous sculptors and architects M.K. Anikushin, S.B. Speransky and V.A. Kamensky. It was inaugurated on May 9, 1975.

THE MENSHIKOV PALACE
The palace for the Prince A.D. Menshikov, the favourite friend of Peter the Great, was built by the architects G. Fontana and G. Shedel in 1710-27.

It is one of the first dwelling houses of the city. Originally it comprised the main building and the outbuildings. A regular garden with fountains and sculptures surrounded palace, and on the Neva there was a pier. The building was reconstructed several times. At present it houses an affiliation of the Hermitage.

THE MINING INSTITUTE
By the time of its foundation (in 1773) the institute was the first in Russia and the second in the world higher technical school. In 1806-11 the architect Andrey Voronikhin combined several houses on the embankment where the Mining Cadet School was housed to become a single building. The main facade which faces Neva is decorated with a portico of twelve Doric columns and bas-reliefs with mythological scenes (the sculptor V.I. Demuth-Malinovsky).

On the sides of the portico stairs there are sculptural groups *The Rape of Proserpine* and *Hercules Strangling Anteus* made by S.K. Sukhanov after the models by V.I. Demuth-Malinovsky and S.S. Pimenov.

THE MONUMENT TO NICHOLAS I
The monument in St. Isaac's Square was erected in 1856-59 after the design by A. Montferrand. Several sculptors took part in the creation of the monument: the model of the equestrian statue of Nicholas I was made by P.K. Klodt, the models of the sculptures for the pedestal were made by N.A. Ramazanov and R.K. Zaleman.

THE MOSCOW TRIUMPHAL GATES
The Moscow Triumphal Gates were erected to commemorate the Russian victories during the Russian-Turkish war of 1828.

The design of the arch was created by V.P. Stasov. The stone-laying ceremony took place in 1834. The gates had the form of twelve cast-iron columns. The sculptured details of the gates — military trophies and figures of genii — were made by the sculptor B.I. Orlovsky in 1835.

In 1935 the gates were dismantled, and in 1958-60 restored (after the design of the architects I.G. Kaptsug and E.N. Petrova).

THE MOSKVA HOTEL
In 1974-77 in a round square in front of the entrance to the St. Alexander Nevsky Monastery, designed in the late eighteenth century by I.E. Starov, one of the largest hotels in Petersburg was constructed — the Moskva hotel (the architects E.S. Goldgor, V.N. Shtcherbin, L.K. Varshavskaya, engineer E.V. Golubev). The squatting extended building with a rounded corner makes a smooth transition from the square to the Neva Embankment and the St. Alexander Nevsky Bridge.

THE MUTUAL CREDIT SOCIETY
The building with its four-faceted dome and a huge vaulted window in the centre of the facade facing the Yekaterininsky Canal is constructed in 1888-90 after the design by P.Yu. Suzor. The sculpture decorations are made by D.I. Yensen and A.M. Opekushin.

THE NARVA TRIUMPHAL GATES
The Gates were erected to commemorate the 1812 Patriotic war.

A wooden triumphal arch was built 1814 after the design by G. Quarenghi to hold the ceremony of meeting the Guards Regiments.

In 1827-34 V.P. Stasov erected the stone gates, preserving G. Quarenghi's composition. The Gates with the chariot of Glory. The horses are made in forged copper after the models by S.S. Pimenov and V.I. Demuth-Malinovsky.

THE NEW HOLLAND
The ensemble of the New Holland (situated on the small island between the Moika and the Admiralty and Kryukov Canals) is a striking monument of the early Russian classical architecture.

In 1732-40 the first timber storehouses were on the island, built after the design by the architect I.K. Korobov. In 1765-80s the wooden storehouses were changed for the stone ones according to the design by S.I. Tchevakinsky. The design of the arch over the channel was made by the architect J.-B. Vallin de La Mothe.

THE NOVOMIKHAILOVSKY PALACE
In 1857-61 the architect A.I. Stackenschneider built the palace for the Great Duke Mikhail Nikolayevich on the Neva Embankment near the Hermitage Theatre. It is a typical monument of the Petersburg architecture of the mid-nineteenth century. In the decoration baroque and Renaissance devices are used such as porticoes and columns. Decorative terracotta sculpture is abundantly used.

THE PASSAGE DEPARTMENT STORE
The building was constructed in 1846-48 after the design by the architect R.A. Zhelyazevich. The prototype for the composition was taken from the Golitsin's Gallery in Moscow (the architect M.D. Bykovsky).

In 1899-1900 the civil engineer S.S. Kozlov reconstructed the Passage and changed its interior planning and facade decoration. He built a third floor, while the ground and the first floor got its huge glass windows. The facade was decorated with pilasters of the Corinthian order and the Renaissance facade shaping was abolished. To face the building, natural stone was used — Radom sandstone.

The concert hall of the old Passage remained after the reconstruction, later it housed V.F. Komissarzhevskaya's theatre which now bears her name in the title.

PAVILION
IN THE MIKHAILOVSKY GARDENS
In 1825 C.I. Rossi built a small pavilion on the bank of the river Moika in the garden of the Mikhailovsky Palace. He managed wonderfully to attain harmony of architecture and nature. Severe forms and elegant proportions, beautiful details of the pavilion harmonize it with the surrounding landscape.

In front of the pavilion there is a terrace-pier fenced with a cast-iron grating.

THE PISKAREVSKY MEMORIAL CEMETERY
The architectural ensemble dedicated to the memory of the Leningraders deceased during the blockade at the time of the 1941-45 Great Patriotic war is created after the design by A. Vasilyev and E. Levinson. The bronze statue of the Motherland in the centre of the ensemble is made by V. Isayeva and R. Taurit. The memorial complex was inaugurated on May 9, 1960.

THE POINT
OF THE VASILYEVSKY ISLAND
The majestic ensemble of the Point of the Vasilyevsky Island was being formed during a long period — beginning from the foundation of the city till the first three decades of the nineteenth century. The compositional centre of the ensemble is the building of the Stock Exchange (at present it houses the Central Naval Museum) constructed by Thomas de Tomon in 1805-10 after the type of ancient Greek temples. The facades are decorated with sculpture groups which emphasize the strickt symmetry of the composition of the ensemble.

On the sides of the building of the Exchange two rostral columns are placed, also made after the design by Thomas de Tomon. The bases of the columns are stone slabs on which colossal allegorical figures hewn in stone are placed; they symbolize four Russian rivers — the Volga, the Dnieper, the Neva and the Volkhov. The sloping descent towards the water is faced with granite, the very «point» of the Island is flanked with powerful granite spheres on pedestals.

THE PUSHKIN DRAMA THEATRE
(THE ALEXANDRINSKY THEATRE)
One of the best works of the architect Carlo Rossi, the theatre was inaugurated in 1832. The attic of the main facade is decorated with sculptures of the Glory and crowned with Apollo's quadriga. The statues of the Muses Terpsichore and Melpomene are in the niches of the main facade.

Inside the building the auditorium is of the greatest interest. Here some fragments of the original decoration remain (the gilded carvings of the boxes by the stage and of the Emperor's box).

PUSHKIN'S HOUSE
(THE CUSTOM HOUSE)
The building created in 1829-32 in the late Russian classical style after the design by I.F. Luchini makes part of the architectural ensemble of the Point of the Vasilyevsky Island. It was built as a result of the enlarging Petersburg port. The main facade is decorated with a portico of eight columns. On its pediments are statues of Mercury, Neptune and Ceres.

In 1927 the building was transferred to the Institute of Russian Literature *(Pushkin's House)* of the Academy of Sciences.

ROSSI PAVILIONS
(THE ANICHKOV PALACE PAVILIONS)
To the west of the Anichkov Palace two single storey pavilions were built in 1817-18 after the design by C.I. Rossi. Their main facades face the Catherine Garden.

Sculpture is used in the pavilions composition — figures of ancient Russian heroes and stucco bas-reliefs made after the models by S.S. Pimenov.

THE RUSSIAN NATIONAL LIBRARY
The library comprises three buildings combined together to present a single whole. The oldest of the three (the one facing the Catherine Garden) was built in 1796-1801 by the architect E.T. Sokolov. The building is typical for the strict Russian classical architecture.

Some old interiors remain in the building, among which is the Gothic Hall known also as «*Faustus Study*», created in 1857 after the design by the architect I.I. Gornostayev. The decorations of the hall, where there should have been kept books made before 1500, reproduce the atmosphere of the library chambers of the fifteenth century castles.

THE SENATE AND SYNODE
The two monumental buildings constructed in 1829-34 by C.I. Rossi to replace the old Senate (the house of A.P. Bestuzhev-Ryumin) are the last major creation of the famous architect. The buildings are connected with an arch thrown over Galernaya Street.

A large group of artists took part in the decoration works. The facade statues are made by the sculptors S.S. Pimenov, V.I. Demuth-Malinovsky, I. Leppe, etc.

At present the buildings house the Central State Archive.

THE SHEREMETEV PALACE
Situated on the Fontanka Embankment, the Sheremetev Palace was built in 1750-55 by S.I. Tchevakinsky and F.S. Argunov. Compositionally, the building complex is conceived to be a kind of country estate — with the interior

court and a garden behind the house. The court is separated from the embankment with a cast-iron grating placed in 1844.

In its outlook the palace is a typical piece of baroque architecture.

SHI-TSU
The granite Petrovskaya Embankment was constructed in 1901-03 after the design by the architect L.I. Novikov and the engineer F.G. Zbrozek. The wide descent towards the water was decorated in 1907 with atone sculptures of the mythological *Shi-tsu* creatures (lion-frogs) brought from Manchuria.

THE SMALLER OPERA THEATRE
(MIKHAILOVSKY THEATRE)
In its exterior the building differs only slightly from the surrounding buildings designed by C.I. Rossi, when he planned the complex of buildings for Mikhailovskaya Square. The interior of the theatre built in 1831-33 was designed by A.P. Brullow, and in 1859-60 reconstructed by A.K. Cavos. In 1918, the Mikhailovsky Theatre became the Smaller Opera Theatre.

THE SMOLNY INSTITUTE
The building was constructed in 1806-08 after the design by G. Quarenghi, as a boarding-school for nobility — the Institute for Noble Girls, and is a striking example of the early nineteenth century classicism. It is connected with the most important events of the 1917 October revolution. The Smolny became the headquarters of the revolution, a place for bolsheviks meetings and conferences. V.I. Lenin worked here for several months (since November 1917 till March 1918). At present it houses the Mayor of St. Petersburg's Office.

THE SQUARE OF ARTS
(THE MIKHAYLOVSKY SQUARE)
The architectural ensemble of the square, one of the best creations of architect C.I. Rossi, is between Nevsky Prospect and the Field of Mars. The conceptual and compositional centre of the ensemble is the **Mikhailovsky Palace** (the **Russian Museum**), built in 1819-25. The main building of the palace constructed in the classical style, with a portico and a majestic colonnade is removed into the interior of the court formed by the two outbuildings and separated from the square with a cast-iron grating.

The opposite facade of the palace faces the Mikhailovsky gardens somewhat re-planned by the architect. On the bank of the Moika he built a small pier and an open pavilion. At the same time, the architect created a rectangular square in front of the palace and made designs to build it.

Rossi laid a new street — Mikhailovsky Street which connects the square with the Nevsky Prospect and opens the view to the palace. He prolonged Sadovaya Street which had run only as far as Nevsky Prospect till the Field of Mars.

There is the Great Philharmonic Hall (the former Nobles' Assembly), the Musical Comedy Theatre, the Smaller Opera and Ballet Theatre in the Square of Arts. In the centre of the square a monument to Pushkin was placed in 1957 (the sculptor M.K. Anikushin), which beautifully harmonizes with the classical ensemble.

In 1895-98, when the Russian Museum was founded to commemorate the Emperor Alexander III, the Mikhailovsky Palace had to be reconstructed to adapt its rooms for the museum exposition. This work was performed by the architect V.F. Svinyin; however, some main rooms of the palace preserved their original aspect (the Main Staircase, the White Hall, etc.).

At present, the Russian Museum is the biggest collection of national art in the country. Besides the Mikhailovsky Palace, it occupies the large building which faces the Yekaterininsky Canal (the architect L.N. Benois, 1912-17). Several palaces which are of a museum value are also transferred to the Russian Museum: the Stroganov Palace, the Marble Palace, the Castle of Engineers, etc.

THE STABLE YARD
(THE KONYUSHENNY DVOR)
The building of the Stable Yard was constructed in 1720-23 by the architect N.F. Gerbel. The complicated configuration of the building with a polygonal interior yard is dictated by the shape of the area where it was built. In 1817-23 the architect V.P. Stasov reconstructed the building while preserving its configuration. Because of its great extent, the building plays the dominating role in the Konyushennaya Square ensemble. Among interior rooms the hall of the former chapel is of the greatest artistic significance. In February 1, 1837 the funeral service of Alexander Pushkin took place in the Konyushennaya Chapel. On the third of February, at night, the coffin with the body of the poet was secretly removed from this chapel to the Svyatogorsky Monastery near Pskov.

THE STATUE OF CATHERINE THE GREAT
The monument in the square in front of the Alexandrinsky Theatre was inaugurated in 1873. The design of the monument was made in 1862 by the artist M.O. Mikeshin, the author of the monument *Millennium of Russia* in Novgorod.

The sculptors M.A. Tchizhov and A.M. Opekushin took part in the works.

The statue of Catherine the Great is placed on a tall base in gray polished granite. At the basis of the statue there are figures of the outstanding Russian statesmen of the late eighteenth century — A.V. Suvorov, P.A. Rumyantsev, G.R. Derzhavin, I.I. Betskoy, E.R. Dashkova, G.A. Orlov, A.A. Bezborodko, G.A. Potyomkin, V.V. Tchitchagov. A peculiar feature of the monument is realism of the figures executed with a striking likeness.

THE STATUE OF PETER THE GREAT
The bronze equestrian statue of Peter the Great is placed in front of the Mikhailovsky Palace in 1800.

The model was made by the sculptor Carlo Bartolommeo Rastrelli, the father of the famous architect, during Peter's life. It was cast only in 1745-47, but the monument was not installed even then.

The pedestal of the monument is covered with white, rose and green marbles and decorated with two bas-relief — *The Poltava Battle* and *The Gangut Battle*.

The legend of the pedestal reads: «*To the Great-Grandfather from His Great-Grandson*» (to Peter the Great from Paul I).

THE STATUE OF PETER THE GREAT
(THE «BRONZE HORSEMAN»)
The internationally known monument to Peter the Great, the «*Bronze Horseman*» glorified by A.S. Pushkin, was made in 1774-78 by the French sculptor E.-M. Falconet to the order of Catherine the Great. The head of Peter the Great was performed by Falconet's pupil — M.-A. Collot.

The pedestal which has the shape of a natural rock is made of a gigantic granite stone (the so-called *Thunder-stone*). This stone was found in 1768 on the coast of the Gulf of Finland near the village of Lakhta by the peasant S. Vishniakov.

The serpent under the horse's hooves was modelled by the sculptor F.G. Gordeyev. He also supervised the installation of the monument.

The monument is justly considered to be a major achievement of world monumental sculpture of the eighteenth century.

ST. ALEXANDER NEVSKY MONASTERY

The complex of the buildings of the monastery occupies a vast area on the left bank of the Neva at the Tchernaya river estuary. According to the legend, it was at this spot that Alexander Nevsky won his victory over the Swedes in 1240.

The construction of the monastery began in 1710 after Domenico Trezzini's design. The oldest building of the complex is the church of the Annunciation (1710-20). The buildings around the monastery court were constructed in 1757-71 by M.D. Rastorguyev. The main building of the complex, the Trinity Cathedral, was erected in 1776-90 by the architect I.E. Starov.

In the graveyard of the monastery many famous scientists, writers and statesmen of Russia are buried (now it is the Necropolis museum).

THE ST. ISAAC'S CATHEDRAL

The present building of the cathedral was erected to replace the two previous ones.

The small stone church created by Mattarnovi was rebuilt after the design by A. Rinaldi later in the eighteenth century. However, the marble destined for the cathedral, in Paul I's time was used to build the Castle of Engineers and the cathedral was built in brick, greatly distorting the original Rinaldi's conception. After the victorious completion of the 1812 Patriotic war, the unsightly building of the cathedral was to be dismantled, and a new majestic building of the cathedral to be erected in that place. The cathedral was being built for forty years (1818-58) after the design by A. Montferrand.

The immence size of the cathedral, the luxury of its interior and exterior decor make it a most splendid monument of world architecture. Columned porticoes surround it from all sides. The building is covered with gray marble. In its interior decoration different kinds of semiprecious stones are used: malachite, lapis-lazzuli, etc. The walls and vaults of the cathedral are decorated with paintings and mosaic pictures executed by the famous Russian artists K.P. Brullow, F.A. Bruni, V.K. Shebuyev, etc.

Inside and outside the building has a rich sculptural decor, made after the models by I.P. Vitali, N.S. Pimenov, P.K. Klodt.

In 1931 the cathedral was converted into a museum.

THE ST.ISAAC'S SQUARE

The St. Isaac's Square ensemble, one of the most impressive ensembles in Petersburg, was taking shape during several centuries, and was definitely formed by the mid-nineteenth century, when St. Isaac's Cathedral was completed. On the opposite side of the square there is the Mariinsky Palace built in 1839-44 by the architect A.I. Stackenschneider for the Great Duchess Maria Nikolayevna, daughter of the Tsar Nicholas I. The Blue Bridge over the Moika in front of the palace, the widest bridge in Petersburg, allowed to expand the space of the square, on both sides of which there are the Ministry of state Properties buildings (at present, the Academy of Agricultural Sciences), designed by N.E. Yefimov after the models of Renaissance palaces. Here there is also the Astoria Hotel, one of the best hotels in Petersburg.

In the late 1850s, the equestrian statue of the Tsar Nicholas I created by the sculptor P.K. Klodt was placed in the centre of the square.

THE ST. PETER AND PAUL FORTRESS

The historical centre of Petersburg, the first building of the city, the fortress was laid down on the small Zayachy (Hares') Island in 1703. This date is considered to be the date of the founding of the city. Originally, the fortifications of the fortress were earthen. Since 1706 they being changed for powerful stone ones, but these works were finished only in 1740s, and facing of the walls and the bastions with granite was only finished by 1786.

Of a sexagonal section, somewhat elongated along the west-east axis, the fortress has six bastions, connected with straight curtains in which the gates are situated; the fortress walls being additionally fortified with ravelins in the west and east, while on the opposite side of the canal in the north there was an earthen bulwark (levelled in the nineteenth century). The main gates of the fortress are in the eastern wall. The other front gates, the Nevsky gates, lead to the pier. During the eighteenth-nineteenth centuries, St. Peter and Paul Cathedral, the Superintendant's House, the Engineers' Buiseness Court, the Boat House, the Mint and other buildings for various purposes were built. It was only towards the end of the previous century that St. Peter and Paul Fortress acquired the appearance that it has today.

St. Peter and Paul Cathedral was built in 1712-33; the construction was supervised by D. Trezzini, and performed after his design. The building has a rectangular section, with a span roof and a campanile at the entrance. The campanile with a spire ending with a figure of an angel with the cross is 122,5 meters tall. Since the burial of Peter the Great in 1725, the cathedral was used as the royal burial vault.

A small pavilion which is built in the square in front of the cathedral — the **Boat house** (1761-62, the architect A.F. Wist) — was especially intended to preserve the boat of Peter the Great, known as «*The grandfather of the Russian Navy*» (at present it is in the Naval Museum). A facade of the **Mint**, placed in the fortress to the order of Peter the Great, faces this square. The present building of the Mint was constructed in 1796-1805 after the design by A. Porto. To replace the bulwark, the architects A.P. Gemilian and A.A. Thon built in 1849-60 a powerful construction of the **Arcenal** (at present the Artillery Museum).

THE ST. PETERSBURG HOTEL

A spacious modern building (the architects S.B. Speransky and N.V. Kamensky) perfectly agrees with the earlier urban constructions. The first building of the hotel was inaugurated in 1970.

THE ST. SAMPSON'S CATHEDRAL

The cathedral built in 1728-40 is one of the oldest buildings in Petersburg. It was built near the site where the church laid down by Peter the Great to commemorate the victory over the Swedes during the Poltava battle (the battle took place on St. Sampson's day, June 27, 1709) previously had been situated.

The composition of the cathedral is traditional for the ancient Russian architecture — on the west a multi-tier campanile and a refectory adjoin the church. The four smaller drums were added to the central dome only as late as 1761: originally the cathedral was one-domed.

THE STROGANOV PALACE

The palace situated at the crossing of the Nevsky Prospect by the river Moika was erected by F.B. Rastrelli in 1752-54. Columns on roost bases, porticoes with pediments, stucco decorations in the form of caryatides, lions' masks, figures of putti are used to decorate the palace. Various shapes of window platbands make a capricious design, which makes a contrasting background for the volumes emphasized by the colonnades.

In 1790s the palace was partly rebuilt by A.N. Voronikhin, many of its interiors were decorated in the classical style.

THE SUMMER GARDENS

One of the oldest gardens in Petersburg occupies the area of about twelve hectares. It numbers as many as three thousand trees, with lime-trees predominating. A major part of the trees remains from the time of Peter the Great.

The laying-down of the garden began approximately a year after the foundation of the city. Simultaneously with the garden, a house for the summer residence of Peter the Great was constructed, as well as galleries, the grotto and greenhouse.

The garden was decorated with numerous marble sculptures and busts acquired by Peter the Great in Italy. Among them were works of D. Bonazza, P. Baratta, A. Tarsia, A. Corradi.

By the mid-1720s the garden acquired a completed aspect. It was an example of the «regular garden» characteristic of the eighteenth century, with straight alley, ponds of geometrically perfect proportions, fountains and numerous statues on pedestals.

In the second half of the eighteenth century the Summer Gardens was greatly changed as a result of regulating the Neva and Fontanka banks. All the trellises were dismantled, the fountains were abolished.

In 1771-86 the garden was enclosed with a grating at the Neva Embankment (the authors of the design were Yu.M. Veldten and P.E. Yegorov). The links of the grating were forged in Tula in 1773-74. The Summer Gardens grating is a masterpriece of the eighteenth century Russian classicism.

In 1826 the architect C.I. Rossi rebuilt Peter's grotto, which became the Coffe-House pavilion.

In 1827 a small wooden pavilion Tea-House was built after the design by the architect L.I. Charlemagne. After the design by the same, the Summer Gardens grating was created from the Moika side. It was cast at the Alexandrovsky factory in 1826.

In 1851-55 the monument to the fable writer I.A. Krylov created after the design by P.K. Klodt was placed in the garden; it was made with money voluntarily donated by the citizens.

THE SUMMER PALACE
The design of the palace was made by the architect D. Trezzini. The construction was completed in 1712; in 1713-14 its interiors were decorated.

The palace facades preserved their original aspect to our day, without any alterations since the early eighteenth century.

Among the palace interiors, the decor of the ground floor entrance hall is of a particular interest. Its main decoration is a wonderfully carved bas-relief of Minerva.

In the study of Peter the Great the tile is preserved depicting genre scenes, landscapes, boats, etc.

At present, the Summer Palace houses a museum of everyday life of the epoch of Peter the Great.

THE TRINITY CATHEDRAL
The present building was constructed by V.P. Stasov in 1828-35 to replace the wooden Trinity Cathedral in the village of the Izmailovsky regiment. A peculiarty of the cathedral is that the placement of the domes makes in their section a cross of equal points. A beautiful decoration of the building is monumental porticoes of Corinthian columns and a sculpted frieze. Figures of angels made by the sculptor S.I. Galberg are placed in the niches.

THE UNIVERSITY
(THE TWELVE COLLEGIA)
The building constructed in 1722-42 after D. Trezzini's design was intended for the Senate and the collegias which were instituted by Peter the Great to replace the former departments. It is an excellent example of the civil architecture of the early eighteenth century.

In 1835 the building was transferred to Petersburg University. For this purpose the architect A.F. Shthedrin made some restructuring.

THE VITEBSKY RAILWAY STATION
Constructed in the early twentieth century after the design by the architect S.A. Brzhozovsky in Zagorodny Prospect to replace the old station building from which the first Russian railway started. The modernist style is used in the decoration of the station.

THE WINTER PALACE
The palace was built by F.B. Rastrelli in 1754-62 to be the winter residence of the Tsar. This is one of the most beautiful monuments of the urban architecture and a major achievement of the Russian and world architecture in the eighteenth century.

The Winter Palace created in the baroque style astounds the spectator with its splendour and magnifience. The palace facades face the Neva, the Admiralteysky Passage and the Palace Square.

Today the palace halls house the collection of a major world museum, the Hermitage.

YEKATERININSKY INSTITUTE
In 1804-07 after G. Quarengi's design the building of Yekaterininsky Institute was erected on the Fontanka Embankment. A serene and simple composition, a severe grandeur of architectural forms characterize G. Quarenghi's work. At present the building houses an affiliation of the Russian National Library.

PAVLOVSK
At the end of 1777 Catherine the Great gave grounds on the banks of the Slavyanka river, the total area of which is about 400 hectares together with villages, to her son Paul. After the owner's name the estate got called Pavlovsk.

After the assassination of the Emperor it became the summer residence of his widow Maria Fyodorovna.

The Pavlovsk ensemble had been being formed during fifty years — since 1777 till the late 1820s — and later did not suffer any important changes.

The Pavlovsk Palace. The palace was in 1782-86 built after the design by C. Cameron and is a logical centre and the biggest construction of the whole ensemble.

The exterior of the central building of the palace, conceived by Cameron, remained till the present day. V. Brenna and other architects who worked later made some changes in the decoration of the rooms.

In 1803 the palace burned down. Due to the selfless efforts of soldiers and inhabitants of Pavlovsk almost all the property of the palace was removed and preserved.

The restoration work of the palace was entrusted to A.N. Voronikhin. In two years he restored the central building and made considerable changes in the decoration of the greater part of the rooms. In 1805-07 he re-created some ground-floor rooms of the southern semi-circular wing: the «Lantern», the Bedchamber and the Stall among them.

Besides the interior planning, Voronikhin created for the palace many designs of furniture, vases and other decorative objects.

The Pavlovsk Park. Charles Cameron designed the territory of the whole estate to be a single complex system of different park zones varying in character but united in a common conception. He created the first large areas in the Pavlovsk Park: the Great Star, the Valley of the Slavyanka river, the Swiss Mountains and the Menagerie.

Cameron shaped the wide valley of the Slavyanka in a pure landscape style. To create large water mirror, dams were installed in the river and ponds were dug.

In 1803 P.Gonzaga reformed the landscape district of the dormer festive field, White Birch and Red Valley, and completed the planning of the Slavyanka valley. All this made the Pavlovsk Park an ensemble of international artistic significance.

Pavlovsk is famous for its beautiful park buildings erected after the design by the leading architects — C. Cameron designed the Open-Air Cage (or, the Poultry Yard), Dairy, **Apollo's Colonnade. The Temple of Friendship** (1779) is especially famous, a circular pavilion which was Cameron's first construction in Pavlovsk.

The **Peel-Tower**, an example of a romantic garden pavilion-belwedere intended for rest during walks, was constructed in 1795-97 after the design by V. Brenna and painted by P. Gonzaga.

A.N. Voronikhin took part in the designing of bridges (the Centaurs' Bridge, 1805), as well as C.I. Rossi (the Cast-Iron Bridge, 1780s), etc.

The palace and the park buildings of Pavlovsk were greatly damaged during the World War II. The main monuments have been restored, but restoration works are still being carried out.

PETERHOF (PETRODVORETS)

The rise of Peterhof is connected with Russia finally taking hold of the Baltic coast in the early eighteenth century.

Several coast farmsteads on the southern coast of the Gulf of Finland were allotted to the Ministry of the Court. Peter the Great used to stay at one of the farmsteads situated in mid-way from Petersburg to the Kotlin island and Cronslott. It got named Peter's Court (Peterhof), and later became one of the best ensembles of palaces and parks in Europe.

The Petrodvorets ensemble is divided into the Higher and the Lower parks.

The fountains of the Lower Park enjoy world-wide fame.

The **Grand Cascade** is the largest completed monument of the mid-eighteenth century. It is erected to commemorate the victorious ending of the Northern war. The length of Cascade is forty metres. There is a terrace above the Cascade. Beginning from the terrace, cascades run in ledges, the mirrors of the terrace wall being decorated with mascaroons of Neptune and Bacchus, sputring water into marble basins. On both sides of mascaroons are marble buts which symbolize seasons.

The big grotto and the cascades rest upon a monolithic stylobate covered with tuff and decorated with decorative hermae, pilasters and mascaroons. The stylobate is adjoined with pedestals with allegorical figures of the Volkhov and the Neva on them. At the foot of the cascade there is the dipper in whose centre rises the bronze group Samson Tearing Lion's Jaws (the sculptor M.I. Kozlovsky). The canal which connects the Grand Cascade with the sea starts at the dipper. The architects J.-B. Leblon, I.F. Braunstein, N. Michetti, M.G. Zemtsov, Yu. M. Veldten took part in the construction of the Grand Cascade.

The sculptural decoration of the Grand Cascade and the grotto is characterized by great diversity. On the sides of the cascade ledges, on the grotto and under the arcades, on the granite boards of the dipper thirty-seven bronze statues are installed. The walls of the cascades are decorated with twenty-nine bas-reliefs and one hundred and eight corbels.

The Great Palace and the Grand Cascade are the compositional dominant of the whole Peterhof complex and the main planning nucleus of the Lower Park. This ensemble includes terraces with fountains, the Great Fountains (the Italian and the French ones), the Voronikhin colonnades, the fountains of the Marble Benches, parterres with flower beds, the Grand Canal, the Fountain Alley, the fountain *Favourite*, as well as boskets with the fountains *Adam* and *Eve*. The central ensemble is connected by its system of radial alleys with the western and eastern ensembles of the Lower Park.

The Cascades of the Dragons, the *Chessboard Mountain*, is the most significant construction in the eastern part of the park, a typical monument of the Russian decorative park architecture of the first half of the eighteenth century. The Cascade was created to replace the Smaller Grotto, one of the first constructions in Peterhof in 1722, headed by the architect I.F. Braunstein. In 1875 after a drawing by N. Benois three dragons were cast.

The **Great Palace** was being shaped during the whole eighteenth century: beginning with the Upper Chambers of Peter the Great (1714-25) which were repeatedly enlarged, and ending with the reconstruction of the whole building and turning it into the Great Palace (1745-55).

The architects D. Trezzini, I.F. Braunstein, J.-B. Leblon, N. Michetti, F.B. Rastrelli worked subsequently to construct the palace.

Besides the fountains, the Lower Park is decorated with pavilions, among which the most interesting are the Hermitage, Monplaisir and Marly.

Damaged during the World War II, the ensemble is completly restored.

TSARSKOYE SELO
(THE TOWN OF PUSHKIN)

The ensemble of the palaces and parks of Tsarskoye Selo was taking shape during one and half century.

Originally it was a Swedish farmstead — Saari Mysa, given by Peter the Great to Catherine. During the years of Catherine I reigning, Tsarskoye Selo (since 1725) remained a small country residence of the Empress. After Catherine's death, the property was inherited by her daughter, Elizaveta Petrovna. She enlarged the stone chambers, built at the time of Catherine I. The architects M.G. Zemtsov, A.F. Kvasov and S.I. Tchevakinsky worked here. Since 1750s the works were headed by F.B. Rastrelli.

The Great **Catherine Palace** is a masterpiece of the Russian baroque architecture of the mid-eighteenth century. The main impression of the palace exterior lies in its length, a complicated rhythm of division, in the luxurious decoration.

The central part of palace, the Middle House, is basically the stone chambers of Catherine I. The side wings of the Palace elongated in a single line are formed by the two symmetrical outbuildings connected by the galleries with the Middle House and with the Chapel and Zubovsky buildings.

A vast vaulted terrace connets the palace with a group of buildings whose role and significance was similar to that of Roman thermae. After the architect's name, they are called the Cameron thermae. The complex includes the Cold Bath with the Agate Pavilion, the colonnade opening a magnificient view of the park and the Great Pod, a sloping descent from the terrace to the Footlights Alley.

In 1756 all the facade and interior decoration works were finished. The main methods of the interior decoration were painting and carving. The Grand Hall, some antechambers leading to it, the Pictures Hall, the Amber room should be mentioned among the interiors.

The leading role in the interior decoration in the second half of the eighteenth century was played by Cameron. He decorated the appartments of Pavel Petrovich and the private chambers of Catherine the Great in the Zubov building and constructed a new main staircase.

In the early nineteenth century V.P. Stasov took part in the decoration works, reconstructing the rooms nearest to the palace chapel in the later classical style. In 1860 I.A. Monighetti changed the Cameron's main staircase for the new marble one.

During the World War II the palace was greatly damaged. After the war, great works to restore the interiors of the palace and its facades were carried out.

Cameron's Gallery. The gallery is named after the architect C. Cameron, who made the design. The gallery was erected by C. Cameron in 1780-93.

The colonnade of the first floor surrounds the glazed part of the gallery — the place for promenades in foul weather. The construction of the staircase completed the overall composition of the gallery. In 1787 on the stone landing of the staircase statues were made after the antique models. The upper landing of the gallery is decorated with bronze busts on pedestals.

The Park. The oldest part of the Yekaterininsky park is the Older Garden that in early eighteenth century got a regular planning. Its composition was conceived by Ian Rozen, the author of the Summer Gardens planning.

The park architects changed the relief artificially, having created three wide terrace-ledges. Here the flower gardens were laid, covered galleries and trelliage summer houses were constructed, two smaller ponds were dug.

In 1722 the construction of the Transverse, or Fish, canal began, which divided the regular and the landscape parts of the parks. In the late eighteenth century tree clipping ceased, and the regular part became one with the landscape part.

The Sculptures. The Older Garden alleys are decorated with sculptures. Only a small part of statues and busts which originally decorated the garden remained to this day.

Statues and busts were placed in the alleys and in green niches. Some of them are signed with the names of the seventeenth and eighteenth centuries' sculptors: Pietro Baratta, Giovanni Zorzoni, Antonio Tarsia, Giovanni Bonazza.

The Tsarskoye Selo park is connected with A.S. Pushkin's name: he studied in the Lyceum which adjoins the Catherine Palace, and many of his youth poems are dedicated to the park.

Like other suburban ensembles, the Tsarskoye Selo park and the Catherine Palace were greatly damaged during the World War II. Restoration works claimed great efforts.

Санкт-Петербург

Альбом на английском языке

Съемка В. СОБОЛЕВА и К. ЖАРИНОВОЙ
Вступительные статьи Д. ЛИХАЧЕВА и Н. ЛАНСЕРЕ
Аннотации Н. ЛАНСЕРЕ
Перевод с русского Т. ТИХОНОВОЙ
Оформление и макет И. ФАРРАХОВА и Л. ЕПИФАНОВА

Генеральный директор издательства
А. КОНСТАНТИНОВ
Директор А. БОГДАНОВ

Редактор В. Волкова
Редактор английского текста Н. Беспятых
Художественно-технический редактор Н. Лакатош
Набор О. Панайотти
Верстка И. Герасимов

•

Подписан в печать 10.07.93.
Формат 70 x 100 1/8. Бумага офсетная «Финнарт Галери».
Гарнитура «Таймс». Печать офсетная.
Печ. л. 21,5. Усл. печ. л. 27,3.
Тираж 9000 экз.
Заказ 9074. Издательство «Библиополис».
198147, С.-Петербург, Бронницкая ул., 17.
Акционерное общество
открытого типа
«Иван Федоров»
191126, С.-Петербург,
Звенигородская ул., 11.